A STAFF
FOR THE
PRESIDENT

Recent Titles in
Contributions in Political Science
Series Editor: Bernard K. Johnpoll

A STAFF FOR THE PRESIDENT

The Executive Office, 1921–1952

Alfred Dick Sander

Contributions in Political Science, Number 229

Greenwood Press
New York • Westport, Connecticut • London

Library of Congress Cataloging-in-Publication Data

Sander, Alfred Dick.
  A staff for the president : the Executive Office, 1921-1952 /
Alfred Dick Sander.
      p.   cm. — (Contributions in political science, ISSN 0147-1066
; no. 229)
  Bibliography: p.
  Includes index.
  ISBN 0-313-26526-7 (lib. bdg. : alk. paper)
  1. United States. Executive Office of the President.
2. Presidents—United States—Staff.   I. Title.   II. Series.
JK518.S26   1989
353.03′1—dc19   88-21339

British Library Cataloguing in Publication Data is available.

Library of Congress Catalog Card Number: 88-21339
ISBN: 0-313-26526-7
ISSN: 0147-1066

First published in 1989

Greenwood Press, Inc.
88 Post Road West, Westport, Connecticut 06881

Printed in the United States of America

∞

The paper used in this book complies with the
Permanent Paper Standard issued by the National
Information Standards Organization (Z39.48-1984).

10 9 8 7 6 5 4 3 2 1

For Helen, Bob and Rick

Contents

Preface

Over thirty years ago Fritz Morstein Marx of the Bureau of the Budget gave a lecture to a group of interns at the National Security Agency about the Executive Office of the President. As a member of that intern group I learned for the first time of this unique organization. My interest in the EOP was furthered by classes taught by Arnold Miles while he was chief of the bureau's Organization Branch. The evolution of the presidential staff has been the subject of much of my research since that time.

This study of the presidential staff is based primarily on the various files in the Hoover, Truman, and Eisenhower presidential libraries, the National Archives, and the Office of Management and Budget. I am much indebted to the skilled archivists in these institutions for facilitating my search. I have also utilized secondary sources, manuscripts from the Library of Congress, oral histories in the presidential libraries, the Columbia University Oral History Collection, and personal interviews and correspondence with some of the participants in the events described herein.

Much of this research was made possible by an individual grant from the Ford Foundation and sabbatical leaves from Purdue University Calumet.

Introduction

Until World War II the American president was about as well served by staff assistants as the executive of a medium-sized company. With little institutional support, the men who occupied the Oval Office were ill prepared as they arrived in Washington with a few aides to manage the executive branch. They soon found themselves engaged in a battle for control with entrenched federal bureaucrats and the powerful chairmen of congressional committees. The presidents' lack of continuity, together with their relative inexperience with the national government's complexities, usually made this an unequal struggle.

During the 1870s and 1880s the presidency reached the nadir of its power and influence—it was considered by many to be primarily a ceremonial office with little impact on national policy. The Republican presidents of the day tended to follow the Whig tradition that limited the role of the chief executive in the legislative process. The small and somewhat sleepy departments were ruled by cabinet members who were able to ignore presidential programs or budgets. The executive power of the president began to grow as the country attained greater influence in the world and the domestic economy developed a national character. Still, with a State Department that had but sixty-three clerks as late as 1901, life was relatively simple. Until

Herbert Hoover tried to cope with the Great Depression the presidency was not a very demanding office.[1]

Presidents-elect typically did not have much understanding of the duties they were about to perform. They entered office assuming that their cabinet would not only administer the departments for them but, as a group, serve as their trusted advisers in carrying out the objectives of the administration. They did not realize that within a short time most of the cabinet members would become the tools of the career administrators in the departments they headed. It was usually late in their terms before presidents recognized that, because of departmental parochialism, the cabinet was unreliable as presidentially focused agents.

It was the development of presidential staffs during the first half of this century that made it possible for the executive branch to move from cabinet to presidential government. Today the exercise of presidential power is critically dependent upon the complex staff structure that serves the chief executive. Surprisingly, presidents were slow to appreciate how they might acquire their own staff of career bureaucrats to help them control the rest of the federal bureaucracy. Initially they were, at best, the reluctant beneficiaries of the staff groups that others brought into existence.

The transitory nature of their incumbency made it unlikely that presidents would view their office from an institutional prospective. Why should they

---

1. The professionalization of the presidential staff began in a modest way when William McKinley, the first of the twentieth century presidents, named George B. Cortelyou, a holdover from Cleveland's White House, as his personal secretary. Profiting from the continuity his experience with a prior administration had given him, Cortelyou soon became the prototype of the modern White House staff aide. After McKinley was shot, Cortelyou was practically the acting president for the eight days McKinley lingered before he died. He guided Theodore Roosevelt as he assumed the office, and so impressed the new president that he named him a member of his cabinet. Cortelyou became the first secretary of labor and commerce when that department was established in 1903. See Louis L. Gould, *The Presidency of William McKinley* (Lawrence, Kansas, 1980), p. 39; Patrick Anderson, *The Presidents' Men* (Garden City, N.Y., 1969), p. 66.

seek the organizational support that could make their successors more effective managers? None did until Harry Truman sought to provide a smooth transition for Dwight Eisenhower.

* * *

The need for a presidential staff complex was eventually recognized by groups of public administration specialists. They were slow to define the problem because it was much easier for them to analyze the roles of bureaus and departments than to consider the immense management task facing the president. Conceptualizing the problem was also inhibited by the peculiar constitutional position of the chief executive, and the intensely personal nature of the office which made it difficult to distill common elements from a variety of presidential experiences.[2]

The first formal presidential staff organization (beyond White House secretaries and clerks) resulted from the efforts of public administrators who were able to convince presidents and congressmen to support some of their ideas. With the establishment of the Bureau of the Budget in 1921 the presidency began to become "institutionalized."[3] Gradually a presidential staff made up of civil servants was created to provide the experience and continuity by which incoming presidents might more equally contest for control of the

2. William Pincus, "Organization of the Executive Office of the President," May 1946, E.O.B. Misc. Memos, 1939–1946, E2–5, Series 39.32, Office of Management and Budget (henceforth OMB).

3. Political scientists have defined institutionalization as "a process whereby sporadic, irregular activities become regularized and governed by norms. Such norms, as they become accepted, reflect established expectations to which relationships and activities respond predictably. In this light, the institutionalization of the presidency refers to the emergence of new and enduring presidential relationships and responsibilities that become continuing obligations of successive Presidents, and integral roles of the presidency." See Lester G. Seligman and Cary R. Covington, "The Comparative Institutionalization of Presidential Roles" (Paper delivered at the 1979 Annual Meeting of the American Political Science Association, Washington, D.C.), p. 3.

national government. In 1939 this staff was formally designated the Executive Office of the President (EOP).

The Executive Office of the President is a most curious organization. With its name emblazoned in the United States Government organization manual as the premier unit of the executive branch, its title could hardly be more impressive. Yet it has no head or separate budget. In any true sense it is not really an organization but merely the name applied to the collection of staff units that directly support the president. The evolution of this amorphous structure is the subject of this study: not because the executive office is of great importance as an organizational entity but because the growth of presidential staff assistance has affected the operation of the federal government in important ways. A modern president could not discharge his many functions without the full range of units that make up the EOP.[4]

* * *

Aside from the acquisition of additional personal aides in the White House, the president's most significant staff organizations have developed around four general functional areas. These involve financial and organizational control, planning, economic mobilization, and diplomatic-military coordination. Although pressures to create these mechanisms were generally prompted by a desire to equip the federal government to cope more effectively with the needs of American society as a whole, proponents of each area were always more interested in their specific remedy, whether it be budgeting or planning or foreign policy development, than they were in the broader problem of the president's capacity to govern. While any study of the growth of the president's staff must of necessity focus on the development of these separate functions, they should be viewed against the background of the total staff needs of the president.

4. John Helmer, "The Presidential Office: Velvet Fist in an Iron Glove," in *The Illusion of Presidential Government,* ed. Hugh Heclo and Lester M. Salamon (Boulder, Colo., 1981), p. 57.

The first area to be developed, and from the president's point of view probably the most essential, was the enhancement of his financial and organizational control of the executive branch. It began with the creation of the Bureau of the Budget (now the Office of Management and Budget).

The second type of staff assistance which evolved was intended to provide the capability to analyze national problems and the development of plans to ameliorate them. National planning has never been very successful in the United States but that does not seem to have discouraged its advocates. During the New Deal, planning was attempted by various incarnations of the National Resources Planning Board but was abandoned during World War II. In 1946 the Council of Economic Advisers was established. Since then federal planning has been limited to economic and financial matters.

The crisis in industrial mobilization that developed during World War I thrust Woodrow Wilson into an economic coordination role. Later, World War II and the cold war again prompted presidential efforts to mobilize the economy. This resulted in a plethora of coordinating agencies during the war and then, in 1947, the creation of the National Security Resources Board.

Lastly, a controversy over the unification of the armed forces together with the growth of worldwide commitments and responsibilities led to the establishment of the National Security Council. The NSC, designed to aid the president in the coordination of diplomatic-military affairs, has become one of his best-known staff groups.

* * *

These four basic presidential staff services had been created by the time Harry Truman left the White House. To discover the origins of the executive office and the forces that shaped it one must examine it in the elemental form it attained during the Truman years. That is one of the reasons why this study concludes with the year 1952. Much of the expansion of the EOP since that time has been in response to pressure from various special interest groups. Presidents have placated groups who have sought assurance that their cause has the presidential ear by adding new staff groups to the EOP or to the White House Office. The significance of these groups has been essentially political rather than administrative.

Basically this book is a study of the institutionalization of the modern presidency. It focuses on the Truman administration because by 1952 that process essentially was completed.[5] Not only did the embryo EOP successfully make the transition from Roosevelt to his successor but Truman tried to make sure that his expanded EOP would be ready to serve Eisenhower. During the Truman years the Bureau of the Budget enjoyed its "golden age"[6] and the Council of Economic Advisers, the National Security Resources Board, and the National Security Council were established as part of the EOP.

* * *

The reader should bear in mind that during the EOP's formative years several basic issues about the proper role of a presidential staff arose time and again as the various staff agencies developed. Because the presidential staff developed piecemeal, rather than according to an overall plan, many central questions were addressed as each unit went through its gestation period. They included such concerns as:

1. Should presidential staff units rigorously confine themselves to purely staff functions? If they did not, would they not eventually dominate the departments?
2. Is the existence of strong presidential staff units compatible with the desire of many presidents to govern through their cabinets?
3. Could presidents resist the temptation to use their institutional staffs as command posts to

5. Fred I. Greenstein, "The Modern Presidency," in *The New American Political System*, ed. Anthony King (Washington, D.C., 1978), pp. 53–57.

6. Larry Berman, *The Office of Management and Budget and the Presidency, 1921–1979* (Princeton, N.J., 1979), p. 42.

subvert the line authority of the department and agency heads?

4. Is the Executive Office of the President forever to be just an impressive addition to the letter-heads of the various staff agencies or can it become a functioning organizational entity?

5. If a president designated a chief of staff, would he become such a powerful figure that he could threaten the authority of the president?

6. Just what should the organizational structure of the executive office be and what are the essential staff services that should be provided to the president if he is to do his job and meet the expectations of the electorate?

7. Should the president alone decide the nature of his staff support or should Congress establish his staff structure by statute and require Senate confirmation of his nominees to head the various staff agencies?

8. Can a total presidential staff system be planned and installed within the American checks and balances system or must it be forged through the political bargaining process?

To discover the degree to which these issues were probed and how they were resolved is one of the objectives of this study.

* * *

Writing in 1949 Clinton Rossiter predicted that the executive office would shape the nature of the presidency "for every century to the end of the Republic."[7] Given the growth of presidential staff groups since that time it seems clear that the executive office, under one name or another, will be a permanent feature of the American presidency.

The development of the Executive Office of the President has been enormously significant because it

---

7. "The Constitutional Significance of the Executive Office of the President," *American Political Science Review* 43 (December 1949): 1215.

inserted an entirely new echelon into the executive branch between the president and the departments. It has given the president a corps of careerists who are immune to departmental parochialism and capable of developing a presidential perspective.

Since the EOP has been established, it has been repeatedly analyzed by individuals, bureaus, and commissions who have devised and proposed various alternative schemes for presidential staffing. But the American political process has defeated all systematic efforts to reorganize the executive office. This book is an account of how and why these forces produced the presidential staff that Dwight Eisenhower inherited in 1953.

1.
Beginnings

Theodore Roosevelt expanded the role of the president in many ways, but it was his successor, William Howard Taft, who first attempted to enhance the institutional character of the office. Taft's interest in government was administrative as well as institutional so he sought to improve the efficient and economical operation of the presidency together with its continuity. In 1911 Taft appointed a Commission on Economy and Efficiency which, for the first time, examined the organization and functions of the executive branch.[1]

During the Progressive Era, municipal reformers began applying concepts of business administration to city government. Taft's commission sought to extend this idea of a "public corporation" to the federal government in which "the democratically elected board of directors, the Congress, was responsible for making policy, but only a strong executive—the President as business manager—could ensure efficient and economical administration."[2]

Among the commission's findings was a recommendation that the president prepare an annual national

1. Barry D. Karl, *Executive Reorganization and Reform in the New Deal* (Chicago, 1963), p. 12.

2. Hugh Heclo, "Introduction: The Presidential Illusion," in *The Illusion of Presidential Government*, ed. Hugh Heclo and Lester M. Salamon (Boulder, Colo., 1981), p. 12.

budget for the operations of the executive branch. The traditional practice then was to require each department and bureau to go directly to Congress each year for their funds. This procedure gave Congress great influence over the programs and operations of the executive agencies, increased the independence of those agencies (especially the Treasury Department) in setting their own agendas, and minimized the capacity of the president to manage the government. Although the president was certainly not a passive bystander in the budgeting process, he was not in charge of federal finances. In addition, he had to compete with some of his own cabinet, particularly the secretary of the treasury, in budgetary matters.[3]

Taft decided to follow the recommendation of the commission since he believed that "if heads of departments are to be considered purely as the ministerial agents of Congress in the preparation and submission of estimates, then as far as the business of the government is concerned, the President of the United States is shorn of his most important executive power and duty." He accordingly ordered his cabinet members to submit their financial requirements to him. Congress immediately perceived the implications of Taft's initiative and responded by ordering the departments to submit their requests to Congress alone. In the end Taft put together the first national budget and Congress, not surprisingly, ignored it. Although Taft did succeed in developing the first integrated national budget, Congress disregarded his efforts and successfully continued their direct relationship with the cabinet officers. Nonetheless, Taft had set an important precedent which was to reach fulfillment during the administration of Warren Harding.[4]

Although Congress was jealous of its budgetary power, it increasingly realized a need to overhaul and centralize what had become a complex and unwieldy process. To improve its own work, Congress, in 1919,

---

3. Allen Schick, "The Problem of Presidential Budgeting," in *The Illusion of Presidential Government*, p. 87.

4. Henry F. Pringle, *The Life and Times of William Howard Taft*, vol. 2 (New York, 1939), pp. 605-608.

enacted a bill that would require the preparation of a national budget, create a general accounting office headed by a comptroller general, and establish a budget bureau under the control of the president. Before it was passed a compromise had to be worked out in a conference committee because of disagreements between the House and the Senate over the organizational status of the proposed budget bureau. The compromise specified that the secretary of the treasury would also serve as the budget director. Woodrow Wilson vetoed the bill because his legal advisers told him that one of its provisions threatened the president's power to remove appointees. Since the House failed, by a margin of a few votes, to override the veto, the establishment of a budget bureau was delayed until the next administration.[5]

Soon after Harding's election, Congress began consideration of a bill that was quite similar to the one Wilson had rejected. Once again the House and Senate disagreed on the proper organizational placement of the budget bureau within the executive branch. And again the issue was compromised, this time by locating the bureau in the Treasury Department but denying its secretary any control over the budgetary process.[6] This unique arrangement ensured that the bureau would have a special relationship to the president.

The bill cleared the way for the budget director to become the president's man when Congress failed to require that he be confirmed by the Senate and

---

5. Larry Berman, *The Office of Management and Budget and the Presidency, 1921–1979* (Princeton, N.J., 1979), pp. 3–4.

6. Senator McCormick of Illinois insisted that the Bureau should be a part of the Treasury Department. However, Congressman Good of Iowa, who served as chairman of the House Select Committee on the Budget, contended that since the formulation of the executive budget was to be an integral responsibility of the president, the director of the budget should report directly to him. Good was discouraged by the compromise Congress adopted, but Taft (who had maintained an active interest in the subject) reassured him that "McCormick gets the shell and you get the meat." See Fritz Morstein Marx, "Some Early Comment on the Organizational Place of the Budget Bureau," 30 October 1947, E2–50/39.3, Series 39.32, RG 51, National Archives (henceforth NA).

neglected to specify his authority. John Nance Garner of Texas and other congressmen claimed that the director of the budget would become the second most powerful man in the executive branch, but Congress ignored the warning. Until the 1970s the director was the only political appointee, other than the White House aides, not subject to approval by the Senate.[7]

The Budget and Accounting Act was signed by President Harding on 10 June 1921. The law created the General Accounting Office (which reports directly to Congress) as well as the Bureau of the Budget. It provided that, with presidential authorization, the bureau could recommend administrative organizational changes in the executive branch and make statistical studies.[8]

The act ordered the departments to prepare annual appropriation requests each year and to provide them to the bureau together with any other data it requested. It removed much of the independence the departments had enjoyed and eliminated the role of the treasury in reviewing their requests to Congress. Instead, the Bureau of the Budget was told to collect, analyze, and adjust departmental requests before sending them to Congress. It is difficult to overestimate the significance of the Budget and Accounting Act in the growth of the president's power to direct the work of the executive branch; as one observer has noted, "Without question the establishment of the bureau was the most important single factor in the evolution of the executive office."[9]

THE BUREAU OF THE BUDGET, 1921–1939

The Bureau of the Budget's first director and founding father was Charles G. Dawes, then a Chicago banker and the next vice-president of the United States. His political standing, personality, background, and rela-

7. John W. Ramsey, "The Director of the Bureau of the Budget as a Presidential Aide, 1921-1952: With Emphasis on the Truman Years" (Ph.D. diss. University of Missouri, 1967), pp. 7-9.

8. Ibid.

9. John Helmer, "The Presidential Office: Velvet Fist in an Iron Glove," in *The Illusion of Presidential Government,* p. 49.

tionship with Harding had a lasting effect on the bureau and its development as the president's first and most important institutional staff arm.[10] An old friend of General John J. Pershing, Dawes had gone to France during World War I to wrestle with the supply problems of the American army. His success in this role convinced him that he was most effective working as the direct assistant of a principal executive, exercising authority in the executive's name over the business management of an enterprise.[11]

President-elect Harding, first offered Dawes the post of treasury secretary but Dawes declined. He told Harding that the only job he would accept was as the "assistant secretary to the President." He was thinking in terms of the function he had performed for Pershing but this time he sought to have a general influence over the business operations of the whole federal government. Harding was determined to attract the "best brains" in the Republican party (such men as Charles Evans Hughes, Herbert Hoover, and Charles Dawes) to his administration. Later in the year when the Budget Bureau was established, Harding asked Dawes to become the first budget director.[12]

Dawes accepted because he believed that as director of the budget he would have the kind of influence he desired. He told Harding that he would leave after one year because he was confident that by then he would have firmly established an economy movement in the government and reduced the expenditures of every department. As the first budget director, he was extremely conscious of the precedents that he was setting. He sought to establish principles of firm presidential control so that "Cabinet demagogues of the future may be discouraged as much as possible

---

10. Dawes, a self-made millionaire and successful lawyer, was something of a Renaissance man who also played the piano and flute. A piece Dawes originally wrote for the violin became the 1950s popular song hit, "Its All in the Game." See Geoffrey Parrett, *America in the Twenties: A History* (New York, 1982), p. 131.

11. Dawes interview by Don K. Price, 9-10 July 1948, E2-50/39.3, Series 39.32, RG 51, NA.

12. Ibid.

in estimating their chances of success in challenging the system."[13]

One of Dawes's first concerns was to break down the natural reluctance of the departments to provide him (and the president) with the information needed to develop a budget proposal for the executive branch. He got Harding to call a mass meeting of all the bureau chiefs within the departments in an effort to get their cooperation. Claiming that "the President is simply putting into effect for the first time in this country a condition which exists in any business corporation," he explained that the corporate head has the right to get information from any source "whether it is from a washer-woman scrubbing the floor, or his first vice-president." At this meeting Dawes enunciated the principles of his budget machinery which must "last as long as the republic." One of these was that the budget director acts for the president in gathering information. By claiming to act in the name of the president Dawes succeeded in enhancing the budget director's power and establishing his political independence from the Treasury Department.[14]

The Harding-Coolidge devotion to frugality and their desire to constrict federal activities had a long-term effect on the attitudes and operations of the bureau. Dawes's complete devotion to the administration's economy effort assured him of Harding's thorough support and allowed the budget director to assume a leadership position, successfully extracting cooperation from the cabinet and establishing himself and his successors as unique presidential agents. Unfortunately, the emphasis on economy carried a price. It fixed the bureau on a narrow path at a time when it might well have developed into the planning and coordinating mechanism the executive branch so sorely needed.

Precedents established by Dawes tended to limit the bureau in other ways. The budget act had given the

---

13. Charles G. Dawes, *The First Year of the Budget* (New York, 1923), pp. 24–25.

14. Ibid., pp. 8–9; Schick, "The Problem of Presidential Budgeting," p. 87.

bureau responsibility for proposing governmental re-organization to promote efficiency. Not only did Dawes fail to direct the bureau into this area, but after meeting with Walter Brown, chairman of the congressional Joint Committee on Reorganization, he told Harding that this function should be left to the committee alone. As a result, twenty years passed before the bureau began to develop expertise in organizational matters. A less enduring precedent was Dawes's practice of inviting the chairman of the House Appropriations Committee to participate in his meetings with department heads working out budget requests.[15] The practice could have undermined the president's budget authority, but fortunately, the practice was discontinued by Dawes's successors.

Dawes left the bureau after its first fiscal year but he stayed long enough to inaugurate its so-called "green eyeshade period" which lasted from 1921 until 1939. During those years, its activities were limited to putting the budget together in an almost ministerial fashion and to being in the forefront of even minor kinds of drives for economy and efficiency.[16] The bureau played essentially a passive role, receiving agency requests, summarizing them, cutting them, and transmitting them to Congress as the president's proposed budget.[17]

Dawes assembled a staff of twenty-two, including clerks and messengers, to do this work. Most of his important appointments went to trusted friends, usually former army associates or men on leave from his bank in Chicago. These included General Herbert Lord and Colonel J. Clawson Roop who became, successively, directors of the bureau for the remainder of the Republican era.[18]

Six months before he left the bureau Dawes got Harding to agree to appoint Lord as his successor. He

15. Dawes, *First Year*, pp. 33, 69.

16. Transcript, Roger W. Jones interview, 14 August 1969, Harry S. Truman Library (henceforth HSTL), p. 4.

17. William Pincus, "Organization of the Executive Office of the President," May 1946, E.O.B. misc. memos, 1939-1946, OMB.

18. Ramsey, "Director of the Bureau of the Budget," pp. 51-66; Dawes interview by Price.

spent much of the remaining time helping Lord build up his own contacts. He left the bureau "with a clear conscience, knowing that its work will go on improving, and that the reorganization of governmental business methods effected through our co-ordinating agencies will be maintained."[19] Roop, who had left the bureau with Dawes in 1922, returned when Herbert Hoover appointed him director in 1929.[20] Lord and Roop proved to be thoroughly imbued with the Dawes heritage and determined to maintain his philosophy of operations.

During the Republican period, the bureau payroll never exceeded forty-eight employees. However, this number was significantly augmented by the practice of detailing employees from other agencies, principally the War and Navy departments, to the Federal Coordinating Service. This organization, which operated under the direction of the bureau director, was established by executive action to monitor the routine business of the government.[21]

The primary function of the bureau was to bring together the material from the departments and agencies for the annual budget submission to Congress. This work was done by the Division of Estimates which consisted of investigators organized into groups. Each group was headed by an assistant to the director and the various government agency budgets were assigned to them on a functional basis.[22]

THE BUREAU, 1933–1939

Much has been written about Franklin Roosevelt's management style. No one who had been assistant secretary of the navy and governor of New York could have been unaware of the basic principles of management, but Roosevelt would not (or could not) follow them. Instead, he adopted what has been called the competitive ap-

19. Dawes, *First Year*, p. 97.

20. Roop interview with Don K. Price, 27 May 1948, E2-50/39.3, Series 39.32, RG 51, NA.

21. Bureau of the Budget, Treasury Department, 1921–1939, B64-2/4, Series 52.2, RG 51, NA.

22. Ibid.

proach. His technique of fuzzy delegation meant that his subordinates frequently found themselves pursuing the same task and eventually were forced to ask FDR to decide which course of action he preferred. Arthur Schlesinger argues that this technique gave Roosevelt great advantages for "it brought him an effective flow of information; it kept the reins of decision in his own hands; it made for administrative flexibility and stimulated subordinates to effective performance." It also extracted a tremendous price in the morale of those who worked for him and in the general inefficiency it produced in his administration.[23]

His organizational methods were antithetical to those advocated by the Bureau of the Budget, yet Roosevelt seemed sympathetic to expanding the scope of bureau operations. He had faulted Dawes for leading the bureau astray by keeping its staff small as an example of economy for the rest of the government. Roosevelt said this caused the bureau to be poorly equipped for even the limited role Dawes established.[24] But when Roosevelt became president he persisted in the practice of economizing at the expense of bureau effectiveness. From 1933 to 1939 the bureau continued to be undermanned and limited to the path Dawes had charted.

Lewis Douglas was named Roosevelt's first budget director. During the 1932 campaign Roosevelt had promised to reduce federal expenditures by twenty-five percent and Douglas not only believed him but thought that it was a good idea. He therefore made strenuous efforts to reverse the "spendthrift" policies of the Hoover administration and so continued the Dawes emphasis on economy as the bureau's raison d' être. Initially Douglas seemed to have great influence with Roosevelt. But as the New Deal moved toward deficit spending and inflation, Douglas predicted the overthrow of capitalism. Roosevelt began to doubt his budget director's loyalty and suspected he was keeping

23. James M. Burns, *Roosevelt: The Lion and the Fox* (New York, 1956), pp. 371–375; Arthur M. Schlesinger, Jr., *The Coming of the New Deal* (Boston, 1959), p. 537.

24. Lewis Brownlow, *A Passion for Anonymity* (Chicago, 1958), p. 338.

a secret diary which might be used to embarrass the administration. Finally, increasingly out of step with the president's policies, he resigned in August 1934.[25]

FDR was upset and hurt by the timing of Douglas's resignation. To the horror of Secretary of the Treasury Henry Morgenthau Roosevelt considered naming Thomas Corcoran to head the bureau. To avoid having an operator like Corcoran in change of the budget, Morgenthau hastily suggested Daniel Bell as the temporary head of the bureau. Roosevelt immediately wrote out a press release announcing Bell's appointment.[26] Bell was asked to become acting director for just a sixty-day period but continued in that position for four years and seven months. He refused to accept a permanent appointment as director because he wished to maintain his civil service status. Bell was a confidant of Morgenthau's, devoid of political ambitions, and devoted to controlling the spenders.[27] By the time Bell took over the bureau Douglas had abolished the Federal Coordinating Service and reduced the bureau staff (professional and nonprofessional) to thirty-one. This number was raised to forty-five the following year and remained at that level throughout Bell's tenure.[28]

The departure of Douglas meant that for the next five years the bureau's director was no longer an intimate presidential adviser. Since Bell was Morgenthau's man it also meant that the bureau was more responsive to the Treasury Department than the president. As a result, Roosevelt tended to rely on White House personal assistants to perform coordinating tasks that the bureau might have done better.[29] Some have argued that Roosevelt deliberately bypassed the Budget Bureau during his first term because if he had permitted them to apply their routine methods to

25. Ramsey, "Director of the Bureau of the Budget," pp. 70–80; Berman, *Office of Management and Budget*, p. 8.

26. Schlesinger, *Coming of the New Deal*, p. 292.

27. Ramsey, "Director of the Bureau of the Budget," pp. 70–80.

28. Elmer Staats in *Portraits of American Presidents*, vol. 2, *The Truman Presidency: Intimate Perspectives*, ed. Kenneth W. Thompson (Lanham, Md., 1984), p. 79.

29. Berman, *Office of Management and Budget*, p. 9.

the coordination of his legislative agenda the bureaucrats might have inhibited his efforts to revive the
economy.[30]

NATIONAL PLANNING

Americans have had an ambivalent attitude toward
national planning since the idea first arose early in
the present century. It somehow seemed foreign to them
because, although it appealed to their desire for efficiency and productivity, they tended to associate it
with autocratic and totalitarian systems. In that sense
planning seemed to contradict their desire for limited
government and democracy.[31]

The concept of national planning was implicit in
the thinking of the Progressive Movement's founders
Herbert Croly and George Perkins. The first president
to involve himself in national planning was Herbert
Hoover who, when he took office, was considered the
embodiment of the progressive statesman. Hoover
appointed a President's Research Committee on Recent
Social Trends to enlist the services of some of the
nation's most prestigious social scientists to apply
the best thinking of this new science to the social
trends and problems of the day. Hoover took an active
part in its meetings and the preparation of its
reports. Unfortunately, for the usefulness of its work,
the committee established the year 1929 as the base
line for their studies. This meant that when their
reports appeared in 1933 they were completely out of
touch with the social and political conditions which
then existed in the depths of the depression.[32]

But the depression also gave the idea of planning new urgency. Between 1930 and 1933 there were six
major legislative proposals made to establish governmental central planning bodies and nine private plans

30. Schick, "The Problem of Presidential Budgeting," p. 88.

31. Barry D. Karl, *The Uneasy State: The United States from 1915 to 1945* (Chicago, 1983), p. 112.

32. Marion Clawson, *New Deal Planning: The National Resources Planning Board* (Baltimore, 1981), pp. 32–33.

which received national attention.[33] One of these efforts resulted in the establishment of the Federal Employment Stabilization Board in 1931. Its purpose was to advise the president on employment trends and business activity that could then be used in the advanced planning of public works by federal agencies. Although Hoover viewed the board as merely "a small statistical body of little significance," the board served as the legal basis for important New Deal planning efforts.[34]

The economic crisis and the consequent increase in the federal public works activity and other recovery measures made inevitable a sharp increase in the level of public planning during the New Deal. The National Industrial Recovery Act of 1933 created a Federal Emergency Administration of Public Works as a device to infuse federal dollars into the economy to support the higher prices planned by the NRA. Harold Ickes, FDR's interior secretary, was also made head of the newly created Public Works Administration. "Honest Harold," in an effort to insure that the funds would be used wisely and efficiently, in turn established, in 1933, a three-member National Planning Board (NPB).[35] Ickes, a devoted follower of Bull Moose progressivism, hoped that long after federal recovery efforts were a thing of the past, national planning would continue as a permanent government institution.[36]

Ickes designated Frederic A. Delano chairman of the NPB with Wesley C. Mitchell and Charles E. Merriam as the other two members. All served on a part-time basis. Since Mitchell and Merriam had served as chairman and vice-chairman of Hoover's social trends committee, there was clearly a direct connection between it and the NPB. Charles W. Eliot II was named the board's executive officer in charge of its full-time staff. Delano, Merriam, and Eliot were involved in all

33. Otis L. Graham, Jr., *Toward a Planned Society: From Roosevelt to Nixon* (New York, 1976), p. 13.

34. Clawson, *New Deal Planning*, p. 36; Udo Sautter, "Government and Unemployment: The Use of Public Works before the New Deal," *The Journal of American History* 73, no. 1 (June 1986): 75.

35. Clawson, *New Deal Planning*, pp. 41-43.

36. Graham, *Toward a Planned Society*, p. 52.

of the succeeding variations of New Deal planning organizations. They were able to provide significant continuity to the policies, organization, and functions of all these units.[37]

Delano had long experience as a city planner in Chicago, New York, and Washington in addition to his work as an engineer, railroad president, and member of the Federal Reserve Board. He was the president's uncle but he was so hesitant to use this family connection that the relationship was probably a handicap to the board. Sixty-nine years old in 1933, Delano continued to chair the New Deal's planning efforts until they were abolished in 1943. By then "Uncle Fred's" physical energy had waned but he remained a brilliant, dedicated planner until the end.[38]

Charles E. Merriam spent his entire professional career as a professor of political science at the University of Chicago. A political practitioner as well as a theorist, he was elected to the Chicago City Council and was narrowly defeated in 1911 when he ran as a Progressive candidate for mayor. Merriam was considered a founder of the discipline of political science.

Adept at raising funds to support his scholarly interests, Merriam helped create the Social Science Research Council as a vehicle to further these interests. Merriam, who had been a member of Hoover's Research Committee on Recent Social Trends, soon transferred his allegiance to the Democrats, got on well with FDR (who apparently found the professor informative, interesting, and stimulating), and became a major force in the New Deal planning effort. Although the university continued to be his base of operations, from 1933 to 1943 Merriam was typically in Washington two days a month for meetings and other board business. Merriam derived his greatest personal satisfaction from giving advice to the president in quiet conversations.[39]

37. "NRPB as an Organizational Device for National Planning," 14 April 1958, E2-50/57.2, Series 52.6, RG 51, NA.

38. Clawson, *New Deal Planning*, pp. 58-59.

39. Ibid., pp. 61-63; Karl, *Executive Reorganization*, pp. 51-55, 81; Richard Polenberg, *Reorganizing Roosevelt's Government: The Contro-*

The third member of the NPB was a Columbia University economist, Wesley C. Mitchell. As a renowned authority on business cycles, he added an economic expertise to the board's deliberations. He was less active on the NPB than either Delano or Merriam so that when he resigned in 1935 he was not replaced for four years.

Charles Eliot, grandson of the famous Harvard president, was only thirty-three when he became the executive officer of the NPB. Before his appointment he was a member of the staff of the National Capital Park and Planning Commission which was headed by Delano, an old family friend. A personal antagonism existed between Eliot and Merriam that contributed to the board's lack of effectiveness.[40]

The establishment of the National Planning Board was in its way an attempt to regularize the planning and advice that the brains trust furnished Roosevelt during the early days of the New Deal.[41] The NPB adopted as its function the following four program areas: (1) planning and programming of public works; (2) a research program for the development of the social and economic aspects of public policy; (3) coordination of federal planning activities; and (4) the stimulation of regional, state, and local planning. The NPB itself only had five employees—most of this work was accomplished by the commissioning of studies and the writing of reports which dealt with such subjects as natural resources, industry, transportation, population, housing and welfare.[42] From the beginning, the NPB sought to elevate planning to a central part of the New Deal.

The NPB only existed under that name for eleven months. FDR had decided the country needed a perma-

versy Over Executive Reorganization, 1936-1939 (Cambridge, Mass., 1966), pp. 12–13.

40. Clawson, *New Deal Planning*, pp. 64–65.

41. Lester Seligman, "Presidential Leadership: The Inner Circle and Institutionalization," *The Journal of Politics* 18, no. 3 (August 1956): 425.

42. Clawson, *New Deal Planning*, p. 43; "NRPB as an Organizational Device for National Planning."

nent long-range planning commission to prepare a program of national development. The NPB sought to become
that commission by recommending in its final report
the establishment of a continuous national planning
agency. In June 1934 the three members and Eliot met
with Roosevelt to draw up a new charter to make the
NPB an independent agency reporting directly to the
president. When Ickes and others learned of the
planned reorganization they objected so strenuously
that Roosevelt added five cabinet members to the
board, named Ickes as its chairman, and called it the
National Resources Board (NRB). The Delano group
retained control of the technical staff and directed
its program. The new board was to help plan the allocation of all emergency relief funds, not just those
funds appropriated for public works. While the committee never achieved its objectives it became a bastion
for those in the administration who believed in a managed economy. Since, like the NPB, the legislative authorization for the National Resources Board was the
National Industrial Recovery Act, when that law was
declared unconstitutional the NRB had to be reestab-
lished. This time it was called the National Resources
Committee and it was attached to the Emergency Relief
Appropriation Act of 1935. It continued to exist in this
form from 1935 to 1939 but nothing really had changed
except the name.[43]

THE BROWNLOW COMMITTEE

Charles Merriam's definition of "planning" was the
relationship between responsibly conducted government
and the provision of reliable information. He firmly
believed that the American government needed the
knowledge residing in the academic community and that
the scholars needed the experience of serving in government.[44] When Roosevelt, in the summer of 1935,
expressed an interest in improving the management of
the burgeoning executive branch, Merriam saw an

43. Clawson, *New Deal Planning*, pp. 44–46; Schlesinger, *Coming of
the New Deal*, pp. 350–352.
44. Karl, *Executive Reorganization*, p. 43.

opportunity to extend the academy's involvement in government planning. He suggested to the president that he have a study made to explore ways to promote "more effective over-all management in the Federal Government, a better integration of the activities of the administrative departments and agencies, and a reduction of . . . jurisdictional conflicts." He offered to have the project undertaken by the Public Administration Committee of the Social Science Research Council. Roosevelt was initially cool to the idea because he was worried about the political implications of Merriam's proposed study.[45]

Merriam's friend Louis Brownlow was the chairman of the council's Public Administration Committee. Brownlow had begun his professional life as a newspaper reporter in Tennessee in 1900. Fifteen years later Woodrow Wilson named him as one of the commissioners who governed the District of Columbia. This led to a career as a city manager in communities in Virginia and Tennessee during the 1920s. As a friend of Ickes's and Merriam's he was used as a consultant by them on various public works and relief projects.[46]

In March 1936 Merriam arranged a meeting between Roosevelt and Brownlow. After a lengthy conference they found themselves "in quite close agreement" about the nature of the proposed study. They defined the problem as how to provide the president "with simple but effective machinery which will enable him to exercise managerial control appropriate to the burden of responsibility imposed upon him by the Constitution."[47] Brownlow wanted to go significantly beyond the concept of the president as a business manager to the doctrine of administrative leadership. That is, the president's role should become a creative one in which he would be responsible for the ends of administration as well as the means. The intent was to establish institutional staff agencies to handle the routine of day-to-day operations so the president would be free to devote

---

45. Polenberg, *Reorganizing Roosevelt's Government*, p. 13.
46. Ibid., pp. 11-12.
47. Brownlow, *Passion for Anonymity*, pp. 329-338.

his major attention to the future direction of government programs.[48]

But while Brownlow and the other committee members were primarily interested in the problem of the general coordination of the top management of the government through improved presidential staff support, Roosevelt wanted to expand their project to include government-wide reorganization. He was able to convince Brownlow that public and congressional support for the study might be secured by emphasizing the need for an examination of the entire federal structure to find a way to integrate the emergency agencies with the regular establishment.[49] Brownlow was not really interested in the broader study nor did he feel competent to carry it out but the president had his way.

Apparently Roosevelt's major concern was always broad reorganization instead of the establishment of a presidential staff. The president also wanted the committee to be his creation—not a private group financed with money raised by Merriam. With some effort FDR found a way to finance the study with federal funds. On 20 March 1936 he created The President's Committee on Administrative Management with Brownlow as its head. The presidential letter that became the committee's charter directed it to study the relationship between the regular departments and the new agencies. To minimize political complications it was agreed that the committee would not report to the president until after the election of 1936, that while it was doing its work the committee would not communicate with Roosevelt, and that the president would be free to accept or reject any or all of the committee's recommendations.[50]

The other members of the committee were Merriam and Luther Gulick. Gulick, who was the youngest of the three, had studied political science at Columbia and had become an outstanding expert on budgetary and

---

48. Heclo, "Introduction" in *Illusion of Presidential Government*, p. 12.

49. Brownlow, *Passion for Anonymity*, pp. 329–338.

50. Ibid., pp. 344–376.

fiscal management. For fifteen years prior to his appointment to the committee Gulick had been director of the Institute of Public Administration in New York.[51]

* * *

Governmental organizational reform efforts before 1937 always had economy as their prime motivation. To the extent that they were intended to aid the president, they sought to streamline his chain of command by strengthening the supervisory agencies outside the White House and by reducing his span of control. The Brownlow committee added a new approach——by expanding the presidency they sought to increase its capacity for control.[52]

Roosevelt accepted the committee's report and, in a White House meeting with congressional leaders in January 1937, sought their support for the concept. This was quickly followed with a formal request that legislation be enacted to implement the committee's recommendations. The most controversial of these proposed: (1) consolidating within twelve major departments all the boards, commissions, corporations, and agencies of the federal government; (2) creating two new departments called Social Welfare and Public Works and changing the name of the Interior Department to Department of Conservation; and (3) including within the Civil Service, on a career and merit basis, all non-policy-making positions reporting to the president.[53] A discussion of the above recommendations is beyond the scope of this book but clearly these were the items that were strongly resisted within the federal bureaucracy and by Congress. They were the recommendations that caused the whole report to be rejected initially by Congress——not the proposal to establish a presidential staff.

Ironically, although the cabinet reorganization aroused the most opposition, Brownlow believed his

---

51. Polenberg, *Reorganizing Roosevelt's Government*, pp. 15-16.
52. Luther Gulick, "Conclusion to Symposium on Executive Office," *Public Administration Review* 1, no. 2 (1941): 139.
53. Brownlow, *Passion for Anonymity*, p. 386.

proposals for the president's staff were far more rev-olutionary.[54] While the concept was new, the proposals themselves were quite modest. In their analysis of the president's needs the committee focused on those clas-sic management tools of budgeting, planning, and per-sonnel. These particular functions were chosen because they were the ones, in the view of the committee, by which an executive could control his organization. They were also the ones most difficult to delegate. As a result they recommended that the president directly supervise a strengthened Budget Bureau and a national resources board that would have the responsibility for national planning and research to improve governmen-tal efficiency. For the White House itself they recom-mended that the president be given a few assistants to help with his work and serve him in a confidential ca-pacity. Personnel issues would be addressed by putting the civil service function under the president.[55]

The committee was criticized at the time because it had not recommended a central administrative offi-cial to be the president's principal assistant and staff coordinator.[56] Really this omission was not the com-mittee's doing. Its first report had suggested the establishment of a secretariat to include all the functions then performed in the White House. It would

54. Some have argued that the committee's part in the establish-ment of a presidential staff has been overrated because their report contained no detailed discussion of the executive office as such. See "Machinery to Assist the President," AM Project 174, June 1944–Novem-ber 1945, E2–5, Series 39.32, OMB. There is a dispute on this point. See Edward H. Hobbs, "An Historical Review of Plans for Presidential Staffing," *Law and Contemporary Problems* 21, no. 4 (Autumn 1956): 674. Richard Neustadt believes that Roosevelt had already decided what staff assistance he needed to enhance his control of the executive branch and that Brownlow's committee was his "chosen instrument" to obtain it. The committee took his ideas and provided, in management terms, a rationale for their acceptance. As Neustadt sees it, "They wrote, he edited." See Richard E. Neustadt, "Approaches to Staffing the Presidency: Notes on F.D.R. and J.F.K.," *The American Political Science Review* 57 (December 1963): 856.

55. Brownlow, *Passion for Anonymity*, pp. 313, 386; Lewis Brownlow, "A General View," *Public Administration Review* 1, no. 2 (1941): 102–103; "Machinery to Assist the President."

56. Hobbs, "Historical Review," p. 675.

be headed by an executive secretary who would establish direct lines of communication with all the staff
agencies except the Budget Bureau.[57] The committee
wanted this individual to serve as the president's primary agent in dealing with current policy problems by
arranging meetings or by direct staff work.[58] It was
Roosevelt who vetoed the idea.[59]

The committee also failed to recommend any
machinery for substantive policy development even
though all the members were probably more interested
in politics and policy than in management. But they
felt that the first step had to be the establishment of
an institutional structure to provide essential information and control. This was a necessary foundation
for a sophisticated system of policy or program development. The mere mention of the latter functions in
1937 would have frightened Congress and probably prevented anything from being authorized.[60] It is also
probable that these recommendations were not made because the committee knew what Roosevelt was likely to
accept and what he would oppose.

57. Brownlow, *Passion for Anonymity*, p. 376.

58. Don K. Price to Director of the Budget, "Presidential or Cabinet
Secretariat," 25 March 1947, p. 3. Copy in possession of Professor
Price.

59. FDR said, "You can't have just one Executive Secretary, the
damn columnists would never let him alone. They are always looking
for the 'white haired boy.'. . ." Instead the president wanted each of
his assistants to handle a separate area and report directly to him.
As he described it: "There would be one for foreign affairs. He would
go out in the morning and see Hull, and then go to the Treasury, to
Agriculture, to Commerce, to the Federal Reserve, and find out what
was up, touching foreign relations where ever it was." Other assistants would similarly deal with business relations, financial affairs,
welfare, and conservation. Brownlow tried to point out that he also
needed a person for personnel and planning and that it would be confusing and inefficient for four individuals to report directly to the
president. One should at least be tacitly designated "primus inter
pares." Eventually FDR agreed to adding a "fellow who never goes
out." As a result of this discussion, and one with Governor Frank Low-
den, the committee decided to eliminate the executive secretary
recommendation from their final report. See Brownlow, *Passion for
Anonymity*, pp. 376, 381.

60. Don K. Price to Alfred Sander, 28 February 1972.

Roosevelt believed he had won the support of congressional leaders for the Brownlow proposals. But, probably because of his landslide victory in November, he was overconfident. The president's court-packing scheme, which had been introduced shortly before the reorganization bill, had so disrupted the Roosevelt coalition that his entire legislative program was endangered. Opponents of the reorganization bill labeled it a "dictator bill" and tied it together with the attack on the Supreme Court as part of a Rooseveltian conspiracy to seize control of the entire government.

After a great effort the president was able to win, in August 1937 by a vote of 283 to 75, House approval of a modified reorganization bill. It was March 1938 before the floor leader, James F. Byrnes, was able to get the Senate to approve by a narrow margin a more severely amended version of the bill. Then it all came to naught when the House refused to accept the Senate version, and the conference committee could not agree on another. The bill was dead. It was another year before Roosevelt was able to work out an acceptable compromise.[61]

There is little doubt that it was the broader departmental reorganization proposals which threatened vested interests that aroused the most resistance in Congress. But it is also true that there was a legislative reluctance to equip the executive with a staff that could contest with the congressional prerogative to establish public policy. Many viewed the New Deal as the crystallization of new executive power and a powerful presidential staff was symbolic of the change. There was also an unwillingness to concede that the presidential staff structure was not a legislative matter.[62]

THE EXECUTIVE OFFICE OF THE PRESIDENT

Despite the congressional rejection of the Brownlow committee's proposals, Roosevelt remained committed to

61. Brownlow, *Passion for Anonymity*, pp. 400–403.
62. Seligman, "Presidential Leadership," p. 421.

their basic purposes. By the fall of 1938, congressional leaders indicated to the president their willingness to try again to pass a reorganization measure. Both the leaders and Roosevelt himself, however, were mindful of the Republican resurgence and the hostility the 1937 bill had aroused. The new bill that emerged, therefore, was shorn of virtually all controversial features. Rather than proposing a dramatic overhaul of the cabinet departments, the new measure merely provided that the president could suggest reorganization plans to Congress which if not rejected by both houses within sixty days would have the force of law—a power similar to one that Hoover had been given seven years before.[63] Twenty-one agencies and bureaus that individual congressmen wanted to protect were exempted altogether from the reach of the bill. And the purpose of the bill was not to produce a more effective executive branch but "to reduce substantially Government expenditures."[64]

In this emasculated form, the bill successfully avoided controversy, passing both houses of Congress by comfortable majorities. In some ways its weakness symbolized the waning of the New Deal. Nonetheless, it contained the seeds of a new form of presidential office. One provision of the bill authorized the president to appoint six administrative assistants, without congressional confirmation, at salaries of $10,000. On this hook, with the power to submit reorganization proposals for congressional review, Louis Brownlow eventually managed to hang a presidential staff structure.

When it became clear that the bill was going to pass Congress, Roosevelt lost little time in reassembling the Brownlow committee and putting it to work preparing several reorganization plans to be submitted under the new law. The committee quickly developed "Reorganization Plan No. 1 of 1939" which, since it was not rejected by Congress, became effective on 1 July

---

63. The Economy Act of 1932 authorized the president to regroup agencies unless within sixty days one of the houses disapproved. See Polenberg, *Reorganizing Roosevelt's Government*, p. 5.

64. Ibid., pp. 183–187.

1939. The plan transferred the Bureau of the Budget and the National Resources Planning Board (the new name of the National Resource Committee) to the "Executive Office of the President."[65] An amorphous presidential staff structure was thus created by this oblique reference to an "executive office" which was not further defined. That could have been the end of it had not Roosevelt, for reasons quite separate and un-related to the establishment of a presidential staff, found it expedient to add other units to this office. Brownlow took advantage of this need to achieve much of his original objective to define a broad presiden-tial staff organization.[66]

65. Ibid., p. 188.

66. Albert A. Blum, "Birth and Death of the M-Day Plan," in *American Civil-Military Decisions*, ed. Harold Stein (Birmingham, Ala., 1963), pp. 79-80.

2.
Roosevelt's Executive Office

As Europe raced toward war during the summer of 1939, Roosevelt was struggling to maintain his control over the industrial mobilization issue raised by the war scare. After World War I the assistant secretary of war had been given the responsibility for developing industrial mobilization plans in the event of another war. Over the years these plans were refined and buttressed by an impressive array of data. The most recent plan developed by the War Department proposed to establish a superagency to direct the nation's economic affairs in time of war. By 1939 it had become the mission of Bernard Baruch, that sometime "adviser to presidents" and ex-mobilization czar, to obtain Roosevelt's support for that plan.[1]

Roosevelt was very suspicious of any mobilization authority recommended by big business. He had a strong instinct against sharing power combined with great confidence in his ability to manage the government. After all, he had a longer period of experience in governmental operations than most of his subordinates. His service as assistant secretary of the navy during World War I had given him a real feel for the

---

1. Robert Cuff, "Ferdinand Eberstadt, the National Security Resources Board, and the Search for Integrated Mobilization Planning, 1947–1948," *The Public Historian* 7, no. 4 (Fall 1985): 39; Bernard M. Baruch, *The Public Years* (New York, 1960), p. 281.

workings of the bureaucracy, and presiding over the complex expansion of the government during the New Deal had added to his self-confidence. He was not in-clined to appoint someone to assume much of the au-thority he felt well qualified to exercise.[2]

Louis Johnson, who in 1937 became the assistant secretary of war charged with industrial mobilization planning, had tried for several years to set up an ad-visory committee of industrialists to work with his office. Roosevelt had several times blocked these ef-forts but he was finally worn down by Johnson's stealthy maneuvering and a fear that war was coming. In August 1939 the president approved the establish-ment of the War Resources Board (WRB) to evaluate the mobilization plan. The board, selected by Johnson and others in the War Department, was made up of business executives from the major banking and industrial in-terests and academics. While the board did not formally report their findings until November, FDR soon learned that they intended to bless the plan and to volunteer to become Baruch's superagency in the event of war.[3]

Widespread opposition to the WRB developed when its membership was announced. Liberal Democrats be-lieved it would be dominated by big business. Many of the president's advisers were suspicious of the "Economic Royalists" who had developed the plan and feared that the superagency would be dominated by the "Morgan interests." Labor and agricultural leaders felt slighted because they were unrepresented on the board. Even many anti-New Dealers saw it as a effort to establish an "iron-heeled dictatorship."[4]

Roosevelt, alarmed by the political uproar and still wary of sharing his power with a mobilization czar, asked Brownlow how he might avoid the WRB trap. When Brownlow discovered that the World War I legis-

2. Robert R. Nathan interview by Kenneth Hechler, 10 June 1946, AM Project 533, 11/45-7/46, Series 39.32, OMB.

3. Brownlow, *Passion for Anonymity*, p. 424; Cuff, "Eberstadt," p. 40; Paul A. C. Koistinen, "The 'Industrial-Military Complex' in Historical Perspective: The InterWar Years," *The Journal of American History* 56, no. 4 (March 1970): 836.

4. Cuff, "Eberstadt," p. 40; Koistinen, "The 'Industrial-Military Com-plex,'" p. 837.

lation that had created the National Defense Council Advisory Committee had never been repealed, he realized that a new advisory committee made up of business and labor leaders of the president's choice could be appointed under the old statute. So he proposed that the president dismiss the War Resources Board as soon as practical and bury its report, reconstitute an advisory committee in its stead, place it within the recently created Executive Office of the President, and assign this new committee the responsibility for the coordination of the mobilization effort. Brownlow explained that in this way the president could avoid the superagency and maintain his control over mobilization. It was the kind of convoluted scheme that was likely to appeal to Roosevelt's devious mind. FDR liked the idea. In late August he asked Brownlow to draw up an executive order activating the Executive Office of the President which had been authorized the previous month in Reorganization Plan No. 1. Then, when the WRB sent in its report in November, FDR thanked them for their work and never convened the group again.[5]

The purpose of the executive order from Roosevelt's point of view was merely to provide a way out of his problems with Baruch and Johnson, but Brownlow used it to spell out the organization and functions of the executive office. For the next several days Brownlow, with help from Harold Smith, the recently appointed director of the Budget Bureau, Donald C. Stone, the new head of the bureau's Administrative Management Division, and Judge Townsend of the Justice Department, drafted Executive Order No. 8248. The final draft proposed a five-part executive office: the Bureau of the Budget, the National Resources Planning Board, an Office of Government Reports, a Liaison Office for Personnel Management, and a White House Office.[6] To deal with Roosevelt's industrial mobilization problem Brownlow inserted in his draft a clause stating that "There should be in that Office in the event of a national emergency or threat of a national emer-

5. Brownlow, *Passion for Anonymity*, pp. 424–428; Cuff, "Eberstadt," p. 40; Koistinen, "The 'Industrial-Military Complex,'" p. 837.

6. Brownlow, *Passion for Anonymity*, pp. 428–429; Donald C. Stone to Alfred Sander, 19 April 1971.

gency such an office for emergency management as the President shall determine."[7]

In the draft Brownlow carefully defined the "White House Office." The passage included a detailed description of the relationship that each of the six administrative assistants would maintain with functional areas within the executive branch. FDR accepted the White House Office but he struck out of the draft the assignments for his assistants.[8] (Roosevelt was never one to limit his options unnecessarily.)

Brownlow was anxious to have the executive order promulgated before war broke out in Europe for two reasons. He thought that the president would have greater flexibility in dealing with the international crisis as well as its possible domestic repercussions if the Office for Emergency Management was in existence. Second, the outbreak of war would probably result in a special session of Congress which might inhibit Roosevelt's ability to organize the executive office on his own authority. Brownlow explained to the president that though "there will be no basis in truth for it, the charge may be made that you have provided in an Executive Order for something that should have been submitted in a reorganization plan which would give Congress the sixty-day veto opportunity." Apparently convinced by this reasoning, FDR agreed to issue the executive order but the war began before he acted. On 8 September 1939, a few days after the German invasion of Poland started World War II, Roosevelt declared a limited emergency and signed the executive order creating the EOP. It went into effect on the 12th.[9]

Roosevelt's biographer has termed the executive office that the order described "the single most important step in the institutionalization of the Presidency."[10] Yet if it had not been for the war and his concern over losing control of mobilization policy, FDR

---

7. Fifth draft of executive order, 29 August 1939, E2-50/39.1, Series 39.32, RG 51, NA.

8. Ibid.

9. Albert A. Blum, "Birth and Death of the M-Day Plan," p. 83; Harold Smith to Roosevelt, 29 August 1939, 2-50/39.1, Series 39.32, RG 51, NA.

10. James M. Burns, *Presidential Government: The Crucible of Leadership* (Boston, 1965), p. 73.

might never had made more than the superficial changes of formally moving the Budget Bureau from the Treasury Department and removing Ickes from the chairmanship of the planning board.

THE OFFICE FOR EMERGENCY MANAGEMENT

The promulgation of Executive Order No. 8248 cleared the way for Roosevelt to inaugurate Brownlow's plan to reactivate the Council of National Defense and set up the Office for Emergency Management (OEM). FDR and Brownlow discussed the structure of the OEM several times during the fall of 1939. But Roosevelt hesitated to act—at first perhaps because he wished to avoid any confrontation with Congress while the Neutrality Act was being revised, and later, because the period of the "phony war" suggested to the public mind that the war would not touch America.[11]

Finally, the German invasion of France provided what Brownlow thought was the right psychological moment to proceed with the mobilization plans. On 21 May 1940 Brownlow wrote to the president suggesting that it was

now necessary to set up this Office for Emergency Management. It should be part of the Executive Office of the President, and should be organized on the basic principle that regular agencies of the Government should be used whenever such agencies exist and to the full extent of their availability. . . . [The office] can be brought into existence at a moment's notice under existing law; it will utilize existing governmental agencies and personnel; it will require only a small number of new setups, only a small number of new persons, and . . . almost no new legislation.[12]

In the same memo Brownlow pointed out that since the new office would operate directly under the president it "would relieve him of the difficulty of adjusting the inevitable friction that would arise if a wholly new emergency organization were set up outside the

---

11. Blum, "Birth and Death of the M-Day Plan," pp. 84–87.

12. Brownlow to the President, 21 May 1940, M1–21/40.1, Series 39.32, RG 51, NA.

existing departments and agencies." This reassurance was bound to appeal to a president who shrank from personal confrontations with subordinates jealous of their prerogatives. Brownlow concluded his memo with another strong selling point: "Such an emergency management organization could be liquidated at a moment's notice by action of the Chief Executive."[13]

The Office for Emergency Management, as recommended by Brownlow, would consist of three elements:

1. The Council of National Defense, established by Act of August 29, 1916, which is composed of the Secretaries of War, Navy, Interior, Agriculture, Commerce and Labor. To these should be added the Secretary of the Treasury and the Director of the Budget;
2. An Advisory Commission of the Council of National Defense;
3. An Administrative Assistant to the President to maintain liaison between the President and Council of National Defense and its Advisory Commission for the purpose of the greatest utilization of existing agencies of the Government, their coordination, and their correlation with such new agencies as may be required. . . .

The president accepted this recommendation, and on 25 May 1940 he established the Office for Emergency Management by executive order. One of his administrative assistants, William H. McReynolds, was designated as the liaison officer in charge of the new office.[14]

Three days later he reactivated the defense council, a legal facade made up of several of his cabinet officers. Finally, on 29 May FDR notified the cabinet that the first meeting of the National Defense Council would be its last and that henceforth its advisory commission could report directly to him through McReynolds. In this way Roosevelt legally obtained an advisory committee made up of experts in various fields of mobilization to help him coordinate the rearmament program.[15]

Why did Roosevelt go to all this trouble to create a specious organization? Perhaps the president

---

13. Ibid.
14. Ibid.
15. Brownlow, *Passion for Anonymity*, pp. 429–430.

sought to counter charges that he was administratively incompetent. Of course, his actions would not convince anyone who understood their lack of substance. Bernard Baruch, for example, was bitter when the plan he sponsored was discarded. He described the whole concept as a tragic error that had been sold to Roosevelt by "some so-called experts or professors on organization."[16] Others, however, were fooled. James M. Burns lauded the two words "emergency management" as summing up "the curious combination of orderly management and crisis government that characterized his early war administration." It was a "peculiarly Rooseveltian instrument—flexible, informal, adaptable."[17]

There is no doubt that it was flexible. Since it was completely undefined it could create the illusion of sound organization without the handicap of regulations, structures, or organizational relationships. The office became a handy place to lodge wartime emergency agencies in a day when it was not politic to hint that war might be coming. But when activated it turned out to be merely an auxiliary or housekeeping agency. McReynolds, its titular chief, had no authority to supervise any of the agencies placed within the office. Although he could be used to help gain the ear of the president, he could also be ignored with impunity. With few exceptions, almost all the wartime agencies were attached to this office at some time during their existence.[18]

The Office for Emergency Management was a temporary expedient. In 1949 Clinton Rossiter observed that it

had a "short happy life" as the administrative sky-hook from which Mr. Roosevelt cleverly suspended the vast hodge-podge of wartime agencies erected in his name as commander-in-chief. The virtually complete postwar abandonment of these agencies left the OEM in its prewar condition, without a head or a place to rest it. If it may be

---

16. Blum, "Birth and Death of the M-Day Plan," p. 89.

17. James M. Burns, *Roosevelt: The Soldier of Freedom*, (New York, 1970), pp. 332-333.

18. Edward H. Hobbs, *Behind the President* (Washington, D.C., 1954), pp. 185-187.

said to exist at all, it is rather as a hazy administrative concept than as a visible office. The OEM is now just a line of type in the *Government Manual.*[19]

THE NEW BUDGET BUREAU

The Executive Office of the President may have come into existence to deal with Roosevelt's war mobilization problems but without a doubt the most significant effect of Brownlow's executive order was the new role it created for the Bureau of the Budget. Allen Schick has written:

The prevailing verdict is that the Brownlow Committee succeeded in augmenting presidential power through the budget process. Within a few years, the Budget Bureau's size increased more than tenfold, and it became the principal staff agency in the new Executive Office of the President. Executive Order 8248 of September 8, 1939, gave the bureau a broad mandate to help the president in superintending the administrative affairs of the federal government. By 1945, the bureau had become a different agency. It still reviewed agency estimates, but it had become the general staff for the president. The institutional presidency was in place, and the bureau's resources, skills, memory, and loyalty to the president could be passed on from one chief executive to the next.[20]

In the spring of 1939 a search had begun for a new budget director.[21] Morgenthau asked Brownlow to recommend someone of the city-manager type who was nonpolitical and who had administrative and budgetary experience. One person Brownlow suggested was Harold D. Smith, who was then the head of the Michigan state budget office.[22]

Roosevelt accepted the Smith recommendation even though he did not know him. Smith's Republican background did not seem to bother the president and

---

19. Clinton L. Rossiter, "The Constitutional Significance of the Executive Office of the President," p. 1209.

20. Allen Schick, "The Problem of Presidential Budgeting," p. 89.

21. The search may have been initiated because congressmen twitted Roosevelt about Daniel Bell's four-year status as "acting" director.

22. Brownlow, *Passion for Anonymity*, p. 414.

eventually a close relationship developed between the two men.[23] Smith took office on 15 April 1939. Since his appointment was part of an effort to revitalize the bureau, it was accompanied by the authorization of fifty-five new positions for the bureau for the 1939 fiscal year.[24]

Harold Smith was a plain man normally outfitted in high laced shoes and inexpensive suits. Slow and deliberate in manner, he worked hard and, more important, he saw the need for a coordinated and talented presidential staff and the role he might play in attaining it. Totally lacking charisma, he nonetheless won respect through the force and conviction with which he moved and spoke once he determined which course to follow.[25] Thoroughly experienced in budgeting, he considered it a device for consolidating the needs, desires, and objectives of the citizens to jointly provide for their safety and comfort. He believed the federal budget was the single most important document in the social and economic affairs of the people.[26] His ambitions for the bureau were not limited to preparing the budget, however. He saw his agency as the logical policy-coordinating arm of the president and his center for management control.[27] With Smith's appointment the Budget Bureau was poised to move into a period of unprecedented competence and authority.

As the bureau staff increased in size, a divisional structure emerged. Expenditure control was strengthened in the estimates division to permit a more searching inquiry into departmental requests for appropriations and the value of departmental operations. A legislative reference division prepared executive orders and proclamations, monitored congressional legislation, and coordinated the development and

23. Staats in Thompson, *Portraits,* vol. 2, p. 79.

24. Harold H. Roth, "The Executive Office of the President: A Study of Its Development with Emphasis on the Period 1939-53," (Ph. D. diss. The American University, 1958), pp. 144-145.

25. Ramsey, "Director of the Bureau of the Budget," p. 92.

26. *Staff Organization Manual,* Frederick J. Lawton Papers, HSTL, p. 33.

27. Herman M. Somers, *Presidential Agency: OWMR* (Cambridge, Mass., 1950), p. 66.

presidential review of proposed legislation. A fiscal division was created to examine questions of fiscal policy and help in the formulation of the president's financial program. The study of administrative problems throughout the government was begun with a small Division of Research and Investigation in 1939 which shortly became the Division of Administrative Management. Lastly, a new impetus was given to the collection and use of economic and social data by the federal government when the Central Statistical Board was transferred to the bureau where it was renamed the Division of Statistical Standards.[28]

Between 1939 and 1942 the Bureau of the Budget was transformed from a fiscal control organization to one involved in the development of substantive policy. This change was due to several factors. Probably most important was the strong leadership of Harold Smith. Another reason was the void that existed in program and policy development in the federal establishment. It was almost inevitable that an agency organizationally close to the president, sparked by imagination and ambition, would move into this vacuum. Lastly, Smith headed a school of thought which believed that budgetary control, administrative management, and policy formulation could not logically, and should not effectively, be separated.[29] As the bureau's capability increased during this period, Roosevelt usually looked to it for the in-depth staff work that he thought his White House aides could not, or should not, take on.[30] It was a self-perpetuating process with the president's dependence on the bureau growing as it demonstrated its competence in serving his needs.

Some feel that the bureau reached the peak of its effectiveness and authority during this period. Smith built the competence of his staff in a systematic manner, recruiting such talents as Wayne Coy, Donald Stone, and Stuart Rice, and skimming the cream of the

28. "The Bureau of the Budget: Its Background," B2-1, Series 52.2, RG 51, NA.

29. Somers, *Presidential Agency,* p. 211.

30. Neustadt, "Approaches to Staffing the Presidency," p. 556.

public administration people out of the colleges.[31]
Harold Smith's great accomplishment was to instill in
the bureau rank and file a sense of service to the
president.

The talented men and women who flocked to the bureau believed that
making government efficient and making it responsive to the president were complementary tasks. For them, the reorganization of an
agency's field offices or the coordination of statistical reports was
presidential business, whether or not the particular matter actually
came to the president's attention.

In this way the bureau became the custodian of the
president's institutional interests. The bureau could
supply the president with the information and advice
he needed and he could trust them to see problems
from his perspective and to protect his interests.[32]
But the bureau was careful to emphasize its institutional role and avoid partisanship. Smith used to tell
his young staff people that "you have to be politically
aware but not politically active." He believed that the
best politics for any president was a nonpolitical Budget Bureau.[33]
　　Finally, and perhaps most importantly, Smith
worked at developing his close personal relationship
with the president. Smith spent so much time with FDR,
sometimes visiting three or four times a day, that the
White House secretaries wondered how he got his own
work done.[34] With probably the best staff in Washington
and an excellent personal relationship with Roosevelt,
it was not surprising that Smith's bureau became the
president's personal technical staff as well as an important policy adviser.
　　The Budget and Accounting Act gave the bureau
responsibility for studying the organization and methods of management of the federal government. But Dawes
took no action so the initiative for executive branch

---

31. Transcript, James L. Sundquist interview, 15 July 1963, HSTL, p.
3.

32. Schick, "The Problem of Presidential Budgeting," p. 89.

33. Staats in Thompson, *Portraits,* vol. 2, p. 87.

34. Confidential sources, personal correspondence, Neustadt Papers, HSTL.

reorganization had remained with Congress. To reclaim this function Smith established the Administrative Management Division and greatly expanded the work of the bureau in this area.[35] It was a daunting task to provide assistance to the agencies in their internal management problems without arousing resentment. The bureau largely overcame this by creating a consulting-type relationship.[36] The management experts were aided in their work by the lines of communication forged with agency administrators over the years through the bureau's budget work. Not surprisingly, the management research greatly improved the traditional budget function since "by getting involved in the internal management of federal agencies, the bureau was able to make informed and acceptable budget decisions."[37]

After a few years of Smith's leadership, "the bureau had moved far beyond its traditional budgetary responsibility and was making ambitious efforts to plan, coordinate, and review the whole war administration."[38] Yet this growth in the power and influence of the bureau reached its peak in 1943 and then began a decline that persisted throughout most of the war. The decline occurred because of the changed climate in wartime Washington and the emergence of a powerful rival in the Office of War Mobilization (OWM). The industrial executives who had come to town to head many of the new wartime agencies were inclined to go their own way either by temperament or because they were unfamiliar with the bureaucratic way of doing business. When their actions were questioned, they tended to go directly to the president for a decision. It was precisely this situation that prompted Roosevelt to delegate much of his power to Jimmy Byrnes and his OWM. Smith never really accepted these developments even as an emergency situation and continued his fight to make the bureau the president's main policy arm.[39]

---

35. Don K. Price, "Staffing the Presidency," *The American Political Science Review* 40 no. 6 (December 1946): 1159.

36. Staats in Thompson, *Portraits,* vol. 2, p. 86.

37. Schick, "The Problems of Presidential Budgeting," p. 108.

38. Burns, *Roosevelt: Soldier of Freedom,* p. 452.

39. Somers, *Presidential Agency,* pp. 66–67.

The bureau had many detractors during the war. For example, Dean Acheson, then an assistant secretary of state, derided the bureau's administrative management unit as the "constant critic and improver of administration," and dismissed the suggestions of the organizational experts, most of whom were trained in public administration graduate schools, as "theoretical nonsense."[40] OWM considered the Budget Bureau merely "a housekeeping agency" and fought the agency's pretensions to be considered a policy-making unit. At least one high-ranking OWM official argued that the bureau simply did not have enough prestige to assume the policy role it sought.[41]

As the bureau's power began to decline, Smith tried to compensate by accentuating his role as presidential aide, turning over many of his administrative duties to his deputy. The influence of the bureau, now increasingly tied to Smith's personal relationship with Roosevelt, suffered another blow when the director had a heart attack in 1943. During that year, Smith and the president limited their meetings to about once a month. In 1944 the two held only eight conferences.[42]

The bureau's loss of influence caused some soul-searching among its leaders. Donald Stone felt that the bureau had become too arrogant in its dealings with the bureaucracy and argued that the bureau should be more conscious "of the day-to-day problems and pressures facing agency administrators."[43] Others suggested that the bureau, being largely staffed by technicians and specialists, tended to overemphasize special interests while losing sight of general objectives. As a result, a bureau staffer was "easily tempted to gratify his self-esteem by forcing his special regulations and his special schemes on operating agencies."[44]

40. Dean G. Acheson, *Present at the Creation: My Years in the State Department* (New York, 1969), p. 44.

41. Robert R. Nathan interview by Kenneth Hechler, 10 June 1946, AM Project 533, 11/45–7/46, Series 39.32, OMB.

42. Ramsey, "Director of the Bureau of the Budget," pp. 99–114.

43. Stone to Hirst Sutton, 27 May 1944, B1–2, Series 39.29, RG 51, NA.

44. Price, "Staffing the Presidency," p. 1159.

Yet before the war ended the bureau began to re-
cover a measure of its former influence. Apparently
the president's declining health (and Smith's partial
recovery), and Roosevelt's increasing involvement in
international matters, revived the bureau's fortunes.
In late 1944 Roosevelt asked Smith to develop the fiscal 1946 budget with little presidential involvement.
Smith demurred since this would require the bureau to
decide a number of policy issues. But Roosevelt insisted and delegated to him total responsibility for
non-war-related matters. Thus the bureau became dominant for a time in establishing the policies of the
normal domestic aspects of the federal government.
Roosevelt also made it clear that he expected the bureau to play the major role in planning for the liquidation of the war agencies and the establishment of a
peacetime administrative structure.[45] Had Franklin
Roosevelt lived, it seems clear that the Bureau of the
Budget would have soon regained its status as the
preeminent presidential staff unit.

An overall evaluation of the Budget Bureau under
Roosevelt is difficult because it was virtually a different agency after 1939. Until the time of Harold
Smith it continued in the mold that Dawes had established. It appears that the Administrative Management
Division began to have a significant impact during the
war on how the federal agencies organized their work.
Even here a note of caution is needed because many
key members of that division became the intellectual
leaders of American public administration and they
were the ones who wrote about the accomplishments of
their colleagues. The economic analysis provided by
the new fiscal division enhanced the sophistication of
the budget messages and the bureau's policy recommendations. And of course there was Smith's role as one of
FDR's corps of advisers. But the budget bureau is not
much mentioned in the literature of the Roosevelt
years.[46]

45. Conference with the President, 18 April 1945, Diary–April 1945,
Harold D. Smith Papers, HSTL.

46. Schick, "The Problem of Presidential Budgeting," p. 89; J.
Weldon Jones to Elmer Staats, 27 March 1952, Reorganization Working
Papers, Lawton Papers, HSTL.

THE NATIONAL RESOURCES PLANNING BOARD

The National Resources Planning Board (NRPB) was essentially a refurbished National Resources Committee. The cabinet officers, including Ickes, were dropped from the membership and Delano became the chairman, but the work of the group continued without interruption. Mitchell's long-vacant seat was filled by George F. Yantis, a lawyer who had been active in regional planning in the northwest. The board's two advisers, Henry Dennison and Beardsley Ruml, continued in that status although they participated in board matters as if they were members. They would have been named members officially except that Roosevelt did not think their formal appointment was worth the political confrontation that might result. He had decided to avoid any issue that might stir up controversy about the board and its activities.[47]

Despite (or perhaps because of) its lofty organizational status, the board was not effective as an advisory or policy-making body. This is not to say it was inactive. On the contrary, during its ten-year life, the board spent a million dollars preparing 1,600 reports running to some 20,000 pages. To produce this volume its staff grew to include 150 full-time Washington employees, in addition to seventy-two in the field, and thirty-five per diem consultants.[48]

The NRPB prepared long-range plans for public works and tried to help states and local authorities to establish their own planning agencies to contribute to the federal program. It also served to bring together leading authorities from both public and private life to prepare reports dealing with the basic objectives of federal policy. The reports were sent to Roosevelt. Some he kept confidential while directing that others be published. Many of the committees that prepared reports included specialists from the federal government

---

47. "NRPB as an Organizational Device for National Planning," 14 April 1958, E2-50/57.2, Series 52.6, RG 51, NA.
48. Ibid.; John D. Clark, "The President's Economic Council," unpublished manuscript, Clark Papers, HSTL, Chapter 3, pp. 2-3.

but they represented their own views, not those of their employing agency.[49]

As time passed the board also began to view postwar planning as its major responsibility. One of its last published studies was "a New Bill of Rights." In it the board proposed broad social guarantees of the right to work; fair pay; adequate food, clothing, shelter, and medical care; personal security; and opportunity for education and recreation. During the war, the board became bolder in advocating its particular views on public policy, issuing a series of reports that reflected the ideas of Alvin Hansen. Hansen was the intellectual leader of those liberals who espoused an ever-expanding capitalist economy that would be balanced by Keynesian fiscal methods and humanized by extensive social welfare programs. His thinking was anathema to many members of Congress. This together with the postwar recommendations increased congressional demands for an end to the NRPB.[50]

Many other things contributed to the board's demise. One Budget Bureau staffer thought it resulted from a

combination of anti-Rooseveltism, of right wing reaction, of lack of awareness by the Board members of the importance of congressional relations, all mixed with considerable intrigue by the Corps of Engineers calculated to remove from the scene a group which threatened its enjoyment of a state of administrative anarchy.[51]

Ironically, shifting the board from Harold Ickes's protective custody to an exposed position on the presidential staff proved to be a fatal move. The board was now vulnerable because it had to seek annual funding from Congress instead of having its expenses covered

---

49. Price, "Staffing the Presidency," pp. 1161–1162.

50. "NRPB as an Organizational Device for National Planning"; Alonzo L. Hamby, "The Vital Center, the Fair Deal, and the Quest for a Liberal Political Economy," *American Historical Review* 77, no. 3 (June 1972): 654.

51. The corps, which over the years had become the main instrument for congressional pork-barrel projects, had always found the public works coordination efforts of NRPB inhibiting. See "Machinery to Assist the President."

by appropriations made for other governmental functions.

Certainly the Budget Bureau did not try to save the planning board. Harold Smith and his colleagues, who saw their own organization as the major institutional staff of the president, were never happy with the competition the NRPB represented. As a result, they were not active in defending it from congressional attack.[52] So the board was left with "no statutory authority, limited funds, and almost no political support. All it had was Roosevelt."[53] But even Roosevelt had grown critical of the NRPB for indulging in lofty schemes, especially in the economic sphere. It was no longer closely attuned to immediate presidential needs or with the closest circle of FDR's relationships.[54] Roosevelt was consumed by the war and the board seemed far removed from it.

The NRPB died on 31 August 1943 when Congress denied it any further funds and prohibited its functions from being transferred to another agency. The end of the NRPB resulted in a serious gap in the supply of academic papers, but its disappearance caused hardly a ripple in the Washington scene. It did not leave much of a void because it had never really gotten involved in the machinery of government except for its assigned responsibility to jointly administer public works with the Budget Bureau. Its public works programming was taken over by the Budget Bureau on a greatly reduced basis.[55]

52. Don K. Price to Alfred Sander, 28 February 1972.

53. Graham, *Toward a Planned Society*, p. 56.

54. Burns, *Roosevelt: The Soldier of Freedom*, p. 353; Seligman, "Presidential Leadership," p. 425.

55. Gerhard Colm to Edwin G. Nourse, 31 March 1952, Colm Papers, Library of Congress; Edwin G. Nourse, *Economics in the Public Service* (New York, 1953), pp. 63-64.

THE OFFICE OF GOVERNMENT REPORTS

The Office of Government Reports (OGR) was probably an afterthought in the executive office. It was primarily an organizational home for Roosevelt's friend Lowell Mellett. In no sense was it a managerial arm of the presidency in the spirit of the Brownlow committee's recommendations, and it was the least significant of the executive office units.[56] Its history highlights FDR's sometime capricious attitude toward the EOP.

The genealogy of the OGR could be traced back to the work of Katherine Blackburn, who in 1932 was in charge of research for the Democratic National Committee. In 1933 FDR brought her to Washington and, financed with "purloined funds," put her to work running his personal press-clipping service. This function soon became the Press Intelligence Section of the National Emergency Council. There it was associated with a general government information service. When the OGR was established in 1939, Roosevelt transferred both services to it.[57]

Mellett, who had been in the newspaper business for forty years, had spent the past twenty as editor of the Washington *Daily News*. As a talented liberal and steadfast supporter of the New Deal, he attracted Roosevelt's attention. In 1937 the president, in an effort to breathe life into the National Emergency Council, named Mellett to head it. The council, which at one time was FDR's idea of a supercabinet, had been moribund since 1936. Now under Mellett it became a whirlwind—coordinating relief and recovery efforts throughout the country, providing information to the media, and producing and distributing motion pictures. A measure of the council's effectiveness was the Republican criticism of it. Congressman Everett Dirksen called it "the biggest piece of fakery in the Government establishment."[58]

---

56. "Machinery to Assist the President."

57. Richard E. Neustadt to Stephen Spingarn, 27 July 1950, Saturday Morning File, Neustadt Papers, HSTL.

58. Graham, *Toward a Planned Society*, pp. 50–51; *Current Biography: Who's News and Why, 1942*, p. 481.

Reorganization Plan No. 2 of 1939 abolished the National Emergency Council and transferred its functions to the Executive Office of the President. Mellett, who had been named one of Roosevelt's six newly authorized administrative assistants, continued as a member of the White House Office when he was appointed to head the OGR. His real job seemed to be to "handle the press" for the New Deal. The OGR gave government officials a day-by-day record of newspaper and magazine information and opinion. Part of its reputation as Roosevelt's propaganda ministry arose because it distributed controversial government films such as *The Plow That Broke the Plains* and *The River* which glorified various New Deal projects.[59]

Mellett, together with press secretary Stephen T. Early, was primarily responsible for carrying out FDR's "informational" propaganda strategy in support of his foreign policy. It consisted of packaging "facts" supportive of the administration's positions and disseminating them through the privately owned mass media. Though the "facts" were accurate, their selection and arrangement made them propaganda because the intent was to build public support.[60] Although Roosevelt may have tried to manipulate public opinion for political purposes, his efforts to use information and propaganda agencies to develop public support for his military and foreign policies has been judged "from first to last a failure."[61]

In 1941 the administration asked Congress to establish the OGR by statute (instead of continuing to have it authorized from year to year by executive order) and to double its appropriation. Mellett's political activities and a fear that he might head Roosevelt's "ministry of censorship" produced some congressional opposition but the bill passed. The OGR then expanded

59. Roth, "The Executive Office," pp. 255–259; *Current Biography, 1942*, p. 481.

60. Richard W. Steele, "The Great Debate: Roosevelt, the Media, and the Coming of the War, 1940–1941," *The Journal of American History* 71, no. 1 (June 1984): 70–71.

61. Richard W. Steele, "Preparing the Public for War: Efforts to Establish a National Propaganda Agency, 1940–41," *American Historical Review* 75, no. 6 (October 1970): 1653.

at a furious pace and planned on a staff of 893 by fiscal 1943. The onset of war led to other information agencies and they soon began to overlap each other and the OGR. Finally, the Office of Government Reports and other agencies were consolidated into the Office of War Information (OWI) on 13 June 1943. Mellett became director of the motion picture bureau within OWI while continuing to serve as one of FDR's administrative assistants. The press saw him as a person who "has silently but steadily become a real power in the Government of the United States."[62]

When the war ended, government information and press intelligence activities were transferred to the Budget Bureau. But the bureau was uncomfortable with this function. In 1946 the bureau got Truman to issue a new executive order that gathered up these activities into a revived OGR with Miss Blackburn as its head. But the Republicans, long suspicious of the political purposes of OGR, soon gained control of Congress and provided only enough funds to liquidate the agency. Truman reluctantly ordered the Budget Bureau to proceed with the liquidation. Miss Blackburn eventually went back to work for the Democratic National Committee.[63]

THE WHITE HOUSE OFFICE

Until the turn of the century the president had to pay for part of his staff from his own pocket. This resulted in a practice, which is still utilized, of detailing personnel to the White House from other departments. When Hoover entered the White House, the president was entitled to a secretary, an administrative assistant, two military aides, and some forty clerks, typists, and messengers. Although it caused a "national sensation," Hoover was able to obtain congressional authorization for two additional secretaries.[64] The official White House contingent remained

62. Roth, "The Executive Office," pp. 255–259, 398; *Current Biography, 1942*, p. 482.

63. Neustadt to Spingarn, 27 July 1950; Neustadt to Herman Somers, 4 August 1949, Chronological File, Neustadt Papers, HSTL.

64. Patrick Anderson, *The Presidents' Men*, pp. 65–66.

at this size until the Reorganization Act of 1939 added six more administrative assistants to the president's staff.

Among the units of the executive office created by the Brownlow executive order was the White House Office. It included the administrative assistants along with the existing presidential assistants such as the executive secretary, correspondence secretary, press secretary, etc. The only thing "institutional" about the White House Office was the name and the positions since it was expected that each president would install his own people in these positions.

Roosevelt was slow in filling the administrative assistant slots Congress authorized in 1939. Mellett of course occupied one of them. He was soon joined by William H. McReynolds, a career civil servant from the Treasury Department, and Lauchlin Currie, an economist who came from the Federal Reserve Board. A former senator, Sherman Minton from Indiana, came aboard to deal with congressional relations along with James H. Rowe, a recent graduate of Harvard Law School. David K. Niles was appointed to handle the important matter of minority affairs. Later, Jonathan Daniels, the son of FDR's old chief in the Navy Department, joined the group. They were all housed in the old State–War–Navy Department Building across Executive Avenue from the White House in what was called "Death Row" because of the high turnover rate among its occupants.[65]

Roosevelt really expected that his assistants would remain men with, in Brownlow's phrase, "a passion for anonymity." James Rowe recalled that one time when he was meeting with the president FDR asked, "Didn't I read in the *Star*, in some social column, that you were at some cocktail party yesterday?" When Rowe confirmed the report, Roosevelt said, "If I read that too often you are going to need another job." The president made it perfectly clear that he was the only one "running

65. Ibid., pp. 78–79; Burns, *Roosevelt: The Soldier of Freedom*, p. 451.

for office" at the White House and his assistants were expected to stay away from newspapermen.[66]

Winston Churchill, who visited Washington in January 1942, was not impressed with Roosevelt's administrative machinery. He described the White House as an isolated place of "Olympian calm." He felt that the president "had no adequate link between his will and executive action." The prime minister compared the White House Office unfavorably with the British Secretariat of the Cabinet.[67]

THE LIAISON OFFICER FOR PERSONNEL MANAGEMENT

One of Roosevelt's administrative assistants was designated the "Liaison Officer for Personnel Management." The liaison officer was one of the six original elements that Brownlow established in the Executive Office of the President in 1939. Its existence was a monument to presidential frustration with the Civil Service Commission and congressional determination to maintain the existing structure.

The commission had been designed to insulate federal employment from partisan considerations by limiting the president's appointment power. But one result of the collegial structure and operation of the commission was to limit the ability of the president to manage federal personnel. The Brownlow committee attempted to remedy the problem by recommending that the commission be replaced by a single civil service administrator who would serve at the pleasure of the president. Even though the report also recommended that a board be established as a watchdog over the new structure, Congress was suspicious. This proposal was a major reason why the Brownlow recommendations were rejected in 1938.[68]

66. James Rowe in *Portraits of American Presidents*, vol. 1, *The Roosevelt Presidency*, ed. Kenneth W. Thompson (Washington, D.C., 1982), p. 10.

67. Martin Gilbert, "The Big Two," *The New York Review*, 14 February 1985, p. 34.

68. G. Calvin Mackenzie, "The Paradox of Presidential Personnel Management," in *The Illusion of Presidential Government*, ed. Hugh Heclo and Lester Salamon (Boulder, Colo., 1981), p. 132.

Roosevelt then tried to improve executive personnel management through a series of executive orders. One order required each agency to appoint a personnel director who became an *ex officio* member of a Federal Personnel Council. The council studied the federal personnel system and made policy recommendations to the president. The Budget Bureau also recommended personnel policies as a part of general responsibility for management improvement.[69]

The Reorganization Act of 1939 specifically denied to the president the right to propose any changes affecting the Civil Service Commission. This eliminated any possibility of restructuring the personnel system. So FDR accepted Brownlow's recommendation that the liaison officer for personnel management be established as part of the executive office to coordinate the activities of the personnel council, the Budget Bureau, and the Civil Service Commission. This was about as close as Roosevelt could come to centralizing authority for management of the federal personnel system in the absence of legislative support.[70]

WAR MOBILIZATION

As the likelihood of American involvement in the war loomed, economic mobilization became an increasingly hot political issue. When Roosevelt's effort to coordinate the effort through the advisory committee failed to produce the desired results, he set up the Office of Production Management within the Office for Emergency Management. It was noted for the unusual (and unworkable) device of having a dual chairmanship composed of an industrialist and a labor leader. Soon dissatisfied with this arrangement, FDR asked his legal adviser, Sam Rosenman, to propose another solution to the mobilization problem. Rosenman's idea resulted in the establishment, in August 1941, of the Special Priorities and Allocations Board (SPAB) chaired by Donald Nelson

69. Ibid., pp. 132–134.
70. Ibid.; Price, "Staffing the Presidency," p. 1159.

of Sears, Roebuck.[71] The lines of authority were now hopelessly tangled with several key individuals serving simultaneously as members of competing organizations.[72]

After the United States entered the war, a War Production Board, still chaired by Nelson, replaced SPAB as the top mobilization agency. Roosevelt now felt that at last he had a completely centralized structure. But the administrative experts were less than enthusiastic over the president's performance. His penchant for giving authority to a few influential advisers who then exercised wide discretion about the issues in which they intervened was particularly troublesome. This practice sometimes resulted in the president being forced to act with only a partial picture before him. The lack of continuity caused inconsistencies over time. Much also seemed to depend upon who saw the president last.[73]

By 1942 it all became too much, even for the master juggler. Roosevelt admitted that "I get so many conflicting recommendations my head is splitting." The disorganizer began to give way to a slowly increasing reliance on the formality of a White House staff. The foundations of a powerful executive office began to emerge as a new system of presidential government was formed.[74]

In October 1942 Roosevelt decided to institutionalize the policy leadership that Harry Hopkins and Sam Rosenman had been providing. He persuaded Supreme Court Justice James F. Byrnes to leave the bench and head the newly formed Office of Economic Stabilization. Byrnes moved into the new east wing of the White House and soon established himself on top of the pile of presidential advisers by making it clear from the

71. I. F. Stone commented that Judge Rosenman "had labored and brought forth a Rube Goldberg gadget" and cautioned his readers not to confuse SPAB with Spam.

72. Samuel B. Hand, *Counsel and Advise: A Political Biography of Samuel I. Rosenman* (New York, 1979), pp. 150–152; Memo from Frederick C. Schuldt to Mr. Zehring, 4 October 1946, Organization of Staff to the President, January–November 1946, Series 39.32, OMB.

73. Donald Stone to Director of the Budget, 13 November 1942, E.O.P. Misc. Memos, Series 39.32, OMB.

74. Burns, *Roosevelt: Soldier of Freedom*, p. 343.

outset that he was the "President's man." He refused to
get bogged down in detail or consider anything but top
policy. He maintained this same basic attitude when in
1943 he was made head of the Office of War Mobilization (OWM), the capstone of Roosevelt's attempts to organize the home front war effort.[75]

Executive Order No. 9347 of 27 May 1943, which
created the OWM, was sweeping in its provisions and
left no doubt that the new organization would control
all the government's economic functions not of a military nature. It was designed, not to provide organizational unification, but to ensure coordination of efforts short of the president. The staff of the OWM was
kept small and care was exercised to keep it out of
operational matters. With a staff of only four profes-
sionals, coordination and conciliation was all that
could be attempted.[76]

Byrnes, together with Admiral William Leahy and
Harry Hopkins, seemed to provide, at least on paper,
the semblance of an effective organization for running
the war.

In fact, Roosevelt was carrying on the old Rooseveltian tradition of
administrative juggling and disorganization. He was no more able in
1944 than in 1940 or 1934 to work through one chief of staff. He had
not three but at least a dozen "assistant presidents," including
Marshall, the more influential Cabinet members, especially Hull and
Stimson, war-agency czars Nelson, McNutt, Land, and others.[77]

THE OFFICE OF WAR MOBILIZATION AND RECONVERSION

Aside from the Budget Bureau, the fullest development
of a presidential staff during the Roosevelt years
came in the Office of War Mobilization and Reconversion (OWMR). Officially it was not even part of the executive office, being established as an independent
agency by Congress on 30 October 1944.[78] The act rep-

75. Price, "Staffing the Presidency," p. 1163; Schuldt memo, 4 October 1946, OMB.

76. "Machinery for Executive Coordination," E.O.P. Misc. Memos, Series 39.32, OMB.

77. Burns, *Roosevelt: Soldier of Freedom,* p. 452.

78. 58 Stat. 785

resented an effort by Congress to direct the administration toward postwar planning. It was unhappy that
the OWM had been established by executive order and
now that the end of the war was in sight wanted to begin to regain many of the powers it had surrendered to
the executive during the war. Aware of the hasty, un-
planned demobilization after World War I, Congress was
determined to dominate reconversion.[79]

Although not legally an element of the EOP, OWMR,
in practice, was a part of the president's office. It
took over the functions of OWM and Byrnes became its
first director. The statute gave the new agency extensive coordination authority, even over the independent
regulatory agencies, but its real authority came from a
recognition by the departments and agencies that the
president was prepared to back up the director's decisions.[80]

The director was appointed for a two-year term
and Senate confirmation of the nominee was required.
Byrnes continued to devote himself primarily to the
adjudication of disputes among departments through
the help of a small staff (less than twenty). But since
the OWMR was now charged with postwar planning as
well as wartime coordination, the size of the staff began to increase after Byrnes resigned and Roosevelt
died. Experienced administrators found that the
"flexibility of the OWMR procedures, and the general
competence and interests of its staff, enabled it to do
work for the President which no other institution has
been able to do."[81]

If a presidential staff group proves itself to be
useful, the president will turn to it regardless of the
wording of the statute that created it or its position
on an organization chart. During the last months of
the Roosevelt administration, the OWMR was quite useful and was given more and more to do. It even tended
to take over the legislative clearance function from
the Budget Bureau. This was partially because much of
the legislation was now war related, and the emergency

79. Somers, *Presidential Agency*, p. 76.

80. Don K. Price to Herbert Hoover, 28 May 1948, Reorganization of
the Executive Branch, Price Memo, George M. Elsey Papers, HSTL, p. 12.

81. Ibid., pp. 12–14.

agencies were the ones most involved in drafting it; they naturally looked to OWMR for policy guidance rather than to the bureau. OWM had confined itself to high-level matters, but OWMR tended to proliferate its interests throughout the government.[82]

ROOSEVELT AND THE EXECUTIVE OFFICE

The growth of the power of the congressional conservatives during the war resulted in the elimination of the Office of Government Reports and the National Resources Planning Board. These were undoubtedly the parts of the executive office in which Roosevelt was most interested. So when the president died, all that remained of the original six units in the executive office were the White House staff, the Bureau of the Budget, the Liaison Office for Personnel Administration (one person), and the collection of wartime agencies in the Office for Emergency Management. OWMR was technically not a part of the EOP but practically fell in the latter category.

Since the White House staff is, above all else, a creature of the incumbent president, and the Liaison Office for Personnel Management was manned by a member of the White House staff, the only institutionalized portion of the executive office to long survive Roosevelt was the Budget Bureau. But since the bureau predated his administration by more than a decade, Roosevelt's only enduring legacy to the institutionalization of the executive office was the concept, the name itself, and the transfer of the Budget Bureau from the Treasury Department to the direct supervision of the president. A more indirect contribution was his part in the creation of an executive branch so vast that his successor would be forced to seek or accept additional staff help to administer it.

But the continuance of the executive office after Roosevelt's death was by no means assured. Harold Smith, who devoted himself to building an organization

82. Richard E. Neustadt, "Presidency and Legislation: The Growth of Central Clearance," *The American Political Science Review* 48, no. 3 (September 1954): 657.

that would serve the presidency no matter who the incumbent, constantly worried that FDR's informal, personality-centered administration would not provide a strong base for the institutionalization of the presidential office.[83] The executive office survived because it was able to make a successful transition from Roosevelt to Truman. That it did so was because of Smith's determination and Truman's needs. It was not the result of Roosevelt's interest in the continuity of his office.

---

83. Fred I. Greenstein, "The Modern Presidency," pp. 52-54.

3.
Truman the Administrator

The year 1945 was a period of great change as the federal government began the complex transition from war to peace. This conversion was accompanied by wholesale changes of personnel in both Congress and the executive branch. It added up to a governmental reorientation unmatched since 1933.[1] From this flux would be born a new concept of the executive office.

Inevitably the accession of Harry Truman to the presidency had an enormous impact on the presidential staff. The contrast between Roosevelt and Truman was so great that it invited comparison in the way they approached their jobs. Sam Rosenman, who served as special counsel for both men, was in a good position to observe their presidential styles. He considered Roosevelt more imaginative but much more cautious politically than Truman—he was always aware of the effect of his actions on his chances for reelection. "He was willing to make many compromises so that he could last to fight another day." Truman, Rosenman believed, did many things that Roosevelt would never have done simply because he thought them necessary or proper. Once he made up his mind on a matter, he gave little thought to its political consequences or his own reelection.[2]

---

1. Richard E. Neustadt, "Presidency and Legislation," pp. 656–657.

2. Transcript, Samuel I. Rosenman interview, 15 October 1968, HSTL, p. 21.

This view was substantiated by Roger Jones, a careerist in the Budget Bureau (and incidentally a Republican). Jones, who worked closely with Truman, found him nonpartisan in the conduct of his office; the president was aware of the politics of issues but was not willing to view them in a partisan sense. Truman's oft-repeated instruction to his aides was: "You let me have it just as you see it from the policy, the programmatic, the substantive, point of view. Let me worry about the politics."[3] His frequent comment to his last budget director was: "If it's the right thing to do, we'll do it."[4]

As an administrator, one of Roosevelt's big advantages was his experience as an agency official. Neustadt believes that

Truman never did acquire Roosevelt's intimate awareness of just how work got done (or stopped) around him and beneath him in the bureaucratic world. . . . Throughout his Presidency, Truman's lack of bureaucratic "feel" . . . left him decidedly less sensitive than FDR to stakes of personal power.[5]

Truman apparently did not feel that he was at a disadvantage because of his past experience. Within six weeks after becoming president he told his wife that he thought he was getting his office and his cabinet better organized. "It won't be long until I can sit back and study the whole picture and tell 'em what is to be done in each department. When things come to that stage there'll be no more to this job than there was to running Jackson County and not any more worry."[6] Despite the confidence Truman displayed to his wife, Sam Rosenman found that: "During Truman's first term, he was overawed, particularly at the begin-

---

3. Transcript, Roger W. Jones interview, 14 August 1969, HSTL, pp. 18–19.

4. Transcript, Frederick J. Lawton interview, 9 July 1963, HSTL, p. 29.

5. Richard E. Neustadt, *Presidential Power: The Politics of Leadership* (New York, 1960), p. 174.

6. Harry S. Truman, *Dear Bess: The Letters from Harry to Bess Truman*, ed., Robert H. Ferrell (New York, 1983), p. 514.

ning, about the responsibility, the authority, and most of all the lonesomeness of the job."[7]

While Truman frequently affected a cocky public attitude, he apparently really believed that his position as an administrator in Jackson County, Missouri, had provided adequate preparation for the presidency. After three years as president he bragged to a group of teachers that: "There isn't any difference in my job there and the one here except that this one is on a forty-eight-state basis, and that one was on a County basis. But the things that have to be done are about the same." He felt he had the reputation of being a good administrator and was obviously proud of it. He added that "they say no good administrator can ever be elected President of the United States," but he was clearly expecting to reverse that trend.[8]

Truman had some traits that enabled him to be a successful executive and he may well have acquired them in Jackson County. Those who worked with him were amazed that this seemingly modest man with a public school education could face the challenges of the presidency. In the fall of 1950 the author John Hersey spent several days in the White House observing the president at work. He later wrote:

President Truman seemed to think of himself sometimes in the first person and sometimes in the third—the latter when he had in mind a personage he still seemed to regard, after nearly four years in office, as an astonishing tenant in his own body: the President of the United States. Toward himself, first-personally, he was at times mischievous and disrespectful, but he revered this other man, his tenant, as a noble, history-defined figure. Here was a separation of powers within a single psyche, and a most attractive phenomenon it was, because Harry Truman moved about in constant wonder and delight at this awesome stranger beneath his skin. And to some extent this wonder and delight must have elevated and purged the mere man.[9]

---

7. Rosenman interview, p. 21.

8. Remarks of the President to a group of government teachers, 23 June 1948, Reorganization folder, George M. Elsey Files, HSTL.

9. Quoted in Thompson, *Portraits of American Presidents*, vol. 2, p. 70. Hersey wrote a five-part profile which appeared in *The New Yorker* from 7 April to 5 May 1951.

This great respect for the office shaped Truman's behavior as president. He had a jealous concern about the power, the prerogatives, and the role of the presidency because he constantly considered the effect of his actions on his successors. He had a quick mind with an impressive ability to recall details which, combined with a willingness to work hard, enabled him to master the routine of the job. He had a knack for making the most complicated problems simple, not oversimplifying them, but getting to the heart of the matter. Frequently he made decisions too quickly but, at least compared to FDR, he was decisive.[10]

Truman's detailed knowledge of the history of the presidency and of his country is well known. When faced with the necessity of making a decision, this knowledge enabled him to draw analogies and gave him comfort. But those who worked with him do not believe that he really used the precedents stored in his mind when he made the truly historic choices of his administration. Instead he seemed to be a case-by-case decision-maker who made no effort to compare choices through time.[11]

* * *

Roosevelt had seemed to his successor to have been a poor administrator. Truman confided to his wife that "the late President had a positive genius for picking inefficient administrators. . . . I've about come to the conclusion that he wanted to do everything himself and get all the acclaim for successful accomplishment and then have a dumb cluck to take the blame for what failed."[12] Soon after Truman entered the White House he decided that at least part of FDR's problem had been his failure to govern through his department heads. In Truman's view he "spent too much of his time doing the

---

10. Elmer Staats in ibid., pp. 89-91.
11. Ernest R. May and Richard E. Neustadt, *Thinking in Time: The Uses of History for Decision Makers* (New York, 1986), p. 252.
12. Truman, *Dear Bess*, p. 526.

work that should have been delegated to the Cabinet."[13]

Actually Roosevelt, like many twentieth century presidents, had entered office intending to use his cabinet in both an advisory and administrative capacity. But the quality of its meetings soon deteriorated. Ickes found the meetings of FDR's cabinet a

sheer waste of time. There was no agenda, Cabinet members were asked in turn if they had anything to bring up; important matters were not discussed because of fear of leaks; a few Cabinet members, like Miss Perkins, bored everyone to tears by airing administrative detail and family gossip of an interdepartmental nature. Organization conflicts were never discussed.[14]

But Truman thought he could use his cabinet to help him meet the challenge of governing. In contrast to Roosevelt, he intended to hold each cabinet member responsible for the affairs of his department and to adhere rigidly to proper administrative channels. He was determined to make it clear that he would not tolerate the kind of backbiting epitomized by Ickes's comments. Neustadt reports that Truman "had an abhorrence of caterwauling, knife-throwing, in-fighting, among his subordinates. And his staff and cabinet learned, perforce, that for their own survival it was essential to keep their quarrels beneath the surface maintaining at least the appearance of good relations with one another."[15]

Roosevelt's administrative methods bothered Truman but not as much as the personnel the late president had selected for his cabinet. Several years later Truman made the following evaluation of some of the cabinet members he had inherited in 1946:

There was Stettinius, Sec. of State—a fine man, good looking, amiable, cooperative, but never an idea new or old; Morgenthau, block

13. Harry S. Truman, *Memoirs*, vol. 1, *Year of Decisions* (Garden City, N.Y., 1955), p. 328.

14. Summary of an interview with Harold Ickes, 28 April 1948, E.O.P. Misc. Memos, 1939–1952, E2–5, Series 39.32, OMB.

15. Richard E. Neustadt, "Notes on the White House Staff," manuscript, HSTL.

head, nut—I wonder why FDR kept him around. . . . He fired himself
from my cabinet by threatening what he'd do to me under certain circumstances. Then there was Stimson, a real man—honest, straightfor-
ward and a statesman sure enough. . . . Frank Walker, P.M.G.—my kind
of man, honest, decent, loyal—but no new ideas. Miss Perkins, Sec. of
Labor, a grand lady—but no politician. FDR had removed every bureau
and power she had. Then Henry Wallace, Sec. of Commerce, who had no
reason to love me or to be loyal to me. Of course he wasn't loyal.
"Honest" Harold Ickes who was never for anyone but Harold, would have
cut FDR's throat—or mine for his "high minded" ideas of a headline—
and did. . . . There was not a man in the list who would talk frankly at
a Cabinet meeting! The honest ones were afraid to and the others
wanted to fool me anyhow.[16]

But apparently he was able to hide these feeling
and succeeded in improving the harmony of his cabinet's meetings. One who had attended all of FDR's cabinet meetings thought that Truman's leadership created
more cabinet teamwork than Roosevelt was ever able to
invoke.[17] But the real improvement came because of a
wholesale change in the cabinet's personnel. After a
few months, only a handful of Roosevelt's old cabinet
remained and within a year all but James Forrestal at
Navy and Henry Wallace had left their posts.

In spite of his firm resolve to use his cabinet
as both advisers and staff, Truman's disenchantment
began before he had been in office a year. Part of the
change was due to friction with individual cabinet
members. For example, during a conference with Harold
Smith in January 1946 Truman took a phone call from
Fred Vinson, his treasury secretary. When he put down
the telephone he complained to Smith:

What a time I am having with some of my prima donnas. I simply don't
understand it. More and more I am beginning to see what President
Roosevelt put up with. Can you tell me why it is that men whom I have
known for some time and with whom I have been accustomed to deal

16. Unsent letter to Jonathan Daniels, 26 February 1950 in Harry S.
Truman, *Off the Record: The Private Papers of Harry S. Truman*, ed,
Robert H. Ferrell (New York, 1980), p. 174.

17. Suggestions made at a luncheon given by the Attorney General,
16 August 1945, H. D. Smith misc. folder, Series 39.27, RG 51, NA.

have now become so touchy? Is there something that the President always does wrong? What is the matter with the Presidency?

Smith, who had never been enthusiastic about Truman's desire to work through his department heads, thought his obvious frustration was but "one phase of the President's developing realism about his Cabinet."[18]

The incident served as background to a most unusual conversation between Smith and Truman a week later. Much of it consisted of, in Smith's words, "an audacious lecture to the President of the United States—one that I had wrestled with mentally for several months." He told Truman frankly that he disagreed with the president's view of his cabinet and that it was disastrous to attempt to use a cabinet as a staff. Smith emphasized that the cabinet should be looked upon simply as operating commanders in their fields who could offer advice gained from their operating experience as well as their general political judgments. However, they could never fulfill the need for a separate presidential staff operating in a detached, objective atmosphere to supply him with information and check the information that came to him.[19]

Smith told Truman that his cabinet members were giving him not objective information but

a mixture of facts and political judgments. . . . More than that, you will find that as time goes on members of your Cabinet will actually be in political opposition to you, either overtly or otherwise, and neither their judgments nor their facts can be altogether trusted . . . because their judgments are colored by personal ambitions and their operating experiences in only a segment of the Government.

During this "lecture" Smith felt that Truman, by his quick remarks, indicated that he had gained a much more realistic attitude toward the cabinet than he had when he first became president.[20]

18. Conference with the President, 31 January 1946, Diary–January 1946, Smith Papers, HSTL.

19. Ibid., 8 February 1946.

20. Ibid.

Although Truman eventually rid himself of much of his illusions about the place of the cabinet in governmental administration, he continued to work at making his cabinet feel they were part of his team.[21] He held cabinet discussions on such issues as price controls, portal-to-portal pay, and tax bills which resulted in a unanimity of view, and this, in turn, led the department heads to support the presidential position with more vigor. Of course the president had to pay a price for this involvement of his cabinet in policy decisions. If he failed to consult them, they were sure to object. For instance, he did not hold a cabinet discussion before he vetoed the Taft-Hartley bill. When Forrestal and Agriculture Secretary Clinton Anderson objected, he felt constrained to promise to "take pains to see that there was no repetition of such a situation."[22]

And of course it is true that although the cabinet does not exist as a legal entity, presidential decisions are not possible without the cabinet members. Individually they have power because of presidential delegation of authority, various acts of Congress, and the alliances they make with congressional committees and public constituencies.[23]

A CABINET CABAL

Disenchantment with Roosevelt's managerial style had led James Forrestal to become a crusader for the development of a form of cabinet government that would adapt some of the features of the British system to the American situation. After FDR's death and with Truman giving verbal support to greater cabinet involvement, Forrestal was able to get some of his colleagues to meet, without the new president's knowledge, to devise some procedures by which the cabinet might become an independent force in the executive branch.[24]

21. Neustadt, *Presidential Power*, p. 174.

22. Walter Millis and E. S. Duffield, eds., *The Forrestal Diaries* (New York, 1951), p. 92.

23. Helmer, "The Presidential Office," p. 51.

24. Princeton Seminars, Transcript of 2 July 1953, Folder I, Dean G. Acheson Papers, HSTL.

The group met several times for lunch and brought others, such as the president's special counsel, Clark M. Clifford, the undersecretary of state, Dean Acheson, and Smith's successor as budget director, James E. Webb, into the discussions. Among their proposals was the suggestion that Clifford assume functions similar to the British cabinet secretary to operate an American cabinet organization. But Acheson and Webb argued strongly against the idea. It was Acheson's position that

we had a presidential government; the President was the only person in the whole group who is elected; we were not his equals, we were his secretaries; and our function was not to try to develop a group which would have any collective coercive effect upon the President. We could advise; we could say whatever we thought was right, but it was his decision and we must operate on that basis.[25]

Among the White House staff there was some sympathy for the idea of a cabinet secretariat. Clifford explained the idea to his assistant, George M. Elsey, who was enthusiastic since it would permit the cabinet "to develop its maximum usefulness as the primary agency for the formulation and coordinated execution of the policies of the executive branch." Elsey believed it would permit the eventual development of an extensive system of cabinet committees that would operate as an integrated administrative machine. However, he did not favor the immediate establishment of an elaborate and formal cabinet secretariat since he believed "its development and growth must be slowly and carefully planned."[26]

Meanwhile Forrestal's luncheon meetings began to get out of hand because as cabinet members began to discuss various issues, they decided on positions and presented a united front at the formal cabinet meetings. The result was to create an enormous psychological pressure on Truman to follow rather than com-

25. Ibid.
26. George Elsey to Clark Clifford, 16 October 1946, Reorganization Executive Branch – Security Secretariat, George M. Elsey Papers, HSTL.

mand.[27] With success it soon became a deliberate practice to establish prior positions in spite of Acheson's
and Webb's arguments against the tactic. At last the
two decided to lay the matter before the president. As
Acheson recalled, they told Truman that they

> didn't enjoy the position of being tattletales, but
> it seemed to us that this was a serious situation. We
> explained to him some of the ideas that were going on,
> and our strong advice to step on this, which he pro-
> ceeded to do, and he made it clear that he did not wish
> his staff to have anything to do with this; he did not
> want this thing to develop; he wished us to spend all
> the time in the world together, but the Cabinet was his
> Cabinet, and when it met, it would meet with him, in his
> presence, and he would lay before it what he wished to
> have before it.[28]

By 1949 Truman's cabinet meetings had become
"useful weekly instruction" but not a place in which
policy was discussed and formulated. It became the
practice for each member, in order of seniority, to inform his colleagues of the outstanding issues of the
week in his department. But as Acheson observed: "no
wise man asked the President's instruction in cabinet
meetings; he would surely find a number of articulate
and uninformed colleagues intervening with confused
and confusing suggestions. The Cabinet, despite its
glamour, is not a major instrument of Government."[29]

So Harry Truman learned, as did presidents before and since his time, that "the Cabinet in this
country is merely the best known interdepartmental
committee in the Government and is thus only an
agency of advice to the President when he wishes to
ask its opinion."[30] As a body the cabinet has not been

27. Somers, *Presidential Agency,* footnote p. 216.
28. Princeton Seminars, Transcript of 2 July 1953, Acheson Papers,
HSTL.
29. Acheson, *Present At The Creation,* p. 736.
30. Arnold Miles's foreword to "The Presidency," vol. 7, 27 September 1947, Case Studies in Policy Formulation and Legislative Clearance, E2-5, Series 39.32, OMB.

an effective council of advisers to the president and has never had any collective responsibility for an administration's policies. One reason presidents soon become disenchanted with their cabinets as policy-making bodies was demonstrated by Forrestal's complaint about lack of consultation on the Taft–Hartley veto. When a president announces his intention to consult with his cabinet on major issues, he surrenders a portion of his flexibility.

The cabinet's status as a recognized, though unofficial, body is another reason presidents hesitate to regularize its advisory function; to do so weakens a president's right to consult with, or to ignore, whichever adviser he chooses. If an issue is brought to the cabinet as a group, all members can express themselves, and though the president still decides, an overwhelming cabinet position is difficult to ignore, if for no other reason than the president has to continue to work with his department heads.

Cabinet members are frequently poor advisers for, no matter what their previous attitudes, they soon become captives of the views of the departments they head. Inevitably cabinets become advocates of the vested interests of the various departments instead of a body that can view issues from a national perspective. As a result, presidents have turned to a kitchen cabinet or to personal unofficial advisers such as Wilson's Colonel House or FDR's Harry Hopkins.

TRUMAN'S STAFF PROBLEMS

The Executive Office of the President is, in one sense, an effort to institutionalize a group of advisers who are insulated from departmental allegiances and capable of rendering advice from the presidential point of view. As the influence of Truman's cabinet ebbed, that of the executive office increased. It was inevitable that an unprepared president would seek help, and over time he found the careerists in the Budget Bureau and OWMR to be more useful than his cabinet.

Truman faced a bigger managerial problem than any of his predecessors. During the depression, the bureaucracy and functions of the government had expanded at a rapid rate. World War II led to an even greater enlargement of both the size and the complexity of the federal establishment. The postwar economic boom and the cold war stimulated further growth. The federal government's "annual growth rate, indeed, was quite as imposing as that of the Gross National Product in the postwar years."[31] The creation of new agencies and functions resulted in vicious infighting between the new and old organizations. All this simply enlarged the already imposing task Truman faced in establishing and pursuing coherent policies. His only hope was to create and to learn to use presidential staff facilities. Neither came easily to him.

Harold Smith, budget director since 1939, continued in that position during the first year of the Truman administration. During his frequent conferences with the new president, particularly after the first few months, Smith repeatedly referred to Truman's administrative problems. As the situation continued to deteriorate, he complained of the "considerable amount of administrative chaos and friction" that had developed around the president. When Smith volunteered to try to improve the situation, Truman seemed receptive.[32]

In another meeting Smith told the president that although he was an orderly person himself there was disorder all around him and it was getting worse. The solution, Smith declared, was good, continuous, organized staff work. Truman agreed that "the situation is getting pretty serious." Smith complained that he didn't "know who does what around here and that is a rather dangerous situation for all of us to be in, . . . none of us can solve any of these problems by a kind of intramural, intellectual exercise." Smith observed that "several times during this outburst the President nodded acquiescence and expressed his own feeling of depression about the apparent difficulty of ensuring a

31. Alan D. Harper, *The Politics of Loyalty: The White House and the Communist Issue, 1946-1952* (Westport, Conn., 1969), p. 233.

32. Conference with the President, 14 January 1946, Smith Papers, HSTL.

steady flow of intelligence concerning governmental problems."[33]

The weakness of the White House staff was apparent even outside the president's immediate circle. Walter Lippman devoted one of his columns to the subject. He wrote that:

While Mr. Truman saw the need to reorganize the Cabinet and to use it, he did not see that he needed also to make the White House itself an efficient department. The Truman Cabinet is by any reasonable standard a good cabinet. . . . But the White House is deplorably weak, and since Mr. Truman is a modest and unpretentious man who must feel his way without benefit of much inspiration through a maze of problems, he has little hope of being a successful President if his own immediate official family remains what it now is. The blunt truth is that the men nearest him do not have enough brains, and have practically none of the wisdom which comes from experience and education, to help him to be the President of the United States.

Lippman felt that Truman had not yet learned that the presidency is not just a man with some secretaries and clerks, but is the central department of the government which must superintend, correct, guide, and make the other departments a team. His assistants must be so able that they cannot only decide what the president must see and prepare him so that he can make a decision, but must be competent to settle many issues in the president's name.[34]

* * *

To understand Truman's staff problems one must consider the situation that existed when he suddenly became president. FDR had, during the war, established Byrnes as his chief assistant for domestic matters, Admiral William Leahy for military affairs, and Harry Hopkins as general troubleshooter. Among the official White House positions that existed before Roosevelt's time, Stephen Early was his press secretary, while William D. Hassett served as correspondence secretary.

33. Conference with the President, 8 February 1946, ibid.
34. *The Washington Post,* 5 January 1946.

Hassett was a tall, erudite, and personable Vermonter "whose prose could soothe raging beasts." He remained in this post until ill health forced his retirement in 1952. FDR's influential appointments secretary had died a few months before Roosevelt's own death. One of FDR's administrative assistants, Jonathan Daniels, continued under Truman for a short time. David Niles, FDR's liaison man for minority affairs, along with his assistant, Philleo Nash, loyally served the new president in the same capacity. Niles, who was known as the "portable wailing wall," died in 1951. He was succeeded by Nash.[35]

For many years FDR had used Sam Rosenman as a part-time speech writer while he served as a New York state judge. By 1943 Roosevelt's demands on the judge's talents had grown and Rosenman's health had declined. Forced to choose between his two jobs, Rosenman decided to leave the bench. Roosevelt then created the title of Special Counsel for his friend and made him a member of the White House staff. When Truman took over, Rosenman offered his resignation but, after some hesitation, the new president asked him to stay on until the war ended. Then, faced with mass staff resignations, Truman decided he needed Rosenman's help. He asked him to stay for another year and began to take him into his confidence. Rosenman's prime contributions to the Truman administration were his detailed knowledge, his great capacity for work, and the liberalism that he represented so vigorously. He developed a loyalty to Truman as great as to Roosevelt and a personal affection that was even greater.[36]

For financial reasons Rosenman decided to leave before his year was up. When he resigned in January 1946, Truman announced that, since the special counsel's position was of wartime origin, Rosenman would not be replaced.[37] His departure marked the end of the continuity with the Roosevelt administration and seriously depleted the capabilities of the White House

---

35. Kenneth Hechler in Thompson, *Portraits of American Presidents*, vol. 2, p. 56.

36. Hand, *Counsel and Advise*, pp. 171-174, 206-208, 222.

37. Harry S. Truman, *Public Papers of the Presidents of the United States, Harry S. Truman, 1946 (Washington, D.C., 1962)*, p. 90.

staff. By the end of February, Smith found Truman completely bogged down in paper work. The president told him that he had to read about 30,000 words in memoranda every night and, now that Rosenman was gone, he feared he was going to have to start writing his own speeches as well. Throughout their conversation Smith noted that "the President expressed various notes of despair about the avalanche of things that were piling up on him." The budget director came away from the White House with his "despair accentuated because of the President's inability to use staff, as yet."[38]

In his efforts to deal with Truman's staff problems Smith had the help of John W. Snyder, a close friend of the president's and then head of the OWMR. This agency, together with the bureau and the White House administrative assistants, represented the sum total of Truman's immediate staff support. The budget director shared his concerns with Snyder and emphasized the need to "get the Executive Office together on doing some real staff work."[39] Unfortunately, Smith was forced to resign before he made much progress on this project.

* * *

Faced with the necessity of building a personal staff almost from scratch, Truman characteristically turned to old friends. Matthew J. Connelly, who had worked for the wartime Truman committee and then served as executive secretary to Vice-President Truman, became the new president's appointments secretary. When Early decided to leave, Truman appointed Charles Ross, a boyhood school friend who was now an experienced and respected newspaperman, as his press secretary. Because of their long association, a close rapport developed between them. Ross was not only effective as a

38. Conference with the President, 28 February 1946. Smith Papers, HSTL.

39. Telephone conversation, 1 March 1946, Daily Record–March 1946, ibid.

press secretary but was one of Truman's valued advisers. He was a force for liberalism in the White House.[40]

As the following diary entry indicates, initially Truman was pleased with his new White House team:

Charlie Ross, straight thinker, honest man, who tells me the truth so that I understand what he means; Matt Connelly, shrewd Irishman, who raises up the chips and shows me the bugs, honest, fair, "diplomatic" with me; Judge Fred Vinson, straight shooter, knows Congress and how they think, a man to trust; Judge Rosenman, one of the ablest in Washington, keen mind, a lucid pen, a loyal Roosevelt man and an equally loyal Truman man; Steve Early, a keen observer, political and other wise, has acted as my hatchet man, absolutely loyal and trustworthy, same can be said as about Rosenman.[41]

He dealt quite candidly with these men and told Ross, Rosenman, and Snyder that "they were most in my confidence and that I wanted frank and unadulterated statements of facts . . . and when they could not treat me on that basis, they would be of no use to me."[42]

But by the end of his first summer as president Truman was clearly less satisfied with his staff support. He complained plaintively to Smith about the unresponsiveness of the bureaucracy and noted in his diary that it "is almost impossible to get action around here even from the most loyal of the close-in helpers."[43] He had appointed an old World War I army buddy, Edward D. McKim, as the "chief" of the White House administrative assistants, but McKim soon developed what the president used to call "Potomac fever." He could not resist the capitol's social scene. Constantly ready to step out, McKim kept his white tie and tails at the office. It was such an obvious malassignment that he "resigned" after a few weeks.[44]

---

40. Hechler in *Portraits*, vol.2, p. 57.

41. Truman, *Off The Record*, p. 46.

42. William Hillman, *Mr. President: The First Publication from the Personal Diaries, Private Letters, Papers and Revealing Interviews of Harry S. Truman* (New York, 1952), p. 120.

43. Conference with the President, 18 September 1946; Truman, *Off The Record*, p. 67.

44. Hechler in *Portraits*, vol.2, p. 54.

George Schoeneman, a close friend of Postmaster General Robert Hannegan, Truman's political ally from Missouri, was then named an administrative assistant and asked to get the staff organized.[45] One of Schoeneman's first moves was to make a survey of the White House staff organization. He concluded that each of the administrative assistants should be assigned to deal with specific departments and agencies so that they would become better informed about their functions and problems. He expected that this would eventually result in a reduction in the president's paper work and enable the aides to be more involved in making decisions.[46]

Initially, Schoeneman's proposal tended to appeal to the president because in theory Truman liked to think of his staff in terms of organization charts and the doctrine of completed staff work. But in practice he never organized his White House staff in a precise fashion. Whatever organizational lines he did establish were likely to be ignored when it came to getting the work done. His instinct was to improvise arrangements around the problems that came before him.[47] Drawing boxes and charts did not solve Truman's staff problems, so in June 1947 Schoeneman left the White House to become a commissioner of Internal Revenue.[48]

Although Truman's staff organization might have been fluid, he had definite ideas about his working relationship with staff members. Donald Hansen recalled his presidential indoctrination:

I'm the man who makes the decision; I'm the man that takes the heat. You do your job faithfully and conscientiously and you can be assured you'll have my full support and protection. . . . I've been criticized a lot for standing up for my friends and my associates, but I always have and I always will and you can be assured that that's what I'll do for you. But . . . I'm the man who takes the publicity; that takes the heat and I want you to stay out of that area altogether. You're to be a

45. Anderson, *The Presidents' Men,* p. 115.
46. Schoeneman to Raymond Zimmerman, 4 January 1946, Zimmerman Files, HSTL.
47. Neustadt, *Presidential Power,* pp. 171–172.
48. Anderson, *The Presidents' Men,* p. 115.

staff assistant. . . . You're to help make decisions; to make recommendations on decisions; the decisions are mine and I do the talking about them.

This was the Truman prescription for the presidential aides that Brownlow said must have a "passion for anonymity."[49]

CLIFFORD AND STEELMAN

After this rocky start Truman made such steady progress in fashioning his personal staff that by the end of his first term he was being served by a group that was energetic, competent, and knowledgeable in the ways of bureaucracy. In the process Truman became "the founding father of the White House staff as we know it." The size of the staff grew with its competence from seven in May 1945 to sixteen in January 1948, and twenty-two by January 1952. Most of the senior members of the group won their positions by promotion from within and almost all had come from other parts of the government, particularly from the Bureau of the Budget.[50]

The real development of Truman's White House staff centered around the rise of Clark Clifford and John Steelman to positions of influence. Clifford was a lieutenant commander in the Naval Reserve when, in July 1945, he was selected by Truman's naval aide, Jake Vardaman, to mind his office while he went off to the Potsdam Conference with the president. Vardaman, incidentally, was an old family friend of the Cliffords. Rosenman, who stayed behind in Washington, by chance asked Clifford to help him with his drafting chores and was very impressed with his work. Told of Clifford's usefulness, Truman had him assigned permanently to the White House staff as assistant naval aide while he understudied Rosenman.[51]

49. Transcript, Donald Hansen interview, April 1963, HSTL, p. 3.

50. Neustadt, "Notes on the White House Staff," p. 4; Harper, *Politics of Loyalty*, p. 242.

51. Roth, "The Executive Office," p. 324.

When Rosenman left in January 1946, Clifford began doing the work of the special counsel. Truman at that point was going through a difficult time with his staff and was not sure that he was going to continue the special counsel position. He did not wish to make any permanent appointments until he had figured out how he wanted to organize his staff. But he did not let Clifford get away. He appointed Vardaman (who had also developed "Potomac fever") to the Federal Reserve Board in April, had Clifford promoted to captain and then designated him to replace Vardaman as the President's naval aide. It was several months before Truman made up his mind to name Captain Clifford as his special counsel.[52]

Clifford probably owed his promotion to special counsel to his skill in rewriting a bellicose speech that Truman had prepared when faced with a nationwide railroad strike. The revised speech, which had a dignity of tone that was entirely lacking in the original version, was well received and Truman realized Clifford had saved him from a serious blunder. Clifford described the relationship that he enjoyed with Truman as a highly personal one which "developed because there was a vacuum in the White House. We were both from Missouri. He was comfortable with me."[53] Compared to today's large White House staffs, it is amazing that for several years Clifford alone was responsible for assembling the administration's proposals, coordinating the legislative drafting and budgetary processes, writing the president's messages and speeches, and guarding his political strategy.[54]

John Steelman, after obtaining a doctorate in sociology in 1928, became a labor relations expert. By 1937 he had been named the director of the Federal Conciliation Service. After several years he "decided it was time to go to New York and make a little money." The day after the elections in 1944 he opened a consulting office in New York.

52. Ibid.; Hechler in *Portraits*, vol. 2, p. 59; *Public Papers, Harry S. Truman, 1946*, p. 313.

53. Anderson, *The Presidents' Men*, pp. 136-138.

54. Helmer, "The Presidential Office", p. 66.

Soon after he became president, Truman found himself faced with severe labor problems. Reconversion to a peacetime economy led to many strikes and he had a labor secretary with little experience in labor matters. Desperate, Truman sent an emissary to sound out Steelman's interest in becoming secretary of labor or of commerce. Although he declined those positions, a few weeks later Steelman got an invitation to meet with the president. Truman told him that "I need help, help, help, and you've got to help me." Steelman agreed to join the White House staff for six months as a special assistant. He arrived in October 1945 and remained in the White House in one capacity or another until Truman left office in 1953. As Steelman recalled, about once a year he would remind Truman that his New York office was suffering, but "my six months never got over."[55]

In July 1946 Steelman replaced John Snyder as the director of OWMR during the last months of that agency's life. When the OWMR was abolished in November, Steelman sought to use the occasion to leave the government. But Truman only agreed to dissolve the agency if Steelman would "stay here with me and keep doing exactly what you're doing now." It is not surprising that Steelman always saw his White House position as an outgrowth of the assignments performed by Byrnes, Vinson, and Snyder at the OWMR.[56]

Steelman was named to a new post Truman created for him on the White House staff. When the president asked the Budget Bureau to draw up a statement describing Steelman's duties they suggested he be called a "Special Assistant to the President." Steelman objected to the title because he planned to be the president's chief of staff. So he crossed out "Special" and wrote in "The."[57] Truman went along with the

55. Ibid., p. 109; John R. Steelman in Thompson, *Portraits,* vol. 2, pp. 36–37.

56. Steelman in Thompson, *Portraits,* vol. 2, pp. 36–37; John R. Steelman and H. Dewayne Kraeger, "The Executive Office as Administrative Coordinator," *Law and Contemporary Problems.* 21, no. 4 (Autumn 1956), footnote p. 693.

57. Steelman in Thompson, *Portraits,* vol. 2, pp. 36–37; Statement of Elmer B. Staats in Francis Heller, ed., *The Truman White House: The*

impressive title of *The* Assistant to the President but he always acted as his own chief of staff. (Later, Eisenhower was to use the same title for a real chief of staff, Sherman Adams.) With the creation of Steelman's position, Truman's White House arrived at the basic configuration it was to maintain until the end of his administration.

During the first several years he was president, Truman was skillful in not permitting any one staff member to be so identified with a particular area that he and others might believe he had the authority to commit the president. To that end he deliberately had the work flow periodically shifted from one assistant to another.[58] Although Truman was chief of his own staff, power within the White House group tended to polarize into recognizable functional areas between Clifford and Steelman and each man jealously guarded his own domain. The junior members of the staff tended to find themselves in one camp or the other "and informally bridging the staked-out gaps between the seniors." The resulting tension created a degree of effectiveness that declined after 1950 when Clifford left the White House to practice law.[59]

THE ASSISTANT TO THE PRESIDENT

Although John Steelman considered himself nonpolitical, his cautious and conciliatory approach to problems caused him to become the main ally of the conservatives in the White House. He and Clifford were natural rivals because of their politics as well as their contrasting personalities.[60] Steelman never lost his active interest in his original assignment as the White House labor expert. This interest sometimes detracted from his main role of dealing with the departments and agencies since the specific, pressing, and familiar character of labor disputes tended to take "precedence

Administration of the Presidency, 1945–1953 (Lawrence, Kans, 1980), p. 169.

58. James E. Webb to Alfred Sander, 3 February 1971.
59. Neustadt, "Notes on the White House Staff," p. 44.
60. Anderson, *The Presidents' Men,* pp. 110–111.

over the vaguer stuff of coordinating 'operations.'"
Steelman's training and experience as an expert medi-
ator instead of as an idea-man or innovator made it
more likely that he would be the troubleshooter of the
staff rather than the policymaker.[61]

Even before Steelman became head of OWMR,
Truman had learned that because of his careful work
he could sign anything he handed him without reading
it. This presidential confidence gave Steelman great
power. Truman believed they enjoyed a close rapport
because they had both sprung from rural middle
America. He once told Steelman:

John. . . you know the soil we came out of. I'm from Missouri and you're
from Arkansas, we understand each other. I know what you are going to
say before you say it or what you're going to decide and you know me
the same way. So take part of this load and don't tell me about it, just
do it. There's too much here for one person.

So Steelman assumed much of the president's burden
and Truman backed him up. On one occasion a cabinet
member asked Truman to overturn a Steelman decision.
When the president said he could not, he was asked for
an explanation. Truman replied that he was "the boss
in general but John issued that order as I understand
it in connection with an assignment I gave him. We had
an understanding that he could call me if he needed
me, I can't call him."[62]

Another of the reasons why Steelman had a dominant position as a presidential aide was because he
had moved directly from heading the OWMR to the White
House. He simply brought the residue of that agency's
problems with him when he took up his new position.
This gave him the lead among the White House staff for
several years in the fields of housing, education, and
the preparation of economic reports.[63]

Steelman spent much of his time sitting on the
lid of the operating disputes. He got into the conflicts
between the pressure groups and the agencies, as well

61. Neustadt, "Notes on the White House Staff," pp. 6–7.
62. Steelman in *Portraits,* vol. 2, pp. 44–47.
63. Ibid.

as the conflicts among the agencies themselves, and tried to resolve them. His style was to try to negotiate acceptable solutions rather than make decisions. He had a deep interest in education, scientific research, shipping policy, resources problems, and labor-management relations. In these fields his views were almost always taken into account.[64]

It was Steelman's job to handle that great range of problems, proposals, plans, denunciations, and hopes that were brought to the White House by the stream of congressmen, businessmen, trade union officials, and interest group representatives who called or wrote. He was also the means of access for many of the heads of independent agencies whose ability to get to the president were more restricted. During his long tenure in the White House Steelman took on many extra assignments such as acting head of other executive office staff units when it was not politic for Truman to appoint a regular head. For extended periods of time he directed the work of the National Security Resources Board and was the defense mobilization chief in addition to his work at the White House.[65]

It is known that Steelman and his assistants were busy, but little of what they did was committed to writing so that it is difficult to determine how much they accomplished. One of Steelman's most useful talents as a presidential assistant was the ability to study a problem until it went away. "A great deal of what went to him was blandly smothered to death in an atmosphere of great interest and good fellowship. Be it said that much of this 'negative' action was undertaken at the President's direct request."[66] He had an amazing ability to listen to his visitors complaints, get their goodwill, and send them on their way convinced that they had been heard, but without having committed himself to any particular course of action in the process.[67]

64. Ibid.; Robert Turner statement in Heller, *The Truman White House*. pp. 57–58.

65. Neustadt, "Notes on the White House Staff," pp. 8–12.

66. Ibid.

67. Robert Turner statement in Heller, *The Truman White House*, pp. 57–58.

CLIFFORD'S ROLE

In theory, the work in Truman's White House was assigned out on a logical, functional basis, but in practice it was much more haphazard. As Richard Neustadt observed, although "Truman theorized like a reserve officer impressed with Army doctrine; he acted like a Senator. His office was decked out with many of the trappings of what became know as a staff system, but he, himself remained incurably informal and accessible."[68] In such an informal atmosphere it was inevitable that the talents and interests of the individual members of the White House staff would have a powerful influence on its organization.

Before Clark Clifford became special counsel he had gotten to know Dean Acheson and James Forrestal well and through them had developed a major interest in foreign policy and national security. Because of his personal relationship with the two men, the custom developed for Clifford to sit in on their meetings with the president. As a result, he developed an expertise in foreign affairs that added a new dimension to the office of counsel. At that time Truman did not have a staff man who filled that capacity other than Admiral William Leahy who had served as FDR's chairman of the Joint Chiefs of Staff. But Leahy was moving out of the picture as World War II ended and he was not well attuned to the problems raised by the developing cold war. (He always called the Russians "those savages.")[69] Clifford alone had any real influence on foreign policy since only he had the self-confidence that permitted easy movement among cabinet officers. When Clifford resigned, this capability was lost because his successor, Charles Murphy, did not develop an equal degree of interest, sources of information, or influence in foreign matters.[70]

---

68. Neustadt, *Presidential Power*, pp. 171–172.
69. Clark Clifford in Thompson, *Portraits*, vol. 2, pp. 8–9.
70. Paul Y. Hammond, "NSC-68: Prologue to Rearmament," in *Strategy, Politics and Defense Budgets*, ed. Warner R. Schilling, Paul Y. Hammond and Glenn H. Snyder (New York, 1962), p. 327.

The domestic program of the Truman administration which became known as the Fair Deal was first articulated in the president's "Twenty-One Point" message to Congress in September 1945. The draft of the message was begun by Rosenman after Truman returned from Potsdam. Rosenman knew that a group (led by John Snyder) who did not believe in the New Deal had great influence with the new president. He was therefore anxious to get Truman committed to a liberal program which would make it difficult for Snyder to turn the new president toward a conservative or even a middle-of-the-road policy. In retrospect Rosenman felt "that the most important thing I did for President Truman, and perhaps through him for the country itself, was to fight without let-up for that twenty-one point message."[71]

Just as Rosenman was responsible for the early political direction of the administration, it was Clifford who maintained this strategic orientation. He was the counsel in the broad sense, since it was he who monitored where the administration's program was going from both the political and substantive viewpoints. He came in as a message writer and sustained his control by retaining his primacy in this field as the size of the staff increased. Since the policy of the administration was primarily articulated in its legislative proposals, his role was a key one. Message writing involved selecting the issues that would receive attention and proposing solutions to them. Most of the recommendations came from the cabinet officers, but it was Clifford who advised the president on these recommendations. As a result, when the department heads got a chance to take a problem to Clifford instead of Steelman, they did so because they recognized the role he played. The more liberal cabinet members especially sought him out. In this way Truman's special counsels, Rosenman and Clifford became the architects of the Fair Deal.[72]

---

71. Rosenman interview, pp. 23–25.
72. "The White House: Three Secretaries," undated note, E.O.P. Misc. Memos, 1939–1952, E2–5, Series 39.32, OMB.

THE CLIFFORD WING

The preparation of messages to Congress has become a major function of presidential staffs. In the Truman White House of 1946 that work was the responsibility of two naval officers, Clark Clifford and George M. Elsey. Elsey a graduate of Princeton and Harvard, had been assigned to the White House during the war as an assistant to the president's naval aide. When Clifford became special counsel in June 1946, Elsey's time was divided between assisting him in his new job and working with the new naval aide. Elsey stayed on at the White House after he left the navy and in 1949 was appointed to one of the administrative assistant positions. He usually worked as a writer and researcher for Clifford and then for Charles Murphy.[73] Later, during the 1948 presidential campaign, Elsey was a key figure in drafting outlines for Truman's whistle-stop speeches.[74]

Although Clifford never wanted a staff of his own, he would occasionally accept temporary help when deadlines approached. Because of the small size of the staff during the early days, Clifford had to turn to the Budget Bureau for help in preparing the 1947 State of the Union message. James Sundquist, who was known as the bureau's writer, was sent over along with David Bell to help out. Soon both men were asked to join the White House staff on a full-time basis. This was the beginning of a gradual migration of bureau employees to the White House staff, a process that was not accidental but part of a deliberate effort by the new budget bureau director, James E. Webb, to subtly increase Truman's reliance on and respect for his agency.[75]

By 1947 the White House staff had grown in both size and stature. An important recruit that year was Charles Murphy whom Truman had first met during his Senate days. Murphy's experience in the Senate legislative counsel's office made him an expert in the writing and analyzing of bills. Truman had recruited

73. George M. Elsey to Alfred Sander, 14 December 1970.
74. Hechler, *Portraits*, vol. 2, p. 60.
75. Webb to Alfred Sander, 3 February 1971.

Murphy to work directly for him on legislative matters, but soon after he joined the White House staff he realized that what he really enjoyed was the kind of work Clifford did. He offered to help and, while Clifford accepted, he was always careful never to give Murphy any instructions or directions.[76]

As others, such as Stephen Spingarn, David Bell, Richard Neustadt, and David Lloyd, joined the White House staff in a junior capacity, Murphy became their informal leader within the Clifford orbit. The core of their work became program development in the form of messages and legislative policy. They also did a considerable amount of legislative campaigning. When Clifford left in January 1950, he handpicked Murphy to be his successor as special counsel. Politically the two saw eye to eye and Murphy was the logical choice. Although he did not have Clifford's taste for power, Murphy was widely regarded as the ablest member of the staff during the last three years of the administration.[77]

As Murphy's job developed, he became responsible for all the president's speeches, major public statements, and messages to Congress. He was also charged with the preparatory work in developing the legislative proposals, selecting issues, reviewing enrolled bills, and preparing executive orders. But Murphy's was not a one-man operation. Instead, he served as the head of a closely knit team consisting, in the last years, of Lloyd, Bell, Neustadt, Donald Hansen, and Kenneth Hechler.[78]

CONNELLY AND DAWSON

Most of the staff was divided into the Steelman or the Clifford/Murphy factions, but there was a third center of power in Truman's White House. It revolved around the appointments secretary, Matthew Connelly, who, with his desk at the door of the Oval Office, controlled

76. Transcript, Charles Murphy interview, HSTL, pp. 449–450.
77. "The White House: Three Secretaries"; Anderson, *The Presidents' Men*, pp. 112–113.
78. Neustadt, "Notes on the White House Staff," pp. 14–16.

both the president's appointments and his incoming telephone calls. He also handled Truman's list of engagements and speeches. Connelly's physical location enabled him to know the president's moods and thinking and to gain his ear at any time. His job was to allocate the president's time "and there is no more precious commodity."[79]

In spite of the advantages of his physical and administrative position, it is doubtful whether Connelly had any direct influence on high policy decisions. Even his occasional advice on the timing and content of speeches was rarely heeded in the later years of the administration. His area of greatest influence was domestic governmental and party matters, such as political tactics, personnel selection, and relations with Congress.[80] Connelly's great strength was his close personal relationship with the president. He was a likable young man who had a knack for politics, could keep his mouth shut, and fitted in well with the Truman circle.[81]

A relic of Roosevelt's original executive office structure that was retained by Truman was the liaison officer for personnel management. Initially Truman named a personnel expert, Raymond R. Zimmerman, to be the liaison officer. Zimmerman spent fulltime on federal personnel policy until he was replaced by Donald Dawson in August 1947. Dawson continued to do the personnel work but subordinated it to his major responsibility as keeper of the patronage for the president. As a result of the association of the liaison officer with patronage, it gained such a bad repute that the title was abolished some months after the beginning of the Eisenhower administration.[82]

Until the end of World War II the selection of political appointees was essentially a political process and only secondarily a managerial one. That slowly began to change under Truman and Dawson.

---

79. Ibid., pp. 26–29.

80. Ibid.
81. Anderson, *The Presidents' Men*, pp. 125–126.
82. Roth, "The Executive Office," pp. 337, 389.

Dawson's small staff handled the routine of nominations, clearances, and endorsements. Some of the candidates were suggested by Truman from among his acquaintances. The president took a personal interest in the process and made a point of individually interviewing final candidates before they were offered a job.[83]

Dawson, in contrast with some of the other members of the White House staff, was a man of proven executive ability before he joined the group. He had originally come to Washington with the New Deal in 1933 and had risen to a top position in the Reconstruction Finance Corporation. He might have been made the chairman of the RFC or the president of the New York Stock Exchange had he been willing to leave the White House but he stayed on the job until the end of Truman's second term.[84]

TRUMAN'S LEADERSHIP STYLE

Even though the formal structure of the White House organization was frequently ignored in that informal and fluid atmosphere, there was a structure to it. As with other human organizations, those who find themselves near the center of presidential power "develop continuities and expectations about division of labor, status and hierarchy, specialization and effective channels of communication, and hence will take on some structure."[85]

The junior members of the White House staff usually found themselves in the camp of Steelman, Clifford, or Connelly. "In Clifford's time this triangle of hostility was marked and continuous, barely kept below the surface." The climate eased somewhat when Murphy replaced Clifford as special counsel because he was not by nature as combative and competitive. Even so, there were times when open warfare between the

83. G. Calvin Mackenzie, "The Paradox of Presidential Personnel Management" in *The Illusion of Presidential Government*, ed. Hugh Heclo and Lester Salamon (Boulder, Colo., 1981), p. 118.

84. Anderson, *The Presidents' Men*, pp. 127.

85. Burns, *Presidential Government*, p. 144.

factions threatened. The disputes were kept under control, however, and did not result in permanent alliances being formed. Instead, the battles were fought over specific issues or individuals and then relative peace returned.[86]

Truman really worked at being his own chief of staff. He always presided over his own staff meetings and there was never any doubt that he was in charge. Around ten o'clock six mornings a week he would meet for half an hour with the senior members of his staff in a semicircle around his desk to lay out the day's work. Connelly would usually begin with a discussion of the day's appointments. Then each member had an opportunity to bring up what was on his mind, interspersed with presidential comments.[87]

Before this regular meeting, the president was likely to go to the offices of his senior staff to discuss a matter that had occurred to him overnight or to give a decision on something that had been discussed earlier. After his regular appointments, Truman was likely to stick his head into various offices to see how things were going. He did not do this to prod or interfere but to offer additional advice or input. He always maintained a personal relationship with and an easy accessibility to even the more junior members of the staff.[88]

As a result of Truman's personal direction of the staff it remained, on paper, an unstructured group. Since no one other than the president had responsibility for the total staff function, no one was responsible for monitoring the activities of the various agencies. For a time it seemed that Steelman intended to lay claim to the leadership of the total staff when he exchanged his OWMR hat for that of "The Assistant to the President" but Clifford's competitiveness and Truman's reluctance to get too dependent on one person made this difficult. Truman did leave the door open for Steelman to assume leadership in the area of policy development, but that was neither Steelman's way

86. Neustadt, "Notes on the White House Staff," pp. 43–44.

87. Hechler in Thompson, *Portraits*, vol. 2, p. 54.

88. Ibid., 62; Neustadt, "Notes on the White House Staff," pp. 47–48.

nor his preoccupation. Murphy, for his part, was always careful about Steelman's titular rights, especially in dealing with the operating agencies.[89] Since the division between the Murphy side and the Steelman wing of the White House existed more in form than substance, there was no little confusion between the two with a relative decline in efficiency as a result.[90]

CONGRESSIONAL LIAISON

The Truman White House never developed a strong legislative liaison function. When Murphy joined the staff in 1947, there was no organized effort to even keep up with the progress of the legislative program in Congress let alone try to influence it. Murphy began to keep a crude record of what Congress was up to. As the staff grew, he convinced Truman to assign Charles Maylon to keep track of developments in the House and Joseph Feeney to watch the Senate. But the two (who worked under Connelly's direction) were rather ineffectual. They were responsible for congressional liaison but this did not mean they were presidential agents authorized to lobby for Truman's proposals. They did more hand-holding than trying to exert leadership for the administration's legislative program.[91]

Whatever efforts were made to get Congress to act favorably on the administration's legislative program were carried out personally by Truman. The president spent many hours with congressmen who came to talk to him about government projects for their districts, the appointment of postmasters, and other minor matters. After the Democrats recaptured control of Congress, the president met weekly with the "Big Four," Vice-President Alben Barkley, Speaker of the House Sam Rayburn, and the majority leaders of both houses. Murphy prepared agendas for these meetings but

89. Neustadt, "Notes on the White House Staff," p. 10.

90. Edward S. Flash, *Economic Advice and Presidential Leadership* (New York, 1965), p. 19.

91. Hechler in Thompson, *Portraits*, vol. 2, p. 62; Murphy statement in Heller, *The Truman White House*, p. 229.

Truman took such a soft approach that their effect was minimal.[92]

It is likely that Truman's attitude about presidential interference in legislative matters was an outgrowth of congressional reaction against Roosevelt's methods. He was a member of the Senate during the years when FDR dispatched "must" bills to the Congress for enactment, tried to pack the Supreme Court, and tried to purge the members who would not support his demands. Truman decided that these methods were neither appropriate or acceptable but perhaps he overcompensated with his hands-off approach. It is ironic that the modern practice of exerting presidential influence on legislation through a well-organized and adequately staffed White House liaison unit was the creation of Dwight Eisenhower, a man without Truman's deep understanding of Congress.

Truman's sensitivity to charges that his staff was interfering in legislative matters was demonstrated by the case of Stephen Spingarn. Spingarn worked for Murphy and specialized in civil rights and civil liberties matters. No member of the staff worked harder or was more devoted to the president's program. He was such a passionate advocate that he was frequently on Capitol Hill propagandizing for the cause. But apparently he pressed Alben Barkley too vigorously. The vice-president complained bitterly to Truman and before long Spingarn, over his protests, left the White House to fill a vacancy on the Federal Trade Commission.[93]

SUMMARY

Truman was proud of the innovative role he played in the development of the White House staff concept. It came about because he desperately needed help.[94] He knew that much of the bureaucracy regarded "the occupant of the White House as only a temporary nuisance who soon will be succeeded by another temporary occu-

---

92. Ibid.
93. Hechler in Thompson, *Portraits*, vol.2, p. 59.
94. Hillman, *Mr. President*, p. 16.

pant who won't find out what it is all about for a long time and then it will be too late to do anything about it."[95] To have a chance to cope with this attitude, he had to have knowledgeable assistants who owed their first loyalty to him.

Before long he insisted upon having all the facts presented to him before making decisions. To get them Truman said he "had to reorganize the office and staff of the President." Truman saw himself breaking new ground by, in his words, "setting out for each assistant a certain kind of work to do, and each confines himself to that task." He also considered himself the chief of his own staff, meeting with them each morning and giving the "instructions for the day."[96]

Truman's personal involvement with the staff was confirmed by the man who wanted to be the chief of his staff. John Steelman admitted that "senior status accrued to certain individuals whose higher rank was generally recognized" but insisted that to "all intents and purposes, the White House Office functioned as a group of senior staff assistants who had direct access to, and operated directly through, the person of the President himself."[97] Like Roosevelt, Truman resisted pressure to have another act as the chief of his staff. Forrestal's abortive cabinet coup may have been partially responsible for this attitude.

---

95. Ibid., p. 47.

96. Ibid.

97. John R. Steelman and H. Dewayne Kraeger, "The Executive Office as Administrative Coordinator," *Law and Contemporary Problems* 21, no. 4 (Autumn 1956): 693.

4.
The
Critical Year
of 1946

The year 1946 was a fateful one for the Executive Office of the President; opportunities for its systematic reorganization were missed and new directions were established in an almost mindless fashion. It was a year that saw the elimination of the Office of War Mobilization and Reconversion (OWMR) and the creation of a significant new addition to the executive office, the Council of Economic Advisers. Because of these changes 1946 was probably the last time when Truman might have been able to restructure the entire executive office in a planned and systematic way to serve the needs of the modern presidency.

THE OWMR

When Truman became president, his most important staff group was, in many respects, the OWMR. It had reached this high status because of Roosevelt's decision to delegate wide powers to Byrnes and the confidence he demonstrated in his "assistant president." In effect Byrnes's OWM served not merely as a staff for the president, but as a substitute for him on the home front.[1] Congress confirmed this grant of power and added postwar planning to the director's responsibility

---

1. Unsigned, undated memo probably by J. D. Kingsley, The Economic Council and Organization of the Presidential Office, Series 39.3, RG 51, NA.

when it created OWMR in October 1944. This statute gave the director more explicit authority to direct executive agencies in certain activities than the president had ever granted. It became the most powerful job that Congress had ever created. In an effort to maintain a measure of control over postwar planning Congress required the director of OWMR to make reports and recommend legislation directly to it. But the statute made clear that the director of the OWMR was subject to the control of the president.[2]

Tension developed between Brynes and FDR when Roosevelt failed to select his "assistant president" to be his vice president in 1944. When the war in Europe appeared to be won, FDR, ten days before his death, permitted Byrnes to resign. He was succeeded by Judge Fred M. Vinson. This was to be but a brief stop in Vinson's rise from the head of the Office of Economic Stabilization to secretary of the treasury and then chief justice in a little more than a year. He handled the OWMR job in much the same manner as had Byrnes, seeing himself primarily as a judge settling conflicts between contending agencies. But Vinson displayed a more aggressive attitude than had Byrnes and built up a somewhat larger staff. He was more interested in the organization of the staff, and more inclined to delegate authority and to rely on his deputies. Even though he only headed the agency for three months, that period, from V-E to V-J Day, when the issues of reconversion were hotly debated, were critical in shaping the direction of the OWMR's work.[3]

In July 1945 Truman and Treasury Secretary Henry Morgenthau had their final falling out. Vinson was appointed to replace Morgenthau in the cabinet while John W. Snyder was named to succeed Vinson as director of the OWMR. Snyder had met Truman during World War I and they had been close friends ever since. A banker in his pregovernment days, Snyder had held positions in the Reconstruction Finance Corpora-

---

2. Don K. Price, "Staffing the Presidency," *The American Political Science Review* 40, no. 6 (December 1946): 1163; John R. Steelman in Thompson, *Portraits,* vol. 2, p. 36.

3. Herman M. Somers, *Presidential Agency: OWMR,* pp. 84–86.

tion and the Defense Plant Corporation before succeeding Vinson as the director of the Federal Loan
Agency. The only similarity between Snyder and his
predecessors at OWMR was his closeness to the president. A shy and retiring director, he was reluctant to
exercise much authority over the agencies. As a result,
he was considered by many to be more a personal adviser to the president than the head of a powerful
agency.[4]

The director of OWMR had an office in the White
House and was considered one of the president's principal assistants. But the first three OWMR directors
did not consider themselves presidential staff aides.
Byrnes and Vinson were men with independent political
careers, and Snyder followed their example when he
accepted his eventual move into Truman's cabinet as a
promotion. So these directors were never very much
interested in creating a coherent organization by
which the presidency might be staffed. Nor did the
staff members of OWMR ever become a closely knit
organization.[5]

The end of the war and, with it, the end of governmental unity and individual selflessness made
Snyder's job much more difficult, in many respects,
than Byrnes's or Vinson's had been. He had to deal with
the toughest postwar problems: economic decontrol, demobilization of troops, recruitment of railroad workers,
stimulation of coal production, cancellation of war
contracts, and the development of administrative
machinery for the control of atomic energy. He served
as head for about a year before he was again named to
replace Vinson, this time as secretary of the treasury.
By the time he left OWMR its staff were resigning
faster than they were being replaced. The agency
seemed to be having more trouble coordinating themselves than in coordinating the rest of the government.[6]

Harold Smith was no friend of the OWMR. He had
opposed the original establishment of OWM in 1943 as

4. Ibid., pp. 87–90.
5. Price, "Staffing the Presidency."
6. Somers, *Presidential Agency*, pp. 88–91.

an "abortion" and a violation of his concept of good government. Considerable tension characterized the relationship between Smith and Byrnes, but there was never any doubt that Byrnes was the top man. As a result, the bureau was gradually pushed out of the area of policy formulation and coordination. This was the choice function of staff groups and one that Smith had been trying to expand since 1939. His frustration mounted as the executive departments increasingly regarded OWM-OWMR as the policy arm of the federal government while the bureau was looked to as the administrative management arm.[7]

Much of the difficulty between the OWMR directors and Smith was because of their differing concepts of the OWMR. Brynes considered himself, as the assistant president, Smith's superior but the budget director treated the OWMR director as merely the head of another top-level agency.[8] The bureau, which believed itself "the central core of the Executive Office," resented any effort by OWMR to intrude itself between the president and the budget director.[9]

THE END OF THE OWMR

By the time John Steelman was appointed director of OWMR in the fall of 1946 it was obvious that an early decision had to be made about its future. The public seemed to be clamoring for the end of all war agencies, of which OWMR was the best known. The agency became even more unpopular when it became embroiled in the political squabbles associated with the end of price and wage controls. In essence, the decline of the OWMR was the result of the country's return to peacetime conditions.

Initially, the most popular proposal for disposing of OWMR, and the one which the agency favored, was to incorporate it into the Executive Office of the President as a policy staff shorn of its directive

---

7. Somers, pp. 67–70.
8. Ibid.
9. Transcript, Roger W. Jones interview, 14 August 1969, HSTL, pp. 31–32.

powers. It was an idea that seemed consistent with a recommendation from the House Special Committee on Post-War Economic Policy and Planning which had suggested that a presidential staff unit be created to coordinate the overall formulation of policy.[10] The bureau, however, viewed this proposal as simply an effort by key members of OWMR to migrate to the White House, there to replace some of the president's administrative assistants and continue to exclude the bureau from matters of policy.[11]

Probably the deciding factor in the bureaucratic battle between the bureau and OWMR for the president's affection and esteem was the election of a Republican-controlled Congress in November 1946. This event made it unlikely that additional funds for an expanded executive office would be forthcoming. Steelman realized the futility of trying to reconstitute the OWMR under these circumstances and so recommended its dissolution.[12] When it became clear that OWMR was not to be continued, James Webb, the new budget director, attempted to get its functions shifted to the Budget Bureau. Truman, apparently determined to try to coordinate the development of policy himself, ignored Webb's efforts.[13]

So an opportunity passed to create a presidential staff for national policy coordination. In retrospect, Donald Stone, who as the bureau's organizational expert had helped bring down the OWMR, thought that the agency had been liquidated too soon. Yet with the country moving into a different stage he did not feel that much would have been gained by trying to continue OWMR in the pattern in which it was functioning.[14]

The War Mobilization Act of 1944 provided for the continuation of OWMR until 30 June 1947. However, at his press conference on 12 December 1946 Truman announced that he was abolishing the agency effective

---

10. Somers, *Presidential Agency*, pp. 98–100.

11. Donald C. Stone to the Director, 7 November 1946, Organization of Staff Assistance to the President, Series 39.32, OMB.

12. Somers, *Presidential Agency*, p. 100.

13. Hobbs, *Behind the President*, p. 191.

14. Donald C. Stone to Alfred Sander, 19 April 1971.

immediately. An executive order, No. 9809, established a new agency, the Office of Temporary Controls, into which was consolidated the OWMR along with the Office of Price Administration and the Civilian Production Administration. The president claimed that the move would result in economies in operation and a more rapid liquidation of the personnel and property of the wartime agencies.[15]

The work of the OWMR continued, after a fashion, because Truman brought Steelman and some of his former agency's staff into the White House. Steelman was named the assistant to the president. His job, in Truman's words, was to "carry on the duties practically as he had been carrying them on; and whatever is necessary to be done in reconversion, he will continue to do."[16]

By putting Steelman, together with a small staff, in the White House, Truman avoided the necessity of seeking a separate appropriation from Congress to maintain the coordination function. And, by eliminating a statutorily defined agency, the president gained more personal control over operations. This last point was not lost on Steelman who now realized that although the "OWMR director had statutory powers over Cabinet members; the Assistant to the President would have to use persuasion."[17] Steelman did not think it would make much difference. As he told Truman: "I've issued about six orders to members of your Cabinet since I've had the job . . . but in every instance I got an agreement first. I don't need that kind of authority."[18] Much of his persuasion now would have to be directed toward the president himself.

V. O. KEY'S ANALYSIS OF THE EOP

The decision to abolish the OWMR was largely a political one but there were efforts afoot to apply public

15. Statement by the President, OF 1173, HSTL.

16. U.S. President, *Public Papers of the Presidents of the United States Harry S. Truman, 1946* (Washington, D.C., 1962), p. 493.]

17. Anderson, *The Presidents' Men,* pp. 109–110.

18. Steelman in Thompson, *Portraits,* vol.s, p. 37.

administration techniques to an analysis of the president's staff needs. Even before the end of the war Harold Smith had directed his organizational experts to study the problem and recommend solutions. They concluded that two of the most obvious problems facing the president's staff were the coordination of the work of the executive office itself and the virtual absence of any mechanism for national planning and policy development.[19]

The bureau experts found coordination was difficult because the executive office was merely "a collection of agencies with no corporate existence beyond a common name." As a result, there was no way to interrelate the inevitable overlaps in the work of the office short of the president himself. When two or more elements of the office happened to be working on the same question, they would not be aware of each other's efforts until one happened to meet the other in an operating agency. Since there was no clear delineation of jurisdiction among the different units of the president's office, the operating agencies had no ready and easy way to seek out the person who would be working on a given problem for the president.[20]

Substantive policy development had never been a part of the work of the executive office because the Brownlow committee had concentrated on the provision of managerial help for the president. The only institutionalized aid the president had in substantive matters was found in the Budget Bureau. This tended to be not too fruitful because the budgeting process emphasizes the translation of established programs and policies into dollars instead of initiating the development of policies to meet emerging problems.[21]

With the end of the European war in May 1945 the bureau made a concerted effort to develop concrete proposals for improving the executive office. V. O. Key, the noted political scientist who worked for the bureau during the war, was assigned the task. He began

19. "Machinery to Assist the President," AM Project 174, June 1944–November 1945, E2–5, Series 39.32, OMB.
20. Ibid.
21. Ibid.

by listing the existing weaknesses of the presidential staffs. Some of the most significant were:

1.   A need to improve the channels and procedures by which presidential decisions were reached. The procedures did not assure that the president had the assistance of the various parts of the executive office on issues coming to him for consideration. This prompted agency heads to try to take advantage of the president by attempting, in an *ex parte* fashion, to obtain decisions from him by offering documents for his signature without opportunity for independent consideration and investigation.

2.   Another problem was the failure to tie closely together the immediate White House staff and the top level advisory agencies. The personal assistants to the president almost invariably sought to operate independently, jealously guarding their access to the president and developing a clientele within the operating agencies. The top-level staff and supervisory agencies were also competitors for status with the president. The functions of the various individuals and groups were unclear. This working at cross-purposes, and sometimes leaving things undone because they fell between unclear assignments, encouraged the operating agencies to bypass coordinating agencies and to seek a decision directly from the president.

3.   A serious defect was the absence of machinery in the executive office for planning how to meet future problems. There was no unit with a specific mandate to watch out for matters that would probably become critical within a year or so, although the NRPB had been an attempt to meet this need.

4.   He also found the apparatus for legislative leadership by the president to be inadequate. There was no effective means by which the advice of the departments could be brought systematically

to the president and used by him in dealing with the party leadership in Congress.[22]

Key believed the task of staffing the presidency had to be thought of in broader terms than that achieved by the Brownlow committee. He called unrealistic the view held by many of the Budget Bureau staff "that the Bureau is, or at least ought to be the Executive Office." Key suggested that the staffing of the presidency was not just a matter of having a few wise men around the White House or of making a functioning institution out of the cabinet, but demanded "large scale institutionalization or even routinized treatment rather than the brilliant, incisive and sometimes erratic action of the lone operator."[23]

To maintain his general constitutional position as the chief executive, Key recommended that the president take the position that the internal organization of the executive office was a matter for presidential determination. That is, agencies that are essentially arms of the president should not be established by statute nor should their leaders be subject to senatorial confirmation.[24] This was to be a position the bureau held to steadfastly over the years, but one which Congress soon violated when it created the Council of Economic Advisers, placed it within the executive office, and made the council members subject to senatorial confirmation.

By June 1945 Key had put together a complete package to achieve a reorganized executive office. It included drafts of a presidential message to Congress on the subject, an executive order establishing the units of the executive office, and memoranda to various officials in the executive branch explaining the

22. Draft memorandum, "Organization of the Executive Office of the President," 7 August 1945, pp. 2-3, AM Project 174, E2-5, Series 39.32, OMB.

23. V.O. Key, Draft Report on the Executive Office, 25 June 1945, p. 40, E2-5, Series 39.32, OMB.

24. Ibid.

role of the various staff components. His work was circulated within the bureau, discussed, and by September
1945 had quietly died.[25]

BUREAU EOP PROPOSALS

The growth and consolidation of the president's power
and the looming problems of the postwar period
prompted others in the bureau to develop proposals to
deal with the policy formulation needs of the chief
executive. According to Don K. Price, then a member of
the bureau, these suggestions usually followed the
blind alleys of a stronger cabinet or joint executive-
legislative organizations or procedures. Price believed
such proposals were futile because of the lack of
political discipline in the American system. His solution was the establishment of committees composed of
agency heads to work out solutions to problems previously defined for them by the president.[26]

Bureau members James Sundquist and Ralph
Burton, because they believed that someone ought to be
thinking about the executive office, volunteered to
devote their spare time to the project.[27] Sundquist
argued that the theory of the executive office needed
to be expanded "since policy leadership and coordination cannot be accomplished satisfactorily through
administrative controls alone." The office had to be
able to ensure the general coordination of national
policy. To do this it would need to be institutionalized
and formed into specific organizational units with
definite functions and systematized interrelation-
ships.[28] He proposed the establishment of four new
staff units in the executive office. Their areas of
responsibility would be economic policy, social program

25. V. O. Key, Progress Reports, Division of Administrative Management, Project 174, ibid.

26. Memo, Don K. Price to Arnold Miles, 19 June 1945, AM Project
174, E2-5, Series 39.32, OMB. Price expanded on these views in
"Staffing the Presidency," pp. 1154–1168.

27. James L. Sundquist to Alfred Sander, 10 June 1981.

28. "A Plan of Organization for Executive Leadership and Coordination," 11 January 1946, Organization of Staff Assistance to the
President, E2-5, Series 39.32, OMB.

planning, national mobilization planning, and military policy. For the development of foreign relations policy, Sundquist recommended that the State Department function as though it were a part of the executive office.[29]

Next, William Pincus was assigned the task of analyzing the presidential staff problem. In reviewing the evolution of the executive office since 1939 he concluded that there were real limitations on the extent to which the presidential office could ever be formally organized. He expected that individual presidents would always vary greatly in their willingness to allow their offices to be institutionalized. Pincus predicted that "the Presidency is too national in scope, too dynamic, too political, too representative of the hopes and aspirations of 140 million Americans, to permit the complete institutionalization and attendant fossilization similar to that now existing in some areas of government."[30]

He suggested the organization of the president's office be limited to three problem areas. One was the need to assure a more definite and orderly coordination of the matters that flow through the executive office. Because modern presidents were more accessible, and as a result more subject to bids for their decisions, it was important for them to know what decisions they had made in the past on the various issues brought before them. The second need was to find a way to bring to bear for the president the vast accumulation of pertinent knowledge and information about the implications of these issues which resided within the executive office but were frequently not tapped in reaching decisions. Lastly, there was the great need for planning to deal with long-range problems. But Pincus knew that the presidency was essentially a political office. No matter how much staff work was done, the work of the staff would be only one ingredient going into the presidential decisions.[31]

29. Sundquist to Burton and Miles, 20 February 1946, ibid.

30. William Pincus, "Organization of the Executive Office of the President," May 1946, E.O.P. Misc. Memos, E2-5, Series 39.32, OMB.

31. Ibid., p. 16.

Pincus opposed too much formal organization in the executive office. He warned that "just as water seeks its own level, so in the political process Executive Office matters will determine their area of consideration by their individual political 'specific gravity.'" Politics made it difficult to categorize matters, for even minor items may have a political implication in the mind of the president. In these circumstances the staff can only offer technical advice while political decisions of a much different kind are likely to be made by the president.[32]

THE FULL EMPLOYMENT BILL

Efforts by public administrators to devise a rational presidential staff system were complicated by the unexpected establishment by Congress of the Council of Economic Advisers. The origin of the council was rooted in the decade before World War II when Americans were haunted by the specter of mass unemployment. The demands of war had provided jobs but the fear remained since there seemed to be little reason to believe that wartime prosperity would not vanish with the return of peace. Many Americans could remember the difficulties of the economic adjustment that followed World War I, and this concern was compounded by the devastation of the Great Depression. In September 1939 there were 46.5 million employed workers in the United States. In 1944 the comparable figure was 65 million. How this expanded labor force would find jobs in a peacetime economy promised to be a major postwar political and economic problem. There were estimates that 18 million Americans might soon be out of work.[33]

Franklin Roosevelt, who had lost none of his political sensitivity, took note of this anxiety and the need to show an awareness of it. In his economic bill of rights speech which kicked off his 1944 presidential campaign, the right to a job was elevated to the level of life, liberty, and the pursuit of happiness. Two days after FDR was inaugurated for his fourth term some

---

32. Ibid., p. 60.
33. Elmer Staats in Thompson, *Portraits,* vol. 2, p. 82.

Democratic senators attempted to redeem his campaign oratory by introducing the Murray–Patman bill. After many changes, this bill became the Employment Act of 1946. The Council of Economic Advisers, an unexpected by–product of that statute, has become its most enduring feature.

Senator James E. Murray's legislative aide, Bertram Gross, coordinated the drafting of what became S. 380 during November and December of 1944. Much of the input for the bill came from Louis Bean, Gerhard Colm, and V. O. Key, all of the Budget Bureau.[34] Harold Smith, who considered the bill "the most important measure since the adoption of the Constitution," was another important bureau influence. Henry Wallace believed that Smith was, to some extent, the "daddy" of the whole idea since it was he who got the fundamental concept of it into Roosevelt's final budget message.[35]

Implicit in the bill's concept was governmental economic planning. Initially, its drafters intended to openly assign this role to the Budget Bureau but, upon reflection, they decided that the threat of an even more powerful bureau might arouse the jealousies of some other agencies. The increased bureaucratic opposition might then be enough to kill the bill. So they hid their hand by specifying that the planning would be done "in the Executive Office of the President under the general direction and supervision of the President, and in consultation with members of the Cabinet."[36]

But the obfuscation was not merely tactical. If the legislation was too specific, it would make it more difficult to implement the executive office reorganization proposals then under study.[37] It was also firm Budget Bureau doctrine that Congress should not

34. Stephen K. Bailey, *Congress Makes a Law: The Story Behind The Employment Act of 1946* (New York, 1950), p. 45.

35. Telephone conversation, Smith and Wallace, 17 December 1945, Daily Record, Smith Papers, HSTL.

36. Bailey, *Congress Makes a Law.* pp. 167–168.

37. Gerhard Colm to E. G. Nourse, March 31, 1952, Gerhard Colm Papers, Library of Congress.

specify how the president organized or made assignments to his staff. Hence the reluctance to invite a statutory assignment of a presidential staff function.

During Harold Smith's testimony before the Banking and Currency Committee, senators tried to get the administration to admit that the Budget Bureau was to become the national economic planner. Smith admitted that his bureau would guide the agencies in the work but suggested that the committee "define the coordinating job to be done and permit the President to work out . . . the particular assignments of function within the Executive Office."[38] In the end, the refusal to specify in the bill the role of the bureau turned out to be a strategic error because it prompted Congress to devise a new organization to carry out the economic planning function.

Another reason the administration bill dodged the question of organizational responsibility for economic planning was because there was a disagreement within the bureau itself on how best to assign this task. Elmer Staats thought the bureau should have the major coordinating role for economic planning because its normal responsibilities included matters involving employment such as budgeting for relief, unemployment compensation, and public works.[39] But V. O. Key, a non-careerist, was able to take a more objective view of the bureau's role. He thought the bureau was already set in "an institutional groove." If it now took on a significant new function, such as economic planning, he predicted that old habits would so mold the new job that it would end up with "just about what we have been doing all along." He advised his colleagues to "recognize that the administration of a new function can often best be undertaken by the creation of a new organization which can be staffed and indoctrinated to meet the necessities of the new program."[40]

As the bill worked its way through Congress, concern mounted in the bureau about its organizational

---

38. Senate hearings, 4 April 1945, Employment Act origins, Edwin G. Nourse Papers, HSTL.

39. Staats to George Graham, 31 March 1945, ibid.

40. Key to George Graham, 24 March 1945, ibid.

provisions. Colm suggested the establishment of a cabinet committee chaired by the president to approve and dramatize the annual national economic plan. But under his scheme the Budget Bureau would still be in control because the bureau's fiscal analysts would serve as the staff for the cabinet committee.

OWMR was another bureau concern. In late 1945 that agency was still very much alive and Staats thought it had an excellent chance of being converted into a permanent agency which would compete with the bureau for leadership in economic policy.[41] Increasingly there was a fear that the failure to specify in the bill that the bureau would plan full employment had been a mistake that would not only threaten the future of the bureau's fiscal division but create the possibility for "a new record of chaos."[42]

Meanwhile, discussion in the Senate ignored the matter of administrative arrangements and focused on the degree to which the bill committed the federal government to a policy of "full" employment. Many senators were determined to avoid any statement in the bill that might imply any official endorsement of Lord Keynes's theory of compensatory spending. Whatever chance the liberal and labor supporters of the bill ever had to commit the United States to such a policy died with the passage of the Hatch Amendment. This compromise provided an escape clause that made any guarantee of full employment dependent upon "the needs and obligations of the Federal Government and other essential considerations of national policy." Since the bill's supporters did not object strongly to the amendment, the conclusion seems inescapable that their real interest was in the establishment of a federal economic planning system rather than a philosophical commitment to Keynesianism.[43]

But if this is true, why did the Senate give so little attention to the kind of organizational structure that would do this planning? Possibly with Truman in the White House instead of Roosevelt the Senate had

41. Conference on Murray–Patman bill, 13 April 1945, ibid.
42. Lyle E. Crane to George Graham, 21 May 1945, ibid.
43. Bailey, *Congress Makes a Law*, pp. 122–123.

less fear of executive usurpation and was more willing
to trust presidential organizational arrangements.
There seems little doubt that the administration deliberately avoided committing itself to a specific organization proposal to maintain its options and reduce
opposition. But by refusing to propose a scheme to
administer full employment, the administration sacri-
ficed the initiative and assumed the risk of being
forced to accept whatever mechanism Congress devised.

Even the senatorial opponents of the bill seemed
unconcerned about the bill's organizational implications and willing to permit Truman wide latitude in
assigning responsibility for producing the annual economic plan. As a result, the administration's proposal
for the preparation of an annual "national budget,"
which would simply forecast the extent to which private investments and expenditures could provide for
full employment, remained a part of the final Senate
version of the bill. S. 380 would also establish a joint
congressional committee on the national budget to receive and evaluate the president's recommendations.
With the support of the Republican leaders Robert Taft
and Arthur Vandenburg, the Senate passed the bill
overwhelmingly by a vote of 71 to 10 on 28 September
1945.[44]

THE HOUSE SEIZES THE INITIATIVE

In the House the bill was assigned to a conservatively
oriented committee which would probably have preferred to see the whole proposal buried. Meanwhile
Truman, who had committed himself firmly to full employment legislation in his twenty-one-point message,
worked to secure its passage. A cabinet committee
headed by Treasury Secretary Fred Vinson was set up
to push the bill through Congress. The president himself met separately with key members of the resistant
House committee, but the only deal he could get from
them was an agreement to report out some kind of a
bill if he would not insist on the Senate version.[45] As

44. Ibid., passim, chapter 6.
45. Ibid., pp. 161–162.

in the Senate, most of the attention of the House committee focused on key words in the bill's declaration
of policy. The committee substituted "maximum" for
"full" employment in their bill and inserted such
qualifying phrases as "sound fiscal policies" and continued devotion to "the American system of free competitive enterprise."[46]

The chairman of the House committee assigned
Congressman Will Whittington the task of preparing the
draft bill. Whittington, a conservative from Mississippi,
was bothered, not only by the Keynesian tone of the
Senate measure, but by its failure to establish a
clear-cut economic planning mechanism. While searching
for such a device, he remembered the testimony of an
economist who had appeared before the committee representing a trade association. This lobbyist had criticized the Senate bill because the economic analysis
and policy recommendations it called for would be
developed by individuals who were unknown to and not
responsible to the public. To remedy this he advocated
"a small independent commission, appointed by the
President and confirmed by the Senate, whose responsibility it should be to make continuous study of the art
of business stabilization through Federal action." The
commission, in his view, should be insulated as much as
possible from political pressures to enhance public
confidence in its work.[47]

When Whittington began drafting an addition to
the bill to create such a "commission," Senator Murray
sought to defeat this effort by urging Truman to
announce immediately how he proposed to administer
the bill once it was passed.[48] Whittington, unwilling to
give up his efforts to establish an economic planning
commission, sent a copy of his substitute bill to

46. J. Joseph Huthmacher, *Senator Robert F. Wagner and the Rise of
American Liberalism* (New York, 1968), pp. 317–318.

47. Unpublished manuscript, chapter 2, pp. 21–22, John D. Clark Papers, HSTL. This manuscript was an outgrowth of Clark's frustration
with Nourse's leadership. He had arranged to have it published in
January 1949, but Truman's unexpected reelection made that inadvis-
able.

48. V. O. Key to George Graham, 5 November 1945, E1-40/44.1, Series
39.32, RG 51, NA.

Vinson for comment. Vinson objected to the organizational philosophy of his proposal, but he did admit that Whittington was "right in believing that some machinery might profitably be inserted in the bill." He insisted, however, that the president should be able to select his own tools for doing this job and should have total control over the agency established to help him. Whittington's bill, he complained, sought to require the president to prepare a national budget "and then force upon him a staff which of necessity will have to do the job or provoke chaos." He termed the proposed council "a second Cabinet" that would have a charter to rove all through the executive branch offering gratuitous advice on matters already under the jurisdiction of the various line officers. Lastly, he objected "most vigorously" to making "this staff agency for the President the handyman for Congress and the Joint Committee."[49]

By admitting that the bill should include a provision for "some machinery," the administration now either had to develop its own alternative scheme or lose by default. Various proposals were considered. One group in the White House drew up plans for a permanent coordinating and planning staff in a reorganized executive office that was similar to the existing OWMR.[50] Another plan, which was developed in the Budget Bureau, suggested a cabinet committee under the nominal chairmanship of the president and including the director of OWMR together with the secretaries of commerce, treasury, labor, and agriculture. This idea of a cabinet committee, which drew heavily on Colm's proposal made the previous spring, would establish the director of the Budget Bureau as the secretary (and presumably prime mover) of the committee.[51] If this suggestion had been adopted, the bureau would have served as the staff for the national budget, and the cabinet committee would have been an elaborate facade to make its recommendations more palatable.

---

49. Fred Vinson to William A. Whittington, 24 November 1945, ibid.

50. Bailey, *Congress Makes a Law,* pp. 169-170.

51. Draft proposal for the administrative structure for the full employment bill, 7 November 1945, Colm Papers, HSTL.

Vinson, for his part, suggested a cabinet committee to be called the "Economic Council," which he, as the secretary of the treasury, would chair. This council would have the "final authority" for the preparation of the president's economic report (as the national budget was now termed). As might be expected, Snyder's OWMR objected to this idea and maintained that the economic council "should serve only in an advisory capacity and that a person similar to the Director of War Mobilization should be responsible to the President for the preparation of the Economic Report." Bertram Gross, who also was involved in these discussions, did not think either proposal workable. He advocated combining the new economic report and the existing budget document with the economic council serving as an advisory body.[52] Most of the disagreement centered around the composition of the economic planning staff, its organizational placement, and its relative influence.

Secretary Vinson took his plan to the president and lobbied to make himself the head of the council. Truman refused to commit himself and sent the proposal on to Snyder and the OWMR for comment. Snyder, motivated by a dislike for the whole idea of full employment legislation and the defense of his staff, chose not to reply and in so doing quietly buried the document.[53]

The failure of Truman to push his staff to agree on an organizational arrangement to counter Whittington's proposal frustrated Harold Smith, whose Budget Bureau would be most affected by the establishment of a new economic planning staff. He complained to Henry Wallace that Congress did not have any idea about how the bill was to be implemented and that there was even "a less clear notion on the side of the administration."[54] Through this internecine feud within the executive branch during a critical period in the bill's

52. Gerhard Colm to J. W. Jones, 17 December 1945, ibid.

53. Bailey, *Congress Makes a Law*, p. 222.

54. Telephone conversation, 17 December 1945, Daily Record, Smith Papers, HSTL.

development, the Truman administration lost an opportunity to influence the character of what eventually
became the Council of Economic Advisers. The new
president's inexperience and insecurity were evident
throughout this episode.

The House passed Whittington's bill with few
changes. Still hoping to restore many of the provisions of the Senate bill in the conference committee,
White House strategists advised the president to apply
pressure to achieve that result. He tried on three
occasions. On 20 December Truman sent letters to the
House and Senate conference managers urging "the
conferees to support the essential characteristics of
the Full Employment Bill as contained in the legislation adopted by the Senate."[55] In a radio address two
weeks later, he asked the country to let their congressmen know that they wanted real full employment
legislation. Lastly, the president's message to Congress
on 21 January 1946 called for a bill like the one the
Senate passed.[56]

In the conference committee the hardest bargaining was over the wording of the bill's declaration
of policy. The battle was usually won by Burt Gross
with his thesaurus. In most instances, he was able to
develop verbal equivalents to the Senate's statements
that won House support.[57]

THE COUNCIL OF ECONOMIC ADVISERS

Since neither the senators nor the administration had
been able to develop an alternative to the proposed
Council of Economic Advisers, this House-devised organization was included almost intact in the final bill.
The bill also established a Joint Committee on the Economic Report to carry out economic studies for
Congress and to comment annually on the president's
economic report. The administration focused its opposition on a provision of the House bill that provided

55. Truman to Senator Robert F. Wagner, Full Employment Bill,
Samuel I. Rosenman Papers, HSTL.

56. Bailey, *Congress Makes a Law*, p. 221.

57. Ibid., p. 224.

that, upon request of the joint committee, the president had to supply Congress with the various studies, reports, and recommendations the council had provided to him. Congressional access to these recommendations would have permitted the playing of factions within the administration against one another in instances in which the president failed to heed the advice of the economic council. Had this provision been retained, it is inconceivable that the council could have functioned as a component of the president's staff. Fortunately the Senate conferees were able to get it eliminated. The conference committee completed its work on 2 February 1946, and four days later the House approved the conference bill. The Senate concurred unanimously six days later.[58]

But even without the eliminated provision there is little doubt that the bill was an effort to limit the president's leadership in economic policy. Clearly, it defined the type of personnel the president could appoint to the council and required that they be confirmed by the Senate. "The requirement that the council be partially responsible to Congress was a device by which Congress could drive a wedge between the President and his staff." To some extent Truman was to be made to pay for Franklin Roosevelt's use of informal economic advisers.[59]

Despite this invasion of presidential power, Harold Smith (who hoped to be named chairman of the new council) told the president that the bill had "emerged in somewhat better shape" than he had anticipated. He urged Truman to sign the bill because the voters needed to be given some assurance that the government was concerned about potential unemployment. Although he still believed that it was "not a very good bill," Truman agreed that politically he could not "do otherwise than sign it."[60]

58. Ibid., pp. 226–227.

59. Lester G. Seligman, "Presidential Leadership: The Inner Circle and Institutionalization," *The Journal of Politics* 18, no. 3 (August 1956): 420.

60. Conference with the President, 8 February 1946, Diary, Smith Papers, HSTL, p. 4.

THE FAILURE OF SMITH'S PLAN

For the Bureau of the Budget, already concerned about the degree to which the OWMR duplicated its functions and competed for presidential favor, the unexpected creation of the Council of Economic Advisers came as a distinct shock. Many of its members began to consider ways to subvert the new organization. Some suggested that it be amalgamated, either formally or informally with the bureau's fiscal division.[61]

Others came up with a bolder plan. Why not persuade the president to appoint Harold Smith chairman of the Council of Economic Advisers while he continued as director of the bureau? Such a scheme would not only enable the bureau to control the council but it a would achieve a measure of the executive office coordination that some had been seeking. Some warned that Congress might view the maneuver as "chiseling in" on its prescription for administering the Full Employment Act, but when Smith was told of the idea he liked it and went to work to sell it to Truman.[62]

The appointment of Smith to head both the bureau and the council would make him, in effect, the chief of the president's institutional staff. This was not a new idea nor was it simply self-serving since Smith really believed the president needed a chief of staff. As early as 1942, when FDR was considering the appointment of someone to serve as his administrative secretary for civilian war business, the bureau floated the idea that Smith be designated "Chief-of-Staff for the Executive Office of the President," but the proposal was not accepted.[63] Later, in testimony before a House committee in 1944, Smith argued that improved planning and coordination in the executive office was necessary

61. Memo, Paul T. David to J. Weldon Jones, 5 February 1946, Administration of Employment Act, Gerhard Colm Papers, HSTL.

62. Memo, Arnold Miles to Donald Stone, 12 March 1946, Council of Economic Advisers, 1946–1948, Series 39.32, RG 51, NA; Telephone conversation, Henry Wallace and Smith, 8 February 1946, Daily Record, Smith Papers, HSTL.

63. Memorandum for the President, 24 September 1942, EOP misc. memos re Organization and Administration, 1939–1952, E2-5, Series 39.32, OMB.

to develop programs that cut across agency lines, to coordinate interrelated programs to maintain their focus on broad objectives, and to continuously appraise the effects of programs.[64] This belief in the need to improve the effectiveness of the executive office together with Smith's concern about Truman's immediate staffing problems and a dash of personal ambition prompted him to make a determined effort to secure for himself the chairmanship of the council.

Word of the plan spread rapidly. The day the Senate approved the full employment bill Smith's friend, Henry Wallace, reported that he had already broached to the president the appointment of the budget director as chairman of the council. Although Truman's reaction was thought to be favorable, he did express concern about the involvement of the bureau in policy matters. Smith told Wallace of support for his candidacy from among his own staff and on Capitol Hill.[65]

That afternoon Smith went to see Truman. After lecturing the president on the inadequacies of his staff and warning him that he could not rely on his cabinet to make up the deficiencies, Smith mentioned that he had heard that he had been suggested for the chairmanship of the council. Truman interrupted to say, "I think it's a good idea. The only thing that worries me is the other two positions."[66]

Thus encouraged, Smith tried to convey the thought that what Truman really needed was a chief of staff to clear up the accumulated administrative disorder that surrounded him. He recalled that Roosevelt had had a concept of the executive office that had never been wholly put into practice and implied that, because "we are entering one of the most crucial periods in American history, now was to time to complete that plan." Smith tried to nail down the appointment by claiming that he had made the bureau into the best

64. Hobbs, *Behind the President*, pp. 218–219.

65. Telephone conversation, Smith and Wallace, 8 February 1946, Smith Papers, HSTL.

66. Conference with the President, 8 February 1946, Diary, Smith Papers, HSTL.

staff in Washington and suggesting that if he was named to head both staff groups it could be the turning point of the Truman administration. The president seemed convinced that the work of the bureau and council would be so related that one person should head both staffs. But Truman probably did not realize that Smith was talking about becoming the chief of his institutional staff. They parted with Truman promising to give the matter his careful consideration.[67] This was probably as close as Truman ever came to offering Smith the chairmanship of the economic council.

The campaign to secure the chairmanship for Smith continued over the next several weeks. Wallace sent the president a list of possible candidates for the council that was based on political rather than administrative considerations, but he continued to insist that "from the standpoint of a workmanlike job, without regard for politics," Smith was the best choice for chairman.[68] This recommendation was reinforced by the chairman of the Federal Reserve Board, New Dealer Marriner Eccles, who tried to convince Truman of the "primary importance that the Director of the Budget be made Chairman of the Council of Economic Advisers if the act is to be effectively administered."[69]

During these weeks, Truman remained noncommittal. Smith tried to open the matter up by writing that he was more and more convinced that the council presented major administrative problems for the president. He told Truman that his own thinking on the subject had matured and asked for an opportunity to present his views to the president but no invitation to do so was forthcoming.[70] There is no indication in Smith's diary that the two ever discussed the appointment again.

Early in March, while Smith was apparently still under consideration for the chairmanship of the council, Secretary of State James F. Byrnes offered the budget director the position of assistant secretary

---

67. Ibid.
68. Wallace to the President, 26 February 1946, OF 985, 1564, HSTL.
69. M. S. Eccles to the President, 15 March 1946, ibid.
70. Smith to the President, 22 March 1946, ibid.

general of the recently organized United Nations. It is not clear whether Byrnes knew that Smith was then angling for the council job, but Smith indicated his interest in the UN position under certain conditions. Thinking he had Smith's agreement, Byrnes broached the subject with the president. He pointed out to Truman that Smith had children to educate and that his current salary of $10,000 would probably force him to leave the government within the year. Perhaps Byrnes was trying to force the president's hand. If so, it did not work. Truman replied that he could better afford to lose Smith in a year or so than now and refused to allow Byrnes to pursue the matter further. Byrnes argued that the assistant budget director, Paul Appleby, was capable of replacing Smith, but the president remained adamant.[71] When Smith learned of the conversation, he was "aggravated about the way the matter was handled, about the way his name was vetoed." He believed it was wrong that the president had turned him down without bothering to consult him.[72]

The incident shows that even though Truman may have decided by mid-March not to appoint Smith to head the economic council, he wished him to remain as director of the budget. But their relationship had been damaged beyond repair, and before long Smith decided to resign. He left the bureau in June when he was appointed vice-president of the International Bank of Reconstruction. In his last meeting with Truman, Smith obliquely referred to the preesident's failure to accept him as his chief of staff when he said "that there was only one element of disappointment as far as he was concerned—namely, that I had not the opportunity to do the job of reorganizing the Executive Office."[73] Within seven months he was dead.

There is no doubt that Smith considered executive office reorganization one of his major objectives

71. Telephone conversation, Smith and Byrnes, 8 March 1946, Daily Record, Smith Papers, HSTL.

72. Telephone conversation, Smith and Ben Cohen, 15 March 1946, ibid.

73. Daily Record–June 1946, ibid.

during the last two years of his term as director. If he had indeed become "chief of staff," and if the system had worked, it seems clear that the institutionalization of the presidency would have taken a different course. Why did Truman fail to appoint him? Did he at last realize what Smith had in mind and fear his dependence on one man? We can only speculate.

Truman, in his *Memoirs*, cites Smith's failing health, not his move to the World Bank, as the reason for his resignation.[74] There is no doubt that Smith's health problems were genuine. He had suffered a heart attack in 1943 and was under heavy medication for a period during the war when Roosevelt had delegated to Smith much of the responsibility for the non-war-related activities of the government.[75] Yet there is no indication that Smith's health declined between early March, when Truman refused to consider his resignation to accept the UN post, and 18 June, when the president agreed to let him leave for the World Bank. There must have been other factors.

James Webb, Smith's successor as director of the budget, suspects that Truman was never as enthusiastic about uniting the leadership of the council and the bureau as was Smith himself. He also points to the concern that White House aides must have had about Smith becoming the de facto chief of staff.[76] It may have been that, alarmed by Smith's play for additional power, Truman's advisers began to campaign against the budget director and succeeded in weakening the president's confidence in him. Then there was Truman's good friend Fred Vinson (who had coveted the chairmanship for himself) and other cabinet members who Smith himself realized would look upon the economic council with jealousy.[77] Webb speculates that this opposition caused Truman "to feel he wanted and needed someone

74. Harry S. Truman, *Memoirs*, vol. 2, *Years of Trial and Hope* (Garden City, N.Y., 1956) p. 33.

75. Don K. Price to Alfred Sander, February 28, 1972; John W. Ramsey, "The Director of the Bureau of the Budget as a Presidential Aide, 1921–1952," p. 101.

76. Webb to Alfred Sander, 3 February 1971.

77. Conference with the President, 8 February 1946, Smith Papers, HSTL.

he and his staff could fully trust to do things differently than Smith had done them."[78] When Smith sensed this loss of confidence and realized he could not achieve the same working relations with Truman as he had enjoyed with Roosevelt he decided to resign.[79]

There are other possible explanations for Truman's change of heart. For instance, Smith was being recommended most strongly by Wallace and Eccles. By March, Wallace's letters to Truman regarding U.S.–Soviet relations had begun to irritate the president. Eccles was an obvious New Dealer. Smith was also close to Harold Ickes, who had publicly objected to Truman's appointment of Ed Pauley and had resigned from the cabinet just a week after Smith had tried to sell himself as the president's chief of staff. It seems that Smith's appointment was being most strongly urged by people increasingly out of favor at the White House. Truman might also have had second thoughts when he realized that Congress might repudiate the combining of the director's and the chairman's jobs. This was obviously not what Congress had intended when it passed the Employment Act, and since senatorial confirmation was required for council appointees, this maneuver could have been blocked.

Perhaps the most likely explanation is that Harry Truman did not want to have a chief of staff and when he finally realized that is what Smith had in mind he would have none of it. Truman never permitted one man to dominate his White house staff, and it is likely that he would be equally opposed to one-man control of the rest of the executive office. He also probably resented the way Smith had tried to maneuver him into appointing him. Four years later Truman most remembered Smith as the "A 1 conniver."[80]

THE KINGSLEY PLAN

If the Budget Bureau was anxious to control the economic council, the OWMR was desperate to do so. It was

78. Webb to Sander, 30 March 1972.

79. Ibid., 3 February 1971.

80. Truman, *Off the Record* p. 174.

struggling, not merely for dominance, but for survival. Even more than the bureau, the council would duplicate much of the economic analysis then being performed by the OWMR and so hasten its departure. Instead, why not use the congressional authorization for a council as the basis for a new organization of the executive office which would contain an expanded version of OWMR's policy coordination function?

J. Donald Kingsley of the OWMR prepared such a proposal and sent it to Director John Snyder in early March 1946. He proposed a thorough restructuring of the executive office to include an office of overhead management, an office of policy coordination and development, and an office of congressional liaison. All these groups would be tied together by the chairman of the Council of Economic Advisers who would serve, not only as the president's chief of staff, but as secretary to the cabinet.[81]

In his memo Kingsley reviewed the evolution of the presidency and the inadequate tools available to the chief executive. He felt that the Brownlow committee had viewed the president primarily in his role as chief executive, neglecting his role as chief legislator. "This astigmatism resulted in recommendations which, while of great importance, failed to touch the most pressing questions and placed an altogether false emphasis upon management."[82] This had been largely due, of course, to externally imposed limitations on the Brownlow recommendations; it was not the committee's preference.

Essentially, both Smith and Kingsley sought to exploit the authorization of the council to strengthen or save their parent organizations while simultaneously dealing with some problems they recognized as existing in the executive office. Smith's idea was the simplest. Through the expedient of heading both staffs, he believed that he could add the dimension of policy formulation, and with this additional power, provide

---

81. Kingsley to John Snyder, 6 March 1946, The Economic Council and the Organization of the Presidential Office, Series 39.3, RG 51, NA.

82. Ibid.

the centralized staff direction he considered essential for the president's office.

Kingsley's proposal was more grandiose. He sought to institutionalize not only policy formulation, but presidential party and congressional leadership. Aside from this fillip, he was suggesting that the Budget Bureau retain its function, and that OWMR be merged with the council and be given a greatly expanded and superior responsibility. In the end, Kingsley had no more success than Smith. The reasons for his failure may have been related to the quality of his proposals, but was probably also affected by White House concern about congressional reaction to a manipulation of its Council of Economic Advisers and Truman's reluctance to depend upon one powerful staff man. In any event, by June, Truman had decided to establish the council along the lines Congress had laid out and had begun an active search for professional economists to be appointed to it.

* * *

Later in the year the bureau came up with one last proposal for reorganizing the executive office, but the new budget director, James Webb, was unable to get Truman to seriously consider it. With the establishment of the council, Republican control of Congress, and the decision to abolish the OWMR, the moment had passed when the executive office might have been thoroughly restructured. The following year, 1947, saw the creation of the National Security Council and the National Security Resources Board. These new staff groups had to be given a chance to prove or disprove their effectiveness before there could be much support for a reorganization of the EOP. Their mere existence was a stumbling block to change because of the vested interests created with them and the legislative sanction they enjoyed.

It is difficult to know what Truman's real attitude was toward the various schemes for reorganizing his office or even whether the various alternatives were ever clearly presented to him. Many of the decisions he was called upon to make may have seemed to him to have revolved around personalities such as Smith or Steelman instead of organizational concepts. Bedeviled by the loss of Congress to the Republicans and Congressman William Fulbright's call for his resignation, executive office reorganization was probably not a high priority item vying for his attention. The movement of events seemed to have overtaken the executive office planners and made their proposals inappropriate for the times.

5.
The
Budget Bureau
and the
Economic Council

The departure of Harold Smith as director of the budget marked the beginning of a new phase in the development of the bureau. Initially, his deputy, Paul H. Appleby, became the acting director. Appleby was a liberal New Dealer who had served as undersecretary of agriculture before becoming the assistant director of the bureau. A professional with a detailed knowledge of midwestern politics, he served as campaign manager for vice-presidential nominee Henry Wallace in 1940. Near the end of the war, Appleby left the government for private business, but Smith did not replace him. Then, less than a year before Smith himself left the bureau, Smith got Truman to persuade Appleby to return to his old job as assistant director.[1] Some think that Smith brought Appleby back because he foresaw his own departure and did not believe that Truman would be capable of choosing a new director. There is no doubt that Smith expected Appleby to be named as his successor or that Appleby expected the job would be offered to him.[2]

But many of those closest to the president at this time were not anxious to have someone as liberal

1. Truman to James E. Webb, 27 July 1946, BOB Misc. 45-53 (1), PSF, Truman Papers, HSTL; Robert A. Caro, *The Years of Lyndon Johnson: The Path to Power* (New York, 1981), p. 629.

2. Ramsey, "The Director of the Bureau of the Budget," note, p. 118 and p. 141.

as Appleby as director. Appleby was further handicapped by his close association with Henry Wallace.
Once it was decided that a new director was to be appointed, a contest developed between Postmaster General Robert Hannegan and Secretary of the Treasury
Snyder over the appointment. Hannegan sought the post
for his protégé, Gael Sullivan. Initially Snyder did not
have a candidate, but knew he did not want Hannegan's
influence in the bureau. As the new treasury secretary, he may have already developed some of the pro-
prietary interest in the bureau that many of his predecessors had displayed. (The people in the Treasury
never quite forgave the fact that the Budget Bureau
was no longer a part of their department.) Naturally,
he would also be interested in having a director in
whom he had confidence and with whom he felt he could
work. Snyder's experience as the director of OWMR had
made him aware of the key position that the budget director occupied and the need for an intimate relationship between the head of the bureau and the president.
When Snyder asked his undersecretary, O. Max Gardner,
for suggestions for the bureau position, Gardner recommended his young assistant, James E. Webb.[3]

Although Webb had met Senator Truman as far
back as the 1930s, he really did not know him.[4]
Hannegan and Sullivan, believing that Sullivan would
be the president's choice as director, had left the
country before the appointment was made. But Snyder,
who had not given up trying to block Sullivan's appointment, suggested Webb's name to Truman. He then
took him to the White House to get acquainted. Snyder
told Truman that this was the young man that he had
spoken to him about. As the conversation lapsed, Webb
volunteered that although he was happy with his work
in the Treasury he would be willing to take the budget
job if Truman wished. The president interrupted to assure him he would be able "to stay on at the Treasury." Webb, assuming his candidacy had been rejected,

---

3. Ibid., pp. 143–144; James E. Webb to Alfred Sander, 3 February
1971; Elmer Staats in Thompson, *Portraits,* vol. 2, p. 86.
    4. Webb to Sander, 30 March 1972.

then left and Snyder and Truman continued their conversation.[5]

Meanwhile, the pressure on Truman to name a permanent successor to Smith was mounting. At his press conference on 27 June 1946, Truman refused to comment on the report that Sullivan was to be named.[6] Sometime within the next month he apparently decided to appoint Webb instead. He announced several appointments at his news conference on 25 July, including two of the members of the Council of Economic Advisers, but became confused and forgot to mention Webb until a reporter asked about the budget vacancy. Truman then found his background material and told of Webb's selection.[7] This incident led some to conclude that this was one of Truman's most casual decisions and that the Budget Bureau was not to play a very significant part in his administration.[8]

JAMES E. WEBB

Webb brought to his position a background of working his way through college, election to Phi Beta Kappa, and studying law in night school. Born in North Carolina, he came to Washington as secretary to Edward W. Pou, chairman of the House Rules Committee, and later joined the law firm of former North Carolina governor Max Gardner. He became assistant to the president of Sperry Gyroscope Company in 1936, and by 1942 when he was called to active duty in the Marines, he had risen to be a vice-president. When the war ended, Gardner became undersecretary of the treasury and took Webb with him as his assistant. He impressed the people in the bureau as being bright, dynamic, aggressive, persuasive, and a "man of tremendous unquestioned integrity." His deputy considered him "a driving management genius." Some felt that because he was a dynamo, an innovator, and a promoter, he never had the

5. Undated note, Conference Notes (personal), Webb Papers, HSTL.
6. *Public Papers of the Presidents, 1946,* p. 316.
7. Ibid. p. 356.
8. Ramsey, "The Director of the Bureau of the Budget," p. 142.

time "to reflect on the really important philosophical questions of the day."[9]

Philosophic or not, Webb shrewdly analyzed the situation in which he found himself, what was wrong with the Smith–Truman relationship, and what could be done to reestablish the bureau as the president's primary staff arm. He came to the bureau with no preconceptions and he was wise enough to take his time. After a short while, he began to get a sense of direction and he devised three guidelines for the bureau to follow to regain its power and influence. First was the need to do the best possible staff work, not only in developing the data, but in trying to consider all the facets of the problems that must concern the president. Second, he attempted to get the bureau to look ahead so the problems would not have to solved on an ad hoc basis. By observing trends he hoped they would be equipped to satisfy the president's needs when they arose.[10]

Third, he saw that it was necessary to improve the personal relationship between the president and the Budget Bureau. Only in this way could Truman's confidence in the bureau be increased, and the antagonism of the president's advisers toward the bureau be counteracted. To do this he tried to meet frequently with Truman and to bring to these meetings some of the senior- and intermediate-level people from the bureau. As a result, according to Webb, "they could get directly from him what was needed to permit the staff of the Bureau to proceed with confidence and . . . he could interact with them . . . and could thus establish a basis of confidence in the leaders of the Bureau."[11]

Truman liked meeting the career staff and he was relaxed with the arrangement for it seemed to fit his informal style of operating.[12] This technique was in direct contrast with Smith's methods of limiting bureau contact with the president to himself, and on occasion,

---

9. Ibid., pp. 144–147; Frank Pace Oral History, HSTL, p. 19.

10. Webb to Sander, 3 February 1971; Staats in Thompson, *Portraits,* vol. 2, p. 81.

11. Webb to Sander, 3 February 1971.

12. Staats in Thompson, *Portraits,* Vol. 2, p. 80.

Appleby. Smith had been jealous of his personal relationship with the president and had channeled all
contact between the White House and the bureau
through himself.[13] Webb thus saw "the need to make
himself and his organization indispensable to the
President and he proceeded to do so with great dis-
patch, great vigor and with tremendous intelligence."[14]

Truman and Webb had their first real private talk
on 15 August. The president took the occasion to explain how he wished his budget director to relate to
him. He said that he considered the post the most important in the executive branch behind the president
and the cabinet. Then he gave Webb his standard lecture on line/staff relationships: calling for the presentation of "the facts" regardless of the pressures,
reminding Webb that when it came to decisions which
deviated from the facts, the president would make them.
Truman reassured his new budget director that "I will
not make decisions about you behind your back——you
can count on that."[15]

Webb's leadership of the bureau resulted in three
major achievements: the improvement in the working
relations and confidence between the White House staff
and the bureau; the establishment of the budget ceilings procedure to increase presidential control; and
the broadening of Truman's concept of the bureau as a
neutral force whose judgement could enhance the quality of his administration. Overall was Webb's attempt to
strengthen the concept of the institution of the presidency.

When Webb assumed the directorship, the bureau
faced competition from the OWMR and the White House
staff for primacy as the president's right arm. As
noted, the OWMR threat disappeared by the end of 1946.
The White House staff was a problem, not because of
its size or quality, but because of its inherent distrust of Smith's desire to have an effect on the administration's policy decisions. Because of this attitude, the White House staff carefully screened all the

13. James Sundquist Oral History, HSTL, p. 2.
14. Roger Jones interview, HSTL, p. 7.
15. Conference notes, A3-4, Webb Papers, HSTL.

bureau's material before it got to the president. The staff's critical comments influenced Truman's view of the bureau's work.

Webb sought to change the attitude of Truman's assistants toward the bureau by being generous in loaning his specialists to the White House staff for special assignments. Charles Murphy recalled that before he had been at the White House many months Webb began to insist that he needed an assistant and offered to give him anyone he wanted from the bureau staff. Murphy asked for Webb's personal assistant, David Bell, and got him.[16] In another instance, the decision to veto the Taft-Hartley Act in 1947 was made after Webb had turned loose three of his staff members without strings to work under Clifford's guidance to develop the president's case.[17] This practice in time resulted in the transfer of many bureau career employees to the White House staff on a full-time basis. The migrants included David Stowe, Richard Neustadt, David Bell, Harold Enarson, and Kenneth Hechler. By 1952 two-thirds of a greatly enlarged White House staff was made up of Bureau of the Budget graduates.[18]

The new budget director was able to alter the president's attitude toward the bureau not only by infiltrating the White House staff with his own men, but by ensuring a high quality of staff work from his agency. Webb was aided in his efforts by the void in staff facilities created by the dispersion of the OWMR staff at the end of 1946, the preoccupation of the economic council with its own birth pains, and the small size and relative inexperience of the White House staff. As a result, the bureau, which had reached its lowest point in the presidential orbit in 1946, was within two years firmly entrenched as the prime presidential staff resource.[19]

16. Charles Murphy Oral History, HSTL, pp. 61-63.
17. Neustadt, "Presidency and Legislation," note, p. 659.
18. Staats in Thompson, *Portraits,* Vol. 2, p. 81.
19. Neustadt, "Presidency and Legislation," pp. 658-659.

STAFFING THE ECONOMIC COUNCIL

In addition to a new director of the budget, the summer of 1946 also saw the appointment of the first Council of Economic Advisers. The Employment Act of 1946 required the president to nominate three members to an economic council who, in turn, were authorized to employ staff assistants and advisory committees to aid them in their studies. The council members, who were to be "exceptionally qualified to analyze and interpret economic developments," were named by the president subject to Senate confirmation. The council was the first presidential staff group placed in the executive office by statute.[20]

Not having any clear concept of the role the economic council would play in his administration, President Truman delayed choosing its members for five months. The delay was not because of a lack of suggestions about whom he should appoint. A few days after the president signed the bill, recommendations began arriving from such sources as Henry Wallace, Senator Robert Wagner, and presidential confidant, George E. Allen. Their candidates ranged from Alvin Hansen and Chester Bowles on the left to Ralph Flanders and Milton Eisenhower on the right.[21]

The members in the House who had cosponsored the employment bill also had their candidates. They recommended, "as the type of men that we thought would help to make the Full Employment bill a forceful and vital measure": Robert Nathan, Frank Graham, Leon Henderson, Max Gardner, John Winant, Ellis Arnall, Major Paul Douglas, and Harold Smith. This list is interesting because it not only demonstrated that Smith had some congressional support for his appointment, but that the House, which had devised the economic council, was not thinking of staffing it with the type

20. Stephen K. Bailey, *Congress Makes a Law: The Story Behind the Employment Act of 1946*, pp. 228–231.

21. For these and other examples see OF 985 (1945–September 1947), Harry S. Truman Papers, HSTL.

of professional economist that later came to dominate it.[22]

Another factor in the delay in appointing the members of Truman's first council was the time the president spent in flirting with and then rejecting the idea of naming Harold Smith as its chairman. It may have been more than coincidence that he waited until Smith had resigned from the bureau before making public his nominees. Edwin Nourse, who became the council's first chairman, and who was probably unaware of the Smith maneuver, thought Truman was slow simply because the council was not high on his list of priorities. He speculated that the president was anxious to leave for another Key West vacation when pressure mounted from various organization to make the council appointments. He imagined that Truman then called in Steelman, Clifford, and Snyder and said, "Who should we appoint to this thing anyway?"[23]

Leon Keyserling later lauded the wisdom of Truman's eventual selections for the breadth of viewpoint they represented while castigating the narrowness of those succeeding councils made up exclusively of academic economists. He saw the combination of a professional economist, a businessman-politician, and (himself) a New Deal lawyer-economist-turned bureaucrat as insuring the broad-gauged economic advice a president should have.[24]

It is doubtful that Truman's choices were made as systematically as Keyserling suggests or as casually as Nourse seemed to believe. Although all of his nominees had formal training in economics, Truman's choices were shaped more by pressures from a variety of sponsors than by a conscious effort to represent various schools of economic thought. The very heterogeneity of their backgrounds also contributed to the dissension that nearly wrecked the council. This was probably one of the reasons why Truman's successors seemed to take

22. George E. Outland to President, 12 March 1946, Full Employment, PSF, Truman Papers, HSTL.

23. Edwin G. Nourse Oral History, HSTL, pp. 17–18.

24. Keyserling in Heller, *The Truman White House*, p. 180.

care to avoid selecting council members who held
disparate views.

Serious efforts to recruit a council apparently
began in April 1946. Among the candidates considered
but not named were George Harrison, Winfield Riefler,
and Alvin Hansen. Harrison, who had been active in the
labor field, was dropped when opposition arose from
other quarters. Riefler, once one of Roosevelt's White
House aides who now headed the Federal Reserve's research unit, was rather a natural for the council, but
he felt himself to be temperamentally unsuited for the
role. Hansen, a protagonist of full employment and a
former staff member of the National Resources Planning
Board, was simply too controversial. He later admitted
to Nourse that he could not have handled the job.[25]
That there were others who were proffered appointment
but declined was indicated by a Truman comment to reporters on 2 May. Some correspondents reminded the
president that it had been two months since he had
last promised to announce his council choices. Truman
replied that his most difficult job was to find capable
men who would give up the higher salaries paid by
private industry.[26]

Although the Employment Act specified that one
of the council members should be designated chairman
and another vice-chairman, it did not assign any additional duties or authority to these positions. However,
Truman evidently considered the chairman's role superior to the other two, and it was this appointment that
caused him the greatest difficulty. In late June the
president offered a place on the council to George W.
Taylor, former head of the War Labor Board and a recent appointment to the faculty of the Wharton School
at the University of Pennsylvania.[27] Taylor declined
because of a personal commitment to the university.
Truman then offered him the chairmanship of the council. Taylor again refused, pleading personal and business commitments that would not permit him to give the

25. Nourse Oral History, HSTL, p. 27.
26. *Public Papers of the Presidents, 1946,* p. 226.
27. Taylor to Truman, 24 June 1946, OF 985, Truman Papers, HSTL.

council the undivided attention required if the new law's concept was to have a fair test.[28]

It was late July before the administration received acceptances from the three new council members. Even then the announcement of the appointments was accompanied by some awkwardness and a last minute substitution. On 23 July the *Washington Post* reported that, according to high administration sources, the council appointments were "almost" definitely settled. The story identified the president's choices as John D. Clark, Leon Keyserling, and Winfield Riefler.[29] But Riefler had declined so the chairmanship was offered to Edwin G. Nourse. It was 29 July before Nourse accepted.[30] While waiting for Nourse's acceptance Truman, at his press conference on 25 July confirmed the Keyserling and Clark appointments and promised to announce the third member in a few days.[31]

John D. Clark had a varied career as a lawyer, businessman, economist, and educator who throughout his life liked to be in the mainstream of political action. During the 1920s, Clark became a vice president of Standard Oil of Indiana and was listed as one of the twenty wealthiest men in America. Then in 1928 he decided on a mid-life career change, divested himself of his business interests, moved his family to Baltimore, and began work on a Ph.D. in economics at Johns Hopkins. Graduating in 1931 at age forty-seven, he spent the next three years teaching at the University of Denver. From 1934 to 1937 he was a member of the faculty of the University of Nebraska, and returned as dean of the business school in 1941.[32]

For his own amusement Clark played a minor role in the politics of Wyoming and in 1941 served as a

28. Truman to Taylor, 26 June 1946, and Taylor to Truman, 3 July 1946, ibid.

29. *Washington Post*, 23 July 1946.

30. Nourse to Truman, 29 July 1946, OF 985, 1564, Truman Papers, HSTL.

31. *Public Papers of the Presidents, 1946*, p. 355.

32. Leon Keyserling Oral History, HSTL, pp. 41–42; Corrine Silverman, *The President's Economic Advisers*, Inter-University Case Program Series No. 48, (Birmingham, Ala., 1959) p. 2; Flash, *Economic Advice*, p. 21.

Democratic representative in the state legislature. He probably owed his appointment to the council to the efforts of Senator Joseph O'Mahoney of Wyoming who was Clark's close friend and a sponsor of the full employment bill. Clark's interest in politics dated back to 1912 when he had served as a delegate to the Baltimore convention that had nominated Woodrow Wilson. From 1937 to 1939 he served as an adviser to the Senate Committee on Government Reorganization. While a member of the council, he frequently sent to White House aides Steelman and Murphy his observations on political conditions and strategy.[33] Clearly, political partisanship influenced Clark's perception of his council role and contributed to the problems the council later had with Congress.

All observers agree that Clark was an able person, but few were impressed with his scholarship. He had had little experience in economic research and analysis before joining the council and seemed to lack the intellectual curiosity and energy needed to acquire the technical qualifications expected of a member. Although he held strong views about economic issues, he was not very precise or articulate in expressing them. Some members of the staff thought him opinionated and arrogant. His midwestern background was evident in the Populist approach he took toward monetary policy and the iconoclastic attitude he had toward American business. Strongly moved by humane purposes, he sought solutions through political action rather than economic analysis. It was this political orientation which made him the natural ally of Leon Keyserling in council deliberations.[34]

Keyserling wanted the council post badly and lobbied actively to secure it. In early July, at a time when the administration was desperately seeking candidates, Senator Robert F. Wagner sent a proposed slate of candidates to the president. Speaking for

---

33. Memos to the President, Clark Papers, HSTL; Homan Sketches, Nourse Papers, HSTL.

34. Flash, *Economic Advice*, 21; David E. Bell Oral History, HSTL, pp. 89-90; Heller, *The Truman White House*, pp. 181-182; Nourse Oral History, p. 20.

"some of the sponsors of the Full Employment Act, and some others much concerned about its success," he recommended three names which he favored only in combination because of the balance they would provide. He stressed that they should be considered only as a package and that he would not advocate "one or two of them if the other one or two were removed from the list." Wagner's candidates were Keyserling, Oscar Chapman, and Sumner Pike. Of the three Keyserling was, in Wagner's judgment, the best equipped.[35] But the senator's effort to dictate the composition of the economic council only succeeded in obtaining the appointment of Keyserling.

Robert Taft may also have been an unwitting factor in Keyserling's appointment. A few weeks before Keyserling was named to the council, Taft had supported his appointment as commissioner of the Public Housing Authority. He spoke of Keyserling's ability, fairness, and courtesy and said that other Republican senators shared these views of the nominee. Truman saw Taft's letter of recommendation, and since it was the one and only time Taft had ever supported a Democrat for a public post, it must have impressed him.[36] It was rare to be able to accede to the wishes of both the New Dealers and "Mr. Republican" in a single appointment

If there was to be a New Deal seat on the council, Leon Keyserling was a natural candidate. The one-time boy wonder graduated from Columbia University and Harvard Law School before returning to Columbia to study for a Ph.D. in economics under Rexford Tugwell. He was lured to Washington by Tugwell in 1933 to join the legal staff of the Agricultural Adjustment Administration. This was followed by service as Wagner's legislative assistant and then as a staff aide of the Senate Committee on Banking and Currency. During this period he helped draft much of the more significant New Deal legislation including the National Industrial Recovery Act and the Wagner Act. From 1937 to 1946 he held various posts with the federal public housing

35. Wagner to Truman, 9 July 1946, OF 985, Truman Papers, HSTL.

36. Taft to Wilson Wyatt, 25 June 1946, PSF, Truman Papers, HSTL.

agencies. He never returned to Columbia to finish his Ph.D.[37]

In 1944 the Pabst Brewing Company sponsored an essay contest on the theme of national postwar planning. Keyserling's entry, which won the second prize of $10,000, was a long essay entitled the "American Economic Goal." It was an exposition of his emerging philosophy which advocated the establishment of national economic goals based on an integrated analysis of the needs and potentials of the economy as a whole. These goals, he suggested, should then be sought through the cooperation of industry, labor, and agriculture with stimulation from the government through tax incentives, research, credit aids, and other policies. He was a Keynesian but he did not believe that government policies were as important as the behavior of investments, profits, prices, and wages in the private economy. He constantly stressed the need to include growth in the norm by which the economy is measured. This placed him in advance of contemporary economic thought, but the economics profession was slow to acknowledge it.[38]

It was Keyserling's proposal for the establishment of national goals and the need for federal long-range planning that had helped stimulate the drafters of the original full employment bill. Keyserling was also involved unofficially in both the drafting and the passage of the bill. There is no doubt that he was well equipped for a place on the council through his broad understanding of the nation's economy and an intimate awareness of the workings of both the bureaucracy and Congress, but his technical qualifications as an economist were rather meager. This was counterbalanced by a quick intelligence and great intellectual stamina which he applied with vigor to whatever interested him. It is clear he had great hopes for the council.[39]

37. Flash, *Economic Advice*, pp. 21–23; Keyserling Oral History. HSTL.

38. Flash, *Economic Advice*, pp. 21–23; Heller, *The Truman White House*, p. 181; Walter S. Salant Oral History, HSTL, pp. 61–62.

39. Flash, *Economic Advice*, pp. 21–23; Homan Sketches, Nourse Papers, HSTL.

The absence of a doctorate made Keyserling very defensive and contributed to his lack of acceptance by other economists who regarded him primarily as a lawyer. Nourse (who did consider Keyserling competent as an economist) thought that the inferiority–superiority complex that resulted from the lack of professional recognition of Keyserling's accomplishments hampered the relationship between the two men. Thirty years after his appointment Keyserling still felt obliged to point out that he had completed all the requirements for a Ph.D. except the thesis, and that his subsequent reports and essays were much more significant than the typical dissertation. As Nourse recalled, it really did "grind him, to think that they talked about *Dr.* Clark and *Dr.* Nourse and *Mr.* Keyserling."[40]

Keyserling's talents, personality, and views aroused strong reaction in others. He was an activist with an aggressive personality who was voluble and articulate in expressing his views. He tried to make the council an instrument to achieve his aims through the widest possible play of his personal qualities. A council staff member characterized him as "a man with the heart of a missionary and the ego of a politician, desiring ardently to be engaged in good works at the center of the Lord's battle for right and justice, but on terms which will afford him prestige and prominence."[41] Such a man was not likely to be long restrained by Brownlow's admonishment that presidential advisers develop a passion for anonymity.

Since the social programs he espoused could only be achieved through political action, Keyserling tended to identify the council's work with the platform of the Democratic party. He also engaged in political intrigue. While a member of the council, he joined the small group (together with Clark Clifford and Oscar Ewing) that is usually given credit for developing the strategy that resulted in Truman's reelection in 1948. Because White House staffer Charles Murphy considered him one of the ablest people he knew, Keyserling be-

---

40. Neil Jacoby Oral History, Dwight D. Eisenhower Library, pp. 17–18.

41. Homan Sketches, Nourse Papers, HSTL.

came an important contributor to presidential speeches
and messages. It is not surprising that the existence
of this informal White House channel and the dual role
he was performing would cause some council members
and staff to distrust him. The politician in him was
interpreted as deviousness by some of his more academic associates. To one of these he was seen as "a
man easy and persuasive with words who turns too
many faces to different people. He has an instinct for
mending his fences."[42]

EDWIN NOURSE

The appointment of Edwin G. Nourse as chairman of the
council was something of a surprise. It certainly was a
surprise to Nourse because he thought it was generally known that did not believe in the full employment
concept. In 1945 Nourse had written an article in which
he called Senator James Murray's original full employment bill "statistically fantastic and economically
naive." Fortunately for his later career, the article
was rejected by both *Harper's* and *Mercury Magazine*
and was never published. It is not likely that Murray,
who was an influential factor in Nourse's appointment,
would have recommended him had he been aware of
these views.[43] Nourse's other major supporter was
Charles Ross, who was then the White House press secretary and a close personal friend of the president's.[44]

When Nourse's appointment was announced, Murray
sent him a congratulatory letter. Implying that he had
been instrumental in the appointment, he attributed his
interest in Nourse to his appearance before his subcommittee in 1944. Murray wrote that Nourse's comments
at that time had helped to develop in him "the philosophy which was finally embodied in the Employment Act

---

42. Ibid.; Charles Murphy Oral History, HSTL, p. 123.

43. A memoir entitled "The Professional Background of the First
Chairman of the Council of Economic Advisers" prepared by Nourse to
accompany his official papers, Nourse Papers, HSTL.

44. Murphy Oral History, p. 121.

of 1946."[45] One can only assume that either the final act was different from the "economically naive" original version, or that Nourse had not been able to convey his attitude when he appeared before the committee.

Twenty years later Nourse learned of the circumstances that led to Senator Murray's sponsorship of his appointment. Bert Gross, who had been Murray's legislative aide, and as mentioned, was the driving force behind both the original bill and the compromise version, revealed that it was he who had engineered Nourse's appearance in 1944. And it was he who had been impressed by Nourse's views and who had pointed out their implications to the senator. Finally, when candidates were being considered for appointment to the council, it was Gross who convinced Murray that Nourse should be named. Gross even drafted the congratulatory letter cited above.[46]

Admitting that Murray's endorsement was important, Nourse, who realized he was not Truman's first choice, believed he was chosen because he did not have any particular disabilities. He had strong support from the agricultural interests and business, and at least a favorable attitude from labor. As vice-president of the Brookings Institution he had many contacts with business executives and professional men, and a long association with chambers of commerce, the National Association of Manufacturers, and the American Management Association. His professional reputation was well established, with service as president at various times of the American Farm Economics Association, the American Economics Association, and the Social Science Research Council.[47] A person of such stature would inevitably provide the council with prestige and a scholarly image. Unfortunately he did not possess the most important attribute for a successful leader in the executive office—the ability to relate to the president.

45. Murray to Nourse, 31 July 1946, biographic information, Nourse Papers, HSTL.

46. Gross to Nourse, 3 October 1966, Nourse Papers, HSTL.

47. Nourse Oral History, HSTL, p. 121.

Nourse, who at sixty-three was twenty-five years older than Keyserling, was probably considered near the close of a distinguished career when he was appointed. After teaching for many years, he had joined the Brookings in 1923. With an office just a few minutes from the White House, he was knowledgeable about the federal establishment. Most important, he was *the* scholar of the original appointees. He knew of the kind of intellectual sweat and tears that was inherent in truly productive economic research.[48] He also knew of the limitations in his discipline. It was probably inevitable that he would attempt to create a council that would serve as a focal point of professional economic views at the apex of the executive branch. It is not surprising that he sought to institutionalize this mechanism by insulating it from the political maneuvering. A council staff member thought Nourse believed "the Council should be sort of a Supreme Court, bringing the best professional judgment to bear on the economic policy problems of the country."[49]

It is difficult to categorize Nourse's economic views. Former White House aide David Bell (who considered Keyserling "a fairly radical reformer") described Nourse as being "from the classical stream of American economics." However, there were few instances of significant disagreement between Nourse and Keyserling in the economic advice they rendered during the period of their joint service.[50]

Keyserling saw Nourse as a Keynesian who "like me, was distrustful of it only in the sense that some claimed too much for it." Nourse, however, gave more "attention to the need for delicate adjustments in the private sector. Accordingly, we were both committed to a combination of vigorous and definitive national policies and national efforts through education---or what some call the jawbone method---to influence the private section." Yet Bell recalls that they had debated at length wide divergences they had on specific policy issues. In the end Nourse usually resorted to ambigu-

48. Homan Sketches, Nourse Papers, HSTL.
49. Salant Oral History, HSTL, p. 52.
50. Bell Oral History, HSTL, pp. 89-90.

ous language in reports to cover up these hard issues.[51] In this way they were able, on almost all occasions, to present a united front in their economic reports. But it was in the area of temperament and the
role they saw for the council that their differences
were fundamental. It was this dissonance that led to
three years of conflict which eventuated in Nourse's
resignation.

Nourse made no secret of the role he expected
the council to perform: "Its prime function is to bring
the best available methods of social science to the
service of the Chief Executive and of the Congress in
formulating national policy." The council would thus
become a scientific agency of the government. Nourse
saw no reason for the council ever to become involved
in advocating particular measures or in the struggles
between various interest groups. He thought it should
limit its political involvement to assessing the probable effect of various proposals being considered by
the Executive or Congress.[52]

The new chairman of the council thought that the
president agreed with his concept of the council's
role. More likely, Truman did not have any clear idea
at the time of what function he wanted them to perform.
When he first offered Nourse the position, Truman described the council as primarily a "fact-finding"
agency. Nourse attempted to correct this impression by
pointing out that facts did not "speak for themselves,"
and while the council might be able to improve the fact
gathering, the primary mission of the council would be
to interpret the facts "into the soundest possible diagnosis as to the state of the nation's health." Instead
of debating this point with Nourse, Truman simply had
a statement prepared that described the role he saw
for the council as twofold. One was fact-finding and
the other was a paraphrase of Nourse's description of
the interpretation and diagnosis role. Truman then
dismissed the matter by telling Nourse that he thought

---

51. Ibid; Heller, *The Truman White House*, p. 181; Salant Oral History,
p. 53, HSTL.

52. Nourse to Truman, 29 July 1946, OF 985, 1564, Truman Papers,
HSTL.

the statement "completely covers the situation" and that he was "looking forward to real results from this set-up."[53] The new chairman was thus led to believe that the president completely supported his concept of the council.

Truman seems to have never developed an appreciation of the council's potential role. Nourse soon discovered that the president was expecting the council to supply him with simple answers whereas the chairman thought Truman should use the council "as a group with whom he could really thresh out problems as a means of arriving at his own decisions."[54] Nourse was never able to reconcile himself to the president's superficial interest in the council.

The council was a graphic illustration of the truism that although Congress can create an advisory body for the president, it cannot force him to take the advice. Lester Seligman has found that:

A facade of conformity to legislation may be maintained while the President seeks effective advice elsewhere. Expressed in terms of a dichotomy of role interpretations, a President may rely heavily upon prescribed staff organization to the point where he becomes the "victim" of his staff. In the other extreme, a President may recruit advisers from many sources, both inside and outside the government, and prefer a staff set-up of wide flexibility.

The experience with the CEA in Truman's administration indicated that Truman was more the latter type of President than the former. . . . Mr. Truman did not wish the Council to serve as an independent agency on the cabinet level but rather to have the same flexible relationship to himself as the rest of the White House aides. But Nourse had no desire to play the role of a politically committed member of the palace guard.[55]

THE BUREAU ENCOUNTERS THE COUNCIL

---

53. Ibid.; Truman to Nourse, 31 July 1946, Daily Diary p. 3, Nourse Papers, HSTL.

54. Memo of conversation with the President, 16 October 1946, Daily Diary, p. 3, Nourse Papers, HSTL.

55. Seligman, "Presidential Leadership," p. 422.

Because of the overlapping functions of the council and the Budget Bureau, the announcement of the Nourse appointment prompted speculation in the bureau about his probable policies. Gerhard Colm, a bureau economist who was soon to join the council, believed that Nourse recognized that the council's resources would be too limited to become involved in policy coordination or program formulation. He thought the new chairman would not be very aggressive, but would quietly build up a small organization in harmony with existing institutions and use their material to appraise economic conditions and make specific policy recommendations to the president.[56]

Another bureau economist soon to join the council staff, Arthur Smithies, proved more accurate in his assessment. He thought that Nourse would have the council make recommendations to the president and report facts and trends to the Joint Committee. He believed that Nourse wished "to set up the Council as a kind of oracle that would bring into the Government the aloof, detached point of view that characterizes . . . the Brookings Institution." Smithies welcomed this attitude but he did not think it would work because of the pressures that would develop on the council to get involved in political issues. He felt that Nourse's predilection for aloofness could win prestige for the council and give it a much better chance for survival than if it plunged into controversial issues. A major reason Smithies approved of Nourse's approach was that the bureau feared the interjection of "three new coordinators of policy . . . into the administrative picture." He felt confident that whatever Nourse chose to do in establishing the council "he will not tread on anyone's toes in doing it."[57] It was fortunate for future bureau–council relationships that the bureau regarded Nourse as a rather benign threat.

The working relationships and attitudes that developed between the council and the bureau were vital to the success of the former. They also provide an interesting case study in bureaucratic survival tech-

56. Colm to Paul Appleby, 1 August 1946, CEA, Series 39.3, RG 51, NA.
57. Smithies to Appleby, 1 August 1946, ibid.

niques. The council began its existence amid rumors that Harold Smith was suspicious of the council idea and "would have been glad to grab the Council off and have it as part of the Budget Bureau."[58] The climate of distrust was dispelled to a considerable degree by the attitude of the new budget chief, James Webb, who made it his policy from the beginning of his tenure to cooperate and work with the council.[59] In spite of good intentions, however, it was inevitable that frictions would develop between the two staff groups because the council had been authorized by Congress to take over functions the bureau regarded as its own; functions which the bureau considered particularly prestigious. And as a respected, powerful, and ongoing organization, the bureau could make life difficult for the council. The creation of the council provided a real test of the executive office concept since the natural instinct of the bureau would have been to "draw into its shell and attempt to buttress its own already well-fortified position."[60]

It was this tendency that Webb sought to counteract. In August, when he and Nourse met to negotiate their new relationship, Webb suggested that the council use the bureau's economists as their staff support. Nourse countered by proposing the transfer of Gerhard Colm, Louis Bean, and one or two other economists from the bureau staff to the council's. Nourse explained that he wanted the council to "take full responsibility for writing those sections of the President's message which comes within [its] jurisdiction." Webb, who was reluctant for the bureau to give up anything until he was certain the council was "a going concern," then turned the negotiations over to the bureau's expert on organization, Donald Stone.[61]

Much of the problem had to do with the overlap between the bureau's fiscal division and the staff of

58. Roger Jones Oral History, HSTL, pp. 29–30.

59. Webb to Alfred Sander, 3 February 1971. This information is confirmed by statements Webb made at his staff meeting on 10 September 1946, B1–2, Series 39.29, OMB.

60. William Pincus, "Organization of the Executive Office of the President," E2–5, Series 39.32, OMB.

61. Webb to Stone, 19 August 1946, B4–1, James E. Webb Papers, HSTL.

economists that Nourse hoped to assemble. Harold Smith had established the Fiscal Division back in 1940 in an effort to develop a comprehensive and intensive view of the economic trends and conditions of the country. The intention was to develop the broad prospective necessary to evaluate the effect of governmental programs on the national economy.[62] Clearly the continued existence of the group was threatened by the creation of the council. (Within a few years much of their work was assumed by the council staff.)

Initially, however, Stone and Nourse were able to arrive at a *modus vivendi* that governed bureau-council relations for the next few years. It was agreed that the fiscal division would continue to perform its function because this work was essential if the bureau was to fulfill its basic responsibilities. But it was also realized that the council had to develop its own staff of economists and not rely on the analysis done by the fiscal division. They were aware of the duplication of effort that would result but they hoped that the two groups would work together and that initially the fiscal division would provide assistance to the council. To permit the council to begin to stand alone it was further agreed that at least one of the economists of the fiscal division would be transferred to the council staff. The bureau member that Nourse selected was one of the originators of the Employment Act, Gerhard Colm.[63]

Stone was also helpful to Nourse as a "management consultant." The Employment Act specified that a member of the council would be designated its chairman and another vice-chairman, but it did not define the responsibility or authority of these posts. Although Truman had named Nourse and Keyserling to these positions, he had not given Nourse any mandate to assume a leadership role. Stone recognized this void and urged Nourse to get the president to specify that the chairman was responsible for coordinating the

62. Hoover Commission, *Task Force Report on Fiscal, Budgeting and Accounting Activities*, Appendix F, p. 55.

63. Stone to Director, 22 August 1946, E1–31/46.1, Series 39.32, RG 51, NA.

council's work. Stone also sought Webb's help in getting Truman to take this step.[64]

Webb followed through at his next meeting with the president by pointing out that it would be difficult for the bureau to coordinate its work with the council unless it was assumed that Truman expected Nourse "to synthesize the views of the Council and operate the Council Staff in such a way as to produce a unified and coordinated result." Truman accepted this view of the chairman's role.[65] In this way the position of the chairman as the first among equals was firmly established. The position of the chairman later became preeminent through an amendment to the Employment Act passed early in the Eisenhower administration.

The bureau was thus of inestimable assistance as the council struggled for its place in the firmament of the executive office. Not all the president's staff was so generous. The council received a lesson in the facts of bureaucratic life while attempting to negotiate a relationship with OWMR. In the fall of 1946 the OWMR was seeking to have itself established on a permanent basis to provide the president with short- and medium-run economic policy coordination. The council believed it had been assigned much of this responsibility under the Employment Act but it feared it might lose by default because it was, as yet, in no position to do the work.

Since Truman was already conditioned to look to OWMR in economic matters, there was also the danger that unless the council was able to stake a claim to a definable area of economic coordination it might end up reporting to the president through the OWMR on all matters. As Richard Neustadt, then of the Budget Bureau, analyzed the coming struggle, the council, "without authority except to advise the President. . . is in a very weak position. It will gain strength only

---

64. Ibid.

65. Conference with the President, 5 September 1946, A3-4, Webb Papers, HSTL.

insofar as it becomes known that the President custom-
arily takes its advice. That is a very long way off."[66]

In October the director of OWMR, John Steelman,
met with the council to discuss their respective roles.
In the meeting the council attempted to "move in with a
heavy hand immediately and deal with a range of subjects in which other persons and agencies had some
responsibility." This caused resentment in OWMR and
prompted Donald Stone to warn the council that it

had to earn its way, that it couldn't expect other agencies or other
persons to take it into their confidence until it had established a
record of behavior which warranted such confidence and that it could
not expect to exercise the kind of influence during the next three
months that it could expect to exert two years hence.

He observed that it was his experience in the executive office "that cooperation at this high level, involving ticklish political factors, was something that
could only be gained by hard work."[67]

* * *

Webb apparently decided early on not to contest the
council's primacy in the area of economic analysis. He
agreed not only to transfer some personnel from his
fiscal division to the council, but to have that division provide the council staff "information on specific
economic problems." To follow through, he designated J.
Weldon Jones, the chief of the fiscal division, his
liaison with the council and told him to work out a
rapprochement with them.[68]

Jones met with the council and, though "the conversations were pleasant," it was not a pleasant time
for the bureau man. He was much more knowledgeable
about executive office procedures than were the council, but as Jones struggled for the continued viability

66. Neustadt to Elmer Staats, CEA-General Administration, Series
39.28, RG 51, NA.

67. Stone to Director, 17 October 1946, E1-31/46.1, Series 39.32, RG
51, NA.

68. Director's Staff Meeting, 10 September 1946, B1-2, Series 39.29,
OMB.

of his division, he was definitely on the defensive. At one point he was reduced to claiming that there was nothing "unlawful" about the economic analysis his division performed because "the Budget and Accounting Act surely sets forth more than an expenditure program; that revenues and proposed legislation was also envisioned." The council agreed, but smugly "pointed out that the Full Employment Act was a later action of Congress."[69]

The bureau's rearguard action thereafter focused on an effort to have the traditional budget message and the proposed economic report of the council combined into one document. If successful in this, the experienced and well-established bureau could expect to become the dominant partner. While Jones was meeting with the council, Webb was telling Truman "that there was much to be said" for combining the budget and economic report. If the council were permitted to prepare a separate report, Webb warned, it might not mesh with either of the other reports that Congress required and the president might be faced with rejecting the work of his statutorily established staff group. The implication of Webb's advice was that the council would be difficult to control unless its work was "integrated" by the bureau before it reached the president's desk. Truman agreed to try Webb's remedy, but in the end the Employment Act's requirement for the preparation of an economic report proved too strong. The bureau thus failed in this effort to relegate the council to a subordinate role.[70] From that point forward the CEA had its fate in its own hands.

69. Jones to Director, 9 September 1946, Series 39.3, RG 51, NA.

70. Conference with the President, 5 September 1946, A3–4, Webb Papers, HSTL.

6.
Truman's Budget Bureau

Harry Truman enjoyed the budgetary process. After ten years on the Senate Appropriations Committee, he entered the White House with a sense of confidence in his ability to manage the budget. He also developed some convictions about how deeply a president should be involved in the process. Truman traced his intense interest in budgetary matters back to 1923 when he was first elected to a government administrative position. As president he estimated that he spent twice as much time with the budget as any of his predecessors.[1]

The president enjoyed displaying his intimate knowledge of the budget figures. Although his press secretary tried to talk him out of it periodically, Truman insisted on having a budget seminar for the press each year. The Budget Bureau would prepare a briefing book, and the day before the press conference, bureau officials would meet with him. Then, with the secretary of the treasury sitting on one side, and the budget director on the other, he would preside at these extremely long sessions, encouraging the reporters to ask him detailed questions about the budget before he sent it to Congress. It was rare that he would have to turn to others for help with the an-

1. Harry S. Truman, *Years of Trial and Hope*, pp. 33–34.

swers. The media were invariably impressed by his performances.[2]

Truman seemed to want everyone to know that the budget was made up of many of his conscious decisions, not just the recommendations of others. He also liked to follow the budget as it was placed in operation. The Budget Bureau accommodated his interest by tailoring a series of chart books that displayed the progress of disbursements. Truman kept these charts in his desk and regularly used them when bureau officials met with him about budgetary questions.[3]

To maintain this detailed knowledge of his budgets required Truman to spend an inordinate amount of time going over the agency requests item by item. This was both an advantage and a problem for the Budget Bureau. The amount of time Truman spent on the budget ensured that the director would have frequent access to the president. His secretary had standing instructions to give the director an appointment anytime he asked for one, and he met with him at least twice a week.[4] But his obsession with the budget meant that Truman initially saw the bureau only as a budgetary agency and tended to resist its intrusion into policy fields.

This was natural because the bureau had been created for the express purpose of coordinating, revising,, reducing or increasing the departmental requests before they were submitted to Congress. This one function was the most important development in the evolution of the executive office.[5] Harold Smith had tried to broaden the bureau's functions to include administrative management and economic analysis, but these efforts were not apparent to most. The business of studying and analyzing the agency budget requests, supplying the president with the facts he needed to make his decisions, and then ensuring these decisions were followed was the responsibility of the bureau's

2. Elmer Staats in Thompson, *Portraits,* vol. 2, p. 88; Frederick Lawton Oral History, HSTL, pp. 2, 8.

3. Staats in Thompson, *Portraits,* vol. 2, p. 88.

4. Truman, *Years of Trial and Hope,* p. 33.

5. Helmer, "The Presidential Office, p. 49.

estimates division. It was by far the largest of its five divisions.[6]

The examiners of the estimates division worked with the various departments and agencies, checking their figures and looking into the nature of their activities, the programs that they represented, and how well they were administered. The process began eighteen months before the start of the fiscal year for which Congress appropriated the funds.[7] By the time Truman became president the procedure was firmly established and is still followed. It was this routine that assured the Budget Bureau an important place in the presidential scheme of things. Since everyone knew that the bureau was in charge of budget preparation, when a new president came into office, the bureau did not have to struggle with the White House staff over budgetary control. The bureau's role was a significant part of the institutionalization of the presidency.[8]

Clearly, much of this work of the bureau was of a negative character. If a president wished to prevent a particular line of action, he could count on the bureau to control it. Since the bureau was primarily a point of review rather than a center for initiative, it was far more difficult to use it to see that something positive was done by the agencies. After all, it was the bureau that blocked appropriations, checked data requests, branded legislative ambitions with the fatal "not in accord with the President's program" label, and interfered with the agencies' organizational schemes."[9]

But the role of the bureau in the budgetary process was not as important as it theoretically seemed to be. The budget has been described "as an iceberg with by far the largest part below the surface, outside

6. Hoover Commission, *Task Force on Fiscal, Budgeting and Accounting Activities*, Appendix F, p. 49; Edward F. Kelley to Mr. Benton, 10 November 1952, General Administration, Series 39.28, RG 51, NA.

7. Radio interview with Harold Smith, 16 January 1944, Series 39.27a, RG 51, NA.

8. Schick, "The Problem of Presidential Budgeting," pp. 91, 101.

9. Machinery to Assist the President," AM Project 174, June 1944–November 1945, Series 39.32, OMB.

the control of anyone."[10] This was because much of the total budget was fixed by the routine functions of government which continued from year to year because of bureaucratic, political, and public demands. (During the Truman years most of the federal budget was still devoted to the expenses and operations of the departments and agencies.) Much of the budget that was supposedly manageable was, in fact, only subject to limited adjustments. This meant that the review process represented mere whittling. The big decisions were made not in the process of putting the budget together but by separate executive or congressional actions. Examples of these decisions included joining the World Bank, the Marshall Plan, the character and dimensions of an agricultural program, and the size of the army and navy. The bureau could make percentage modifications but large determinations were not systematically organized by it, only systematically reflected.[11]

LEGISLATIVE CLEARANCE

Since the budget is not the only device for making financial decisions, it was natural for the bureau to try to coordinate it with other decision-making processes. The best example is its development of legislative clearance. This began as an effort to plug fiscal loopholes but developed into a process for formulating the president's legislative program.[12]

The process began in November 1921 when the chairman of the House Appropriations Committee suggested that the bureau examine all the legislative requests of the departments and agencies for their fiscal implications. Soon a budget circular was issued by Dawes that required all agencies to send to the bureau all of their legislative proposals that involved money. There they would be examined for harmony with the president's financial program. The departments' violent reaction to this procedure caused Dawes to rescind the

10. Aaron Wildavsky, *The Politics of the Budgetary Process* (Boston, 1964), p. 13.

11. "The Budget Bureau and the Economic Council," C4-11, Council of Economic Advisers, Webb Papers, HSTL.

12. Schick, "The Problem of Presidential Budgeting," p. 106.

requirement. He said the bureau would limit its review to routine matters but cautioned the departments to check with the president on important issues.[13]

For the next twenty-five years there continued to be a legislative reference office in the bureau but it did not develop beyond the routine. "It reviewed various bill that came up for presidential signature summarizing the pros and cons and the departmental positions on those bills but it was not a positive role in the sense that it had any outreach functions."[14] The resurgence of the bureau's legislative clearance function coincided with the appointment of James Webb as director in the summer of 1946 and his efforts to prove to the president that the bureau had the ability to provide staff assistance far beyond that which Truman envisioned. The new director used his legislative clearance machinery as the principal means of demonstrating the bureau's utility in meeting the president's needs. The weakness of the White House staff at this time facilitated the movement of the legislative clearance group into a position of real influence in a relatively short period. As the bureau developed a measure of control over policy formulation, its influence grew.[15]

In 1947 bureau leaders decided to set up a legislative program for the president in addition to the budget program. This was done not merely because legislation cost money, but in an effort to have the executive branch speak with one voice before Congress. They set up a small group called the Legislative Reference Office headed by Dr. Elmer Staats. Roger Jones was brought into the office to be his deputy. These two, together with Richard Neustadt, set to work to develop the program. Soon their office became virtually an adjunct to the White House, working closely with Clifford and later Murphy.[16]

In November 1946, when the Republicans won control of Congress, the legislative clearance group began

13. Neustadt, "Presidency and Legislation, pp. 641–658.
14. Staats in Thompson, *Portraits*, vol. 2, p. 81.
15. Edward H. Hobbs, *Behind the President*, pp. 60–61.
16. Staats in Thompson, *Portraits*, vol. 2, pp. 80–81.

to be used as an institutional channel to the congressional committees. Truman and Webb used the group to work with the clerks and staff directors of the committees, supplying information, explaining the relationship of bills to the president's program, serving as stalking horses to see what the committees were up to and to report back on the legislative climate they found. One reason Roger Jones was chosen to work in legislative reference was because he was known as a Republican and so, it was hoped, more likely to be well received. The process soon became a two-way street. Many of the committees began to seek opinions from the bureau about how bills that originated in Congress related to the president's program. Much of the reciprocity was due to Senator Robert Taft's support of the process.[17]

The legislative reference group also got involved in the preparation of presidential messages to Congress. In 1947 the White House staff persuaded Truman to ask each of the department and agency heads to send him their suggestions for items to be included in the next year's State of the Union Message and Economic Report. The result was a great flood of paper descending on the White House. Because the staff there was shorthanded, the bureau's legislative reference office was given the job of going through the pile. This improvisation established the precedent for the bureau to become the coordinator of all phases of the president's legislative program. From that time forward the legislative clearance group

served as back-up staff to Truman's Special Counsel, drafting the program call, checklisting agency responses, identifying open issues, stimulating working teams and acting as their secretariat, collating phraseology in message drafts, providing linkages among their drafters—all this done by the prospective interpreters of presidential programs: the clearance agents gaining a firm footing for their clearances.

Helping to put together the president's legislative program and messages grew rapidly and soon was the

---

17. Roger Jones Oral History, HSTL, pp. 24-26.

heart of the entire legislative clearance function. The power of collecting legislative ideas, recommending those considered important to the president, sifting and sorting out others, and attempting to coordinate the departmental positions into a consistent program was very great.[18]

It soon developed that whenever a bill was being prepared the bureau was instructed to do the basic draft. It was then reworked into final form by Clifford or Murphy after many meetings with budget people and other members of the White House staff. The relationship between the special counsel's office and legislative reference became so close that the bureau people were never quite sure whether they were working for the budget director or the counsel.[19]

* * *

Truman relied on the bureau, as did Roosevelt, to advise him on what action to take on enrolled bills. Roger Jones recalled that:

He wanted institutional advice, he wanted someone to analyze for him the views of the departments, to give him the pros and cons, to stand aloof from the normal departmental attitude toward pieces of legislation, which heavily tended to reflect the attitude of the department's constituency, and do objective analysis of the issue for the President.

An analysis of the bill file during the Truman years indicates he usually accepted the recommendation of the bureau over the departments in deciding whether to sign or veto bills. This was particularly true of private bills (for which the bureau served as the president's court of equity). He told the legislative referencepeople to look at legislation from the point of view of Harry Truman and what they thought they knew of his convictions. They even tried to emulate a

18. Neustadt, "Presidency and Legislation, pp. 1003–1013.
19. Staats in Heller, *The Truman White House*, pp. 227–228.

Truman-style prose when they drafted his veto messages.[20]

Later, when Roger Jones headed legislative reference, he tried to avoid getting his group involved in
partisan considerations. He attempted to limit the bureau role to pulling together the agencies comments
and its own technical views. He thought only the
president and the White House staff should consider
the political angles. Jones was willing to consider the
political dimension if specifically instructed to do so,
but feared that if it happened too often the word
would get "around that the Budget is a stopping point
on the lobby trail."[21] The White House staff reviewed
all the bureau's veto recommendations, but only
changed them infrequently. If the bureau did not know
what to recommend, they usually asked the president's
staff what they thought he would like to do.[22]

In making their recommendations the legislative
reference office normally involved the other parts of
the bureau. As a result, they got a broad view of a
bill's economy, its relationship to the budget, and general problems of organization and administration which
it might entail. By tapping all of the talent in the bureau, legislative reference was able to get the examiners to make a major contribution to the analysis of a
bill's budgetary and program implications, the fiscal
division furnished information on its impact on the
national economy, and administrative management gave
advice on managerial aspects.[23] Don Price believed that
if a president did not have this help "a great many
independent and irresponsible agencies in the executive branch would have been created, and many costly
and unwise provisions would have been included in
proposed legislation."[24] By using this machinery, the

20. Roger Jones Oral History, HSTL, pp. 14–20; Frank Pace to Frank
Pace, Sr., 25 June 1948, Frank Pace Papers, HSTL.
21. Richard Neustadt to Stephen Spingarn, 12 June 1950, Misc. on
Executive Office, Spingarn Papers, HSTL.
22. Donald Hansen Oral History, HSTL, p. 16.
23. "The Legislative Clearance Function of the Bureau of the Budget," 16 August 1948, p. 13, in The Presidency, vol. 6, Facilities and
Systems Required by the President, E2–3, Series 39.32, OMB.
24. Price to Herbert Hoover, 28 May 1948, Elsey Papers, HSTL.

Truman administration became the first to have a well-coordinated legislative program.

THE BUREAU AND CONGRESS

A statutory relationship between the Budget Bureau and Congress was established by the Budget and Accounting Act of 1921. Section 212 stated that, at the request of any committee of either house that has jurisdiction over funds, the bureau shall "furnish the committee such aid and information as it shall request." Over the years Congress made increasing use of this provision on a multiple variety of subjects.[25]

The bureau and Congress typically regarded each other with a cautious ambivalence. The bureau realized that congressional control over appropriations for the executive branch was a serious obstacle to the bureau's position of leadership among the agencies. The agencies could, on occasion, make "end runs" around the bureau to gain support directly from Congress. If this happened too often, the bureau lost face and power. In self-defense the bureau tried to watch for consistent congressional biases in favor of certain agencies and raise their budget ceilings to minimize defeats.[26]

Many congressmen regarded the bureau as a necessary evil in a day of big and complex government, but they resented its power and its loyalty to the president. One congressman reminded a secretary of defense that while he was "a very important man in the Government . . . you are a minor deity . . . compared to the Director of the Budget. He is the Poo-Bah of this town.[27]

Other congressmen grudgingly accepted the presidential staff role of the bureau, but resented their dependence on it. They believed that since the bureau was legally required to provide "aid and information" to congressional committees, its reports to them should be impartial and not reflective of presidential pro-

25. Testimony of Frederick Lawton on S. 913, 17 May 1951, Lawton Papers, HSTL.

26. Wildavsky, *The Politics of the Budgetary Process*, p. 41.

27. Ibid., p. 38.

nouncements.[28] Because of the organizational pressures
that existed this was an unreasonable expectation. The
basic fact was that on most items the bureau's product
was in the president's name rather than its own. According to a bureau staffer this meant that:

On matters of a controversial nature in which heavy interests are involved, such as organizational relationships, the Bureau's position is
essentially what the President desires. This does not mean that the
Bureau does not have to do a real staff job so that the President may
have the greatest area of choice in reaching his decision, but it does
mean that the element of decision does not rest with the Bureau staff.
Consequently, the whole climate and tenor of Bureau-Congressional
relationships will inevitably be dependent upon President-Congres-
sional relationships.[29]

Although both were presidential staff groups, the
bureau's dealings with Congress were on a different
plane than the White House staff's. The budget director
was a personal adviser to the president but he also
had close relations with Congress and frequently appeared before its committees.[30] Webb also encouraged
his division chiefs to appear before Congress "once we
get policy lines straightened out on a subject." He
thought this would help develop the personal capabilities of these men and create more respect for them in
their dealings with cabinet members.[31] But in testifying
before committees it was sometimes difficult to stick to
the policy line. Congressmen usually tried to bore in
on bureau people to draw out impressions and recommendations. Frederick Lawton counseled that:

As long as we are on the main line of our general proposal and not
deviating from the main line of the Presidential program we are all
right, but when we begin to give aid and comfort to certain specific

---

28. Hoover Commission, *Task Force on Fiscal, Budgeting and Accounting Activities*, Appendix F, pp. 48–49.
29. C. B. Stauffacher to Frank Pace, 28 September 1948, Staff Meetings, Lawton Papers, HSTL.
30. John Clark, unpublished manuscript, chapter 4, p. 2, Clark Papers, HSTL.
31. Telephone conversation between Donald Stone and Webb, 2
February 1948, Calendar, Webb Papers, HSTL.

ideas we get ourselves into trouble. In some cases there are compromises to be made, but they should be made on an institutional rather
than a personal basis.[32]

Although his relationship to Congress was a formal one, there were instances in which congressmen
privately contacted the budget director to apply pressure, get information, or seek favors. Since Webb was
from his state, North Carolina senator Clyde Hoey frequently asked "Jimmy" for favors. They ranged from
trying to get the president to sign the Taft-Hartley
bill to using the bureau to get national income figures
for a speech the senator was preparing. Webb complied
but tried to mend his own fences by using the contact
as an excuse to put the bureau's congressional liaison
person in touch with the senator's legislative aide.[33]
Planning parliamentary strategy with congressmen and
their aides was also a feature of Webb's relations with
Congress.[34]

THE REORGANIZATION OF 1952

One of the problems the bureau faced during the last
years of the Truman administration was the critical
evaluation of much of its operations by the Hoover
Commission. The bureau had cooperated fully with the
commission during its fact-finding stage and furnished
all kinds of background information to the various
task forces. Webb pleaded with Truman to accept the
commission's recommendations and Lawton served as a
member of the task force on budgeting and accounting.[35]

Yet this task force, headed by well-known accountants from some of the large firms, was most critical of the bureau's operations. It accused the bureau
of neglecting its primary budgeting responsibility to

32. Staff Meetings, 29 September and 7 October 1948, Staff Meetings, Lawton Papers, HSTL.

33. Telephone conversation between Webb and Lawton, 11 March
1948, Calendar, Webb Papers, HSTL.

34. Telephone conversation between Joe Winslow and Webb, 18 March
1948, ibid.

35. Lawton Oral History, HSTL, pp. 15-16.

pursue more glamorous functions. It criticized the bureau because the jungle of legislation defining the budgetary process, "some of it dating back almost to Alexander Hamilton's time, had not been cleaned up." The report charged that the bureau had failed to provide congressional appropriations committees with the information they needed to act expeditiously and wisely.[36]

Another target of the task force was the excessive compartmentalization which it believed was encouraged by the bureau's organizational structure. It suggested that if the bureau integrated its staff it could more readily bring all of its talents into play. Although the full Hoover Commission did not accept the task force's view that budgeting was being neglected by the bureau, it did support the idea that the bureau should be reorganized.[37] In response to this recommendation the bureau put in place a major reorganization in 1952.

The basic outlines of the new organization had been suggested by the task force on budgeting. It proposed that:

The division lines, as between Estimates, Fiscal and Administrative Management, should be obliterated, and the work now performed by these divisions redistributed on a functional basis. Ten or a dozen functional groups should suffice to form the nuclei of gravitational centers, around which the staff would operate in the formulation and execution of the budget. . . . The nucleus of each group would consist of budget examiners, administrative and fiscal analysts, management specialists and economists.[38]

The reorganization abolished the existing divisional structure and created five new divisions: International, Military, Resources and Civil Works, Commerce and Finance, and Labor and Welfare. In this way the work was "grouped in terms of broad sectors of the Government's total range of activities." Each division

36. Hoover Commission, *Task Force on Fiscal, Budgeting and Accounting Activities*, Appendix F, pp. 61-62.
37. Hoover Commission, *Budgeting and Accounting*, p. 23.
38. Hoover Commission, *Task Force on Fiscal, Budgeting and Accounting Activities*, Appendix F, pp. 61-62.

was no longer limited to the budget process, but sought to help the operating agencies improve their internal management and organization. They also tried to help the agencies identify emerging problems and issues in their work.[39]

Each of the new divisions reported directly to the director along with four new "offices." The four were Legislative Reference, Management and Organization, Budget Review, and Statistical Standards. It was the responsibility of these offices to: (1) advise the director on policy in their functional areas; (2) coordinate and guide the divisions in the area of their competence; and (3) to handle the work that could be done more efficiently on a centralized basis. The Office of Legislative Reference and the Office of Statistical Standards were little affected by the reorganization other than changing their names from division to office. Most of the work once done by the fiscal analysis division was now the responsibility of the Council of Economic Advisers. What was left was assigned to the economic adviser in the Office of Budget Review.[40]

THE DIRECTOR AND THE PRESIDENT

The budget director's relationship with the president was one of privilege and obligation. In return for the opportunity to present his views on governmental matters to the president he owed him unbiased information and loyalty. The information was necessary to balance the one-sided pleadings of the departments so the president could make more objective decisions. Loyalty was essential to the director's exercise of his decision-making authority. He needed to discover the president's values, attitudes, and priorities so that he

39. Edward F. Kelly to Mr. Benton, 10 November 1952, General Administration Folder, Series 39.28, RG 51, NA; Staff Organization Manual, Lawton Papers, HSTL, p.2.

40. Organization Manual, ibid.

could make his decisions within these parameters rather than his own views.[41]

It was this loyalty that was the main source of the director's power. According to Don Price, the bureau became the most important part of the presidential staff because, since the time of Dawes, "no Congressman or columnist has ever been able to make an important political issue of the fact that the incumbent Director . . . had offered advice that the President had failed to follow. Budget Directors have given critical and independent advice, but as confidential advisers."[42] Of course these words were written before the days of David Stockman.

Harry Truman worked with four budget directors. Harold Smith's tenure was a transitory period during which he provided continuity, battled OWMR for presidential favor, and made progress in educating Truman in the capabilities of the bureau. Webb understood the president and his concept of the presidency.[43] He was also Truman's first appointment to the office. Building on the resulting rapport, he was able to reestablish the bureau as the president's most powerful staff arm. Aware of the bureau's institutional role, he consulted with all the previous directors. General Dawes was particularly helpful to him. Webb made a point of visiting him about every six months. Their meetings were typically followed by a Dawes statement to the press commending Webb's work. This support was helpful to Webb as he dealt with the Republican-controlled Eightieth Congress.[44]

During Webb's two and a half years as director, there was a steady increase in presidential confidence that the bureau could be relied upon to provide him with the institutional background, precedents, and framework he needed.[45] This rise in bureau influence

41. Kermit Gordon, "The Budget Director," in *The Presidential Advisory System*, ed. Thomas E. Cronin and Sanford D. Greenberg (New York, 1969), pp. 58–59.

42. Don K. Price, "Government and Science, Their Dynamic Relation in American Democracy," pp. 180–182, Nourse Papers, HSTL.

43. Roger Jones Oral History, HSTL, p. 30.

44. Webb to Alfred Sander, 3 February 1971.

45. Ibid.

was based on three developments: the increasingly close White House Office–Budget Bureau relationship; the increasing effectiveness of the bureau's legislative clearance work; and the ability of Webb to sell himself and his bureau's services to the president.

When Truman was surprisingly reelected in 1948, Webb immediately tendered his resignation.[46] This was not a *pro forma* gesture because earlier Webb had decided it was time for him to leave government service. But in the end he accepted Truman's offer to become the undersecretary of state. Dean Acheson, the newly designated secretary of state, took Webb as his deputy at Truman's request. Because of Truman's high regard for Webb, Acheson hoped his appointment would increase the president's confidence in the State Department's efficiency. He expected Webb's administrative talents would compensate for his lack of background in foreign policy. Although he performed well in his new post, Acheson did not believe Webb was ever happy in the State Department.[47]

FRANK PACE

Webb recommended that his assistant, Frank Pace, Jr., be named to replace him as budget director. Born in Arkansas, Pace graduated from Princeton and Harvard Law School. At Princeton he was an avid athlete but an indifferent student. He practiced law and then, during the war, served in the Army Air Corps. After the war, he became an assistant attorney general in the Justice Department's tax division. From there Attorney General Tom Clark sent him over to "run the post office" for Hannegan. When Hannegan was leaving government, he arranged for Truman to offer Pace the chairmanship of the Civil Aeronautics Board. Meanwhile, even though he knew Webb only casually, Webb had asked him to become his deputy. Pace decided to turn down the CAB job to join the Budget Bureau. There Webb treated Pace as though he were a younger brother and groomed him as his eventual replacement. During his apprenticeship,

46. Webb to Truman, 5 November 1948, Folder C2-1, Webb Papers, HSTL.

47. Acheson, *Present at the Creation*, p. 250.

he spent two or three hours a day just learning about the bureau.[48]

Pace projected a country-boy manner but he was really quite urbane. An excellent speaker, his quick mind enabled him to create the impression that his remarks were spontaneous, but they were well prepared. His warm, friendly, informal manner contrasted markedly with Webb's intense, hard-driving approach. Because of his personality he was probably Truman's favorite director. As Pace explained their relationship, "He came from Missouri and I came from Arkansas and that gave us a little commonality." Roger Jones recalled that Truman "was very comfortable with Frank. He liked to have Frank around. . . . Frank was his kind of politician."[49]

But Jones was never sure that Pace "appreciated the presidential-institutional relationship in the sense that others did."[50] Many in the bureau felt that Pace had considerable political ambitions and that he regarded the bureau as a stepping stone. Since Pace left the directorship after just fifteen months to become secretary of the army, this may have been an accurate assessment.

There were not many new departures under Pace, but there did not need to be because Webb had already brought the bureau to the pinnacle of its power. The new director soon found that his job covered every area of the government and that there was "nothing that does not come within its scope." He felt it impossible to lose interest in it because the problems he faced, from veterans hospitals to atomic energy, were so varied and manifold.[51] Though interesting, much of the work of the director was a day-to-day grind which did not suit Pace's temperament. So Pace used his fondness for public speaking to project the bureau's public image while delegating much of the work of running the agency to his deputy, Frederick J. Lawton.[52]

---

48. Ramsey, "The Director of the Bureau of the Budget," pp. 178–198; Pace in Thompson, *Portraits,* vol. 2, pp. 146–147.

49. Ramsey, ibid.; Roger Jones Oral History, HSTL, pp. 30–31.

50. Roger Jones Oral History, HSTL, p. 31.

51. Pace to Frank Pace, Sr., 18 July 1949, Pace Papers, HSTL.

52. Ramsey, "The Director of the Bureau of the Budget," p. 192.

Rather than innovate internally, Pace sought to expand the influence of the bureau as a policy maker. He wanted "the Bureau not only to continue to assist the President in solving problems, but also to provide some directional force for the President's program." He urged his staff to suggest items that the president could take up with the congressional leadership as one method by which the role of the bureau might be broadened.[53]

Near the end of his tenure, Pace summed up his stewardship as one of "substantial accomplishment." Although concerned about a budget deficit which would bring the bureau into more prominence, he assessed relations with the cabinet and agency heads as being "at an unprecedented high level." As to the president, Pace reported his "reliance on the bureau was constantly increasing."[54]

Pace's major contribution to the bureau was to maintain the position of the director in the president's circle. As such, he was a transitional figure between the dynamic Webb and the stabilized period that characterized the bureau during the Korean conflict.[55] He considered himself primarily a doer, not an innovator, so his long-term influence on the bureau was not great.[56]

As a fiscal conservative, Pace's natural allies in the administration were John Snyder and Edwin Nourse. It was Nourse's resignation that led to his own decision to leave the bureau. He believed that Leon Keyserling's policies as chairman of the economic advisers would be "much too loose" for his taste, so he told Truman to get a budget director who had more philosophical rapport with the economic council. When the president was unable to change Pace's mind, he offered to name him secretary of the army. Without much hesitation Pace accepted the new assignment.[57] He was a natural executive and much more at home with the ma-

---

53. Staff meeting items, 7 April 1948, Meetings and Conferences, Series 39.29, OMB.

54. Staff Meeting Items, 19 January 1950, Lawton Papers, HSTL.

55. Ramsey, "The Director of the Bureau of the Budget," p. 198.

56. Frank J. Pace Oral History, HSTL, pp. 19-65.

57. Ibid.

jor operational responsibilities entailed in his new job.[58]

FREDERICK J. LAWTON

Truman eventually realized how important the institutional character of the presidency was to the continuity of the federal government and that the Budget Bureau was probably the most important element in that continuity. By the time Pace left the bureau in 1950 the president thought it unlikely that he would run again, so his next budget director should be a man who could strengthen the bureau's institutional character. This would serve to enhance the possibility of a smooth transition to the next administration. Frederick J. Lawton, Truman's last budget director, was the first careerist to hold that position. He was ideally suited for this task by background and his commitment to Truman's constitutional views about preparing for the transition.[59] Elmer Staats, another career bureau employee, became deputy director under Lawton.[60]

Lawton had spent his entire adult life in the federal government. Born in Washington, he entered government service after graduation from Georgetown University. Later he picked up a law degree in night school. In 1935 he began his long career in the bureau. As one of his first assignments, he was selected by the Brownlow committee to work with the Senate committee preparing reorganization legislation. The next ten years found him in either the number three or number two position in the bureau. In 1948, while serving as the bureau's acting assistant director, he was appointed for a time as an administrative assistant in the White House Office. After five months on the president's staff, he returned to the bureau to become assistant director under Pace.[61]

58. David Bell Oral History, HSTL, pp. 8–9.

59. Roger Jones Oral History, HSTL, p. 31.

60. Staats interview, 11 September 1979.

61. Ramsey, "The Director of the Bureau of the Budget," pp. 202–203; Chronological File, 1948, Lawton Papers, HSTL; Hobbs, *Behind the President*, p. 30.

Fred Lawton was widely respected for knowing more about the details of the government than any other man. Quiet, cautious, and introspective in manner, he was a striking contrast to Webb and Pace. His long service and his contacts in Congress and throughout the bureaucracy gave him advantages they did not possess. Having served on the White House staff and having accompanied Webb and Pace to their meetings with the president, Lawton already knew Truman well when he became director. Lawton felt he had received his appointment because Truman "had been accustomed to seeing me, and I knew most of the answers to his questions."[62]

Under Lawton's leadership the bureau functioned competently but not brilliantly. Since he was not comfortable working on the major issues of government policy, he had much less effect on economic policy than his immediate predecessors.[63] More important than Lawton's personal interests in altering the bureau's role was the Korean War and the stage that the Truman administration had entered when he became director. As during World War II, it was inevitable that the bureau's influence would decline as mobilization agencies were created and moved to center stage. Domestic considerations were muted and the New Deal became an anachronism. The last two years of an eight-year administration were, not surprisingly, not a time for innovation and challenge, but for consolidation.

62. Ramsey, "The Director of the Bureau of the Budget," pp. 203–205.
63. David Bell Oral History, HSTL, p. 9–10.

7.
Economic Advice

The fall of 1946 was a precarious time for the embryonic Council of Economic Advisers. It was already late in the year and the economic report, which had to go to Congress in a few months, imposed an unavoidable deadline. To establish its territorial claims in the firmament of the executive office, the council was under great pressure to acquire a competent staff and begin producing worthwhile advice for the president.

The establishment of the council was clearly an experimental move on the part of the Congress. And there was little consensus among those legislators most involved in the council's creation about what kind of an organization it should be. But there was agreement that it should be a small organization; an annual ceiling of $345,000 for salaries was written in the Employment Act. Throughout the Truman years appropriations never reached that level and usually were far below it.[1]

Because of the staff's small size each appointment was critical. But it was difficult to attract high-caliber people to an organization whose future was in doubt. Yet if recruiting was slowed to obtain the most qualified personnel, the quality of the first economic report, which was so important in establishing the

1. Bertram Gross and John P. Lewis, "The Evolution of the President's Economic Council," May 1952, Series 39.28, RG 51, NA.

council's reputation, would likely suffer. If people were hired too quickly, the council faced the possibility of operating with second string talent for some time into the future.[2]

The problem of balancing these concerns and recruiting a staff of economists fell to the council's chairman, Edwin Nourse. The other council members, Leon Keyserling and John Clark, took the attitude that Nourse should do the hiring because he knew the people in the field better than they did. As the only practicing economist among the three, Nourse was better equipped to choose technical people. Nourse was particularly anxious that the staff be representative of the whole spectrum of the economics profession so he was careful not to select only people who agreed with his opinions. Most would agree that he put together a high-quality staff.[3]

As the recruiting process unfolded, it took on a certain character. Staff members were chosen in part because of the breadth of their previous personal contacts in their respective fields. As a whole, the background of these economists was predominantly analytical or advisory rather than operational. Their views, over a period of time, tended to coincide with those of Keyserling. Almost all of the senior economists were government careerists who knew their way around and had established reputations and contacts quite apart from their positions as members of the council staff.[4]

The acquisition of Gerhard Colm from the Budget Bureau was a key move in Nourse's attempt to build an outstanding staff. Not only did he have seven years of experience in the government, but Colm had originated the concept of the national economic budget which FDR had included in one of his budget messages. He was also one of the original group who had drafted the Murray full employment bill. As one of the senior ana-

2. R. E. Neustadt to Elmer Staats, 7 October 1946, Series 39.28, RG 51, NA.

3. Edwin Nourse Oral History, HSTL, pp. 34-35.

4. Homan Sketches, Nourse Papers, HSTL; Don K. Price to Herbert Hoover, 19 July 1948, Don K. Price Papers, Herbert Hoover Library; Edward S. Flash, Jr., *Economic Advice*, p. 31.

lysts of the bureau's fiscal division, he provided the council with both Budget Bureau know-how and valuable operations-level contacts. His own point of view tended to be near the center of gravity of the council as a whole, and eventually he developed an undefined leadership role among the staff members.[5]

Nourse tried to establish a climate in which the council and its staff worked together in a seminar discussion fashion. So long as he was chairman, the council members and the staff economists met periodically to discuss economic problems and issues. This practice frustrated the action-oriented Keyserling who wanted the staff to spend their time writing drafts for the council to consider.[6] In an effort to get expertise without the domination of a single technical approach (while catering to the egos of the senior staff members who, as fairly distinguished scholars, would resent the idea that any one of them could be put in charge of the others) Nourse devised a tripartite staff arrangement. He encouraged one group to focus on analysis, another on statistics, and a third to draft the reports.[7]

The Employment Act did not assign any special responsibility or authority to the chairman of the Council of Economic Advisers so Nourse took these actions by default. He did this on the advice of Donald Stone of the Budget Bureau who told Nourse to make all of the personnel appointments on his own and not to take them to the council for a vote. Stone also suggested that he acquire an assistant to plan the work of the staff and maintain contact with various other agencies.[8] But Nourse soon learned that Keyserling had, without consulting him, offered Bertram Gross, Senator Murray's aid, the post of assistant to the chairman.

5. Flash, *Economic Advice*, pp. 28-29; Walter Salant Oral History, HSTL, pp. 30-31.

6. Walter Salant Oral History, HSTL, pp. 52-55.

7. Nourse to Paul T. Homan, 3 October 1955, Nourse Papers, HSTL; Salant Oral History, HSTL, pp. 50-59.

8. Stone to Director, 22 August 1946, E1-31/46.1, Series 39.32, RG 51, NA.

Nourse honored the commitment but told Gross, "I'm not going to turn the running of the Council over to you. . . . You've all sorts of connections here in Washington, you know the ropes, and you can be of great help to me in that connection, but policies and decisions will be mine. You're not gong to make them independently."[9] Although not a professional economist, Gross, first as assistant to the chairman, and later as executive secretary, was to play a far more creative role in the council's activities than his titles might indicate. The aggressiveness, initiative, and knowledge that characterized his effort in behalf of the Employment Act were now directed to establishing the council as an important element in the executive office.[10]

THE ECONOMIC REPORT

The preparation of reports was very important to the council because it was their most significant statutory function. A president could accept its advice or ignore it, but the Employment Act specified that the council should prepare for the president an annual report of its activities and assist and advise the president in the preparation of the Economic Report. This meant that at least once a year the council would have the opportunity of presenting its views to the president and he was under some obligation to listen. There was no guarantee, however, that these views would be incorporated into the Economic Report. If they were not accepted, the stature of the council would be seriously diminished so they fought hard to have their first report endorsed by the president. It proved to be a difficult struggle.

The annual State of the Union and Budget messages are significant mileposts in any administration. The deadlines they impose tend to actuate the bureaucracy and force decisions. They become creative exercises characterized by intense competition among would-be policy makers for presidential approval. The fashioning of these messages engaged the bulk of the

9. Nourse Oral History, HSTL, p. 36.
10. Flash, *Economic Advice*, pp. 30-31.

attention of both the White House staff and the Budget Bureau during the last two months of the year. Now Congress had added an Economic Report. Since all three messages ostensibly represented the views of the president, a measure of consistency was expected among them even though they were essentially written by different groups. To coordinate the writing, Truman set up a committee composed of Steelman, Webb, Nourse, and Clifford. Neustadt, who witnessed their confused and chaotic efforts, thought the process had "a distinct Gilbert and Sullivan air—with serious overtones."[11]

Three different groups, each unaware of the other's efforts, took a stab at rewriting the Economic Report which the council had labored so hard to prepare. When the council learned what was happening, it protested so strongly it was at least able to have a major voice in the final version. Even so, it was not their document that emerged and they had to accept the diversion of large chunks of their original draft to the State of the Union message.[12] In retrospect Keyserling thought that the strong stand the council finally took on the authorship of the Economic Report was all that prevented the CEA from becoming "an adviser to Steelman rather than the President."[13]

By mid-January 1947 the first Economic Report had been delivered to Congress. It was generally well received by the nation's editorial writers and radio commentators. Even though it was in many ways the work of others, the report helped establish the council as an ongoing operation in the eyes of the public. The council also began to find a place within the president's staff structure.

* * *

In future years the production of the Economic Report was a more systematic procedure. By 1949 it had begun to parallel the process for preparing the Budget and

11. Neustadt to Staats, 20 January 1947, Series 39.28, RG 51, NA.

12. Daily Diary, 14 January 1947, Nourse Papers, HSTL.

13. Unpublished manuscript, chapter 4, pp. 4–8, Clark Papers, HSTL; Heller, *The Truman White House*, pp. 187–188.

State of the Union messages. It was in September of that year that the White House staff first invited the departments and agencies to submit topics for inclusion in the three messages.[14] Once the CEA developed its draft of the Economic Report it was circulated to appropriate agencies for comment and clearance. If there were disagreements that could not be resolved at the staff level, they were negotiated between the agency heads and the council members. If this failed, the issue was referred to the cabinet or, as a last resort, to the president. Virtually all the recommendations the council advanced in its draft to the president developed from interagency discussions.[15]

Steelman always sat in on the discussion between the CEA and the White House when the final draft of the Economic Report was submitted, but increasingly the task of preparing the final version shifted over to the message-writing group headed by Clifford and Murphy.[16] Once David Bell of the Budget Bureau joined the White House staff as an assistant to Murphy, he was assigned the job of smoothing the process by which the council's draft was transformed into the President's Economic Report. To do this he sat in on the debates the council engaged in as it considered the suggestions of its staff. His purpose was not to control these discussions but to keep Murphy informed as to the direction they were taking. Because of Bell's involvement, Murphy and Truman had advance knowledge of the issues that would face them when the council presented its draft. While he sometimes interjected questions that the White House wanted considered by the council, only infrequently did he engage in straight-out arguments with the council members at these sessions.[17]

When the draft of the Economic Report was completed, the council sat down with the president to discuss and explain it. Murphy and Bell usually sat in on these sessions. After hearing the arguments, Truman

14. State of the Union Message—1950, Clifford Papers, HSTL.

15. Flash, *Economic Advice*, p. 34.

16. Leon Keyserling Oral History, HSTL, pp. 105-106.

17. David Bell Oral History, HSTL, pp. 90-92.

would give Murphy instructions as to what he wanted done with the draft. Murphy and Bell would then sit with the three council members and put the final draft together. It was a time-consuming process character-ized by a great deal of discussion and friendly argu-ment. Out of it arose policy issues in the fiscal, tax, credit, labor, and agricultural areas. The report-writ-ing process became an important device by which presidential policy in these fields was determined.[18]

The first two Economic Reports were long docu-ments containing program recommendations supported by thorough economic analyses. However, it was incongru-ous for the president to sign a document of that length. So it was decided to break the document into a short "Economic Report from the President," containing the program recommendations, with the supporting analysis in the "Annual Report of the Council of Eco-nomic Advisers." In a sense, the Economic Report was a summary of the council report cast in a presidential style.[19]

The idea for two reports came in response to a complaint from a Commerce Department committee that the president's Economic Report was always too "political." It was suggested that the council periodi-cally issue over their own signatures a "factual and objective report." But the decision to divide the re-port into two parts caused some bitter discussion among the council members. Nourse opposed the idea because he feared it would reveal differences between the council's conclusions and the president's policy decisions. Keyserling and Clark not only favored two reports but wanted to include in the council's document considerable interpretive material to supplement the factual data. Clark dismissed Nourse's concerns be-cause, since the president had always followed the council's advice, there were no differences to hide. Keyserling believed the council could always phrase its analysis so it would appear to agree with the president's views. The discussion raised another fun-damental question: must the council members always

---

18. Ibid.
19. Keyserling in Heller, *The Truman White House*, pp. 58-59.

agree when they were advising the president or should they tell him when they disagreed? Nourse argued they should disclose their differences if they were important and irreconcilable. Keyserling thought they should always speak to the president with one voice, determined by majority vote if necessary.[20]

THE COUNCIL AND THE WHITE HOUSE

The relationship between the council and the White House staff was a dynamic and evolving one which varied with the personalities involved and the needs of the moment. When the council was sworn in, Truman told Nourse that Steelman would be his primary contact. This was a natural assignment because the president thought of Steelman, who was then director of OWMR, in terms of economic matters. Nourse considered the channel as a "sort of shunt off right away," and in a sense it was. Organizationally Nourse was on the same level as the budget director and he knew that Truman had not directed that official to report to him through the White House staff.[21]

Although Steelman monitored the work of the CEA until the end of the Truman administration, his greatest involvement was during Nourse's tenure as chairman. *Dr.* Steelman, who considered himself something of an economist even though his training was in sociology, got on well with *Dr.* Nourse. He, along with John Snyder and James Webb, became the council chairman's principal advisers and contacts. Nourse did not consider Steelman "a skilled technician in any field of economic analysis, but he was at the level of communications between professional economics and the President's political policy making." As such he served as a presidential surrogate for those discussions of economic problems that Nourse always yearned to have with Truman but which the president refused to engage in. Steelman typically ended their meetings with a promise to explain the council's views to Truman. While Nourse realized that Steelman would not fight hard to

---

    20. Daily Diary, 27 November 1948, Nourse Papers, HSTL.
    21. Nourse Oral History, HSTL, pp. 58–59.

convince the president to accept them, he also knew that Truman had full confidence in Steelman and saw him every day.[22]

When Keyserling became chairman, he wore two hats: one as the leader of the CEA and another as an individual, politically oriented idea man, speech writer, and operator. As chairman his contact was Steelman, but as a political operator it was with the Clifford–Murphy wing of the White House. At times the distinction was blurred.

Although Keyserling characterized his contacts with Steelman as "inconsequential," he admitted that they were regular and that Steelman always sat in on meetings in which the Economic Report was discussed. Keyserling may have minimized Steelman's role because he considered conservatives generally as the enemy, and, while he knew Steelman was not particularly ideological, he also knew that he tended to line up with the more conservative wing of the president's advisers. Still, Keyserling admitted that Steelman "was very hard working, had great ability along some lines and was . . . fundamentally honest." Perhaps Keyserling was chary of Steelman simply because he had been Nourse's confidant and was known to be a rival of Clifford and Murphy.[23]

THE COUNCIL AND CONGRESS

The most exciting potential relationship created by the Employment Act was between the economic council and the congressional Joint Committee on the Economic Report. The committee, composed of seven members from each house, was authorized to continuously study and report on matters relating to the Economic Report. To do this it could draw on the work of executive agencies, private research organization's and its own staff. The committee, together with the CEA, was the congressional answer to the problem of long–range economic planning in the federal government. But the act did not specify how the committee and the council

22. Ibid.
23. Keyserling in Heller, *The Truman White House*, pp. 193–194.

were to work with one another. That relationship became an evolving one much affected during the Truman
years by the Republican congressional victory in 1946
and personalities in Congress, the CEA, and the White
House.

Bert Gross, while still a member of Senator
Murray's staff, worried that the committee would tend
to think of the CEA as its own agency unless the
president took some action to impose himself as a
buffer between the two. He thought this could be done
if Truman would initiate periodic meetings with the
joint committee to establish the idea that the committee's contact with CEA should be through the White
House.[24] In actuality, the committee never tried to
dominate the council but the situation was very fluid
in 1946.

The Republicans controlled Congress when the
joint committee was first organized and their leader,
Senator Robert Taft, became its first chairman. This
had several implications for the council-committee relationship. First, the opening of the Eightieth
Congress marked, in many ways, the beginning of the
1948 presidential campaign so the Economic Report
could become a factor in the political maneuvering.
Second, a situation in which the White House and
Congress were controlled by different parties was
hardly an auspicious way to begin the experiment in
legislative-executive cooperation envisioned in the
Employment Act. And third, Taft, leading a party long
out of power and exercising an individual dominance
over Congress seldom seen, was too busy getting organized to have much time to lead the joint committee.
Without the chairman's full attention and with no
precedents to guide its work, the new committee floun-
dered for several months. As a result of these circumstances, the inherent congressional suspicion of executive planning, which was so evident in the abolition
of the National Resources Planning Board, was exacerbated. As Clark Clifford observed, Congress had always
resisted "strong and highly centralized control over

---

24. Weldon Jones to the Director, 20 March 1946, E1-40/44.1, Series
39.32, RG 51, NA.

the Executive Branch by the Chief Executive and [displayed] even stronger resentment against 'planning' by the President to improve his executive position."[25]

Shortly after the first Economic Report was dispatched, Truman and Nourse talked about what attitude the CEA should assume toward Congress. Upon the president's suggestion, Nourse tried to set up an informal meeting with Taft, but when the senator failed to return his phone call he stood on ceremony and refused to place another call.[26] For his part Taft released a statement from the committee claiming it did not yet have sufficient staff to study the long-range recommendations in the Economic Report. He referred the short-range recommendations in the report to the various congressional standing committees. Neustadt termed the committee's action "a clean and beautiful by-passing operation."[27] As a result, 1947 passed without any significant progress in joint executive-legislative planning.

It was the appointment of a professional staff by the joint committee that first triggered significant collaboration with the CEA. The council members encouraged their staff to confer with their opposite numbers on the committee staff. Soon CEA staffers were invited to attend meetings that the committee economists held with various advisory groups. Collaboration between the staffs grew, but Nourse tended to maintain a standoff attitude toward the joint committee. When the committee staff asked the CEA to undertake special studies, Nourse refused because the joint committee had

a lot more money than we had to staff itself and conduct its studies and ponder our findings. The Council of Economic Advisers had a small staff of experts to service the President, not to service the committee or other committees of Congress. They had a good American separation of powers there which I respected and honored.[28]

25. Clifford to Forrestal, 5 April 1948, Unification folder, Clifford Papers, HSTL.

26. R. E. Neustadt to the files, 21 March 1947, Series 39.28, RG 51, NA.

27. Neustadt to Staats, 3 February 1947, ibid.

28. Nourse Oral History, HSTL, pp. 65-66.

It was clear, even at this early stage of its development, that the CEA was to be the servant of the chief executive and not of the Congress.[29]

By requiring the president to annually submit an Economic Report, Congress ensured it would have better and more consistent information. But the Employment Act did nothing to enhance the likelihood that Congress would act on the advice. None of the prerogatives of Congress or its standing committees was affected, so the way the legislature acted on the advice was unaffected.[30] The joint economic committee "was deliberately conceived as sterile: it cannot originate legislation of any kind, for that, of course, would impinge on existing committees. It can only report to Congress on the President's budget and economic report and offer some general recommendations of its own on priorities and financial sanity."[31]

Another reason the joint committee did not fulfill the expectations of its proponents was its difficulty in establishing its influence in a Congress dominated by legislative committees. Each of these had carved out an area of power based on a particular concern such as labor or foreign affairs. These areas were in turn supported by special interest groups and client agencies. To a lesser degree the appropriations committees faced the same problem as the joint committee since their area of interest encompassed the total spectrum of congressional activity. But the appropriations committees controlled the purse strings whereas the joint committee could only offer advice—often unwanted advice. The joint committee's influence was also weakened by a partisan membership which usually produced both majority and minority reports. As a result, the joint committee did not become the unifying force that could represent Congress in the development of national

29. Roger B. Porter, "The President and Economic Policy," in *The Illusion of Presidential Government,* ed. Hugh Heclo and Lester M. Salamon (Boulder, Colo., 1981), p. 209.

30. James L. Sundquist, *The Decline and Resurgence of Congress* (Washington, D.C., 1981), p. 67.

31. Warren Weaver, Jr., *Both Your Houses: The Truth About Congress* (New York, 1972), p. 266.

economic policies. Instead, by providing a forum for the discussion of the Economic Report, it tended to enhance the CEA's role rather than the congressional role.

The Joint Committee on Atomic Energy is the only joint committee that is allowed to report legislation. The others can only examine ideas and conduct inquiries. Bicameralism seems to foster jealousies between the houses so they have been very reluctant to deal with major functional matters via the joint committee mechanism.[32]

THE ROLE OF THE CHAIRMAN

The antagonism between Nourse and Keyserling was celebrated at the time but in retrospect both men felt their differences were overplayed.[33] As their dissension became general knowledge, proposals to alter the council's structure increased. From the beginning many public administrators had criticized the concept of using a board to head a staff agency. Most would agree with Neustadt's observation that "the Council's difficulties are probably inherent in the three-man structure but, undoubtedly, these particular three men have exacerbated them far beyond what would be strictly necessary."[34]

Suggested changes ranged from abolishing the council completely to replacing it with an economic adviser on the White House staff coupled with an independent economic commission of from five to seven members.[35] A popular proposal would keep the council intact but elevate the chairman to a position of true primacy. Nourse admitted that the ambiguity of the chairman's position made practical operations difficult, but he did not think that the time was ripe for making

32. William L. Morrow, *Congressional Committees* (New York, 1969), pp. 37–38.

33. Nourse Oral History, HSTL, p. 39; Keyserling in Heller, *The Truman White House*, pp. 180–181.

34. Neustadt to Herman Somers, 4 August 1949, Chronological File, Richard E. Neustadt Papers, HSTL.

35. "A Way to Clarify the Functions of the Economic Council," E1-1, Series 47.3, RG 51, NA.

that change. He feared to suggest it because "it might have stirred up the animals so much it would have been harder."[36]

The Hoover Commission studied the CEA intensely when it analyzed the executive branch. It expressed its concern over the public disagreement among the members which it found made cooperation with related agencies more difficult. The commission's recommendation was to abolish the council and encourage the president to vest its functions in a single economic adviser in the White House.[37] The effect of this recommendation on the members of the council was to unite them in defense of their organization. They argued that since their work was advisory rather than administrative the single-head proposal was not germane and that it was quite appropriate to have advice rendered by several men with varied backgrounds and experience. They also claimed that the institutionalization of the CEA was enhanced by the multimember structure. A single personal economic adviser would inevitably be replaced by a new president.[38]

Truman agreed that the existing CEA structure should be retained. He said he preferred receiving various viewpoints and he did not want to be confined to one person for economic advice. One economic adviser would mean that all recommendations would be channeled through him and necessarily colored by his opinions.[39] With both the president and the council opposed to the Hoover Commission CEA recommendations they were ignored by the Truman administration. But one of the first actions of the Eisenhower administration was to submit a reorganization plan that made the chairman of the economic council preeminent. Except for this change the characteristics and functions of the council have remained remarkably constant.[40]

36. Nourse Oral History, HSTL, pp. 109-110.

37. Herbert Hoover, *General Management of the Executive Branch* Part II, *The Executive Office of the President*, (Washington, D.C., 1949), pp. 16-17.

38. Council to President, 16 March 1949, John D. Clark Papers, HSTL.

39. Frederick J. Lawton Oral History, HSTL, p. 10.

40. Roger Porter, "The President and Economic Policy," p. 208.

THE COUNCIL AND POLITICS

The basis of most of the disagreements among the three council members was temperamental rather than economic. This was clearly why they were split over whether to appear before congressional committees as advocates. Their attitudes were related directly to their deep-seated disagreement as to the proper role of the CEA collectively and its members individually.[41] Nourse was determined to create a "professional" economic council which, by avoiding political controversy, would become institutionalized and move intact from administration to administration. He believed this nonpartisan role would be jeopardized if CEA members appeared before committees in support of specific proposals.

As early as January 1947 Nourse broached the subject with the president:

I pointed out that other members of the Council were inclined to welcome a rather active relationship [with the joint committee], whereas I was somewhat apprehensive as to the possibility that the Committee might seek to draw us out into discussion of policy positions taken by the President in his report, some of which might not be precisely in line with the views of the Council. . . . I suggested that we should establish a practice from the beginning which could be followed consistently and with safety in subsequent years when conceivably, there might be considerable divergence between the Council's recommendations and the President's policy statement to Congress.

Truman agreed with the danger but still he did not want the council to remain aloof from the joint committee. He advised Nourse to elucidate points of fact or interpretation for the committee but to avoid being drawn into policy discussions.[42] This of course did not settle the issue within the council. It continued to simmer throughout 1947 with Nourse insisting that if he appeared before a committee he would either have to disagree with the president or defend presidential policies he consid-

41. Paul T. Homan to Nourse, 3 June 1955, Nourse Papers , HSTL.
42. Daily Diary, 14 January 1947, Nourse Papers, HSTL.

ered unsound. Keyserling and Clark, on the other hand, argued that since the Economic Report was largely the work of the council they should accept the responsibility of explaining it to Congress. They told Nourse that

to enjoy being chairman of the Council of Economic Advisers but avoid tasks which he temperamentally regarded as onerous was like trying to have one's cake and eat it too. We felt that men of integrity were obliged to support the president for whom they worked when the differences between the president and themselves were slight, and to resign when they were sufficiently great, and that the chairman of the council was indistinguishable in this matter from a cabinet secretary, the budget director, or the head of the military establishment.

They also resented Nourse's insistence that the chairman could act unilaterally and his refusal to be bound by a majority vote on the matter. At the root of the disagreement was the fact that Keyserling and Clark were extreme partisans who yearned to be in the thick of the political battle. Pressure to resolve the question increased when Nourse advertised their differences in the media. Keyserling feared this left the impression that he and Clark were too political while Nourse had maintained his objectivity.[43]

The issue was discussed repeatedly at Truman's daily staff meetings. In January 1948 Charles Ross, the president's press secretary, reported that Nourse had called him and threatened to resign if he was forced to appear before a committee. Ross agreed with Nourse that the council would inevitably become involved in politics and see much of its value impaired if it became an advocate before Congress. Steelman reported that "Clark particularly wanted to go to the Capitol and had said he was going to go."[44]

In an attempt to mediate the situation Steelman sought a neutral opinion from the Budget Bureau. Webb took a middle-of-the-road position. He suggested that the council should not seek to testify nor should it

43. Keyserling in Heller, *The Truman White House*, p. 182.
44. Diary, 13 January 1948, Eban Ayers Papers, HSTL.

accept every invitation to do so, but "it can not make a practice of refusing to testify without provoking Congressional irritations." The real problem, according to the bureau, was how the council could testify without destroying its integrity. This, they maintained, was "a matter of technique and not a matter of principle."[45]

Others tended to support the Nourse position. Don Price told Hoover that the council might limit themselves to

informal meetings with the Joint Committee on the Economic Report to advise and help its members, but for the Council to undertake to carry the principal burden of defending publicly the President's economic program would put it in a position that ought to be occupied by the President's principal political officers, the heads of the executive departments.[46]

The Hoover Commission agreed that the council "should not take public leadership on issues of policy in its own right."[47]

The issue boiled over during the summer of 1948 as the presidential campaign heated up. In July Truman, as a political tactic, called the Republican-controlled Congress into special session. The council was asked to prescribe an antiinflation program for presentation but, in the highly charged political atmosphere, the council's remedy was not well received.[48] In frustration Clark wrote to Truman lamenting the "confusion, the lack of conviction, and the buck-passing exhibited by administration officials in the Senate committee hearings" on the antiinflation proposal. He pleaded for the president to:

Permit the members of the Council to assume responsibility for their advice to you. Allow them to justify their anti-inflation proposals by

45. Webb to Nourse, 15 January 1948, Daily Diary, Nourse Papers, HSTL.

46. Price to Hoover, 19 July 1948, Price Papers, Herbert C. Hoover Library.

47. Hoover, *General Management of the Executive Branch*, Part II, pp. 16-17.

48. Unpublished manuscript, chapter 5, pp. 14-15, John D. Clark Papers, HSTL.

economic analysis which no one else in the administration is offering or can offer. Two members of the Council, who have had long experience with Congressional hearings, are prepared to do this. By the time they have cited chapter and verse of their public reports . . . it will be perfectly clear that you have not been engaged in political maneuver but have been meeting your responsibility under the Employment Act. . . . It will be equally clear that all three members of the Council joined in recommending the program originally, and in urging you to send it to Congress repeatedly. This is too good a hand to yield to any bluff by someone that he will join the other officials who have run out on you.[49]

This appeal was well designed to strike a responsive chord in a candidate engaged in a desperate campaign for reelection. By this time Clark and Keyserling were openly charging that Nourse was trying to avoid being identified politically with Truman so he could continue on the council under President Dewey.[50]

Truman responded by designating Paul Porter to coordinate the presentations to Congress. Porter in turn applied "considerable pressure" on Nourse to appear before the committee in support of the program. Nourse replied that he did not support the entire program and that the White House was aware of those areas in which he dissented. When Porter delicately raised the question of a congressional subpoena, Nourse bristled that he would then have to appear as a "scholar discussing the economic issues on their merits." He threatened that after he had been on the stand a couple of hours, Porter "would probably regret that he had had me called." Nourse threatened to resign if Truman used the council in that way.[51] When the White House asked Nourse what he would do if just Keyserling and Clark testified, the chairman said he could accept that. So Truman finally concluded that the wisest course was "to permit the members to be guided by their own convictions."[52] Keyserling thought the president had taken a very weak stand.[53]

49. Clark to Truman, 31 July 1948, CEA, PSF, Truman Papers, HSTL.
50. Leon Keyserling Oral History, HSTL, p. 54.
51. Daily Diary, 27 November 1948, Nourse Papers, HSTL.
52. Truman to Nourse, 3 August 1948, CEA, PSF, Truman Papers, HSTL.
53. Keyserling in Heller, *The Truman White House*, p. 183.

This action relieved the immediate tension but did not bury the issue. Even before Truman made his decision Keyserling had begun burning the midnight oil preparing for his appearance before the Senate Banking and Currency Committee. After his presentation, Keyserling ebulliently told Truman that the committee chairman had said that he was the best witness he had ever seen.[54] But Nourse, after reading his testimony, said he shuddered to think what would have happened if certain able economists of a somewhat different philosophy had been there to comment.[55]

In April 1949, with the Democrats back in control of Congress, Nourse received an invitation from Senator Claude Pepper to testify on some fair labor standards proposals. Convinced that the White House had been disappointed by Keyserling's appearances before the banking committee, Nourse sought to use Pepper's letter to raise anew the question whether CEA members should testify. He wrote Truman that he hoped

that you will have no objection if I ask to be excused . . . on the basis of the principles on which I have thus far been excused. . . . Is it your wish that Mr. Keyserling and Mr. Clark should be free to accept this invitation if they so desire? I have a strong feeling that their participation in Congressional hearings a few weeks back was seriously harmful to the position and future usefulness of the Council. . . . It is my hope that . . . we may have a clear-cut statement from you that it is your wish that in future no member of the Council shall appear before a Congressional committee to discuss specific legislative proposals dealing with issues of economic policy.[56]

Nourse apparently hoped that Truman's instinct to protect the presidency from legislative inroads would overcome whatever political advantage he saw in Keyserling's appearances. But he was disappointed, for Truman replied that whatever the members wanted to do "is perfectly all right with me." Curiously, the president then observed that "other members of the President's staff . . . do not appear before Congressional

---

54. Keyserling to President, 6 August 1948, CEA, PSF, Truman Papers, HSTL.

55. Daily Diary, 27 November 1948, Nourse Papers, HSTL.

56. Nourse to Truman 6 April 1949, CEA, PSF, Truman Papers, HSTL.

Committees."[57] This could mean that he really did not think that council members should testify, or it might merely have been an effort to keep his policy in regard to the council from being used as a precedent that would weaken executive privilege for his other staff people. Nourse, as might be expected, interpreted this statement as further proof of Truman's lack of interest in the CEA.[58]

NOURSE AND TRUMAN

Nourse had definite ideas about the role of the economic council. It should be a professional body that would institutionalize the synthesized views of the economics professional at the apex of the federal executive establishment. Only a nonpartisan council would be able to endure from one administration to the next. The prime responsibility of the members of the CEA was to draw on the material developed by thousands of economists, statisticians, and other social scientists working in the government and in private business, labor, agricultural, and academic organizations to clarify economic issues for the president. Since the members were not policy makers, Nourse was not disturbed by differences between their views and the president's actions.[59]

But, even if Nourse did not mind if the president did not follow the council's advice, he did not want him to simply ignore it. Nourse never felt that Truman was willing to listen to the views of the CEA. Nor did he feel that the president could have understood the kind of economic analysis the council provided even if he were willing to listen. It was not that Truman was rude or inaccessible. He frequently told Nourse of the high regard he had for the council's work, and how important it was for the chief executive to have its advice. He always promised to read carefully the reports that the CEA prepared for him. But Nourse learned later

57. Truman to Nourse, 8 April 1949, ibid.

58. Nourse Oral History, HSTL, pp. 83–84.

59. Nourse speech, American Society for Public Administration, 14 March 1947, OF 985, Truman Papers, HSTL; Nourse to William Haber, 23 August 1946, CEA Staff File, Nourse Papers, HSTL.

that many times Truman had handed these reports to Webb with the comment, "Here's the report that the Council brought me, I can't make anything of it. You tell me what it is all about."[60] Apparently Nourse did not think it was the responsibility of the CEA to provide advice in terms the president could understand.

Nourse was something of an intellectual snob toward the president. Perhaps it was related to his realization that Truman had never accepted the CEA as a very significant part of his staff. Nourse dismissed the president as a "formal" supporter of the full employment bill who never really knew what the legislation was all about. He resented Truman's tendency to turn to businessmen, politicians, and lawyers rather than economists for advice and for his heavy reliance on Clifford and Webb.[61]

Just as Truman enjoyed getting into the details of the budget, he was pleased by the CEA's development of a quarterly report called the "Economic Indicators" which permitted him to indulge his fascination with numbers. Pointing to his copy he told Nourse, "Yeah, I keep this here all the time, and when people come in and talk to me about this, I say, 'Here are the figures' and I pull that out." But instead of building on this interest and approaching the president on his own terms, Nourse complained because Truman did not say, "Here's the reasoning about these matters that the Council has given me." That, according to Nourse, would have been "beyond his intellectual ken."[62]

Truman must have sensed something of Nourse's attitude toward him, but he always seemed somewhat in awe of the chairman. In private he referred to him as "the old gentleman" even though they were both about the same age. The president probably was relatively ignorant of the terms and techniques used by economists so it is not surprising that he sought to avoid displaying his lack of background by avoiding technical discussions with the CEA. Although Nourse did not think Truman could comprehend abstract

---

60. Nourse Oral History, HSTL, p. 106.

61. Ibid.

62. Ibid.

thinking, he kept trying to establish an intellectual dialogue with him. The president always gave Nourse an appointment when he asked for one "but when he met me, it was on a folksy basis of talking about trivia instead of saying, 'Here's a precious half hour when I might get some enlightenment on what the issues are.'"[63]

Nourse never seemed to try to adjust his approach to one that would be congenial to the man he wished to influence. As Walter Heller has pointed out:

The Council's access to the President is potential, not guaranteed. Unless personalities click; unless the economic adviser is both right and relevant; unless he gets off his academic high horse without falling obsequiously to the ground—his usefulness will be limited and his state of proximity to the President will gradually wither away.[64]

NOURSE RESIGNS

Nourse's decision to resign was a long and tortured process. He had been disenchanted with Truman's handling of the council from the very beginning; yet he stayed more than three years. In the end he did not leave because he disagreed with the president, but because of internal tensions within the council which he could not resolve in his favor.

The campaign year of 1948 was a stressful one for Nourse. It was then that he was overruled on the issue of testifying before Congress, and he was struggling to maintain a council that could survive a transition to a new administration. He probably began to see in Truman's defeat a solution to his problems with Clark and Keyserling. With this in mind, he quietly passed the word to the Dewey camp that he would like to continue as a member of the CEA in the new admin-

---

63. Ibid.

64. Walter Heller, "Economic Advisers," in *The Presidential Advisory System*, ed. Thomas E. Cronin and Sanford D. Greenberg (New York, 1969), p. 37.

istration.[65] According to Keyserling, the defeat of Dewey was a severe disappointment to Nourse.[66]

Nourse wrote to the president categorically denying that he had "devoted a major part of my time and effort to 'saving my skin' in the event there was a change in administration."[67] He included a letter of resignation, but Truman did not respond to either. When Webb learned of Nourse's offer to resign, he urged him to stay on. He told him of the forthcoming Hoover Commission recommendation that the CEA should be replaced with a single economic adviser. Webb suggested that if Nourse became the adviser it would be a way out of the council's internal tensions. Nourse agreed that he would continue if circumstances were different, but that he just could not go

through another annual or midyear report struggle with the present set-up. After two years and a half experience, I regard it as impossible both internally and externally. We cannot organize and operate a staff satisfactorily or produce a product which will stand the time test of any reasonably professional economic standards. Nor can we maintain proper external relationships.[68]

When the Hoover commission recommendations were made public in February 1949, Nourse initially saw them as "the easy way out." If Truman would accept the proposal to replace the CEA with a single economic adviser, Nourse thought he would get the job. If this happened, he believed Keyserling would become head of the Housing Authority and Clark would be appointed to the Federal Trade Commission.[69] But when it became clear that the commission's CEA recommendations would not be accepted, Nourse joined his colleagues in opposing them.

Nourse told his allies, Steelman, Webb, and Snyder, that a change in the membership of the council was the only solution to the problem. Probably the

65. Daily Diary, 27 November 1948, Nourse Papers; Nourse Oral History, HSTL, pp. 105–109.

66. Keyserling in Heller, *The Truman White House*, p. 183.

67. Nourse Oral History, HSTL, pp. 102–103.

68. Daily Diary, 11 January 1949, Nourse Papers, HSTL.

69. Ibid., 8 February 1949.

only reason he did not resign at this point was because he feared Keyserling might become chairman by
default.[70] His concern proved to be justified.

With spring Nourse began to feel sanguine about
his future with the council. He was working closely
with Truman in developing new ceilings for the defense
budget while Keyserling, at least in Nourse's view, had
seriously overstepped himself in his presentations to
Congress. Although Nourse realized it would be awkward
for Truman to move Keyserling, he thought it would
eventually happen. He reduced his demands for remaining to having "at least one other member of the
Council who is capable of taking a substantial share
in organizing and directing our professional work program." Nourse set 1 November 1949 as the deadline for
Truman to make the change.[71]

After battling with Keyserling and Clark over the
midyear report and then seeing the president virtually
ignore it, Nourse again became quite discouraged. He
felt that the physical and nervous strain was so great
that his breaking point was near. He tried to force the
issue by reminding Truman of his resignation letter
and urging an early selection of his successor.[72]

Part of the strain Nourse felt was due to his
belief that Keyserling was working through Clark
Clifford to short-circuit his relations with the White
House. He recalled seeing White House material all over
Keyserling's desk and accusing him of not going
through council channels. But Keyserling merely
"looked up bland as a baby and said, 'It isn't that
way.'" Since Nourse did not believe him he decided he
had no choice but to resign.[73]

In early August Nourse discussed his impending
departure with Steelman over lunch. Steelman assured
him that "the Boss will not under any circumstances
move Leon up to be Chairman." But Nourse told him that
no one of any caliber would take the job so long as
Keyserling remained as vice-chairman. Steelman said he

---

70. Ibid., 21 February 1949.
71. Ibid., 13 March 1949.
72. Ibid., 9 August 1949.
73. Nourse Oral History, HSTL, pp. 59-60.

had been trying to find another post for Keyserling since February, but "doggoned if I can find any place where we could move this boy." He promised to keep trying, however, and suggested that Nourse stay another year to train a replacement.[74] Hearing nothing further from Steelman, Nourse wrote to the president that he planned to resign in November. Truman's only response was to have Steelman take Nourse to lunch again to get suggestions for a possible successor.[75]

Although David Bell believes that Truman let Nourse go because Keyserling's views were more compatible with the administration's economic objectives, this ignores the president's known concern with inflation and defense budgets.[76] It seems more likely that Truman, faced with an unresolvable personality clash on the council, took the line of least resistance and accepted the only resignation he received. If Nourse was right that Truman did not regard the council very highly, then his main concern was the political impact of Nourse's resignation. Keyserling accused Truman of spending three years in "tender temporizing of Nourse" for political reasons because he overestimated Nourse's public prestige.[77]

CHAIRMAN KEYSERLING

With the departure of Nourse, Keyserling assumed active direction of the council. But Truman waited six months before formally elevating him to the chairmanship. Keyserling was told that when the president received Nourse's resignation he had remarked: "Now we can appoint Leon." But nothing happened. Later Truman sent word to Keyserling through Oscar Ewing: "Tell Leon not to worry and to keep his shirt on." Keyserling was greatly embarrassed by the delay because Truman normally filled top vacancies very quickly. He felt it was the one ungenerous act in the president's behavior toward him.[78]

74. Daily Diary, 12 and 13 August 1949, Nourse Papers, HSTL.
75. Nourse Oral History, HSTL, pp. 60–61.
76. Flash, p. 96.
77. Keyserling in Heller, *The Truman White House*, p. 184.
78. Ibid., pp. 194–195.

The opposition to Keyserling's elevation was centered in two camps: the academic community and Truman's more conservative advisers. The academic concern focused on Keyserling's credentials and his political activism. Those in the White House circle who disapproved of him were Steelman, Webb, Pace, Sawyer, and Snyder.[79] At least two candidates were approached for the position before Keyserling was decided upon. The general reaction of these economists was that if Nourse, with his long experience in Washington, had not been able to make a success of the CEA, they would not have a chance.[80]

Keyserling may have been a little too radical for Truman's taste. During 1949 Bert Gross and Keyserling were active in an attempt to resurrect many of the concepts of the full employment bill that were then before Congress in the form of the Spence and Murray bills. Truman opposed these bills, but Keyserling had agreed to speak in favor of them to a group of businessmen in New York. Truman instructed Clifford to "tell your friend, Leon Keyserling, that if he makes that appearance, I will regard it as an very unfriendly act." When Clifford relayed the message, Keyserling was quite shaken. He realized he might have been fired and quickly called off the talk.[81]

It is not clear from the available evidence why Truman finally named Keyserling chairman. It may have been that he always intended to do so but needed to allow the conservatives a chance to search for another candidate to ease their disappointment. Or Nourse's analysis may have been right. No other suitable candidate could be found and Keyserling inherited the job because it was awkward to continue him indefinitely as an acting chairman. It is also possible that it simply took six months for Clifford, Murphy and company to convince Truman that Keyserling was the best choice.

The decision to name Keyserling chairman caused some interesting comments in the press. The columnist

79. Ibid., p. 194.

80. Nourse Oral History, HSTL, pp. 61-62.

81. Flash, *Economic Advice*, p. 24; Keyserling Oral History, HSTL, p. 187.

J. A. Livingston thought the change was made because the council had been created to deal with depression and unemployment, but instead had found itself faced with full employment and inflation. As a result "the Council was and is like a fire department in a fireless town." To get into the public eye it will be necessary for the CEA to create issues and problems to make headlines. Nourse, he felt, was unsuitable for this part but Keyserling, a sloganeer accustomed to the hurly-burly of government infighting, would be adept at the role. He predicted the council would soon become the main protagonist of the administration's policies.[82]

In an editorial the *Washington Post* said the CEA should confine itself to a dispassionate analysis of economic problems. It was critical of Keyserling and Clark for becoming propagandists for the administration and interpreted the elevation of Keyserling as putting "the stamp of approval on this misconception of the proper role of an advisory group."[83]

BLOUGH AND TURNER

The designation of Keyserling as chairman was accompanied by the announcement of Roy Blough's appointment as the third member of the economic council. The consideration of Blough for the post had begun in January 1950 when Grover Ensley, the associate director of the staff of the joint committee, brought his name to the attention of Donald Dawson, the White House personnel man. Blough's name had surfaced two weeks earlier when he had given a paper before the American Economic Association on the role of the CEA. In it Blough defended the appearance of council members before Congress and disputed Nourse's belief that the council should become institutionalized. He proposed that council members be considered "as expendable, each carrying forward the work as far as he individually can, then . . . drop by the wayside." In this way he attempted to resolve the conflict between a council member's obligation to actively defend the president's

---

82. *Washington Post,* 18 May 1950.
83. Ibid., 21 June 1950.

policies and maintaining his professional integrity. He simply suggested that council members resign if the disagreement became significant.[84]

In many ways Blough was admirably suited to fill the void left by Nourse's departure. He was a respected academic from the University of Chicago who had had governmental experience on both the state and federal level. A reticent moderate, he avoided controversy yet supported the Keyserling-Clark position on testifying. Those who worked with him at the council found him ill at ease there and not anxious to exert much leadership.[85]

In September 1952 Blough was replaced by Robert C. Turner who had served from 1946 to 1948 on the White House staff under Steelman. Turner had begun his governmental career in 1941 with the War Production Board. In 1948 he joined the faculty of Indiana University and for the next twenty years was able to combine an academic career with government service. Sometimes he did his government work just during the summer or as a consultant, but periodically he became a full-time government employee, first as a member of the CEA in 1952 and again in 1961 when Kennedy named him assistant director of the Budget Bureau.[86] He joined the council as a lame-duck appointee. As he recalled, "my service was at the end of Mr. Truman's second term, when few initiatives were being undertaken. During those closing months, the council operated pretty much on its own with very little contact with the President."[87]

EVALUATION

With a president that did not appreciate its work, the council had a difficult time establishing its place in the Truman White House circle. When compared with the bureau, the role of the council was anomalous because of necessity it carried on its work remote from an in-

84. Grover W. Ensley to Donald Dawson, 12 January 1950, OF 985-A, Truman Papers, HSTL.

85. Flash, *Economic Advice*, p. 36.

86. *The Purdue Exponent*, 6 December 1978.

87. Turner in Heller, *The Truman White House*, p. 57.

timate knowledge of the president's other problems and his points of view about them. Being a council of three equal members was another handicap. As Seligman has pointed out, "a council almost by its very nature cannot integrate itself into the confidential relationships of the President. Committees and councils are too unwieldy and prone to disunity to mesh with such close relationships."[88] Were it not for the Employment Act's requirement for an annual Economic Report to Congress, a president could totally ignore his council. But even the need to develop an Economic Report was not enough during the Truman administration to make the council an influential part of the president's staff.

And Truman's economic council (like all of its successors) was handicapped by the limits in the ability of economists to operate in a political environment. Typically, the profession was bold in predicting remote future conditions but was reluctant to deal with the kind of near-term forecasting useful to political leaders.[89] A president is too busy to devote much attention to a staff group that is not very useful to him. A staff unit's effectiveness is directly proportional to the need a president feels for its services.

In retrospect it does not appear that the CEA, as an institution, had a continuing or decisive impact on the economic decisions of the Truman administration. This is not surprising given a president who did not put much faith in the advice of economists and a council at war with itself during much of his administration. Truman in many ways only went through the motions with his Council of Economic Advisers.

This does not mean that the council did not perform useful services for the president. The work that was done in coordinating the economic policies of the executive branch marked a significant advance over prior practices. The studies it performed in the areas of foreign aid, inflation control, and budget ceilings provided important rationales for decisions already taken and helped gain congressional and public support for these programs.

88. Lester Seligman, "Presidential Leadership," p. 421.
89. Unpublished manuscript, chapters 2 and 3, Clark Papers, HSTL.

But it would be difficult to demonstrate that any of Truman's major economic decisions would have been different if the council had never existed. This president simply did not include the council's views in his frame of reference in making these decisions, but instead relied on his White House aides, budget directors, and cabinet members. The council might have been more successful in influencing policy decisions if it had been more aggressive in pushing its recommendations. Instead, it simply sent its recommendations to the president and hoped that someone would study them and be influenced by them.[90]

The Truman council did have a decided effect on the economic councils that followed it. The contrasting styles and philosophies of Nourse and Keyserling provided models that helped their successors avoid some of the same difficulties. The widely publicized differences between the first two chairmen also emphasized the structural flaws in the council's organization which led to remedial action. Similarly, the council's internal dispute concerning advocacy before congressional committees conditioned the attitudes of succeeding council members. Most importantly, the Truman CEA survived those critical years, and so provided a basis and precedents upon which future councils were able to build.

---

90. David Bell to Charles Murphy, 3 October 1950, CEA, Murphy Files, Truman Papers, HSTL.

8.
The
National Security Act

The National Security Act of 1947 established the National Military Establishment headed by a secretary of defense, the Central Intelligence Agency, and two new presidential staff units, the National Security Council and the National Security Resources Board. The statute abolished the departments of War and Navy and established three subcabinet departments, Army, Navy and Air Force, in their place. A complex and significant enactment, it was the product of many forces.

World War II gave rise to increased demands to unify the armed forces. The war had accentuated inter-service rivalry and the greatly expanded Army Air Corps was demanding parity with the army and navy. Unification had the powerful support of General of the Army George C. Marshall, the army chief of staff. The general had stated as early as May 1944 that "he was unshakably committed to the thesis of a single civilian Secretary with a single military Chief of Staff."[1]

Marshall was very bitter about what had happened to the army in the 1920s when it was hamstrung for lack of money. He feared it would suffer again after World War II when the peacetime army would have to compete for appropriations with a more glamorous navy and air force. A solution might be found in a single Defense Department that might allocate the monies on

---

1. Walter Millis and E. S. Duffield, *The Forrestal Diaries* ,p. 60.

the basis of military priority rather than congressional popularity.[2]

The war was also a significant factor in the creation of the Central Intelligence Agency. In spite of a few outstanding successes in cryptanalysis, the United States was woefully behind in intelligence capability at the time of Pearl Harbor. When the war began, the existing intelligence efforts maintained by the War, Navy and State Departments and the FBI expanded their activities. The intelligence picture was complicated when, in 1942, the energetic "Wild Bill" Donovan set up his Office of Strategic Services (OSS). Each of these activities was carried on with little regard for preventing duplication, sharing information, or providing an overall analysis of the operations. In 1943 Donovan began to exert pressure to establish a centralized agency to coordinate the work of all the intelligence organizations. The military condemned this proposal as an attempt to establish an "American Gestapo," and the fight was on.[3]

Since the war was in its final stages when Truman became president, he was under great pressure to make an early decision as to how the postwar intelligence effort should be organized. His often repeated view that the "country wanted no Gestapo under any guise" was evidence that he had been impressed by the arguments of the military.[4] The first proposal he received came from the Budget Bureau which had studied the intelligence problem and recommended that the president transfer the bulk of the OSS personnel to the State Department. The bureau believed the secretary of state should be the focal point for leadership in all intelligence activities.[5] The army and navy, backed by the Joint Chiefs of Staff, countered with an alternate plan that called for a new national intelligence authority and a central intelligence group composed of staff from the State, War and Navy depart-

2. Don K. Price interview with Marshall, 6 July 1948, Cabinet Secretariat Concept, First Hoover Commission, Herbert C. Hoover Library.

3. Dean Acheson, *Present At The Creation*, p. 158.

4. Harry S. Truman, *Year of Decisions*, pp. 99, 226.

5. Hoover Commission, *Task Force Report on Foreign Affairs*, Appendix H, pp. 91–92.

ments to plan, develop, and coordinate all foreign intelligence work.[6]

In January 1946 Truman held a series of meetings
to examine the various proposals for centralized control of intelligence. Since only the Budget Bureau still
supported the State Department position, the president
decided to accept the army/navy scheme. By the end of
the month, an executive order had been issued which
established the Central Intelligence Group and the
National Intelligence Authority.[7] The later creation of
the Central Intelligence Agency in the National Security Act was intended to strengthen this concept.

THE ORIGIN OF THE NSC

The origin of the concept of the National Security
Council can be traced to many divergent sources. The
desirability of coordinating foreign affairs and military policy was apparent at the time of the Spanish-
American War, but until World War I cooperation was
limited to letters exchanged between the secretaries
of state, war, and navy and whatever time or expertise
the president might provide. During World War I, the
army and navy did establish a joint board as a means
of coordinating their efforts but when, after the war,
the State Department was asked to send a representative to the board's meetings, it refused.[8]

In the 1930s FDR set up a "Standing Liaison Committee" composed of the undersecretary of state, the
chief of naval operations, and the army chief of staff
to consider "matters of national policy," but it rarely
even met before being abolished in 1943. As World War
II drew to a close, the need for military government
directives led to the creation of the State-War-Navy
Coordinating Committee (SWNCC). Because many of the
committee's discussions involved military matters, a
representative of the Joint Chiefs of Staff worked with
the committee's staff. Theoretically, the SWNCC could,

---

6. Acheson, *Present At The Creation*, p. 159.

7. Truman, *Years of Trial and Hope*, pp. 56–57.

8. Ernest R. May, "The Development of Political-Military Coordination in the United States," *Political Science Quarterly* 70, no. 2 (June
1955): 161–180.

subject to presidential approval, make policy, but they did not because that was beyond the authority of the assistant secretaries who made up its membership. Because it was not organized at the highest level and had an inadequate secretariat, it never reached its full potential, but it at least provided a mechanism to discuss questions that one of the departments might raise.[9]

General Marshall also contributed to the development of the NSC. His painful realization that the British did a better job of planning and coordination than the Americans led him to gather information about how they managed it. He then attempted to popularize the concept of their cabinet secretariat system among American policy makers. Those he sought to influence included Harry Hopkins, Admiral William Leahy, who was chairman of the Joint Chiefs of Staff, Secretary of War Henry Stimson, and Secretary of the Navy James Forrestal.[10] The administrative chaos of the Roosevelt administration made some of these harried wartime leaders particularly receptive since they wanted to avoid such confusion in any future wars. They became even more anxious when Truman succeeded Roosevelt because many of them did not trust him. After all, "He had been chairman of the War Investigating Committee and he wasn't another Roosevelt." This group supported the idea of a national security council more as a mechanism to restrict the president than to give him help.[11]

Because of these developments the British cabinet ideal had considerable vogue among American governmental reformers in the immediate postwar years. They began to envision a national security council together with a mobilization agency as the basis of a

9. Ibid.; John F. Meck, "The Administration of Foreign and Overseas Operations of the United States Government, A Staff Memorandum on the National Security Council" (Brookings Institution, March 1951), p. 1.

10. George M. Elsey to James Lay, 16 January 1953, OF 1290, Harry S. Truman Papers, HSTL.

11. Staats in Thompson, *Portraits,* vol. 2, p. 93.

war cabinet.[12] Forrestal particularly was convinced of
the need for such an arrangement in the American
system. He began a long-term effort to bring the defense services together with the State Department and
other vital agencies in the formulation of coordinated
foreign policies.[13] In November 1944 he told Hopkins
that an organization similar to the Joint Chiefs of
Staff needed to be established on the civilian side of
government. Without it he did not think the United
States would be able to deal with its postwar problems.[14] The integration of military and diplomatic planning was considered by Forrestal to be vital to the
national security.

There would have been no National Security
Council without James Forrestal. But whether his desire
to establish an American version of the British war
cabinet in Washington was his prime motivation in advocating it is doubtful. The navy secretary also was
determined to prevent the unification of the armed
forces. He suspected that both Congress and the public
were sympathetic to Marshall's suggested Defense Department so he knew it would happen unless the navy
made a counterproposal.[15] Forrestal claimed that if a
council was established to coordinate not only the
army, navy and air force but the State Department as
well, unification would not be necessary. The idea of
suggesting interdepartmental committees as a substitute for departmental unification was not new. The
army and the navy, threatened with unification for
reasons of economy after World War I, had proposed
committees instead, and had successfully withstood the
challenge.[16] Forrestal's advocacy of an American war
cabinet mechanism preceded, but neatly (and suspi-

12. Robert Cuff, "Ferdinand Eberstadt, the National Security Resources Board, and the Search for Integrated Mobilization Planning,"
p. 46.

13. Joseph M. Jones, *The Fifteen Weeks* (New York, 1955), pp. 118–
119.

14. Millis and Duffield, *The Forrestal Diaries*, p. 19.

15. Forrestal to Palmer Hoyt, 2 September 1944, ibid., p. 60.

16. Paul Y. Hammond, "The National Security Council as a Device for
Interdepartmental Coordination: An Interpretation and Appraisal," *The
American Political Science Review* 54, no. 4 (Dec. 1960): 899.

ciously) dovetailed with, the navy's substitute for unification.

MOBILIZATION PLANNING

World War II and Franklin Roosevelt also contributed to the suggestion that planning wartime industrial mobilization be the full-time concern of a peacetime board. Richard Neustadt found that:

The pain Roosevelt inflicted in the war years has left a lasting imprint on our government. Officialdom retaliated, after he was gone. To some degree or other—oftener than not to a large degree—organizations at the presidential level which were written into statute in the latter 1940s were intended to assure against just such Rooseveltian freewheeling. . . . It is no more than a mild exaggeration to call NSC "Forrestal's Revenge," or NSRB . . . "Baruch's Revenge" with Eberstadt as agent.[17]

The concept of a peacetime mobilization agency was a product of the unpreparedness experience of World War I. In 1916 the Council of National Defense together with an advisory board was set up to coordinate industrial mobilization. But after war was declared the mobilization program faced collapse, so Wilson transformed the advisory group into the War Industries Board and gave it broad powers. The new board's director, Bernard Baruch, thought that his organization "was doing a pretty good job when the war ended."[18] Based on Baruch's recommendations, the National Defense Act of 1920 made the assistant secretary of war responsible for planning economic mobilization for future wars. The Army-Navy Munitions Board, created in 1922, was given the task of developing the actual mobilization plans. Its first blueprint for mobilization was published in 1931, revised in 1935, and again in 1939. These plans were all based on the assumption that the direction of economic mobilization would be dominated by American industrial leaders.

17. Alan A. Altschuler, *The Politics of the Federal Bureaucracy* (New York, 1968), p. 116.

18. Bernard Baruch to Arthur M. Hill, 31 August 1948, Baruch folder, Entry 1, RG 304, NA.

Baruch was the leading proponent of this approach during the 1930s.[19]

Roosevelt opposed this concept and his efforts to keep mobilization planning in his own hands was one of the reasons for the establishment of the Executive Office of the President.[20] Many were unhappy with FDR's organizational arrangements during the war. Baruch thought that the failure to follow his advice had "cost millions of lives and billions of dollars" during World War II.[21] Baruch and others sought to correct this error after Roosevelt's death. One of these was Ferdinand Eberstadt.

Eberstadt and Forrestal knew each other as undergraduates at Princeton and after graduation both went to work for the Wall Street investment firm of Dillon, Read. Forrestal eventually became president of the firm. In 1939 he left Wall Street to join the Roosevelt administration. Eberstadt made millions with Dillon, Read and then set up his own investment firm. After his old friend Forrestal went to Washington, he periodically offered him advice and assistance. In December 1941 Eberstadt also entered the government as chairman of the Army–Navy Munitions Board (ANMB). With great tenacity and drive, he made the ANMB a powerful advocate for the military.[22]

Before long Donald Nelson, because of pressure from the army and navy, appointed Eberstadt vice-chairman of the War Production Board. But in 1943 Nelson fired Eberstadt to save himself from those same pressures.[23] Eberstadt was considered the brains of the group that favored the control of production by the business–military people rather than by the government. His abilities profoundly impressed official Washington.[24]

19. Hobbs, *Behind the President*, pp. 156–157; Rowland Egger, *The President of the United States* (New York, 1969), pp. 36–37.

20. See Chapter 2.

21. Baruch to Hill, 31 August 1948, Baruch Folder, Entry 1, RG 304, NA.

22. Cuff, "Ferdinand Eberstadt," pp. 38–39.

23. "Machinery for Executive Coordination," Executive Office of the President, Miscellaneous Memos, Series 39.32, OMB.

24. *Washington Star*, 8 September 1948.

Roosevelt's sabotage of Baruch's plan had a traumatic effect on Eberstadt and convinced him that industrial and economic mobilization planning should never again be associated in the public mind with the military. He believed it had to be clearly in civilian hands and integrated with the rest of the executive branch so that in case of war it would not be necessary to set up so many special agencies. Because of his wartime experience, Eberstadt wanted to see an OWM type of organization established to link strategic planning to national resources.[25]

Eberstadt was not alone in calling for mobilization planning. Many others felt the country should profit from its World War II experience by undertaking peacetime planning for mobilization in the event of another war. The Bureau of the Budget already had done extensive work on how best to organize the government for national mobilization planning. In November 1945 Truman, informed of the bureau's efforts, encouraged them to develop their plans and present them to him. By January 1946 general agreement had been reached within the bureau on a proposal for an "Office of National Mobilization Planning," but Harold Smith, then director, decided not to send it to Truman just yet.[26] Smith probably decided that a new proposal might divert attention from his plans to completely reorganize the EOP.[27]

Meanwhile, John D. Small, head of the Civilian Production Administration (CPA), which in 1946 included the residue of the various wartime mobilization agencies, was concerned that once his agency was liquidated, its skills, experience, and personnel would be lost forever. In December 1946 he told the president of his worries and urged him to use his powers under the Reorganization Act of 1945 to set up a civilian agency within the executive office "to plan during peace-time for the economic mobilization of the country in the

25. Cuff, "Ferdinand Eberstadt," pp. 39–41.

26. Arnold Miles to Director, 21 August 1946, E2–58/46.1, Series 39.32, RG 51, NA.

27. James Sundquist to Arnold Miles, 20 February 1946, E2–5, Series 39.32, OMB.

event of war." To this agency, Small wrote, should be transferred a skeletal staff from CPA since it still contained a nucleus of organization units of modest size which could be expanded quickly into a full-fledged war production board. He emphasized that the CPA had "maintained alive the framework of industry advisory committees without whose cooperation, advice and assistance the miracles of war production could hardly have been achieved."[28] Truman did not act on this proposal, probably because by then the navy alternative to unification in the form of the Eberstadt Report was under active consideration.

THE EBERSTADT REPORT

Soon after Truman became president it became clear that he favored the military unification plan proposed by the army. Perhaps he was influenced by his own army background and his great respect for Marshall. A few months after Roosevelt's death, Forrestal attempted to feel out the new president on the subject. Truman said he did not contemplate abolishing the War and Navy departments but did not deny that he had a plan to unify them in some fashion.[29]

Although Forrestal had a strong distaste for partisan politics, he was a consummate political operator in bureaucratic Washington.[30] He knew that he had to have a a suitable occasion to launch his counterattack on the army's unification plan, and that he had to provide a constructive alternative. A letter from the chairman of the Senate Naval Affairs Committee, David I. Walsh, provided the opportunity. Walsh suggested that the navy undertake a thorough study to "determine whether or not it would be desirable . . . to propose the establishment of a Council of National Defense as an alternative."[31] Forrestal's reply in-

---

28. J.D. Small to President, 5 December 1946, Security Resources Board, Clark Clifford Papers, HSTL.

29. Millis and Duffield, *Forrestal Diaries*, pp. 62-63.

30. Paul Y. Hammond, *Organizing for Defense: The American Military Establishment in the Twentieth Century* (Princeton, 1961), p. 232.

31. U. S. Congress, Senate, Committee on Naval Affairs, Ferdinand Eberstadt, *Report to the Secretary of the Navy*, "Unification of the

dicated his agreement to the idea and his concern that the navy had been "merely taking the negative in this discussion."[32]

So in the spring of 1945, as the war in Europe was drawing to a close, Forrestal enlisted the services of Eberstadt to undertake the study suggested by Walsh. He was charged with determining whether unification would improve national security, and, if not, what forms of organization should be created to achieve that result.[33] Eberstadt assembled a staff of bright young men who were then junior officers in the Navy Department. By mid-July Forrestal, Eberstadt, and Walter Laves, an organization expert from the Budget Bureau, had arrived at some basic conclusions. They agreed that the cabinet could be made more effective if served by a secretariat, and that two new bodies were needed: one composed of representatives from the State, War, and Navy departments to define national policy, and another to keep up-to-date information on the national resources for war.[34] These last two ideas eventually emerged as the National Security Council and the National Security Resources Board.

The Eberstadt Report was sent by Forrestal to Senator Walsh in October 1945. It did not break much new ground, most of it being "foreshadowed by Forrestal's own thinking, by the new President's unsettled views about his cabinet, . . . by Navy traditions about the relationship of the Navy to policymaking, and by reforms already underway, such as in the strategic intelligence community." The contribution the report did make was to draw many of these ideas together for the first time in one document that recommended a precise plan of action.[35] To maintain his flexibility Forrestal did not publicly endorse the recommendations in the report when he forwarded it.[36]

War and Navy Departments and Postwar Organization for National Security," 79th Cong., 1st sess., 22 October 1945, pp. iii-iv.
32. Ibid., p. v.
33. Ibid., p. 1.
34. Millis and Duffield, *Forrestal Diaries*, p. 87.
35. Hammond, *Organizing for Defense*, p. 206.
36. Eberstadt, *Report to the Secretary of the Navy*, p. 7.

The report was designed to provide an alternative to the army plan for merger of the armed forces. It proposed instead a loose confederation of the services. This pallid version of unification was to be headed by a national security council rather than a secretary of defense. In this way Forrestal sought to remedy the inadequate coordination he believed existed between military and diplomatic policy and, with the same device, parry the army pressure for unification. When he was later forced to concede the necessity for a secretary of defense, Forrestal suggested that this official serve as the deputy president in all matters having to do with national security.[37] He thought the secretary should dominate the national security council, protect the country from presidents who were inadequate administrators, and incidentally, be far too busy to interfere in the affairs of the navy.

Eberstadt put his report together from papers prepared by members of his team. Myron P. Gilmore prepared the study of foreign and military policies in which he lauded "the peace time machinery of the Committee of Imperial Defense, which had been transformed in both World Wars into a War Cabinet, . . . well adapted to the conduct of a major war." Based on this British model, Gilmore proposed a national security council that "would be formally described as advisory" but, since the council would be headed by the president, the "advice" would always be accepted. His council would also recommend the annual budgets for the State and military departments to the president. To increase the likelihood these recommendations would be final, they would be made public and made available to Congress as well as to the president. The Budget Bureau would have no input into these budgets. Eberstadt followed Gilmore's guidelines in his own report.[38] Neither man showed much understanding of the difference between cabinet and presidential government or the relationship between a president and his advisers.

---

37. Sidney Souers to Calvin Christman, 22 December 1970, Sidney W. Souers Papers, HSTL.

38. Hammond, "The National Security Council As a Device for Interdepartmental Coordination," pp. 899–900.

A resources board was also proposed in the report. This board was to have two basic functions: (1) formulating mobilization plans and programs and keeping them current; and (2) "maintaining a skeleton organization for the prompt and effective translation of military plans into industrial and civilian mobilization." The chairman of this board would be appointed by the president and given "full power of decision" much like that then exercised by the head of the OWMR.[39] Baruch and Eberstadt were obviously hopeful that Truman would be more willing than Roosevelt to share his power.

TRUMAN'S UNIFICATION MESSAGE

Although Eberstadt, in preparing his report, held long talks with Harry Hopkins, he neglected to consult and enlist the aid of such obvious White House contacts as Admiral Leahy or the president's naval aide. Their views were not sought, and they were not sent copies of the final report.[40] Copies of the report were sent to Rosenman before being sent to Walsh, but there was no attempt at formal coordination with the president. This may have been a tactical error for, while there was probably no chance that Truman would have endorsed the report at this stage of the battle, the fact that the navy sent it directly to its friends in Congress gave the impression that they were avoiding the usual administrative channels.

It was obvious that a new offensive in the unification battle had been launched. Soon two unification bills were introduced in Congress, and the Senate Military Affairs Committee opened hearings on the issue. As the hearings dragged on into December, Truman decided to intervene by sending a message to Congress recommending his plan for unification. Judge Rosenman, who had spent the previous five months trying to convert the navy to the army plan without success, was asked to write the message.[41] The judge, who person-

---

39. Eberstadt, *Report to the Secretary of the Navy*, pp. 8–9.
40. Note, 15 October 1945, Postwar Military Organization, Source Material Folder, George M. Elsey Papers, HSTL.
41. Truman, *Years of Trial and Hope*, p. 49.

ally favored the army plan, did not believe that a message would break the deadlock, but the president was adamant.[42]

The battle over unification moved to the White House while the message was being drafted. There the navy had some strategically placed allies in Clark Clifford and George Elsey who still wore the uniforms of naval officers. Clifford was not yet Truman's special counsel but he had attended some of the president's regular morning staff meetings. There, Elsey recorded, he was appalled

by the casual and haphazard manner in which decisions of the utmost importance were being made. He found that there was no policy-making body; merely a collection of not-too-well-informed men, each intent on his own job. In interdepartmental affairs, the President is floundering around for assistance and support. . . . CMC [Clifford] said to me on 12 Dec. that he felt that there must be some type of policy committee of Head Men, with all questions of policy referred to that committee. The committee should meet for discussions and it should have sources of information open to it. The Committee should submit recommendation to the President. The Committee, after discussions with the President and after all necessary parties had agreed to it, could formalize policy. . . . Of course I concurred emphatically with CMC, because I have felt the same need for a very long time and have watched similar situations arise often.

Elsey agreed to prepare a recommendation for a committee to remedy these flaws for Clifford to pass on to the president.[43]

Both Elsey and Clifford tried to influence Truman's unification proposal by bombarding Rosenman with memoranda commenting on the judge's draft of the message. Clifford told him that Truman liked the national security council idea because "he knows the need of a body like this." He claimed the NSC was "one of the most vital recommendations of the Eberstadt re-

---

42. Samuel B. Hand, *Counsel and Advise: A Political Biography of Samuel I. Rosenman*, p. 223.

43. Elsey's typewritten note, 4 January 1946, Reorganization Executive Branch – Security Secretariat, Elsey Papers, HSTL.

port, and the one with which I agree most strongly."[44]
Together the two men did their best to get the council
included as one of Truman's recommendations to
Congress.

The president's message on unification was discussed at a cabinet meeting a few days before it was
sent to Congress. During the meeting, Postmaster General Robert Hannegan tried to dissuade Truman from
sending it. With key members of Congress opposed to
the president's plan, Hannegan thought that "the President was inviting an unnecessary fight which he might
lose, with the resultant loss of prestige." Truman
replied that there had been ample opportunity to discuss the issue and that it was his duty to recommend
unification because "it represented his conviction."[45]

After Rosenman finished his final draft of the
message he sent it to various cabinet members for comment. He noted on Forrestal's copy that since the
president realized the navy secretary was opposed to
the whole project, he should limit his comments to cor-
recting any misstatements of facts.[46] Forrestal replied
that he was "so opposed to the fundamental concept
expressed in the message that I do not believe there
is any very helpful observation that I could make." He
recommended that no message be sent until the committee had completed its hearings.[47] At his press conference a few days later Truman had to deny that
Forrestal was resigning and to express the hope that
he would remain in office.[48]

TRUMAN COMPROMISES

Truman sent his message to Congress on 19 December
1945. In it he recommended that there should be a sin-

44. Clifford to Rosenman, 13 December 1945, Unification Folder No.
1, Postwar Military Organization, Elsey Papers, HSTL.

45. Millis and Duffield, *Forrestal Diaries*, p. 117.

46. Rosenman to Forrestal, 17 December 1945, Unification Folder
No.2, Samuel I. Rosenman Papers, HSTL.

47. Forrestal to Rosenman, 18 December 1945, Unification Folder No.
3, ibid.

48. U.S. Presidents, *Public Papers of the Presidents of the United
States: Harry S. Truman, 1946*, pp. 565–566.

gle department of national defense and a single chief
of staff. The three services would become "branches of
the Department," each headed by an assistant secretary. There was no mention in the message of a national security council or a national security resources board which Forrestal and Eberstadt had said
would make a single defense department unnecessary.[49]
Rosenman, who had told Clifford that he would include
the NSC in the message, later explained that Truman
"did not want to get into that subject at that time."[50]

Clifford and Elsey were dismayed when they read
the message. Elsey thought Truman had taken the army's
side completely. Clifford was discouraged because his
memoranda had succeeded in getting only a few "small
crumbs." Both men were fearful that Forrestal would be
disappointed by their efforts in support of the navy.[51]
Truman had indeed clearly chosen the army plan over
that of the navy. He did not even compromise to the
extent of incorporating some of the navy suggestions,
such as the national security council or resources
board.

Throughout the spring of 1946 the controversy
grew more bitter. In their arguments both sides dis-
guised their real interests. Army spokesmen, who
wanted unification because they thought it would provide them with a greater share of the defense budget,
said they supported it because it promised greater
efficiency and a stronger national defense. Navy
spokesmen, fearful of being submerged by the larger
army, held up the specter of a military takeover. They
claimed that the job of directing the armed forces was
too big for any one man; therefore, the civilian secretary would be forced to rely more and more on the
military until eventually civilian control of the services would cease to be a reality. Meanwhile, a Senate
subcommittee had been established to take the president's message and fashion it into a bill. The subcom-

---

49. Ibid., pp. 546-560.

50. Elsey note, 4 January 1946, Reorganization Executive Branch –
Security Secretariat, Elsey Papers, HSTL.

51. Notes, 17 and 19 December 1945, Postwar Military Organization,
ibid.

mittee described the bill which they produced in early April as a compromise, but the navy did not regard it as such.[52]

The "compromise" was called the Thomas bill (S. 2044) when it was reported to the Senate by the Military Affairs Committee on 13 May 1946. It provided for a "Council of Common Defense" which was analogous to the national security council of the Eberstadt Report with one significant difference. This council would be presided over by the secretary of state rather than the president. This was an important distinction because it would remove the automatic acceptance of the council's advice which was an essential, if unstated, part of the Forrestal–Eberstadt proposal. The bill also provided for a national security resources board which would be subordinate to the Council of Common Defense. The other members of this council would be the secretary of common defense and the chairman of the national security resources board.[53]

The navy and its supporters in Congress viewed the Thomas bill with suspicion. As a tactical move, Walsh, chairman of the Naval Affairs Committee, obtained the authority near the end of April to have his committee hold hearings on the matter. These public hearings had the effect of heating up the controversy still further. Forrestal appeared on 1 May and criticized the bill for its lack of specificity. He called it a proposal to "merge now and organize later." The problems were too great, he felt, to be susceptible to this kind of an approach.[54]

With the gulf seeming to widen rather than narrow through the congressional infighting, the president called for a meeting of the administration's principals on 13 May in an attempt to push them toward agreement. He asked the army and navy to get together, identify their points of agreement and disagreement, and report back to him by 31 May. Both Secretary of War Robert Patterson and Forrestal agreed to try. When

52. Millis and Duffield, Forrestal Diaries, pp. 146–151.
53. Meck, "The Administration of Foreign and Overseas Operations of the U.S.," p. 2.
54. Millis and Duffield, *Forrestal Diaries*, p. 159.

the two secretaries met next day, they found they were able to agree on a large number of points, including a council of national defense and a national security resources board.[55]

When Harold Smith learned of the progress that Patterson and Forrestal had made, he was alarmed. In a memo he tried to warn the president of the dangers inherent in the council concept and outline his own prescription for "real" unification. He cautioned Truman that

the compromise discussions appear to be accepting the organization devices of the "Eberstadt plan.". . . The greatest threat is the Council of Common Defense [NSC]. This Council is presented as a means of relieving the President of work. This it does—but by divesting the President of authority and responsibility which he cannot lose and still be President under our form of government. Beyond that it gives the military an undue control, in effect a veto power, over foreign policy.

The budget director found the proposed resources board to be almost as ill conceived as the council:

This Board has the unworkable feature of bringing almost the entire Cabinet into a Board chaired by a person other than the President—which chairman is supposed to speak in meetings of the Council of Common Defense for the Cabinet members not on the Council. The greatest danger in this whole approach is that the formulation of basic national policy will be dominated by the military under the guise of a civilian committee structure.

Smith told Truman that these proposals would result in the most drastic changes in the top structure of the government since the days of Washington. They were conceived, he warned, not from the president's point of view, but from the perspective of one secretary. He concluded by recommending that Truman ask his advisers to develop a "President's plan" in its stead. He volunteered the services of his bureau in laying out such a plan.[56]

---

55. Ibid., pp. 159–163.

56. Smith to the President, 22 May 1946, BOB Military 45–53, President's Secretary's File (PSF), Truman Papers, HSTL.

These were strong words and couched in arguments that normally aroused Truman to battle. This time they did not. Smith's credibility with Truman was at a low point and he was to leave office in a few weeks. The president may also have discounted Smith's warning because he knew that the bureau was unhappy at being excluded from the unification organizational discussions. Truman had not yet realized that the bureau was the one unit in the government that considered itself the guardian of presidential power from departmental usurpation.

TRUMAN ACCEPTS THE COUNCIL AND THE BOARD

In a joint letter Forrestal and Patterson reported to Truman that, while they still disagreed on the basic question of the power to be given an overall secretary of defense, they had reached agreement on eight of the twelve issues that had divided them. Significantly, Forrestal won Patterson's support for a council of common defense which was to

integrate our foreign and military policies and . . . enable the military services and other agencies of the government to cooperate more effectively in matters involving our national security. The membership of this council should consist of the Secretary of State, the civilian head of the military establishment (if there was to be a single military department), the civilian heads of the military services, and the Chairman of the National Security Resources Board. The resources board would, "establish, and keep up to date, policies and programs for the maximum use of the Nation's resources in support of our national security." Their plan would have made this board, composed of representatives of the military services, subordinate to the security council.[57]

Truman was unable to get to get his defense chiefs to totally agree, so he proposed a compromise. The president submitted his second unification plan to Congress in the form of a letter to the chairmen of the Military and Naval Affairs committees of both houses. His recommendation regarding the council of national

---

57. Forrestal and Patterson to Truman, 31 May 1946, Unification: Correspondence—general, Clark Clifford Files, Truman Papers, HSTL.

defense and the resources board was lifted from Forrestal and Patterson's joint letter.[58] This signaled Congress that the president was willing to accept these bodies in substantially the form of the Thomas bill. The major deviation in the president's proposal was the addition of the service secretaries to the council's membership.

In taking this action Truman reversed his stand on what was to become the National Security Council (NSC). Why did he reject it in December and propose it in June over the strong objections of his budget chief? There appear to be several good reasons. First, it was part of a hard-won compromise between the army and the navy. If he now began to pick and choose on the various points, the whole accord might disintegrate. Second, it provided a mechanism to meet the navy demand that the civilian heads of the services should have access to the president. Truman held firm against their membership in the cabinet, but he could now say that they would be able to represent their services's point of view to the president through the medium of the Council of National Defense. Third, it permitted him to appear to concede to a major navy demand (the NSC), while maintaining his determination to have a single civilian head of the armed forces. The navy, which in trying to defeat unification had inflated the council concept beyond its real significance, found the ground cut out from under it. Last, perhaps because of Smith's warning, the council that Truman recommended did not include the president as one of its members. He thus avoided the trap (at least temporarily) of setting up an advisory committee whose advice could not be rejected by the president because he had been a part of the decision-making process.

THE FOURTH DRAFT OF THE NATIONAL SECURITY ACT

Once Truman had decided, over Harold Smith's objections, to accept the NSC concept, the Budget Bureau sought to find a way to limit its threat to presidential authority. The bureau was also anxious to regain the

58. *Public Papers of the Presidents, 1946*, p. 305.

initiative and to reestablish its position as the president's primary adviser on organizational matters. It planned to achieve both objectives by persuading the president to establish the council and the resources board by executive action rather than trusting to congressional caprice.

Creating these bodies by executive order would permit the president to ensure that they would not infringe on the position and authority of the chief executive. Arnold Miles, one of the bureau's organizational experts, warned that

if their creation is left to law, the President will get whatever happens to be included in the bill which will be considered primarily for its unification provisions and only secondarily for its basic reorganization of the President's coordinating machinery. In the framing of that bill, the Congress has been listening primarily to Army and Navy officers, not the President.

Further, Miles argued, the use of an executive order would provide a degree of flexibility that legislation could not. He suggested that the order could be followed in about six months by a reorganization plan in which Congress would be asked to endorse the council and the board as statutory bodies. The hiatus would provide a period for experimentation to refine the role of these units before their charters were codified. He urged quick action on his proposal because he believed coordinating machinery was needed in both areas immediately and Congress could not be expected to pass unification legislation for at least six months (actually it took another year).[59]

In order to convince the new budget director, James Webb, to take the plan to the president Miles added some arguments that appealed to the bureau's self interests:

In view of our convictions as to the need for changing the basic concepts embodied in both agencies as now being proposed, we are particularly anxious that the Bureau participate to its maximum effect

---

59. Miles to Director, 21 August 1946, E2–52/46.1, Series 39.32, RG 51, NA.

in planning the establishment of the new agencies. Our opportunity would appear to be much better to influence an Executive Order than to influence legislation. . . . The Bureau of the Budget should determine its position on both agencies proposed, within the limits of the President's commitments, and should participate in the development of Executive Orders to create the agencies.[60]

Miles had prepared the way for his proposal by skillfully maneuvering the Navy and War Departments into supporting the idea. Forrestal had appointed a committee to study organization problems, and this group had concluded that the council and the resources board should be created immediately. Miles assured the committee that the president's war powers could be used for that purpose. A short time later (at Miles's urging) Acting Secretary of War Kenneth Royall formally proposed that the bureau create an interdepartmental committee to study the establishment of these agencies. A precedent for executive action already existed in the creation of the Central Intelligence Group by presidential order and the establishment of a Joint Research and Development Committee by the service secretaries.[61]

Miles reminded Webb that Senator Thomas, the leading Senate supporter of unification, had suggested that the president had ample war powers to create both the council and the resources board. In fact Thomas had proposed that Truman implement by executive order all of the eight points that Forrestal and Patterson had accepted in their May letter. The president rejected the suggestion because he thought it would lessen the possibility of getting Congress to pass a unification bill.[62]

In mid–September 1946 Webb met with Truman to change his mind about issuing executive orders to set up the council and the board. It was only the second time that Webb had met privately with the president since being appointed budget director and they had not yet developed the close rapport that later character-

60. Ibid.
61. Ibid.
62. Ibid.; Millis and Duffield, *Forrestal Diaries*, p. 204.

ized their relationship. Webb presented the plan for setting up the NSC and NSRB by executive order as a navy idea instead of a scheme hatched in the Budget Bureau. But Truman rejected the notion by curtly declaring, "I will not sign such an order." He explained that he believed unification "was a legislative problem and that any piecemeal approach would make it more difficult or impossible to obtain a legislative solution in the next Congress."[63] It may well be that Truman saw the council and board as a price he had to pay to get unification but he wanted to make sure he got his quid pro quo before he allowed them to come into existence. It was another indication that Truman did not see the need for coordinating mechanisms such as the NSC and NSRB. His outright refusal to consider the idea made it difficult for Webb to pursue that tack further.

It was now late in the congressional session, and no further action was taken on the unification bills that year. At the Pentagon, General Lauris Norstad and Admiral Forrest Sherman had begun to draw up a draft unification bill based on the views of Forrestal and Patterson. It included a provision that would make the head of the Munitions Board the chairman of the NSRB as well. In this draft the decisions of the resources board, which would include cabinet officers among its members, would be binding on these immediate subordinates of the president. James Webb was alarmed at this attempt of the services to direct the heads of other departments. To prevent this, Webb, supported by Secretary of State George Marshall, prevailed upon Truman to move the bill-drafting process to the White House.[64]

A few days later, Truman summoned the military and civilian heads of the two services to the White House to make plans for the introduction of merger legislation in the next session of Congress. He announced that Clifford and Admiral Leahy would write a bill and send it to Congress as the doctrine of the administration. He expected everyone to support it. When the president called for a frank exchange of

63. Conference with the President, 15 September 1946, Conference Notes A3-4, James E. Webb Papers, HSTL.

64. Hammond, *Organizing for Defense*, pp. 221-222.

views, Secretary Patterson affirmed that he still did not believe that unification could be achieved through committees and boards, but he said he would agree to see the secretary of defense limited to broad areas of policy. Forrestal suggested a deputy to the president who would make decisions on such fundamental questions as defense budgets, missions, personnel and command disputes. But he emphasized that he was opposed to the involvement of this "deputy president" in the administration of the service departments. When the navy secretary implied that he would resign before supporting proposals that did violence to his principles, the president indicated he did not think that would be necessary. There was no discussion of such agreed upon matters as the Council of National Defense or the Resources Board.[65]

The drafting of the national security bill took about six weeks. The president's limited participation involved attendance at two formal meetings. The actual drafting of the bill was done by Charles Murphy, representing the White House, together with General Norstad and Admiral Sherman. Stuart Symington joined the group later to speak for the soon-to-be-independent air force.[66] One change that resulted from the White House participation was to make the NSC and NSRB coordinate and equal bodies. This was done at the behest of Elsey who wrote, "it just doesn't make sense to have Sec State doing supervision of resources!"[67] By mid-January 1947 the group had agreed on a draft bill and a letter to be signed by Forrestal and Patterson reconciling their views on unification.[68] The military officers, satisfied that their work was complete, sent certain congressmen copies of their draft bill. The implication was that since the services had

---

65. Millis and Duffield, *Forrestal Diaries*, pp. 203-205.

66. Notes for a talk on Executive Office Reorganization, 21 November 1949, Elsey Papers, HSTL; Elsey to James Lay, 17 April 1951, Unification Folder No. 15, ibid.

67. Handwritten note, Unification (1), Elsey Papers, HSTL.

68. Millis and Duffield, *Forrestal Diaries*, pp. 229-231.

agreed to the draft it would inevitably be the bill that the president would recommend to Congress.[69]

At this stage of its development the proposed legislation was designated the fourth draft of the army-navy bill. The Council of National Defense was now called the National Security Council, but otherwise this provision was in substantially the same form as the previous summer. Although it provided that the president could, at his discretion, attend meetings of the council and would preside when he attended, he would not be a statutory member. It also provided that the council should direct the work of the CIA. The council's membership included the secretary of state as chairman, the secretaries of the army, navy, and air force, and the chairman of the resources board. The council was directed to report to the president on its work and to make recommendations respecting the formulation and execution of foreign and military policies. Its key power was "under the direction of the President, to coordinate the foreign and military policies of the United States."[70]

THE FIFTH DRAFT

Had not the bureau intervened at this point it is likely that Truman would have sent this draft to Congress without the president realizing the extent to which it would limit his power.[71] But Donald Stone, head of the bureau's Division of Administrative Management, had been following the progress of the bill's preparation in an effort to protect the president's position.[72] Stone reported to Webb that Murphy "was doing only a drafting job," and was not concerning himself with the substance of the legislation. He feared that no one was representing the president's interests in the matter. So Webb asked Stone to draft a memorandum summarizing

69. G. F. Schwartzwalder, Postwar Organization of Armed Forces, Richard E. Neustadt Papers, HSTL.

70. "Title II – Coordination for National Defense," Unification Folder No. 1, Elsey Papers.

71. G.F. Schwartzwalder, Postwar Organization of Armed Forces, Neustadt Papers, HSTL.

72. Stone to Alfred Sander, 19 April 1971.

the president's previous position with respect to unification and the bureau's concern over provisions in the bill's fourth draft.[73]

Stone's memorandum was particularly critical of the national security council provisions of the bill. It said that the draft bill would delegate presidential authority to others but, in the American constitutional system, only the president can be responsible for the ultimate formulation of foreign and military policy. Despite the saving clause, "under the direction of the President," Stone felt the provision was a usurpation of the president's power.[74]

The bureau also feared that the bill would practically ensure that foreign policy, and much of the domestic economic policy, would come under the domination of the military. Although the council would be composed of civilians, five of the six would have a military orientation by virtue of their departmental responsibilities, and would have their staff work done by military officers. The transitory nature of their tenure and the general excellence of military staff work would weaken civilian control even more. In the fourth draft there was no provision for a separate NSC staff, the implication was that this work would be done by the Army-Navy Munitions Board, a military agency.[75] Stone suggested the following specific changes in the draft bill's council provisions: (1) it should be made advisory to the president; (2) statutory reference to the president's right to meet with the council should be eliminated; (3) delete reference to Senate confirmation of the council's executive secretary; and (4) the council should have no statutory functions since it should be solely advisory.[76]

These comments were quite significant. Until now the NSC idea had evolved as a result of the struggle by the army and navy to reach agreement on unifica-

73. Minutes of the Director's Staff Meeting, 28 January 1947, Meetings and Conferences, Series 39.32, OMB.

74. Paper dated 30 January 1947 with pencil indication of Bureau of the Budget origin, Unification Folder No. 3, Elsey Papers.

75. Ibid.

76. Donald C. Stone, "BOB Analysis of Proposed Functions," 3 February 1947, Unification, Correspondence: Comment, Clifford Papers, HSTL.

tion. Their agreement had been the critical test, and there had been little attempt to look at the proposal from the point of view of the presidency. The White House staff and the Bureau of the Budget were the only governmental agencies inclined to view the problem from the presidential standpoint. In this case, the bureau was the more perceptive because of its institutional framework. Comments such as these were almost certain to get a favorable reaction from a president as much concerned with the institutional aspect of his office as Truman was.

Over the next week Stone's material was discussed with the president and the White House staff.[77] This resulted in reworking the offending sentences in the fifth draft of the bill to read

The function of the Council shall be to advise the President with respect to the integration of foreign and military policies and to enable the military service and other agencies of the government to cooperate more effectively in matters involving national security. . . . In addition to performing such other functions as the President may direct for the purpose of more effectively coordinating the policies of the departments and agencies of the government and their functions relating to national security, it shall, subject to the direction of the President, be the duty of the Council: (1) to assess and appraise the objectives, commitments, and risks of the United States in relation to our actual and potential military power, in the interests of national security, for the purpose of making recommendations to the President in connection therewith; and (2) to consider policies on matters of common interest to the Department of State, the Department of National Defense, and the National Security Resources Board, and to make recommendations to the President in connection therewith.

Elsey was involved in getting the navy to accept this revision of the council's function. On his copy of the redraft Elsey noted: "Sherman and Forrestal O.K. and say better than draft 4. This is a great concession by them."[78]

77. G.F. Schwartzwalder, Postwar Organization of Armed Forces, Neustadt Papers, HSTL.

78. Fifth Draft, 11 February 1947, Unification Folder No. 3, Elsey Papers, HSTL.

The bureau was also critical of the fourth draft's description of the functions of the NSRB. Stone insisted that the board's job should be the concern of a full-time adviser under the president's direction and that this individual should be the chairman of the NSRB. The board should "assist" the chairman in his responsibilities. He recommended that the board's staff should be employed by the president rather than the military departments and the NSRB should be completely separate from the Munitions Board.[79] The fifth and final draft of the unification bill accepted Stone's suggestions and described the NSRB as follows:

There is hereby established a National Security Resources Board . . . to be composed of the Chairman of the Board and such representatives of the various executive departments and independent agencies as may from time to time be designated by the President. . . . (b) The Chairman of the Board, subject to the direction of the President, is authorized to appoint . . . such personnel as may be necessary to carry out the functions of the Board. (c) It shall be the function of the Board to advise the President concerning the general coordination of military, industrial and civilian mobilization.

This was a far different organization than that envisioned by Eberstadt, but, as Elsey noted in the margin of this draft, "Sherman and Norstad accepted, after explanation, the fact that the Board is made strictly advisory to the President."[80]

At the behest of the bureau, Truman circulated the fifth draft to the interested departments for comment before it was sent to Congress. For the first time the State Department was asked for its views about unification. George C. Marshall, who had been installed as secretary of state the month before, was thoroughly disgusted with the direction that the legislation had taken since he left the Pentagon in 1945. Marshall particularly opposed the language creating the NSC because he felt it had gravely overloaded the council

79. Analysis of NSRB, 3 February 1947, Unification: correspondence, Clifford Papers, HSTL.

80. Fifth Draft, 11 February 1947, Unification Folder No. 3, Elsey Papers, HSTL.

with military people.[81] He pointed out to Truman that since the work of the council would be primarily concerned with foreign policy its "membership should be limited to the Secretary of State, the Secretary of National Defense and the Chairman of the Council." He suggested that the bill designate the secretary of state chairman of the council.[82] But the strong objections of Marshall and the Budget Bureau were not enough to persuade Truman to change the membership of the council. He realized the inclusion of the service secretaries had been a key part of the bargain with the Pentagon. The White House felt it had to stand firm "to keep the Navy in the person of Forrestal from kicking over the traces."[83]

The State Department's failure to participate more actively in the negotiations leading to the establishment of the National Security Council is surprising. Other than Marshall's memorandum and comments by the department's legal adviser at a fairly advanced stage of the bill, it does not appear that the State Department gave any attention to the proposal. Nor does it seem they gave any real thought about how the State Department would relate to it, or the scope of the problems it would consider.[84] Probably the department considered the whole unification bill an interservice squabble which did not really concern them and the council as a Forrestal ploy which would never assume any significance.

CONGRESS ACTS

The fifth draft was forwarded to Congress on 26 February 1947 with the assurance that it had the approval of the civilian and military heads of the army and navy.[85] The major effort of the White House now shifted

81. Marshall interview by Don Price, 6 July 1948, First Hoover Commission, Cabinet Secretariat Concept, Herbert C. Hoover Library.

82. Marshall to Truman, 25 February 1947, Unification, Correspondence-comments, Clifford Papers, HSTL.

83. Elsey to Clifford, 17 November 1948, Unification Folder No. 11, Elsey Papers, HSTL.

84. Meck, p. 3.

85. Hobbs, *Behind the President,* p. 131.

to riding herd on the testimony of various members of the administration while guarding against any major congressional alterations in the proposal.

Navy strategists began to focus on obtaining congressional membership on the NSC to counterbalance presidential attempts to enforce a ceiling on their budgets. It was not a new idea since the Eberstadt Report had called for close relations between congressional leaders and the NSC.[86] Forrestal and others were invited to testify at the Senate Armed Forces Committee hearings which began in the spring. The navy secretary wanted to recommend that the "Chairman of the Foreign Affairs Committees or of other Congressional committees . . . might, at appropriate times, sit with the National Security Council." When a draft of Forrestal's testimony was sent to the White House for clearance, objections were raised. Murphy and Elsey feared this practice would weaken the president's control of executive branch policy. Webb then convinced Forrestal to drop the suggestion.[87]

When Admiral Ernest J. King appeared before the committee, he proposed an elaborate council system that would include appropriate congressmen and the secretary of the treasury among its members. King's testimony indicated that at least some elements of the navy still had not given up hope of substituting the NSC for unification. He stressed that his council system should be tried before any further steps were taken toward unification.[88]

The progress of the bill through Congress was carefully watched by the White House and the Bureau of the Budget. The bureau was distressed by two changes in the NSC approved by the Senate. One made the president a member of the council and its chairman. The other eliminated the position of executive secretary and provided that the council's staff would be headed by the secretary of national security

86. Eberstadt, *Report to the Secretary of the Navy*, p. 13.

87. Elsey to Clifford, 19 March 1947, Unification Folder No. 2, Elsey Papers, HSTL; "Draft of testimony Forrestal was to give before Senate Armed Forces Committee, 18 March 1947, Ibid.

88. Hobbs, *Behind the President*, pp. 132-133.

(secretary of defense). The bureau believed if the president presided at council meetings it would weaken its advisory role, inhibit deliberation, and cause NSC procedures to be too formalized. It was viewed as an undesirable invasion of the president's right to decide where to invest his time and energy. Since Congress could not force a president to attend council meetings, the bureau's concern was more with form than substance.[89]

The bureau was more distressed by the elimination of the executive secretary. It did not like the substitution of the part-time efforts of a very busy executive for the full-time, high-level staff assistance envisioned in the administration's bill. The secretary of national security would be in the awkward position of holding full membership on the council while at the same time being its staff director. The orientation of the staff would also be narrower if directed by a member of the council whose area of responsibility would be inevitably less broad than that of the council as a whole. Finally, the secretary would tend to reflect his preoccupation with military considerations in the total national security picture.[90]

The House restored the provision for a civilian executive secretary, and much to the relief of the Budget Bureau and Clifford, it was the version that was finally approved.[91] In fact, the only change Congress made in the fifth draft that affected the NSC was the inclusion of the president among its membership as the presiding officer. It added, however, that he could designate another member to preside in his absence. As the bureau pointed out, Congress could not force him to attend the meetings. The only limitation on the president's appointment of additional members to the NSC was the stipulation that they had to have been confirmed by the Senate for the office which made them eligible for appointment to the council.[92]

---

89. "Revisions Affecting the National Security Council," Bureau of the Budget Folder, Clifford Papers, HSTL.

90. Ibid.

91. Clifford to Truman, 22 July 1947, Unification: Correspondence: Comment, ibid.

92. *U. S. Statutes at Large*, Title I, sec. 101, pp. 496–497.

EVALUATION

The biggest potential loser in the establishment of the NSC was the State Department. During the years that Congress spent debating unification the State Department had few defenders and the department did very little to protect its own turf. Don K. Price believes that the Foreign Service came out of the war interested only in a very restricted political function whereas superpower status and the cold war had imposed worldwide military and economic responsibilities on the country. So executive office coordinating machinery arose in "an effort to make up for the fact that the State Department, not by doing anything specifically but rather by negative action, abdicated its primacy."[93] This analysis explains much of the lack of opposition to the council in the Congress and elsewhere, but the driving initiative that produced the NSC was deeply rooted in interservice rivalry.

Although Congress accepted the administration's specifications for the NSRB, there is a real question whether they understood what they approved. Many congressmen were uneasy about the possibility of "industrial regimentation" by the government, but they accepted the need for mobilization planning because they were told that the next war would probably leave little time for the trial and error methods that had been used in the past. Congressional fear of military domination of the economy helped the administration convince them that the NSRB should not be subordinate to the NSC, which was then looked upon as a semimilitary body. The pertinent parts of the act that established the NSRB stated:

There is hereby established a National Security Resources Board . . . to be composed of the Chairman of the Board and such heads or representatives of the various executive departments and independent agencies as may from time to time be designated by the President to be members of the Board. . . . The Chairman shall be appointed from

93. Henry M. Jackson, ed., *The National Security Council* (New York, 1965), pp. 250–251.

civilian life by the President. . . . It shall be the function of the Board to advise the President concerning the coordination of military, industrial and civilian mobilization. . . . In performing its functions, the Board shall utilize to the maximum extent the facilities and resources of the departments and agencies of the Government.[94]

The board, which existed for six years, was never able to agree on what these words meant or what its mission was.

Unfortunately, because of the larger issue of unification of the armed forces, neither the National Security Council or the National Security Resources Board received the consideration by Congress they deserved. A contemporary study of the legislative history of the National Security Act observed that the original unification proposal which came from the War Department focused on the armed forces alone. The navy's counterproposal in the form of the Eberstadt study which was designed to divert attention from merger emphasized "security" rather than "defense." No one in Congress seriously challenged the assertion that the armed forces alone cannot ensure national security. So they acted on the concept as an afterthought without much discussion. In so doing, the Congress ignored the still undigested lessons of World War II which was rich in expensive experiments in coordination.[95]

Probably the biggest factor in the passage of the legislation by Congress was their realization that it represented the best compromise the president could obtain from the War and Navy departments. To most members of Congress the National Security Council and the National Security Resources Board just happened to be a part of that compromise.

---

94. Public Law 253, 80th Cong., chapter 343, p. 5.

95. "Some Observations on Relations of Military Agencies to National Security," 21 June 1948, M1-21/48.1, Series 39.32, RG 51, NA.

9.
The National Security Council, 1947-1950

The National Security Act became law on 26 July 1947. It created a National Military Establishment, a National Security Resources Board, and a National Security Council. After Robert Patterson decided to leave the government, Truman named James Forrestal as the first secretary of defense.[1] Because the legislation provided little more than a structure for these new organizations, the stage was set for the struggle that would ultimately determine their character.

Whether the idea for the NSC came from the British Committee on Imperial Defense or from the navy's effort to substitute a council for unification now made little difference. Forrestal still assumed the NSC would be a tool of the secretary of defense but this was based on his misconception of the American system. The power of the presidency cannot be embodied in a committee. "Once the NSC was established, the divergent purposes which had brought it into being all yielded, of necessity, to one: the Presidential purpose. For while the NSC could be less, it could be no more than what the President wanted it to be, if he knew his mind."[2] The role of the NSC was ultimately determined by the president's attitude toward it. For this reason,

1. Walter Millis and E.S. Duffiels, eds., *The Forrestal Diaries*, pp. 295-296.

2. Paul Hammond, "The National Security Council As a Device for Interdepartmental Coordination," p. 901.

each of Truman's successors has created his own version of the council.

The contest to determine Truman's attitude toward the NSC was between Forrestal and the Bureau of the Budget. The defense secretary began to plan his attack at a Pentagon conference held on 8 August 1947. Eberstadt and the others in attendance decided to draft a directive to guide the council's operations and send it to the president for his approval.[3] They and Forrestal wanted the NSC to be much more than an "advisory" body to the president. The defense secretary believed

that when, in the absence of the President, there was consensus within the Council on a particular matter; when the departments or agencies represented on the Council were able to carry out the decision reached; and when that decision was within the scope of previously approved Presidential policies, it would not be necessary to take the matter to the President for decision.[4]

This Pentagon group, who really viewed the NSC as simply a part of the defense establishment, wanted the president to designate the defense secretary as the member to preside over meetings in his absence. Of course they expected the council to be located in the Pentagon close to Forrestal's office. Marx Leva, one of Forrestal's aides, was put to work drafting a memo to support these recommendations. To do so, he cited the precedent of the British war cabinet; the wording of the National Security Act which stated that the "Secretary of Defense shall be the principal assistant to the President in all matters relating to the national security"; and the legislative history of the act

3. Anna Kasten Nelson, "President Truman and the Evolution of the National Security Council," *The Journal of American History* 72, no. 2 (September 1985): 364.

4. "Organizational History of the NSC," James S. Lay to J. Kenneth Mansfield, 30 June 1960, NSC files, p. 5. This document, written by Lay and Robert H. Johnson of the NSC staff was prepared at the request of the Senate Subcommittee on National Policy Machinery.

which implied that the secretary should preside over the council.[5]

THE BUREAU'S MEMORANDUM

At about the same time that Forrestal was establishing his position toward the council, the bureau was also preparing a document. Drafted by Charles B. Stauffacher of the administrative management division, it was this memorandum that eventually fixed the president's basic attitude toward the NSC.[6] The memorandum discussed generally both the problems and opportunities the president faced now that Congress had presented him with a security council. It concluded with a list of eight suggested actions he should take. Stauffacher pointed out that the stated purpose of the council was to advise the president on matters of national security—an important part of his total job—but reminded him that the creation of this new agency neither increased his authority nor decreased his responsibility. In a practical way it meant he would gain the assistance of a high-level executive in the person of the secretary of defense and the council's full-time staff. These could be used to complement and support the forms of committee assistance that traditionally had been available to the president. But these gains were far overshadowed by the problems inherent in the complex organizational and personal relationships that the council created.[7]

The memorandum warned Truman that the council "should in no sense restrict or circumscribe his freedom to reach a 'Presidential position' . . . without pressure of publicity or implied commitment." He should remain free to take any of the council's recommendations under advisement and to consult other advisers.

5. Anna Kasten Nelson, "National Security I: Inventing a Process (1945-1960)," in *The Illusion of Presidential Government*, ed. Hugh Heclo and Lester M. Salamon (Boulder, Colo., 1981), p. 234.

6. "Suggestions on the Organization and Utilization of the National Security Council and the National Security Resources Board," draft, C.B.S., 7 August 1947, E2-58/47.2, Series 39.32, NA.

7. Memorandum for Truman, 8 August 1947, Unification file, Elsey Papers, HSTL.

"The Executive responsibility to determine program and enforce coordination should not be impaired." The recommendation suggested that the best way to attain these objectives would be for the president to avoid attending most of the council meetings and to designate the secretary of state to preside in his place. This would assure that the actions of the council would be advisory in nature and protect the president from being pressed to resolve issues on the spot.[8]

Stauffacher observed that in a sense it would be difficult to separate the NSC from the cabinet. "National security" was such a broad subject that it could be considered a matter of concern to all the departments of the government. But if all those who had a legitimate interest in national security were included among the council members, it would result in the re-creation of the cabinet plus the service secretaries and the chairman of the NSRB. Not only would this be unwieldy but it would also produce a cabinet operating under statutory law, a condition that no president would welcome. So the bureau recommended that the council be considered a cabinet-level subset instead of a replacement for the cabinet. The particular usefulness of the NSC would be its ability to focus on the problems of national security without the inhibiting effect of the full cabinet's presence.[9]

The relationship between the president and the NSC's executive secretary was another question that the memorandum explored. It saw this official as "the President's man," not the council's, and suggested he be considered as one of the president's administrative assistants with full access to him. The executive secretary, under the president's direction, should establish the council's formal agenda and reporting procedures and provide the NSC with staff support.[10]

Budget director Webb gave this memorandum to Truman the same day that Forrestal was meeting with his advisers at the Pentagon. Webb had previously discussed with the president the problem of ensuring that

---

8. Ibid.
9. Ibid.
10. Ibid.

the NSC did not exercise "power over" him. He pointed out that three of Stauffacher's recommendations were particularly important in preserving his independence. These were:

1. Designation of the Secretary of State to act in the absence of the President as Chairman of the Security Council;
2. The appointment of the Executive Secretary of the Council prior to the approval of plans for its organization, insuring his participation under [presidential] direction in establishing those plans;
3. The establishment of the Executive Secretary of the Security Council and the Chairman of the Security Resources Board in the same relationship to [the president] as other key assistants in the Executive Office of the President.[11]

The president accepted and acted on this advice. He consistently adhered to its strictures for the remainder of his administration.

Truman adopted the views of the Budget Bureau because, while Forrestal sought to diminish the president's position, the bureau was committed to enhancing it. The institutionalization of the presidency was a matter of bureau doctrine as well as its self-interest. All other elements of the government sought to use presidential power to support their more parochial goals. Truman, with his sense of history, was determined to turn over his office to his successor intact, and he recognized the bureau as an ally in pursing this goal.

ORGANIZING THE NSC

The first step in organizing the NSC was to appoint its executive secretary. Truman's choice, Admiral Sidney W. Souers, through the strength of his personality and the relationship he developed with the president, became a key player in the evolution of the council.

In civilian life an investment banker like Forrestal and Eberstadt, Souers had known both men

---

11. Webb to President, 8 August 1947, C2-1, James E. Webb Papers, HSTL.

during the 1930s. A member of the Naval Intelligence Reserve for many years before the war, he was ordered to active duty shortly before Pearl Harbor. In 1944 he was named assistant director of naval intelligence plans. The following year he became the deputy director of naval intelligence and was promoted to admiral. When Forrestal organized the Eberstadt committee, Souers was asked to write the report's chapter on intelligence. Eberstadt became one of his strong supporters.[12]

Truman first met Souers in 1945 during the controversy over the postwar organization of foreign intelligence. The president eventually chose to follow the "navy" plan which was endorsed by the joint chiefs and presented by Souers. Then the admiral, who was a close personal friend of Clark Clifford's, was named the director of the National Intelligence Group (CIG) which the navy plan had recommended. Although Souers was from Missouri, until this time Truman only knew him as "a pillar of the Democratic party in St. Louis." When the National Security Act abolished the CIG, Souers was available for a new assignment. He probably owed his appointment as the executive secretary of the NSC to his friendship with Clifford, the confidence that Admiral Leahy had in him, and as a peace offering to Forrestal who was not likely to be pleased with Truman's concept of the security council.[13]

Souers soon realized that "Mr. Truman did not look upon the NSC with much favor" and that the role of the council would be much different from that planned by Messrs. Forrestal and Eberstadt.[14] There is no doubt that Souers initially sympathized with the Forrestal view, but apparently he had a facility for adapting his views to those of his boss. Even though Forrestal was pushing to have the NSC in the Pentagon, Souers decided "that the Executive Secretary could serve the President and members of the NSC better

---

12. Souers to Calvin L. Christman, 22 December 1970, Sidney Souers Papers, HSTL.

13. Souers to Allen Dulles, 25 February 1964, ibid.; Nelson, "Truman and the Evolution of the NSC," p. 367.

14. Souers to John Osborne, 19 August 1963, Souers Papers, HSTL.

being directly under the President." Souers soon became a loyal and skillful supporter of the president's
position. Within a few years even Eberstadt admitted
the admiral had made the right decision.[15]

When Truman appointed Souers, he asked him to
begin developing "an assistant who is a careerist in
government and who could be considered . . . for subsequent appointment as Executive Secretary."[16] Truman
apparently had decided from the beginning of the NSC
to institutionalize the executive secretary position so
that it could survive a change in administrations or
even parties. Perhaps he too had the model of the
British cabinet secretariat in mind, or possibly he
simply recalled how difficult it had been to pick up
the reins of foreign policy when he had suddenly become president. Souers selected as his heir apparent
James S. Lay, Jr., whom he had known as a division
chief in the CIG and as a member of the State Department. Lay, who Neustadt thought was almost a carica-
ture of a career civil servant, was initially appointed
the assistant executive secretary of the NSC.[17]

After accepting his appointment, Souers returned
to St. Louis to put his business affairs in order. Before leaving, he turned over to Lay the Budget Bureau
memorandum of 8 August and implied that the memorandum outlined approved policy for the operation of the
council. Lay thereupon set out to consult individually
with the members to develop with them a plan of operation that was acceptable to the president. When he
talked to Forrestal, he was dismayed to learn the defense secretary held a view of the council significantly different from that of the Budget Bureau.[18]
Forrestal believed that efforts by the Budget Bureau
to protect the authority of the president were really
aimed at destroying the council.

Forrestal had been continuing to make plans for
the operation of the NSC. In late August he met with
General Norstad and Admiral D. C. Ramsey to discuss

15. Souers to Christman, 22 December 1970, ibid.
16. Souers to President, 17 November 1949, ibid.
17. Neustadt, unpublished manuscript, HSTL, p. 40.
18. Arnold Miles to Donald Stone, 9 September 1947, NSC, M1-21, OMB.

the relation of the council to the president, the cabinet, and the Budget Bureau. Norstad confirmed Forrestal's suspicion that the State Department, "under Acheson's leadership had been very dubious about the creation of the council and would undoubtedly try to castrate its effectiveness."[19] These reports tended to confirm the moody Forrestal's belief in a conspiracy involving the State Department, the Budget Bureau, and the White House staff.

After his encounter with Forrestal, Lay sought moral support and advice from Arnold Miles of the administrative management division of the Budget Bureau. This was the unit that had written the memorandum from which Truman and Souers had derived their NSC policy. Miles suggested that Lay seek the support of Robert Lovett who had recently replaced Acheson as undersecretary of state. Then Miles and Lay drafted a paper, based on the bureau memorandum, outlining the policies and procedures that should govern the activities of the NSC and its staff. Anticipating the reception this document was likely to get at the Pentagon, Miles suggest that "Souers reinforce himself with Clifford or possibly the President on the views of our memo before carrying the paper around to Council members for signature."[20]

The Miles–Lay paper took the form of a presidential memorandum to the executive secretary. It limited NSC membership to those officials whose membership was mandatory under the act and emphasized that the "Council is purely an advisory body and has no policy making or supervisory functions, except in its direction of the Central Intelligence Agency." Nor was the NSC "to be used as an instrumentality for reaching interdepartmental decisions or supervising interdepartmental agencies." The agenda of the council was to be limited to matters that required the president's consideration and no information about the council's affairs was to be released to the public without his specific authorization. The executive secretary was

19. Millis and Duffield, *Forrestal Diaries*, pp. 315–316.
20. Miles to Stone, 9 September 1947, NSC, M1–21, OMB.

made responsible to the president for the performance of his functions.[21]

Fearful of Forrestal's reaction to such a council, it was decided to break the news to him en masse rather than to have Souers alone collect his signature. A meeting was held between the defense secretary and a White House staff delegation on 17 September. They discussed the proposed agenda for the first meeting of the council, where it should be held, and the Lay-Miles draft of procedures and policies. They also discussed the potential membership of the NSC and the NSRB and the concept of a central secretariat for the council. Elsey noted that "Forrestal did all we were afraid of—he assumed his decision would be final, and that he was going to run these affairs. [Clifford] had to speak up in firm disagreement to keep him from reaching decisions in final fashion without consultation with State Department."[22]

Later that day Forrestal confided to his diary that it was

apparent that there is going to be a difference between the Budget, some of the White House staff and ourselves on the National Security Council—its functions, its relationship to the President and myself. I regard it as an integral part of the national defense setup and believe it was so intended by the Congress. As I have said earlier I regard it also not as a place to make policies but certainly a place to identify for the President those things upon which policy needs to be made.[23]

Earlier there had been a disagreement about the physical location of the NSC staff. Forrestal and Eberstadt were adamant that the NSC office should be in the Pentagon.[24] The Budget Bureau just as strongly recommended that the council staff be housed with the rest of the executive office in the old State-War-Navy

21. Draft memorandum to the Executive Secretary, NSC, Security Council Folder, Elsey Papers, HSTL.

22. Conference with Forrestal, 17 September 1947, "Agenda," Unification folder no. 6, ibid.

23. Millis and Duffield, *Forrestal Diaries*, p. 316.

24. Souers to Christman, 22 December 1970, Souers Papers, HSTL.

Building next to the White House.[25] Miles hoped this would limit military influence in the NSC and encourage the council staff to integrate their work with the activities of the EOP.

Souers initially planned to have his own office and that of four or five of his immediate staff in Old State, but the rest were to be at the Pentagon and serviced by Forrestal. The defense secretary had offered his hospitality and Souers did not know where to get the funds to do otherwise. The bureau soon found an alternative source of money by arranging for the CIA to provide necessary services for the council staff.[26]

The location problem, which the bureau considered a matter of "high policy," proved to be more difficult to solve. The aid of Charles Murphy was enlisted to get Truman's attention to this detail. Initially Murphy suggested getting someone at the State Department to plead the case with the president, but it was soon realized that there was "no one in State who has these [NSC] problems on their minds full time."[27] In the end Truman supported the bureau but, at Forrestal's urgent request, allowed the executive secretary to have a second office at the Pentagon next door to the defense secretary. This proved to be a temporary arrangement because Souers did not use his Pentagon office.[28]

This early confrontation helped establish the pattern for presidential domination of the NSC. It demonstrated that a president can use the council for whatever purpose he wishes. It wa also a remarkable demonstration of the detachment of the State Department from NSC matters at this stage of the council's development. Although ninety percent of the business of the NSC was to involve foreign policy considerations, but for the vigilance of the Budget Bureau it might have become an adjunct of the Pentagon.

---

25. Miles to Stone, 9 September 1947, NSC, M1–21, OMB. The NSC was not formally incorporated into the EOP until 1949.

26. Stone to Webb, 17 September 1947, M1–21/40.1, Series 39.32, RG 51, NA.

27. Miles to Stone, 9 September 1947, NSC, M1–21, OMB.

28. Souers to Christman, 22 December 1970, Souers Papers, HSTL.

PRECEDENTS

The first meeting of the NSC was scheduled for 26 September 1947. The day before, in an effort to dominate the proceedings and establish some useful precedents, Forrestal held a rehearsal meeting in his Pentagon office. In attendance were the three service secretaries, the joint chiefs, Souers, and from the State Department, Robert Lovett. They discussed the issue they intended to raise as the first substantive matter for NSC consideration.[29]

The first official meeting was held in the Cabinet Room of the White House. The NSC was to meet here irregularly for the next ten months.[30] The statutory members at this time, in addition to the president, were the secretaries of state, defense, army, navy, and air force, and the chairman of the NSRB. All except Marshall attended the first meeting along with Executive Secretary Souers, the new director of the CIA, Admiral Roscoe Hillenkoetter, and the president. Lovett attended in place of Marshall.

Truman evidently decided to preside at this meeting so he could impress his concept of the council on its members. He told them "that he regarded it as *his* council and that he expected everyone to work harmoniously without any manifestation of prima-donna qualities." Forrestal replied that, while he understood that the president and the secretary of state would make the final decisions in foreign policy, he expected that they would give the advice of the council "due consideration."[31]

From this meeting until the outbreak of the Korean War, Truman attended only twelve of the fifty-seven meetings of the council.[32] In this way the presi-

---

29. Nelson, "Truman and the Evolution of the NSC," p. 360.

30. Stanley Falk, "The National Security Council Under Truman, Eisenhower and Kennedy," *Political Science Quarterly* 79, no. 3 (September 1964): 407.

31. Millis and Duffield, *Forrestal Diaries*. p. 320.

32. U. S. Congress, Senate, Committee on Government Relations, Report of the Subcommittee on National Policy Machinery, *Inquiry on*

dent followed the advice of the Budget Bureau to avoid most of the NSC meetings to emphasize its advisory character. He also adopted their suggestion that he name the secretary of state to preside at NSC meetings in his absence and insisted that the undersecretary of state preside when both he and the secretary were absent. These actions were in direct conflict with Forrestal's view of the NSC. The National Security Act had specified that the defense secretary was to be the "principal assistant to the President in all matters relating to the national security." Forrestal naturally assumed that this would at least include presiding at NSC meetings when the president was absent.[33]

In its first formal action the NSC adopted policies and procedures to govern its activities which the bureau had developed. Next, the council approved a memorandum that outlined the function of the NSC staff. Most of the staff's duties were secretarial but it was also authorized to develop a program of studies and recommendations for consideration by the council.[34]

Italy became the first substantive matter considered by the NSC through an agreement between Forrestal and Lovett. A few days before the first council meeting the two had been discussing the Italian problem. What should the United State do, they wondered, if, when American forces were withdrawn from Italy, the Communists formed a republic in the northern provinces? Lovett said the State Department could not propose a policy because they did not know what military capabilities were available to implement various options. Forrestal replied that the Defense Department could not propose a policy because its job was to state capabilities and await instructions. Lovett then suggested that this was the type of question that should come before the NSC. The two agreed to meet and prepare a proposal for the council to consider.[35]

National Policy Machinery, vol. 2, "Studies and Background Materials," 86th Cong., 2nd sess., 1960, p. 421.

33. James Lay, "Suggestions for Further Strengthening NSC," 19 January 1953, M1–1, Series 52.1, RG 51, NA.

34. Minutes of the First Meeting of the NSC, PSF, Truman Papers, HSTL.

35. Millis and Duffield, *Forrestal Diaries*, p. 320.

Lovett then led a discussion of the Italian problem at Forrestal's rehearsal for the first NSC meeting.[36]

A paper entitled "The Position of the United States with Respect to Italy" was developed. It was adopted by the NSC at its second meeting as "NSC 1/1." When it was approved by the president on 17 November 1947 it become the first in a long series of foreign policy statements processed through the council system. The paper consisted of a statement of the problem, an analysis, and conclusions. This structural arrangement became typical of the format of NSC studies for many years. Unfortunately, its vapid conclusion also became typical of too many of the council's policy statements. It declared that "the United States has security interests of primary importance in Italy and the measures to implement our current policies to safeguard those interests should be strengthened without delay."[37] It is difficult to see how this policy could have provided much guidance to Lovett and Forrestal if the hypothetical problem they had posed a few months earlier had materialized. But for the first time in the nation's history an effort had been made to guide governmental actions by identifying national objectives and how they might be achieved.

Over the next several years four types of policy papers were developed. These included: general policy and strategy for dealing with a broad range of problems; papers bearing on geographic areas such as NSC 1/1; functional topics such as mobilization or arms control; and organizational questions involving intelligence activities. The topics arose from the interests of Souers, the NSC staff, or from suggestions by the members. During the early years, most of the papers were of the geographic variety.[38]

It soon became standard practice for the president to approve just the conclusions of the policy documents. When he approved the statement on Italy, Truman directed that it be "implemented by all departments and agencies concerned, under the coordination

36. Nelson, "Truman and the Evolution of the NSC," p. 360.

37. NSC 1/1, 14 November 1947, PSF, Truman Papers, HSTL.

38. Falk, "The National Security Council," pp. 409-410.

of the Secretary of State." Phraseology similar to this became a part of almost all future presidential policy approvals, and the State Department was normally designated as the implementation coordinator.

One precedent not established by NSC 1/1 was the method by which presidential approval was secured. Truman had simply told Lovett that he approved of the council's paper on Italy and one of Lovett's aides told Souers. Clifford and Elsey thought this an "atrocious procedure." They got Souers to agree that in the future (1) he alone would present NSC papers to the president; (2) he would submit two copies to the president and ask him to indicate his approval or disapproval on one copy for the NSC files; and (3) assume the responsibility for informing "the members of the President's decision on the Council's recommendation, and inform them of the manner in which a recommendation is to be implemented."[39]

THE STAFF

The NSC staff that was authorized at the council's first meeting was to be made up of career employees supplemented by people detailed full-time from the participating departments. Although a maximum of thirty career staff was fixed by the council, the number never exceeded twenty-three during the Truman years. At first the career staff did the secretarial work while the detailed members, who were usually referred to as "The Staff," developed the studies and policy recommendations for council consideration. The detailed people typically had offices in their agencies as well as in Old State and were attached to the office of chief planners in their departments. Those from military agencies were at the colonel or lieutenant colonel rank and the civilians had an equivalent civil service grade.[40]

---

39. Truman to Executive Secretary, 17 November 1947, NSC Meeting #2, PSF, Truman Papers, HSTL; Elsey to Clifford, 5 November 1947, Unification folder, Elsey Papers, HSTL.

40. Lay, "Organizational History," pp. 10–11; Lay, "Suggestions for Further Strengthening NSC; Souers, "Address to the Joint Orientation

At Souers's request Marshall sent one of his senior Foreign Service officers to the NSC to serve as the "coordinator" or leader of the staff. Another State Department official was transferred to the NSC on a permanent basis to become the assistant to the coordinator. At its first meeting the council specified that:

This staff would be responsible for mapping out assigned projects, obtaining necessary facts, views and opinions from appropriate departments and agencies, analyzing these facts, views and opinions in an effort to devise a generally acceptable solution, attempting to reconcile any divergent views, and finally, preparing reports for the Council which present clearly and concisely the facts, conclusions and agreed recommendations or, alternately, the majority and minority recommendations. In performing these duties, this staff must maintain close and constant contact with all departments and agencies concerned with national security. . . . The staff members detailed from the four departments . . . will undoubtedly need to spend the majority of their time within their respective departments.[41]

The rationale for organizing a staff composed of both permanent and detailed employees was "to steer a course between two undesirable extremes." Souers felt that if the staff was made up entirely of permanent council employees they might develop an ivory tower attitude. If, on the other hand, there were no permanent staff members, excessive turnover could result in inadequate continuity. It is probable that the practice of keeping half of the staff on the rolls of the member agencies was partially a budgetary device to conceal part of the council's costs. But more important, the departments were likely to be more receptive to policy recommendations that they knew included the views of their own detailed officers. By November 1948 the size of the combined staff, including secretaries, messengers, and professional members, numbered thirty individuals, about half of whom were on detail.[42]

Conference of the National Military Establishment," 8 November 1948, Unification folder, Elsey Papers, HSTL.

41. NSC Action #2, "Policies of the Government Relating to National Security, 1947–1949," vol. 1, PSF, Truman Papers, HSTL.

42. Souers, "Address to Orientation Conference," Unification folder, Elsey Papers, HSTL. Much of this address later appeared as an

Unwittingly, the small size of the NSC helped ensure its domination by the State Department. The staff really did not have the capability to develop the policy studies the council expected from it. But the Policy Planning Staff (PPS), which Marshall had set up in the State Department shortly before the National Security Act was passed, was well equipped to do this work. As a result, it was soon the usual practice for the Defense Department to suggest the topics for exploration and for the PPS to write the papers. In this way the State Department heavily influenced the conclusions endorsed by the NSC.[43]

The final element of the early NSC staff system was called the "consultants." In early November 1947 Souers got the service secretaries to name the chiefs of their plans and operations divisions as consultants to him. Then Marshall agreed to have the chief of his PPS join the consultant group while Forrestal contributed the services of General Alfred Gruenther, the director of the joint staff. The director of central intelligence decided he would personally represent his agency in the consultant group. This high-level unit contained, from time to time, such luminaries as George Kennan, Dean Rusk, Lauris Norstad, and Albert Wedemeyer. The consultants role was essentially a passive one: to tell Souers whether a paper that had been developed by the staff was ready for council consideration. Since they rarely met as a group, Souers normally gathered their input on an individual basis.[44]

During the early years of the NSC, the development of a formal policy paper normally followed a prescribed sequence. Possible topics for development as papers were initiated by the member agencies or by the NSC staff pursuant to a long-range agenda to develop a series of area, country, or subject reports. Since Truman always insisted on controlling the agenda, the

article by Souers entitled, "Policy Formulation for National Security" in *The American Political Science Review* 43, no. 3 (June 1949): 534–543.

43. Nelson, "Truman and the Evolution of the NSC," p. 370.

44. Lay, "Suggestions for Further Strengthening NSC" and "Organizational History," p. 11.

executive secretary's first step after receiving a suggested topic was to check with the president to see if
he wished the council to consider it. After obtaining
Truman's approval, a working draft was prepared, us--
ually by the State Department and its policy planning
staff. This draft was then worked over by the NSC
staff until they were satisfied with it as individuals
(that is, they did not check with their departments).
The draft was then considered by the consultants.
These men were senior enough to be able to reflect the
views of their departments but not to speak defini-
tively for them. If the consultants approved, the paper, or an acceptable version of it, was sent to all the
members of the council before being considered at one
of its regular meetings. If the paper had strategic
military implications, and most of them did, it was cir--
culated to the Joint Chiefs of Staff as well. The last
step was to discuss the paper at a NSC meeting, and if
it was approved there, it was presented to the president by the executive secretary along with the comments of the joint chiefs.[45] The approval or rejection
by the president completed the policy formulation process.

SIDNEY SOUERS

The oil that permitted this machinery to work, to the
extent that it did, was supplied by Sidney Souers. He
decided that his job, as "an anonymous servant of the
Council," was to be "a broker of ideas in criss-cross-
ing proposals among a team of first-rate minds."[46] He
believed the executive secretary had to be objective
and willing to subordinate his personal views on policy to the task of coordinating the views of all the
responsible officials. He realized that his work would
be jeopardized if he ever took sides among the members of the council. As a facilitator he always had to
keep in mind that he shared neither the responsibility

45. Souers, "Address to Orientation Conference," Unification
folder, Elsey Papers, HSTL.
46. Ibid.

nor the authority that had been invested in the council.[47]

Frank Pace thought that the remarkable job that
Souers did, in spite of flaws in the council mechanism,
was due to "the strength of his personality and relationships to the President and other key executive
branch officials."[48] Another budget director remembered
the "lunches with Forrestal, the friendship with Webb .
. . the association with Clifford; the loyalty to the
president" that contributed to Souers's ability to keep
open communications to all the participants in the
process.[49] It was fortunate that he had enough stature
and presidential support to work on an intimate basis
with the council members.

Souers's ability to relate to Truman was the key
to his effectiveness. Although the functions of the executive secretary were outlined in the National Security Act, as a practical matter the job was whatever
the president chose to make it. (And Truman did not
believe he needed a national security adviser.) The
executive secretary saw the president daily and
Souers soon became Truman's personal nonpolitical
confidant.

The practice of giving the president an intelligence briefing each day had begun during World War II.
Roosevelt had used Fleet Admiral William Leahy for
this purpose and Leahy continued in this role under
Truman. When Souers became executive secretary, he
joined Leahy in briefing the president until Leahy re-
tired in March 1949. Souers then carried on the practice alone. Truman seemed to view Souers primarily as
his liaison with the intelligence community rather than
as his NSC agent—usually referring to him as his
"intelligence man" or his "cloak and dagger" man.
Souers noted that he was described in Truman's memoirs
as the president's special assistant for top-level intelligence. He rationalized the president's slighting of

47. Executive Secretary Qualifications, NSC 1947–1949, Souers Papers, HSTL.

48. Conference with Frank Pace, 22 June 1950, NSC, Series 47.3c, RG
51, NA.

49. Nelson, "Truman and the Evolution of the NSC," p. 377.

his NSC function by suggesting that Truman may have "considered my briefings as 'intelligence' covering the views of his cabinet officers and other officials."[50] It is more likely that Truman's perception of Souers's role was further evidence that he did not consider the NSC to be a very important body.

Despite the president's attitude, Souers took his position as the link between the council and the chief executive seriously. He saw himself as a facilitator who was to ensure that the views of all interested departments were reflected in the advice given to the president. To do this, he participated in the meetings of the council, worked with the consultants in their deliberations, and served as head of the NSC staff. As the president's agent he controlled the NSC agenda and methods of operation. He was the linchpin that articulated the council mechanism.

As an administrative assistant to the president, Souers was technically part of the White House staff but he maintained a discreet separation from the other staff members. Avoiding Truman's regular morning staff meetings, he briefed the president alone after the others had left. He probably thought this was necessary to maintain the nonpartisan neutral image he was trying to establish for the council. Although he made a point of discussing the domestic implications of NSC matters with Clifford and later with Murphy, this channel was not used extensively.[51] Souers was viewed as close-mouthed and distant by the White House staff who were effectively excluded from foreign policy matters by the executive secretary. Neustadt thought his attitude had "serious consequences for the evolution of the NSC and for its utility as Presidential staff machinery; consequences of which Souers and Lay were not unaware."[52]

50. Elmer Staats in Heller, *The Truman White House*, p. 171; Meck, "The Administration of Foreign and Overseas Operations", pp. 8-9; Souers to John Osborne, 19 August 1963, Souers Papers, HSTL.

51. Souers to Paul Y. Hammond, 14 December 1959; Nelson, "Truman and the Evolution of the NSC," p. 369.

52. Neustadt, "Notes on the White House Staff," HSTL, pp. 40-41.

NSC AND THE BUDGET

During its lifetime the NSC has repeatedly struggled (but never very successfully) with the problem of determining the proper level of military budgets. The issue first arose in the NSC in 1948. In May of that year Truman imposed a ceiling on the military budgets for fiscal 1950 which Forrestal thought unreasonably low. The defense secretary tried to get Secretary of State Marshall's support for a higher figure by raising the issue in the council.[53]

In early July Forrestal, in a long memorandum addressed to the members of the NSC, claimed that his budget needs were dependent upon many factors beyond his control. To determine these needs more accurately he asked for a statement of the national policy toward the Soviets which would "specify and evaluate the risks, state our objectives, and outline the measures to be followed in achieving them." Because of the differences between Truman's concept of the proper role of the NSC and his own, Forrestal carefully quoted from the National Security Act in support of the view that the preparation of the statement he requested was "clearly a function" of the NSC. He concluded by suggesting that the State Department be asked to draft a statement that could be used as the basis for discussion by the council.[54]

Forrestal sent Truman a copy of the memorandum with a covering letter. Neither admitting that the president controlled the NSC or asking him to put the matter on the council's agenda, the defense secretary said he thought "this project is one in which you will be interested and which should be given the highest priority." He justified his action as a device that would help the president make the ultimate decision about the proportion of the nation's resources that

---

53. Warner R. Schilling, "The Politics of National Defense: Fiscal 1950," in *Strategy, Politics, and Defense Budgets* ed. Warner R. Schilling, Paul Y. Hammond, and Glen H. Snyder (New York, 1962), p. 184.

54. Forrestal to the NSC, 10 July 1948, Department of State, *Foreign Relations of the United States, 1948*, vol. 1, part 2 (Washinton, D.C., 19), pp. 589–592 (henceforth *FRUS*).

would be devoted to military purposes.[55] It seems clear that Forrestal did not really think the NSC had the capability of producing a clear-cut statement of policy that could be translated into military budget levels. He was simply trying to apply pressure to have his ceilings raised, and Truman knew it.[56]

The president saw the incident as a challenge to his control of the NSC and as a budget issue rather than a foreign policy question. He turned to the Budget Bureau to draft his response to Forrestal and accepted without change the letter the BOB prepared. In it the president announced that he was putting the matter on the NSC's agenda because it would be desirable to have the factors that Forrestal outlined as influencing the size of the defense budget "reduced to writing." In this way he indirectly reasserted his control over the NSC. Truman's letter was careful to point out that the factors that Forrestal asserted affected his budget had been considered in determining the ceilings.[57]

In the same letter the president told Forrestal to expedite his budget preparation. Although Truman agreed to have the council attempt to develop the policy statement Forrestal requested, he was determined not to permit the NSC to be used as a ploy to delay the imposition of the budget ceilings. Next day his order was reinforced by Webb when he confirmed to Forrestal the previously imposed ceiling.[58]

One reason behind these maneuvers was the desire of the military, because of the way it did its own planning, to get the diplomats to state in precise terms the measures that should be undertaken to achieve foreign policy objectives. This conflicted with the State Department attitude, most strongly articulated by George Kennan, that such a statement would lead to a dangerous rigidity in responding to international situations. Forrestal's gambit did not cause the

---

55. Ibid., pp. 592-593.

56. Schilling, "The Politics of National Defense," p. 185.

57. Truman to Forrestal, 15 July 1948, BOB-Military, PSF, Truman Papers, HSTL.

58. Ibid.

State Department to support a larger military budget in fiscal year 1950 or result in any easing of Truman's determination to maintain his budget ceilings, but it did move Kennan to eventually produce (as NSC 20) the first comprehensive statement of the United States' objectives in its dealings with the Soviet Union.[59]

With the departure of Forrestal, Truman seemed to feel more comfortable with the NSC, and decided to use the council to help him make national security budget decisions for fiscal year 1951. In July 1949 he asked the council members to recommend the relative priority and emphasis for programs ranging from the military budgets to Point Four. For this discussion the president invited Edwin Nourse, the chairman of the economic advisers, to sit with the NSC.[60]

The results of this exercise were probably not helpful to a president trying desperately to restrain the federal budget. The NSC, joined by the acting secretary of the treasury, the Economic Cooperation administrator, and the chairman of the economic council, apparently were not able to establish the relative priority of the programs Truman asked them to look at. Instead, over the dissent of Nourse and the Treasury, they recommended that the ceilings be raised by over two billion dollars. Truman never formally approved or disapproved of this report from the NSC. It was still pending nine months later when it was superseded by NSC 68 and the Korean War.[61]

THE HOOVER COMMISSION AND THE NSC

The first systematic evaluation of the NSC by an outside group was made by the Hoover Commission in the summer and fall of 1948 while the NSC was still in its formative first year of operation. Two of the commission's task forces, representing the divergent views of the diplomats and the military, looked at the council's performance. The first focused on NSC activity related to foreign affairs. The second included the council in

59. *FRUS, 1948*, vol. 1, Part 2, p. 662.

60. *FRUS, 1949*, vol. 1, pp. 350–352.

61. Ibid., pp. 385–396.

its charge of examining the "national security organization." The latter task force was headed by Eberstadt who still held to his original concept about the proper role of the NSC and the NSRB.

One of the compromises Truman had to make to secure passage of the National Security Act was the designation of the secretaries of army, navy, and air force as permanent members of the NSC. This led to persistent criticism of the council's overwhelmingly military composition. Even Forrestal, who had insisted on their inclusion when he was the navy secretary, had changed his mind now that he had become secretary of defense. Two of the three service secretaries also thought they should be dropped from the council. Stuart Symington, the air force secretary, testified before the national security task force that the NSC was a good mechanism for distributing information but it was "too much military" to be a top-level policy agency. Secretary of the Army Kenneth Royall, was even more specific and critical in his comments:

The National Security Council wastes a tremendous amount of time and Mr. Royall says he is glad to be out of town when they have a meeting. It is a fine concept which can work but it is not working now as it should. There is a tremendous duplication of effort among more or less the same people discussing the same problem, first in an individual military department, then in the War Council, then in the joint Chiefs of Staff, then with the Secretary of Defense, and then with the National Security Council. It would work better if it were composed only of the Secretary of State (and Under Secretary), the Secretary of Defense (and Under Secretary), a Single Chief of Staff, and Chairman of the NSRB with the president a non-voting member.[62]

The task forces developed opposing recommendations regarding the NSC. The national security group adopted much of Royall's view when it proposed that the secretary of defense should be the sole representative of the military on the council. It suggested that the joint chiefs attend NSC meetings but not be

62. Testimony at meeting on 10 June 1948, OBEG 20 and 56, Dean Acheson Papers, HSTL.

accorded full membership.[63] The foreign affairs task force questioned the logic of a NSC mandated by law and clearly resented the council's intrusion into "foreign policy questions over which the Secretary of State might be expected to have principal control." It did not believe that Congress should tell the president where to get his advice.[64] The full commission ultimately endorsed this view that the NSC should not be statutorily defined.

Souers thought a statutory NSC was necessary to ensure its institutionalization. Otherwise he feared it might get lost during changes in administrations. Although Souers favored a minimum statutory membership, he pointed out that Congress could not prevent the president from inviting others to sit with the council since he could always "call them in on the side and take their advice instead of the council's"[65]

Congress was receptive to dropping the service secretaries from membership, but was not inclined to give the president complete flexibility in the selection of the members of the NSC. In January 1949, before the Hoover Commission even filed its report, a bill was introduced into the House to change the NSC membership. H.R. 1945 provided that the the service secretaries would be dropped as statutory members but added the vice-president. This presented a problem for the White House which the Budget Bureau delicately summarized in a memo for the president:

The thinking of the Bureau for a number of years has been that the statutory creation of and designation of membership on interdepartmental committees should be avoided. You have agreed with this position in a number of instances. The Hoover Commission has fully adopted this position and given it forceful statement. . . . H.R. 1945 contradicts this general principle. . . . This bill obviously raises a question of relationships between yourself and the Vice President. It is suggested that you may wish to discuss this matter with him in order that the position which both of you consider wisest can be deter-

---

63. Hoover Commission, *Task Force Report on National Security Organization*, Appendix G, p. 16.

64. Hoover Commission, *Task Force Report on Foreign Affairs*, Appendix H, pp. 62-63.

65. Jackson, *The National Security Council*, p. 109.

mined and that any action which you take on the measure can be handled in an informal way.[66]

Truman evidently decided that his relationship
with his newly elected vice-president, Alben Barkley,
was more important than preserving presidential prerogatives in the EOP. When H.R. 1945 became law, the
membership of the NSC consisted of the president, the
vice president, the secretary of state, the secretary
of defense, and the chairman of the NSRB.[67]

The change in membership did not significantly
affect the operation of the council during the Truman
administration because the service secretaries had not
been particularly effective council members. Royall
tried to avoid NSC meetings if he could, Symington was
antagonistic, and Secretary of the Navy Francis P.
Matthews was isolated into ineffectiveness by suspicion and distrust.[68] Nor did the addition of Barkley
contribute much to the NSC discussions. He attended
regularly but was habitually late because of the press
of what he considered more important business in the
Senate.[69]

In its final report the Hoover Commission recommended that the NSC and the NSRB be incorporated into
the Executive Office of the President. Souers did not
think this technicality warranted official action but
Truman decided to pursue it.[70] To effect these changes
Reorganization Plan No. 4 of 1949 was sent to Congress
in June. The rationale was that many of the problems
dealt with by the NSC and NSRB required collaboration
within the EOP with the Budget Bureau and the economic
advisers.[71] In fact, Truman had always considered the
NSC and NSRB as de facto elements of the executive

66. Frank Pace to President, 15 February 1949, M1-21/40.1, RG 51,
NA.

67. Public Law 216, 81st Cong., 1st sess., chapter 412.

68. Paul Y. Hammond, "NSC-68: Prologue to Rearmament," in *Strategy,
Politics, and Defense Budgets* ed. Warner R. Schilling, Paul Y. Hammond,
and Glen H. Snyder (New York, 1962), p. 295.

69. Hobbs, *Behind the President*, p. 155.

70. Souers to President, 16 March 1949, E2-50/49.1, Series 39.32, RG
51, NA.

71. Press release, 20 June 1949, Truman Papers, HSTL.

office and had located them all in what is now the Executive Office Building to facilitate their working relationships. The reorganization plan simply brought their legal status into accord with existing administrative practice.

Other reorganizations based on Hoover Commission recommendations were carried out in the State and Defense departments. Some of these served to improve the relations between these departments and the NSC. However, the most serious problems of the council in 1948 and 1949 arose from competing departmental personalities, jurisdictions, and philosophies. These were not amenable to organizational remedies.

KENNAN AND THE NSC

To a large extent the rationale for establishment of the NSC was the inadequacy of the State Department.[72] State's ineffectiveness was evident when the department failed to participate constructively in the design of the council. Once the NSC was set up, the State Department tried to take the stance that nothing should ever be considered by the council that could be handled by direct negotiations between State and one of the departments or with the president.[73]

When George Marshall became secretary of state in 1947, he created a Policy Planning Staff (PPS) in the department and charged it with anticipating future problems and suggesting solutions to these problems. George Kennan became the first chief of the PPS. As the council began to function, it naturally turned to the State Department for help in the preparation of policy papers and Marshall assigned this work to the PPS. When Forrestal demanded that the NSC provide the Defense Department with a national policy toward Russia, it was inevitable that the NSC staff would turn to the PPS for help.

The staff took a paper drafted by Kennan for another purpose and fashioned it into the first coherent statement of American objectives in its relations with

72. Jackson, *The National Ssecurity Council*, pp. 250–251.
73. Paul David to James Sundquist, 29 August 1950, M1–21/50.1, Series 39.32, RG 51, NA.

the Soviets. In the paper Kennan approached the subject in his usual analytical and philosophical fashion. The military wanted their guidance in terms of specific actions to be taken, not philosophy, but Kennan had little sympathy for this approach. The paper that was approved by the council and the president in late November 1948 (and designated NSC 20/1) reiterated, in modified form, the conclusions in Kennan's original paper. To mollify the Defense Department, the NSC asked its staff to develop a list of detailed measures that the United States should undertake to achieve the objectives outlined in NSC 20/1.[74]

This action by the council resulted in a confrontation between the NSC staff and a State Department that was philosophically and jurisdictionally opposed to detailed implementation papers. Nor did State think that the NSC staff had the ability to develop policy papers. As the staff began to work on the assigned "measures" paper, the State Department representative resisted its efforts. He "consistently advanced the view that no useful purpose would be served by attempting to draft a paper of this kind." But eventually a paper was developed and sent to the NSC consultants for review. Kennan, State's consultant, recommended that his department oppose the document in the NSC "on a point of principle concerning the basic approach to foreign policy problems."[75]

James Webb, who was now under secretary of state, sought to avoid a confrontation in the NSC. When he explored the issue with the department's senior officials, Kennan took the position that the president's approval of NSC 20 should be adequate to guide policy and end the involvement of the NSC. He argued that the measures paper simply reflected the inability of the military to understand that foreign affairs planning was not susceptible to the kind of detailed implementation that they were accustomed to. Most of the others at the meeting were unsure about the purpose of the NSC and joined Kennan in roundly condemning the measures paper as an extremely dangerous precedent.

74. NSC Meeting #27, PSF, Truman Papers, HSTL.
75. Kennan to Webb, 14 April 1949, *FRUS, 1949*, vol. 1, p. 282.

Webb, who had only recently joined the State Department, took a less provincial view. He tried to counteract the negative direction of the discussion by suggesting that the department work with Souers to help shape the president's use of the NSC.[76]

Admiral Souers, aware of the degree to which his NSC was dependent upon State Department cooperation, was anxious to placate them. He was also enough of a politician to realize that he would have to make some concessions. Souers and Lay met with Webb and the PPS on 4 May. Webb, who had helped form Truman's view of the council, began by questioning the role and composition of the NSC staff. He stated that the function of the NSC staff had never been clearly defined and that his department "doubted that it served any useful purpose." When Webb also expressed concern about the continued detailing of two State Department people to this staff, Souers quickly agreed that the NSC could manage with only one. The admiral thought that "a good man" could serve as both the State staff member and staff coordinator.[77] The two positions were combined in July.[78]

The admiral admitted that the accomplishments of the NSC staff had not been impressive so far. He even agreed that his staff "should not generally attempt to draft papers and . . . State should not have to submit its papers to the Council through the Staff." Souers suggested that the proper role of the staff should be to serve as a "forum for analysis of problems and a bringing together of military and political views to be taken into consideration by State in its drafting of papers." This would effectively remove the NSC staff as a potential competitor in the formulation of foreign policy. Souers did not explain how this process would work, but his apparent willingness to make concessions so pacified Kennan and Webb that they both agreed that his concept of the staff's proper role had merit

---

76. Record of the Undersecretary's meeting, 15 April 1949, ibid.
77. Memo of conversation by Webb, 4 May 1949, ibid., p. 297.
78. Lay, "Organizational History," p. 11.

and they expressed a willingness to give it a thorough trial.[79]

On the basis of this discussion, Souers issued instructions on 26 May that the staff was

(a) to conduct a periodical review of all current national security policies in order to determine what revisions were necessary; and (b) to undertake a program of studies on major aspects of those problems and analyze alternative courses of action open to the United States, without, however, making policy recommendations.

These two functions: reviewing existing policies and analyzing alternatives, became a recurrent part of council business from that time forward.[80] The directive removed the NSC staff from the perilous position of recommending policies for the departments to follow.

STATE AND THE NSC

This episode came near the end of the Policy Planning Staff's involvement with the NSC. Antagonism toward the PPS had been developing in the State Department for some time among the substantive action units. These critics complained that the PPS had not consulted enough with them about council matters and that preoccupation with NSC work had diverted the PPS from its primary mission. In July 1949, as part of a general organization of the department, a deputy undersecretary of state for substantive matters was established. He was assigned responsibility for coordination with the NSC. Henceforth, the preparation of papers for the NSC was done by the area desks in the department that had the primary responsibility for the particular problem under study instead of centrally by the PPS.[81]

That fall Kennan asked to be relieved as head of the PPS. The ostensible reason for his departure was a dimunition in the role of his staff group. Under General Marshall the PPS reported directly to him. The new

79. Memo of conversation by Webb, 4 May 1949, *FRUS, 1949*, vol. 1, p. 297.

80. Lay, "Organizational History," p. 13.

81. Meck, "The Administration of Foreign and Overseas Operations", pp. 12–13.

secretary of state, Dean Acheson, required the PPS to coordinate its work with the substantive bureaus instead of reporting its work directly to the secretary. The philosophic differences between Kennan and Acheson together with Souers's disenchantment with Kennan were probably more basic causes for his resignation. By the end of the year, Kennan had been replaced by Paul Nitze.[82]

In November 1949, Dean Rusk, the deputy undersecretary, was designated the department's NSC consultant. Max Bishop was appointed coordinator of the NSC staff as well as serving as the department's representative on the staff. He was responsible for coordinating NSC papers within the department at the staff level and serving as Rusk's assistant. A new position of special assistant to the secretary was created for William Sheppard, who was made responsible for a continuing review of the department's involvement with NSC, NSRB, CIA, and the Defense Department.[83]

John F. Meck made a study of the NSC for the Budget Bureau in the spring of 1951. He found that the State Department reorganization had greatly improved its relations with the council. He reported a definite improvement in the speed with which the department arrived at positions and in the completeness of their staff work.[84] It seems likely that Souers had a hand in the reassignment of NSC work within the department. He decided that Kennan had become less and less the type of man he wanted handling these matters because he had become so "wrapped up in the implementation of NSC policy."[85] Although its working relations with the council improved, the State Department's basic attitude remained unchanged. It continued to view the NSC with suspicion and tried to restrict its area of involvement

---

82. George F. Kennan, *Memoirs, 1925-1950* (Boston, 1967), pp. 466-468.

83. *FRUS, 1949*, vol. 1, p. 410.

84. Meck, "The Administration of Foreign and Overseas Operations", pp. 12-13.

85. Conversation of Arnold Miles and Ralph Burton with Sidney Souers, 22 June 1950, NSC, Series 47.3c, RG 51, NA.

to those problems involving considerations of national security resources and military strategy.[86]

DEFENSE AND THE NSC

In April 1949, when Louis Johnson succeeded Forrestal as secretary of defense, the State Department persuaded him to improve the department's attention to politico-military affairs. An Office of Military Affairs under Najeeb Halaby was set up to ensure that policy papers were coordinated with the three military departments and the Joint Chiefs of Staff (JCS). This tended to improve effective relationships between the two departments until Johnson became disaffected with Halaby in early 1950.[87]

Halaby named his liaison man with the JCS to be the Defense Department's representative on the NSC staff. As part of the effort to enhance defense attention to foreign policy Johnson was advised by an assistant to the secretary on foreign military affairs and military assistance. This officer, General James H. Burns, worked closely with the defense consultant to the NSC.[88]

The National Security Act had made the joint chiefs "the principal military advisers of the President, the Secretary of Defense, and the National Security Council." In 1949 the position of chairman of the JCS was established. General Omar Bradley, the first chairman, began to sit with the NSC to carry out the chiefs advisory responsibilities.[89] Still the council and the Defense Department had difficulty integrating the views of the JCS into their deliberations. According to Marshall, part of the JCS's problem was the delay built into their procedures "because of the Navy's

86. Meck, "The Administration of Foreign and Overseas Operations", p. 14.

87. Conversation with William Sheppard, 22 June 1950, NSC, Series 47.3c, RG 51, NA.

88. Meck, "The Administration of Foreign and Overseas Operations", p. 20.

89. "Relations of SECDEF to NSC," draft, 31 October 1960, M1-21, Series 52.6, RG 51, NA.

determination not to be coordinated."[90] Their reluctance to reach a common decision also bothered Souers. He thought the JCS had trouble agreeing upon a strategic plan because of strong differences between the air force and the navy. But, he complained, in the absence of a strategic plan, budgeting became "a matter of splitting up, or adding up, the total dollar pie."[91]

The great difficulty with the organization of the joint chiefs was that they were all equal but they had to speak with one voice. Acheson recalled the situation this created in the NSC:

. . . in the truest possible sense of the word, the JCS do not know what they think until they hear what they say. And that means that the Joint Chiefs only know what they think when a paper is brought up, put through them, and signed by them. Now, at that point you have reached a situation where discussion is almost impossible, because the Joint Chiefs have spoken, and it is like the Pope: the Pope has spoken, and they are infallible, and you can't go back on this thing. You can't discuss this matter with the Pope before he has spoken, because the Pope isn't a person; it is a collegium, and no member of the collegium can speak for anybody at all, so you have infinite discussion with all their representatives, you think you understand what they say, a paper is prepared, some fellow who knows nothing about it but is one of the Joint Chiefs of Staff says something, this is incorporated in their final decision, and you have got a result which is completely contrary to weeks and weeks of work. Now that is brought up in the National Security Council, and the Secretary of Defense presents the view of the Joint Chiefs of Staff. These aren't his views. I sat beside him for four years, and I know he didn't believe a damned word he said, but he reads out a paper, and he seeks to defend it.[92]

The inability to get a firm agreement with the Defense Department, or even to know what its position would be until the time of the council meeting, was a source of great frustration for the State Department.

90. Don K. Price interview with George Marshall, 6 July 1948, Cabinet Secretariat Concept, First Hoover Commission, Herbert C. Hoover Library.

91. Conversation with Souers, 22 June 1950, NSC, Series 47.3c, RG 51, NA.

92. Princeton Conference, 10 October 1953, folder 1. Dean G. Acheson Papers, HSTL.

This probably colored Acheson's views and is evident in William Sheppard's comment that:

No one can commit the JCS. Basic policy issues can be carried all the way to the top and be buttoned up by Rusk of State and Burns of Defense; yet on the morning of the day of NSC consideration of the matter, along can come a JCS paper stating its own independent position apart from agreements reached by Rusk and General [93]

This practice continued throughout the Truman administration and greatly weakened the NSC's ability to serve as a coordinating committee.

Acheson was also critical of the process by which the JCS reached their decisions:

What they tend to do, being greatly overworked, is to wait until a problem is entirely worked out and you've got a paper, and this has to come into the NSC Wednesday afternoon and they will meet on Monday, and without any great knowledge, except what they get in a hasty reading over the weekend, they will come to conclusions on a paper which their secretary takes down, and they don't like this, they want to change this conclusion this way, this one should be cut out, there should be inserted the following, signed Omar Bradley, Chairman, Joint Chiefs of Staff.[94]

Acheson was particularly bothered by the effect this procedure had on the president's ability to make sound decisions. It resulted, he said, "in all sorts of undigested issues coming up to the NSC, being presented in a way which was wholly improper to the President."[95] Of course Acheson was not a totally objective reporter on Defense Department matters, but it seems clear that the unwillingness of the JCS to produce their views at an earlier stage in the process seriously inhibited the healthy cross-fertilization of political-military views that should have been one of the great strengths of the NSC mechanism.

93. Burns Conversation with Sheppard, 21 June 1950, NSC, Series 47.3c, RG 51, NA.

94. Princeton Conference, 2 July 1953, folder 2, Acheson Papers, HSTL.

95. Princeton Conference, 10 October 1953, folder 1, Acheson Papers, HSTL.

Although organizational arrangements respecting NSC matters were improved within both the State and Defense departments during 1949, these changes were not able to counteract the serious deterioration of co-operation between the two departments that flowed from the personal antagonism between secretaries Johnson and Acheson. In many respects the council was simply an interdepartmental committee that was heavily dependent upon personalities for its effectiveness as a co-ordinating mechanism. It had managed to function during its formative first year because of the relationship between Forrestal, Lovett, Kennan, and Souers. But now the key departments were headed by two men who rarely even spoke to each other.[96]

Johnson had been an important political figure in the Democratic party for years and had, as campaign finance chairman, played a key role in Truman's re-election in 1948. Truman, according to Frank Pace, "was personally over impressed with Mr. Johnson." Pace, who served as secretary of the army under Johnson, did not think that he had enough breadth to be an effective secretary of defense; nor did he think that Johnson paid enough attention to the details of his department's operations.[97] Acheson probably held similar views in addition to being his competitor for the ear of the president and a persistent critic of the Defense Department. The ability of the two secretaries to work together was even more seriously compromised when Johnson began to attack Acheson for his position on the Alger Hiss case.[98]

Because of worsening relations with Acheson and because he did not trust many of his own subordinates, Johnson issued orders that all communications between the Defense and the State Department had to have his personal approval and be limited to the Acheson-Webb level. This proved to be unworkable, so State gradually and experimentally ignored this proclamation.[99] Al-

96. Nelson, "Truman and the Evolution of the NSC," p. 371.

97. Frank Pace Oral History, HSTL, p. 80.

98. Averell Harriman in Heller, *The Truman White House*, p. 154.

99. Conversation with Sheppard, 21 June 1950, NSC, Series 47.3c, RG 51, NA.

though there were few repercussions to the violation of this order, its proclamation clearly inhibited staff-level discussions between the departments and tended to increase confrontations at the NSC level. Relations were further strained when the Defense Department began to adopt a more aggressive attitude in the NSC by raising more than half of the policy questions.[100] In a real sense, the problem between the two departments was much more one of attitude and approach than it was of organization. Sheppard summed this up: "Defense is primarily concerned with winning the next war___ State is trying to prevent it."

EVALUATION

As 1949 drew to a close, it was obvious that the effectiveness of the council had declined. The NSC staff continued to perform the same duties but the detailed members of the staff were increasingly regarded as "foreigners" by their parent departments. The consultants continued to function, but they all had heavy departmental responsibilities so they tended to give less and less attention to council matters. These developments caused NSC members to begin to bypass the NSC staff and send policy issues directly to the council. As a result, the council frequently found itself faced with papers that had not been worked through the member organizations. To obtain the necessary staff coordination, the NSC began to refer these matters to ad hoc council committees. Delay and inadequate staff work were the result.[102]

At this low point in the council's development Admiral Souers decided to resign as the executive secretary. In his letter of resignation he said that this was an appropriate time for him to step aside because "the Council is now well integrated into the governmental structure and is actively and wholeheartedly supported by the members and their Departments and

100. Meck, "The Administration of Foreign and Overseas Operations", p. 20.

101. Conversation with Sheppard, 21 June 1950, NSC, Series 47.3c, RG 51, NA.

102. Lay, "Organizational History," p. 18.

Agencies."[103] Although it was true that Souers had created an NSC staff and had succeeded in getting the
State and Defense departments to adapt their internal
organization to this new mechanism, he knew that his
council was not as healthy as his letter implied.

Souers's ostensible reason for leaving at this
particular time was to help ensure the continuation of
the council into the next administration. For the sake
of long-range continuity he thought it important for
the executive secretary to personally bridge administrations. Because he felt that as a lifelong Democrat
he was too closely identified with partisan politics to
be acceptable to a Republican president, Souers arranged with Truman to appoint James Lay as his successor. He considered Lay "the kind of long-enduring
career man the council should have."

Both Truman and Souers probably realized that
Lay did not have either the prestige or the personality needed to rescue the council from its current difficulties. So they agreed that Souers would maintain an
office next to those of the NSC and would spend several days each week in Washington as a presidential
consultant. Neustadt described Souers's new position
as

a sort of informal father-confessor and guardian for Lay, an elder-
statesman kind of personal advisor to the President, and an informal
link between them, confidant to both. . . . Souers served as a sort of
super-secretary of the NSC, not a personal substitution for the secretariat's neutrality, but part of it himself. He did not function as
the presidential alter ego on the NSC.[105]

This new arrangement probably had the effect of further weakening the council.

In retrospect, the years of Souers's stewardship
as the executive secretary were an important but not
particularly successful period for the National Security Council. While it is true that it functioned as a

103. Souers to Truman, 17 November 1949, OF 1290, Truman Papers,
HSTL.

104. Broadcast by Frank Bourgholtzer, WRC, 16 January 1950, Souers
Papers, HSTL.

105. Neustadt statement in Heller, *The Truman White House*, p. 112.

broadening influence and a coordinator in the arena of political-military affairs, the NSC had not developed into the deliberative body that many had hoped it would become. It had survived, but that was not a great accomplishment for an organization that was firmly embedded in the National Security Act. (It would have probably required a dramatic failure for Congress to abolish it after so brief a trial.) Most important, it had not become an important factor in presidential foreign policy decisions—its stated purpose. To fulfill this role would require a better organization, improved personal relationships, and a new presidental attitude—1950 was to be a critical year.

10.
NSRB:
An Agency in Search
of a Mission

The establishment of the National Security Resources Board was a considerable achievement for Ferdinand Eberstadt. It raised the economic mobilization planning function from a minor responsibility of the War Department to the presidential staff.[1] But the idea of a peacetime agency devoted to a continuous assessment of the nation's economic capacity for war in the end proved a failure. Eberstadt's NSRB was abolished during the first months of the Eisenhower administration when its functions were assumed by the Office of Defense Mobilization. However, the idea did not die so quickly; a direct descendant of the NSRB lived on into the Nixon administration as the Office of Emergency Preparedness.

There were several reasons why the NSRB failed but one of them was its inability to clearly establish itself from the very beginning as a civilian organization. Instead, Forrestal, who regarded it as a part of his Defense Department, tried to have the NSRB housed in the Pentagon, financed it from service appropriations, and got Truman to name one of his wartime aides as the board's first chairman. Robert Cuff, who has studied economic mobilization in two wars, does not understand why Eberstadt, who participated in these de-

---

1. Robert Cuff, "Eberstadt and the Search for Integrated Mobilization Planning," p. 42. The NSRB was formally incorporated into the Executive Office of the President in 1949.

cisions and who understood the necessity of distancing mobilization planning from the military, did not try to dissuade Forrestal from these moves.[2]

Soon after the National Security Act was passed, the president appointed Arthur M. Hill chairman of the NSRB. Like Souers, Hill owed his position to the recommendation of Forrestal. He had worked as head of the navy's transportation branch during the war and at one time as an assistant to Secretary of the Navy Forrestal. At the time of his appointment he was the president of the Atlantic Greyhound Bus Company.[3] Hill could be expected to view the NSRB from the perspective of Forrestal, Eberstadt, and Baruch.

Hill took office in late September 1947 amid reports that some of Forrestal's immediate assistants were serving the new chairman unofficially on matters of personnel, office space, and procurement. This raised a "widespread fear among certain people," wrote one of Steelman's assistants, that the board would become an appendage of the military and depend upon the Munitions Board for its staff. The mere fact that the NSRB initially took up residence in the Pentagon was a symbol of military control to the other agencies.[4] Such fears were not entirely groundless.

HILL'S POWER PLAY

Another reason for the failure of the NSRB was its unique organizational structure. The National Security Act said there would be a board consisting of a civilian chairman "and such heads or representatives of the various executive departments and independent agencies as may from time to time be designated by the President." This board was to advise the president about the "coordination of military, industrial and civilian mobilization." In doing this work the NSRB was to "utilize to the maximum extent the facilities and

---

2. Ibid.

3. *New York Times*, 30 August 1947, p. 5.

4. John L. Thurston to Steelman 24 September 1947, NSRB, OF 1295, Truman Papers, HSTL.

resources of the departments and agencies of the Government."[5]

The statute raised many more organizational questions than it answered. For example, was the NSRB staff responsible to the president through the chairman or was it primarily a servant of the board? Again, did the chairman have an independent responsibility to the president or did he merely speak for the board? Truman himself was worried about the composition of the board. He was opposed to the idea of naming most of his cabinet to this body because of the possible effect on the cabinet system and his own authority. It was only with great difficulty that his staff persuaded him to appoint the department heads themselves to the board instead of their subordinates.[6] Since some of Truman's cabinet members had sought to organize unauthorized meetings of the cabinet in the past, his concern was understandable.

There was also a real question about the authority of the chairman and his relationship to the board. Eberstadt wanted the power of decision conferred on the chairman, subject only to the president, as was the case with the OWM/OWMR model he sought to follow. But the National Security Act seemed to vest the authority in the board itself. Eberstadt advised Forrestal to ask Truman to issue a letter conferring all the board's authority on the chairman. If this was not done, Eberstadt warned, the chairman would have to get presidential support for each decision he made. He said this did not make sense since the purpose of the act "was to relieve the president of such burdens"[7]

Before the board held its first meeting Hill clumsily tried to follow this advice by asking Truman to issue an executive order he and his staff had drafted. The paper defined the functions, duties, and powers of the chairman quite apart from the statute. The effort resulted in the first confrontation between Hill and

5. Public Law 253, 80th Cong., chapter 343, p. 5.

6. George Elsey to Clark Clifford, 30 October 1947, Unification Folder No. 8, Elsey Papers, HSTL.

7. Cuff, "Eberstadt and the Search for Integrated Mobilization Planning," p. 47.

the White House staff/Budget Bureau. There were to be several more of these during Chairman Hill's fifteen-month tenure.

To support his request for an executive order, Hill argued that since the chairman was the only board member devoting full time to board activities he needed to be able to act between board meetings without having his authority challenged. As chairman, he believed he should be able to make decisions as to how the board's purposes should be accomplished. He thought that the board members should limit themselves "to policy decisions, familiarity with over-all procedures and approval of the plan." The draft executive order would authorize the chairman to issue instructions to other agencies requiring them to provide information in their possession to the NSRB.[8]

When George Elsey of the White House staff saw the draft order, he suggested Hill be told "no soap" until Truman had appointed the members of the board and they had a chance to consider the issues. Charles Murphy and the Budget Bureau shared Elsey's view so the following reply was drafted for Clark Clifford to pass on to Hill:

1.   The Attorney-General raises grave legal objections. The statute vests functions in the Board; the President could not give them to the Chairman, even if he chose.

2.   The President is always opposed to the "sandbag" approach. To give the Chairman or the Board the authority to direct the work of any or all government agencies is to give one man, or one group more authority than has ever been given before, and gives it in a way that will inevitably result in conflict and confusion, with numerous appeals to the President. No Board, no staff, no one man, can have authority to direct "studies, investigations, and reports" throughout the Federal government.

3.   The way to make rapid progress in your work is to get out an Executive Order similar to the one we now propose, appoint your staff, and start in. The President is concerned at the

8. "The Organization and Position of the NSRB," NSRB Functions, Entry 1, RG 304, NA; Draft executive order, 7 October 1947, Unification Folder No. 6, Elsey Papers, HSTL.

delay in getting underway, several cabinet members have expressed their unalterable opposition to the type of language
you have in paragraph three, and he is firmly convinced that
"you can't do business by force."

4.   I am convinced that Executive Order of the type you proposed
         wouldn't work. It is, I believe, contrary to the intent of the
         Act, and certainly contrary to our understanding at the time
         the Act was drafted as the manner in which the Board would
         function. It was not intended to be a group which could direct
         all the resources of the Government into mobilization plan-
         ning, regardless of the desire or obligation of the several de-
         partments and agencies to fulfill their statutory functions.[9]

Which departments should be represented on the
NSRB was another question Truman had to resolve. It
was clear that the departments of Defense, Commerce,
Labor, Treasury, Agriculture, and Interior all had a
part to play in mobilization planning. But what of the
State Department and some of the independent agencies? Forrestal particularly thought that the State Department should hold membership on the NSRB. Initially
the offer was rejected, but the State Department had
second thoughts and Marshall became a member in
February 1948.[10]

Hill, who felt strongly that the cabinet members
themselves should give their personal attention to
board business, sought to have them specifically named
as members in an executive order. Most of the department heads were agreeable to being the de facto members of the board if the NSRB set up a working group
made up of departmental assistant secretaries to assume most of the work involved. The Budget Bureau advised Truman that such a compromise was "not incon-
sistent with the view that the Board as a whole is a
junior body of both the National Security Council and
the Cabinet."[11] Rather than decide between Hill and his
department heads, Truman had his White House aides

9.   National Military Establishment, Security Resources Board,
Clark Clifford Papers, HSTL.
   10. Press release, 19 February 1948, OF 1290, Truman Papers, HSTL.
   11. Hill to Truman, 21 January 1948, ibid.

arrange a meeting with the prospective board members to work out the conflicts.

Clifford and Elsey got Forrestal to invite Marshall, Secretary of Commerce Averell Harriman, John Snyder, Attorney General Tom Clark, and Lovett to a luncheon meeting in his office. The two White House aides then set down the strategy they would follow at the meeting. First, they would try to make the point that the NSRB must be under civilian control and that the best way to assure this was to name cabinet members to the board. Second, since Truman was concerned lest the NSRB weaken his cabinet, Clifford would insist that cabinet members participate in long-range planning which in turn would insure that their departments were involved. Their third objective would be to instill Elsey's concept of NSRB operations: "Hill would do the work & run the staff; Cabinet members would meet, say, once a month to go over what has been done & to iron out amicably whatever difficulties may have arisen."[12]

At the luncheon meeting Forrestal urged the acceptance of an executive order Hill had drafted, but the others objected that the order would bypass the authority of the department heads. Marshall reminded the group that Budget Director Dawes had raised the same issue when he tried to get the authority to require cabinet officers to report to him on budgetary matters. Although no firm agreement was reached at this meeting, Harriman suggested the compromise that was eventually adopted. He proposed that the president vest all of the authority in the board and that the board in turn, at its first meeting, pass a resolution vesting most of its authority for actual direction of the NSRB staff in the chairman. Progress was also made in convincing the cabinet officers to come to board meetings rather than sending their subordinates.[13]

The next day Hill drafted a new proposed executive order. He attempted to satisfy departmental concerns that the NSRB would order them about by sub-

---

12. Handwritten note, 30 October 1947, Unification Folder No. 8, Elsey Papers, HSTL.

13. Elsey to Clifford, 30 October 1947 ibid.; Millis and Duffield, *Forrestal Diaries*, p. 332.

stituting "shall" for "are directed" in the new draft.[14] But this failed to meet the objections of Harriman and others, so "shall" became "request." At a final meeting of the potential NSRB members, Hill agreed to this wording when the others accepted the text of a resolution vesting the chairman with NSRB's powers. It was understood that this resolution would be passed at the board's first official meeting.[15] According to Hill, "that seemed to make everyone happy and is predicated upon the membership and attendance by the Cabinet members themselves."[16]

In accord with this agreement the executive order (No. 9905) was duly issued on 13 November. The first meeting of the NSRB was held at the White House and, with the president in attendance, the resolution granting authority to the chairman was passed.[17] However, this solution to the dilemma meant that the chairman got his powers from the board instead of from the president. It is little wonder that Hill was confused about his relationship to the president and to the board. Who was he working for?

BELSLEY'S ADVICE

When Hill appeared before a Senate committee in October 1947 he attempted to explain the role of the NSRB. He proclaimed his independence of the Pentagon by stressing that mobilization planning was to be a civilian responsibility and reminding the committee that he headed a civilian agency that reported directly to the president. He defined his task as threefold. One was to take inventory of the status of the nation's resources—industrial, materials, and manpower—and compare these to the projected requirements the nation would have in time of war. A second responsibility was to foresee problems that might

---

14. Hill to Clifford, 31 October 1947, NSRB Functions, Entry 1, RG 304, NA.

15. Millis and Duffield, *Forrestal Diaries*, p. 332.

16. Hill to H. Strueve Hensel, 7 November 1947, NSRB Functions, Entry 1, RG 304, NA.

17. NSRB press release, 10 December 1947, OF 1295, Truman Papers, HSTL.

threaten economic readiness for war and propose solutions to these problems to the president. The third
basic function of the NSRB was to develop detailed
plans for policies, regulations, organizations, etc. that
would be necessary in case of war. Taken together, Hill
said these actions would give the nation continuous
mobilization planning.[18]

Admittedly, the definition of the NSRB's function
and relationships was a difficult problem. It was a
unique organization in the American experience. There
was no clear understanding of peacetime mobilization
planning, and whether it should be a military or
civilian responsibility was still controversial. The
awkwardness of a presidential staff unit that consisted of seven of the nine cabinet officers was a
further complication. Perhaps the greatest disagreement concerned the extent to which the NSRB should
assume operational responsibility in time of emergency.
All of this confusion over the board's mission made it
especially difficult for a new agency to establish its
place in the federal bureaucracy.

Hill received a great deal of advice on how he
should proceed. One of the more remarkable efforts to
help the chairman to define the board's role was made
by G. Lyle Belsley. Belsley, a career civil servant who
had been a member of the staff that had helped the
Brownlow committee to prepare its report, joined the
NSRB as the board's secretary in October. He worked
closely with the organizational experts in the Budget
Bureau in developing his concept of the NSRB mission.[19]

In early February 1948 Belsley sent Hill a
twenty-page memorandum reviewing the factors affecting the work of the NSRB and suggesting the approach
he thought Hill should take in establishing the board's
role. He defined the NSRB's work as "the development of
the overall strategy for appraising the status of the

18. Testimony of Hill before the Senate Special Committee Investigating the National Defense Program, 24 October 1947, Unification
Folder No. 8, Elsey Papers.

19. Harry B. Yoshpe, *A Case Study in Peacetime Mobilization Planning: The National Security Resources Board, 1947–1953* (Washington,
D.C., 1953), pp. 32–33.

Nation's many resources, for recommending such action as will ensure their balance with requirements, and for recommending such plans as will permit their effective and orderly mobilization in time of war or emergency." He saw the concern of the board as wide-ranging since security resources encompassed the total resources of the nation, both physical and human. Its work was complicated because it had to simultaneously plan for peace, the transition to war, and wartime, and these general time periods could not always be clearly marked.[20]

Belsley stressed that the sole function of the NSRB was to advise the president. He tried to educate Hill, in basic terms, on the meaning of the staff function, and particularly on the role of a specialized staff in the president's executive office. He believed the key to the success of such a group was to maintain the president's confidence. This would be more difficult for the NSRB because of its unique organizational structure. He cautioned Hill that the board's

inclusion of a majority of Cabinet members creates delicate problems of which the Chairman and individuals must be aware. It is true that the members sit on the Board because they are department heads, not because they are members of the President's Cabinet. Nonetheless, the Board members cannot readily split their official personalities and disregard, for security resources deliberations, their roles as Cabinet members. . . . The President will not find useful and thus will not support any agency that interferes with his responsibility for security resources policies. The temptation to such interference may be strong because the Board's members, being department heads and reflecting the concerns of broad segments of the Nation's economy, could readily settle major issues by agreement without referral of the issues to the President. This must not happen. . . . The President cannot support any agency that prevents his reliance on the Cabinet individually and collectively for frank counsel. The Board, therefore, must not serve as a caucus of a majority of the Cabinet. The Board's recommendations will stem from its mission and should give emphasis to the national security aspects of the matters on which it gives advice. It must not so fully commit its members as to prevent the Presi-

20. Belsley to Hill, 4 February 1948, NSRB Interdepartmental Staff Group, Entry 1, RG 304, NA.

dent's turning to his Cabinet or to individual Cabinet members for advice on the larger political, economic, financial, and social implications of the Board's recommendations.[21]

It seems clear that Belsley's advice was based on the Budget Bureau's analysis of Truman's latent opposition to a majority of his cabinet meeting under the chairmanship of a person other than himself. The NSRB was the first instance in which a portion of the cabinet had been given a major statutory responsibility on a permanent basis.

The memorandum then analyzed the sources of the board's strength. These pages could well serve as a primer for any part of the EOP. Belsley explained that the NSRB's real and apparent strength were quite different. Most crucial was the board's ability to win and keep the president's confidence.

The size of the Board's staff, its volume of reports, the frequency of recommendations to the President, the elaborateness of its structure of advisory or interdepartmental committees, are all meaningless in terms of real influence unless the Board has the support and respect of the only man whose decisions will stick.

Belsley advised Hill that the president's confidence depended upon the adequacy of the staff work provided by the NSRB and the soundness of its judgment. He would also be influenced by the clearness with which it recognized its role as a helper and adviser to the president. The board must therefore resist any temptation to be an independent advocate of policies, to sulk when its recommendations are not accepted, or to become an operating agency that attempts to build up power in its own right. It must preserve the president's freedom of decision.[22]

The president's attitude toward the NSRB would, he cautioned, be affected by the degree of confidence exhibited toward it by the rest of the executive office and the executive departments. The other parts of the EOP were influential because they had easy access to

---

21. Ibid.
22. Ibid.

the president and they were obligated to protect him from inadequate advice. It would be necessary for the board to win their respect if it wished to retain the president's respect. Belsley predicted that the board's ability to work with the executive departments would also condition its success. Since the NSRB was merely the president's instrument for bringing to focus the research and thinking of the departments on security resources policies, it was dependent on them for much of the basic research. As a staff unit, the NSRB was obligated to reflect the views of all the agencies. Belsley warned that

if nearly every Board recommendation to the President results in in-dependent protests by other agencies directly to the President, he will become convinced that the Board is not canvassing other agen-cies' views adequately and is failing to do a good staff job of in-forming the President of the areas of agreement and disagreement.[23]

Hill would have been well advised to have fol-lowed the suggestions of this Washington-wise bu-reaucrat, but the chairman never seemed to understand the role of a presidential staff person. With only a hazy idea as to how to organize his staff and get un-derway, he was sure that he did not want to accept as narrow an interpretation of his agency's role as Belsley advocated. He and most of his staff could not resist the temptation to develop an operational compo-nent in the NSRB. They construed their mission to in-clude not only the preparation of mobilization plans but the development of a skeleton organization for im-plementing the plans in times of emergency.

STAFF VERSUS OPERATIONS

In February and March 1948 a Communist takeover in Czechoslovakia and a bellicose Truman speech to Congress created a war-scare climate in Washington. These events occurred at a crucial time in the devel-opment of the NSRB while Hill was searching for a di-rection to lead his agency. With an appropriation of

23. Ibid.

three million dollars and a rapidly burgeoning staff
that was to increase from 64 in January to 207 in June,
Hill was under intense pressure to set a course. Yet
there was still sharp disagreement within the NSRB
staff as to what the mission and organizational
structure of the agency should be.[24]

The president's speech brought the period of debate about the board's mission to an end. Hill decided
to shift from long-range planning to an immediate mobilization effort.[25] Ralph Watkins, who had joined the
NSRB in January as head of the program division, urged
Hill to "draft" Eberstadt to come to Washington to prepare an organization plan "for the mobilization emergency period and for any war emergency that may develop."[26] It was hoped that an analysis of the various
factors governing organization for war mobilization
would yield a body of doctrine that could guide the
development of the NSRB.[27] On 29 March the board's
patron, Bernard Baruch, appeared before the Senate
Armed Services Committee calling for America to "make
up its mind where it stands." Among the more radical
measures he advocated was a "work or fight" wartime
draft. This stance further impelled the NSRB toward an
emergency mobilization position.[28]

Eberstadt decided that the war scare might provide an opportunity to fashion a role for the NSRB in
line with his original concept. That spring he arranged
to devote all of his energies to that cause. He took up
residence at the Shoreham Hotel and began to make the
rounds.[29] His official excuse for this intervention was

24. Overall Problems and Issues of the NSRB, 29 November 1948, M1-
2, Series 39.32, OMB; Reappraisal for Steelman, 21 December 1948, Entry 4, RG 304, NA.

25. Yoshpe, *Case Study*, p. 53.

26. Watkins to Hill, 24 March 1948, Eberstadt Folder, Entry 4, RG
304, NA.

27. Organization for War Mobilization, 24 March 1948, M1-2, Series
39.32, OMB.

28. Matthew Robinson to Hill, 9 April 1948, Program Division, Entry
1, RG 304, NA.

29. Cuff, "Eberstadt and the Search for Integrated Mobilization
Planning," p. 48.

a letter from Hill asking for assistance with the following projects:

1. Based on consideration of the National Security Act of 1947, and its legislative history and other relevant data and experience, prepare recommendations concerning the authority and functions of the [NSRB] through its evolution and development as the Nation may experience (a) the threat of an emergency, (b) a mobilization emergency, and (c) war.

2. The organizational pattern of the necessary civilian mobilization agencies of the Government, including their respective functions and authorities, and the inter-relations of these various agencies, as the Nation may pass through the phases referred to above.

3. The basic and essential legislation, executive orders, rules, regulations, and instructions necessary to provide the [NSRB] and related organizations with authority to perform the responsibilities contemplated in Paragraphs 1 and 2.

4. The organizational pattern of the [NSRB] best suited to its present duties and to meeting the need for its evolution and development to adapt itself to the changing circumstances.[30]

It is clear from these instructions that Hill was determined to base his agency's mission on "legislative history and other relevant data" instead of the statute. Many believed he would fail. Forrestal called former secretary of state James F. Byrnes to explain Hill's plan and ask his advice. Byrnes warned Forrestal to stay aloof because Baruch's statement to the Senate committee had made a "bad impression." He told the defense secretary that "there isn't any use for you to go 'tink' for something that you know in advance is going to be turned down . . . it will hurt your other things."[31]

Had Hill been more astute he would have realized Truman was determined to adhere to the Budget Bureau's interpretation of his agency's mission. When the president had ordered Hill to move the NSRB offices from the Pentagon to the Executive Office Building he

30. Hill to Eberstadt, 19 April 1948, Eberstadt Folder, Entry 1, RG 304, NA.

31. Exerpts from telephone conversation, 28 April 1948, ibid.

had included with the order a brief lecture (written by the Budget Bureau) on the need for executive office cooperation and the importance of completed staff work. Like Belsley's memo, Hill ignored these hints.[32]

TRUMAN REBUFFS EBERSTADT

When Eberstadt began working full time at the NSRB he seemed to galvanize the organization into making some decisions. He drafted a document (R-7) that listed the steps the president should take to minimize the dislocation, inequities, and inflationary effects the international crisis was imposing on an already heavily occupied economy. The steps were:

1. Ask Congress for standby authority to allocate resources.
2. Try to achieve voluntary cooperation before imposing these controls.
3. Ask Congress for standby authority to control prices, wages, profits and rents, and impose rationing.
4. Set up a central agency to coordinate mobilization efforts.
5. Make the NSRB that central agency because of "the legislative history of the National Security Act, past experience, and the preponderance of opinion of leading authorities in this field."
6. Call for legislation to enable businesses "to cooperate with the Government and with each other."
7. Request legislation to facilitate getting people to run the program.
8. Reestablish the Reconstruction Finance Corporation.[33]

Both Webb and CEA chairman Nourse expressed reservations about some of the proposals and the Commerce Department raised objection to most of them. But

---

32. Truman to Hill, 27 March 1948, ibid.

33. Recommendation to the President on Steps and Measures Essential to the Fulfillment of the National Security Program, 30 April 1948, M1-21/45.1, Series 39.32, RG 51, NA.

Hill, with some difficulty, got the board to approve the document.[34] Despite this opposition and without any knowledge of Truman's attitude, Hill sent the document to the president on 30 April. Assuming approval, Hill asked that the document be made public to help the board recruit key personnel.[35]

But Truman told Hill to keep the document secret and to take no action based on the assumption that it would be approved. Meanwhile the White House sent the document to the Budget Bureau for analysis.[36] The bureau warned that "in the absence of specific and unmistakably clear decision by the President, the NSRB under its current leadership, is almost sure to proceed to take steps consistent with the recommendation, on the assumption that absence of disapproval implied approval."[37] While waiting for the president's response, the board indeed was making preparations to become the central force in a mobilization effort.

After the NSRB sent its R-7 document to Truman, Eberstadt lobbied hard at the Budget Bureau, the economic council, and the Commerce Department to sell his program. Webb told him that mobilization planning must not be permitted to attenuate the presidential power or the prerogatives of the departments. Eberstadt confided to his diary that "Webb continued rather confused and is somewhat affected by a constitutional reservation toward NSRB." Discouraged by the reactions, Eberstadt angrily decided that:

As a result of conditions down here I see the same type of thing developing as occurred in 1940. Just as Roosevelt concealed the War Resources Board report, Truman has concealed the report which the National Security Resources Board made to him and their recommendations. They are dilly-dallying and fussing with expedients and failing to face the issues squarely. All this in spite of the fact that

---

34. Yoshpe, "Planning for Defense: A History of the Role and the Accomplishments of the National Security Resources Board." Draft, NSRB General Administration Folder, Series 39.28, RG 51, NA, pp. 43-44.

35. Hill to Truman, 30 April 1948, President, Entry 1, RG 304, NA.

36. Yoshpe, "Planning for Defense," p. 44.

37. Draft memo for the President, M1-21/45.1, Series 39.32, RG 51, NA.

billions have been allocated for the European Recovery Program, billions for atomic energy, more billions for military. . . . It seems once more we are moving in the atmosphere of lipstick and soda preparations.[38]

Webb was put in a difficult position when Truman asked for advice on the organizational and administrative implications of R-7. He was determined to restrict the NSRB to an advisory role, yet he had to try to maintain cordial relations with the NSRB and attempt to strengthen the EOP. He approached the problem by having his staff hold several conversations with Hill and Eberstadt in which they sought both an amplification and a moderation of the recommendations in R-7. The bureau then made a detailed analysis of the organizational and administrative aspects of the proposal and obtained the approval of Hill and Eberstadt to the resulting "interpretation" of the recommendations. They were rephrased by the bureau to: (1) create a control source for the coordination and integration of policies; (2) designate the NSRB as the control source; and (3) create skeleton mobilization organizations.[39]

The first of these points meant that an agency should be designated to maintain a running balance of civilian and national security requirements for critical items in short supply and to recommend measures to correct or alleviate the imbalance. The bureau believed that this function was currently being performed by several agencies. The Commerce Department objected to assigning the function to the NSRB because the board could then give orders to the departments.[40]

In the end Webb advised the president to disapprove much of what the NSRB requested. The bureau drafted a letter for the Truman to send to Hill if he approved of Webb's recommendations. Truman totally accepted the bureau view and immediately dispatched the letter to Hill. In unmistakable terms it stated:

---

38. Cuff, "Eberstadt and the Search for Integrated Mobilization Planning," p. 49.

39. Attachment A, Mobilization Folder (1), James E. Webb Papers, HSTL.

40. Ibid.; Webb to Truman, 24 May 1948, M1-2, Series 39.32, RG 51, NA.

I do not intend to vest in the National Security Resources Board any responsibilities for coordination of the national security programs of the Government which require the exercise of directive authority over any department and agency, or which imply a final power of decision resting with the Board. It is my view that the proper role of the Board is the exercise of its statutory duty to advise the President. Therefore, to the extent that recommendations Nos. 4 and 5 of NSRB-R-7 imply coordinating authority, they are not approved.

The letter emphasized that the presidential policy was not one of mobilization for war but of maintaining a firm foundation of preparedness on which mobilization could be based if needed.[41]

The bureau then tried to help Hill sort out his mission by listing some tasks the president wanted the board to undertake. The first of these should be the preparation of long-range programs necessary to maintain an adequate state of preparedness. In doing this job, the NSRB should use the existing agencies as much as possible. The board "must consider itself a Presidential advisory agency and conform its actions and recommendations to producing information and advice upon which Presidential action may be taken." Hill was encouraged to work with the other units of the EOP and particularly to join with the director of the Budget Bureau in studies of plans for organizing the government in case of war. In regard to procedures, the bureau, through the president's letter, advised Hill that on short-range problems "it may frequently be advantageous to present a staff view instead of obtaining formal Board action on all points."[42]

A few days later Webb wrote to Forrestal to explain Truman's action and the bureau's part in it. He sent him a copy of the analysis the bureau had prepared for the president and tried to ameliorate the strong words in the letter to Hill by adding:

The only denial implicit in the President's letter and from my talks with him is the denial of directive authority. As I indicated earlier,

---

41. Truman to Hill, 24 May 1948, Mobilization folder (1), Webb Papers, HSTL.
42. Ibid.

our contacts with the Board Chairman and his advisers indicated that they do not consider this an important point. In considering the President's letter a distinction must be drawn between a "coordinating function" and a "Coordinating Authority," for that is a point of major concern to the President.

Forrestal had told Webb that he wanted the NSRB to direct him in respect to the placing of contracts. The budget director said that the president's position was that, even if the president wanted to do so, "there is no way by which the President could empower the NSRB to direct you in the full authoritative sense of that word."[43]

This explanation was less than candid because later, during the Korean War, Truman did delegate to Charles E. Wilson, then the director of the Office of Defense Mobilization, the authority to direct the executive departments in mobilization matters. In summary then, the president's (and the bureau's) position at this time was that the NSRB should focus upon developing basic policy and programs for the president while encouraging the departments to concentrate on operational detail.

To consider the other recommendations in R–7 the White House staff set up an *ad hoc* committee chaired by Robert Turner who was one of Steelman's assistants. Based on this group's recommendations, Truman refused to approve a request that Congress enact standby controls (items 1 and 3). He also vetoed the proposal that Congress be asked to waive the antitrust laws in time of war. The only two recommendations in R–7 that got even partial presidential support were proposals that Congress reestablish the RFC and strengthen the stockpile program.[44]

According to press reports, Truman objected to the NSRB recommendations on two grounds. He felt that they were too belligerent in tone and imbued with a crisis atmosphere which he was trying to discourage. He also dissented from the Eberstadt philosophy which

43. Webb to Forrestal, 1 June 1948, E2–58.47.2, Series 39.32, RG 51, NA.

44. Steelman to Hill, 3 June 1948, White House, Entry 1, RG 304, NA.

he thought assigned too much mobilization authority to businessmen and the military and not enough to the regular government departments.[45] So Truman passed the word that he did not want to hear any more about the imposition of controls and administrative authority for the NSRB. The president reportedly told his friends that he had a better plan, "one that makes him umpire, lets board enforce his decisions".[46] There is no doubt that R-7 was perceived by many of the agencies as a power grab on the part of the NSRB and further isolated its staff from the bureaucracy.[47]

While the White House and Budget Bureau were analyzing R-7, Eberstadt continued his work with the board's plans and programs section. By late May his work at the NSRB began to taper off because he had been named to head the Task Force on National Security Organization for the Hoover Commission.[48] Before he left, with help from Walter Millis and E. F. Willett, he finished a report and presented it to Hill on 4 June. In it he reviewed the historical background of mobilization from World War I to the creation of the NSRB, the board's statutory functions, and the role he thought it ought to play in the current situation and in time of war. He concluded by noting that during his stay with the NSRB

one perceives a certain remoteness—remoteness from the President, from executive departments and agencies, from Congress, from the civilian and industrial world, from labor. A resulting lack of understanding in many places has handicapped the Board's operations. It extends even to high levels of the government, where a tendency has at times appeared to regard the Board as a rival of established powers and prerogatives. . . . The National Security Resources Board . . . does not and should not compete with or supplant the functions of any existing department or agency nor interfere within their jurisdictions. Equally, it can and should perform essential functions for which no other provision exists within the governmental structure. . . . The best way . . . in which to bring the Board to its full potential

---

45. Doris Fleeson in the *Washington Star*, 8 September 1948.
46. "In the Offing," *Washington Daily News*, 27 November 1948.
47. Russell Porter in *The New York Times*, 7 July 1948.
48. Eberstadt to Ewalt T. Grether, 25 May 1948, Entry 1, RG 304, NA.

value . . . is to give it real and vital current responsibility in the current context of events. To waste the NSRB now would be a grim anomaly.

Eberstadt probably hoped that the report would cause the president to reconsider his decisions on R-7 for he ended by quoting from Truman's March speech to Congress: "There are times in world history when it is far wiser to act than to hesitate. There is some risk involved in action——there always is. But there is far more risk in failure to act."[49]

* * *

One of the legacies of Eberstadt's work with the NSRB was a new internal organization which was put in place in mid May. It was based on the concept that each of the offices of the staff should serve as the nucleus for an operating office under mobilization conditions.[50] There were four basic units in the new Mobilization Planning Staff that were to deal respectively with production, transportation, human resources, and economic management. Under conditions of mobilization, these would provide the cadre for offices of war production, war transportation, war manpower, and economic stabilization.[51] Even though Eberstadt's concept of the NSRB was rejected by Truman, this organizational structure remained in place until August 1949 and hampered it conversion to a strictly advisory staff for the president. As a result of misguided enthusiasm, the NSRB, during a period of rapid staff expansion, recruited personnel whose expertise was in operations instead of planning. These individuals were poorly equipped to carry on the work for which the NSRB was intended.

From his position as the chairman of the Hoover Commission task force on national security Eberstadt continued his efforts to strengthen the NSRB. One of

49. Report to Arthur Hill, 4 June 1948, M1-21/45.1, Series 39.32, RG 51, NA.

50. Reappraisal for Steelman, 21 December 1948, Entry 4, RG 304, NA.

51. Responsibilities of the NSRB, 22 October 1948, ibid.

his first actions was to invite Hill to testify before the group. In early June Hill, in his remarks, came close to insubordination when he stated that "the NSRB had not been supported adequately by either the White House or the Budget Bureau and that the proper functioning of the NSRB has been hindered thereby." He claimed there was a need to coordinate the mobilization program but "the President is against giving the Board the necessary powers." While admitting that "other governmental circles" did not support his concept of the NSRB, Hill saw the most important need was to "sell the President on the role of the NSRB."[52]

Hill's comments reflected the view of many of the key members of the NSRB staff who had participated in Eberstadt's work and committed themselves to his ideas. Now they were confused and embittered by Truman's rejection of their proposals and slow to accept his decisions. Baruch added to the discontent when he criticized the president's decision during an address he delivered in late June at the Industrial War College. He reviewed the tortured history of mobilization planning that culminated in the creation of the NSRB and then complained that "when it attempted to act, it was prevented from doing so. . . . What is lacking is a will to decision. . . ." Baruch insisted that the "people are entitled to a full report of the status of these plans." The White House staff was upset when it learned that these remarks had been distributed throughout the military establishment.[53]

Eberstadt continued to press his case. At an interdepartmental meeting he warned that the Munitions Board would take over the NSRB functions if the resources board failed to take a more active part in coordinating mobilization. "He said that this would happen not because of military intentions or wishes to take over but because the Munitions Board is strong and old and would pick up the default of the new and weak." Eberstadt moderated his position somewhat when he drew a distinction between an "active function" for

52. Meeting of the National Security Organization Committee of the Hoover Commission, 10 June 1948, Dean G. Acheson Papers, HSTL.

53. Charles Schwarz to Steelman, 27 June 1948, Entry 1, RG 304, NA.

the NSRB and an "operating function." He said he no longer favored the latter and tried to reassure the departments that the NSRB was not a "dangerous staff" but was the "Safe Cabinet."[54] Despite these efforts, Eberstadt was unable to get the president to reconsider his decision.

HILL RESIGNS

Baruch told Hill that if *he* had been turned down by the president in that way "he would have had my resignation with a good strong letter."[55] But Hill did not resign, at least not yet. He stayed for another six months and tried to salvage what he could from the situation. He had a lot of work to do if he was to bring the organization into line with Truman's concept of the board's proper role. It would require a major reorientation of the staffing pattern, the work program, and relationships with other agencies. But old habits were hard to break. Hill seemed to conscientiously try to redirect his agency, but he lacked conviction and a clear understanding of how to proceed.

The staff continued to grow in size through the recruitment of career government employees, but it remained top heavy in key positions with business executives who had joined the agency with the expectation that they would be directing the mobilization effort. These men inevitably continued to be preoccupied with operational near-term matters rather than planning. However, a positive step was taken in July when the staff moved from the Pentagon to the Executive Office Building.[56]

Hill was continuously in conflict with many of the board members over the nature and extent of their involvement in directing the work of the NSRB and the role of their departments in the planning process. Most of the eleven formal meetings of the board held during his tenure were probably unnecessary. They

54. J. Weldon Jones to Division Chiefs, 26 July 1948, NSRB, Series 39.9, RG 51, NA.

55. Baruch to Hill 31 August 1948, Baruch folder, Entry 1, RG 304, NA.

56. Yoshpe, "Planning for Defense," pp. 47–48.

dealt too much with substantive details for which the members had not been adequately prepared. Many times these items were put on the agenda simply to give the impression that the NSRB was a going concern.[57] The Commerce Department, under both Harriman and Charles Sawyer, consistently insisted on the board's right to consider the details of the staff's operations. Sawyer berated Hill for the haphazard way in which he determined which matters should come before the board and complained that "as a member of the NSRB I should like to know what is going on and I should like to know before and not after the event, what the Board's program is."[58]

To a degree, this friction was the inevitable result of the impracticability of having a cabinet committee serve as the policy group for a presidential staff unit. The paradox they faced was described by Richard Neustadt while he was a Budget Bureau analyst:

NSRB's functions as a body advisory to the President are vested by statute in its agency members collectively. This means that a recommendation to the President from the Board can be expected to represent the views of the membership meeting as the Board. But it does not automatically follow that the views of the Board are necessarily the same as those of its individual members in their capacities as heads of single departments. The members must wear two hats, psychologically as well as legally, if the Board is to have any identity and cohesion whatever. Further, whether as a group of department heads or as a group of powerful members of the Administration's top leadership, the Board must operate in reaching decisions like any other board, with some degree of "horse-trading," "log rolling," "tours de force," and "going along for the ride." The results will not reflect all of the delicate shadings of views and degrees of interest which exist around the Board table, and the vote of an individual member may easily fail to reflect the precise point of view which he would hold with his other—departmental—hat on.[59]

---

57. Ibid. p. 20.

58. Sawyer to Hill, 26 July 1948, Department of Commerce, Entry 1, RG 304, NA.

59. Neustadt to Elmer Staats, 27 October 1948, Chronological File, Richard E. Neustadt Papers, HSTL.

Hill finally gave up trying to work with the board after its meeting in September 1948. It was not to meet again until the spring of 1950, by which time Congress had redefined its role and established it as an advisory body to the chairman. In its stead, Hill established an Interdepartmental Staff Group made up of representatives designated by each board member. It first met in June 1948 and began serving as the principal point of contact between the NSRB staff and the departments. After September it in effect replaced the board as a coordinating mechanism.[60]

Throughout the summer and fall of 1948 Eberstadt's task force held hearings that indirectly pressured the administration to assign the NSRB an "active" role. Robert Turner of the White House staff testified that good relations had not developed between the president and the NSRB because

any presidential adviser or advisory agency achieves a position of influence and responsibility and confidence of the President, only after it has demonstrated by actual performance its capacity for such a position. The NSRB is a relatively new agency, and to date does not seem to have demonstrated such capacity.

He also believed that the relationship had been strained because the NSRB had been perceived as "largely a mouthpiece for the Secretary of Defense."[61]

There is some evidence that at last the board's staff began to realize that their success would ultimately be based on their performance rather than legislative authority or executive orders. Kenneth Johnson, the NSRB general counsel, advised Hill that the power the NSRB needed to do its job "will not generate by reason of detailed legislative authority so much a it will from the sheer force of its cumulative influence—an intangible force that will inevitably result from doing its job wisely and well."[62]

As 1948 drew to a close, little progress was made in resolving or defining the NSRB mission. At that

60. NSRB Document #82, M1-2, Series 39.32, OMB.

61. Personnel File, 25 August 1948, Robert C. Turner Papers, HSTL.

62. Johnson to Hill, 16 September 1948, Hoover Commission, Entry 1, RG 304, NA.

point the Budget Bureau summarized the basic questions about the board's character as:

1. Should the NSRB attempt to develop as a nuclear
   staff for war agencies?
2. To what extent should NSRB engage in current
   operations?
3. What is the mobilization planning role of the departments?
4. What is the role of the chairman?

On these points the bureau found no agreement among
the board or its staff and it doubted whether the
president had ever been given an opportunity to express his opinion on these questions.[63]

After Truman was unexpectedly reelected in
November and the administration began to gear up for
another four years, the blame for the NSRB's problem
was increasingly directed at Hill. Elsey charged that
he had not

acted as a presidential staff man, nor has he allowed the Board to act
in the fashion contemplated by the Security Act—that is, advisory to
the President. Hill had behaved as though he were the head of an independent agency, with only the slightest sense of responsibility to
the President. The fault lies with both the Act and the individual.[64]

This White House attitude was probably a factor
in Hill's offer to resign by mid December. Truman
promptly accepted his decision. Hill's final act as
chairman was a full-dress oral presentation to the
president on the NSRB's recent activities. It contributed little to a clarification of the agency's direction.[65]

---

63. "Overall Problems and Issues of the NSRB," draft, 29 November
1948, M1-2, Series 39.32, OMB.

64. Elsey to Clark Clifford, 17 November 1948, Unification Folder
No. 11, Elsey Papers, HSTL.

65. Hill to Truman, 29 November 1948, OF 1295, Truman Papers, HSTL;
Agenda for Presentation to the President, 10 December 1948, Entry 1,
RG 304, NA.

STEELMAN TAKES OVER

If Truman knew what he wanted the NSRB to do, the naming of a new chairman would be his chance to point the agency in that direction. But the president did not have a clear concept of the board's role so the appointment of a successor to Hill was just another chore. He explored with Hill the possibility of simply naming one of the cabinet members currently on the board as its chairman. Hill was shocked and considered the idea impolitic, unwise, and illegal. He did not believe that a person could detach himself enough from his department's interests to have the confidence of the other board members, nor did he think one person would have the time to do both jobs. He also believed such an appointment would be a violation of both the spirit and the letter of the National Security Act. In discussing the qualifications of his successor, Hill emphasized that the individual should have the closest personal relationship with the president and "that relationship should be well known, especially to the members of the Board."[66] By implication Hill attributed part of his own failure to the president's lack of confidence in him.

But Truman apparently believed that the chairmanship of the NSRB was no more than a part-time job. He finally decided to give his aide, John Steelman, another hat when he named him acting chairman of the board. He promised to appoint a regular chairman after the NSRB and its staff had been fitted "into the broader framework of total Presidential responsibilities."[67] That is, he would rely on Steelman to reorient the board before entrusting it to another political appointee. Steelman was the ideal man to direct the rebuilding of the NSRB because he saw Truman daily, knew his wishes, and had his support.

Much of the press interpreted the Steelman appointment as a presidential slap at the NSRB, but it was probably not so intended. On 7 February 1949 Truman nominated his old Senate friend Mon C. Walgren

---

66. Hill to Truman, 7 December 1948, OF 1295, Truman Papers, HSTL.
67. Press release, 10 December 1948, ibid.

to be chairman of the NSRB. But Walgren did not make a good impression in his confirmation hearings and the Republican senator from Walgren's home state of Washington viewed the nomination as a violation of senatorial courtesy. When it became clear Walgren could not overcome these obstacles, Truman reluctantly withdrew his name. But he was so angry that he did not nominate a new candidate for over a year. As a result, Steelman remained as part-time "acting chairman" for seventeen months.[68]

During this period, Steelman devoted most of his time to his regular job as the assistant to the president but usually spent several hours a day in his NSRB office. While he was acting chairman, the board itself lapsed into a state of suspended animation and did not meet as a group. He scheduled two board meetings but they were cancelled before they were held. Since Steelman saw the board members frequently in his other capacity, he was able to transact required business on an individual basis or through the inter-departmental staff group.[69] This method reflected a growing conviction in the White House that having a cabinet committee run a presidential staff was a flawed concept. But it did not seem appropriate to ask that the statute be amended until a permanent chairman was installed.

THE STOWE REORGANIZATION

The departure of Hill and the appointment of Steelman led to the resignation of several of the NSRB's key people. Belsley transferred to the Federal Security Agency in February. Vice-chairman Reginald Gilmor left a few days later. In March Chief Counsel Kenneth Johnson joined the faculty of Columbia University. The general unhappiness among the staff began to be reflected in the press. Jack Anderson, who was then a legman for Drew Pearson, reported that five employees had called Pearson to say the board was a year behind in its work. The informants gave Anderson a list of

68. Hobbs, *Behind the President*, pp. 164–165.

69. H. Dewayne Kraeger to Symington, 1 May 1950, Entry 4, RG 304, NA.

resignations they said were due to the chairmanship situation.[70]

During the Steelman period, David Stowe, a White House aide who normally reported to Steelman, was the day-to-day manager of the NSRB. Stowe, who had worked for several years at the Budget Bureau before moving to the White House, had a broad background in handling manpower and industrial problems.[71] Steelman named Stowe to head a task force to study the NSRB and recommend changes in its program, objectives, and organization.[72] Stowe began by conducting a series of interviews with members of the NSRB staff and discovered many instances of mismanagement. An office chief reported that when he started work he "wasn't given any instruction as to what the job was, though down in the corner of the organization chart I read that my office might become a WPB in time of war. So I started to develop my own ideas. Ten days later I went to Mr. Hill to find out the overall plan. The answer was, 'There is no plan.'" Another office chief reported "that each office of the NSRB has its own philosophy as the mission of the agency."[73]

Stowe decided that the fundamental problem at the NSRB was that there was no definition of the mission and no understanding of how a staff agency to the president should operate. He found a lack of leadership and direction and a top-heavy management staff. There was, he reported,

a very interesting conglomeration of self-contained units. In planning any operation one of the most important things is the interrelationship of the staff operation. No staff member should be allowed to go off in a vacuum and come out with his own pet idea. But there were eight of those compartments, each operating on its own particular assumptions. In fact if we had gone on, we might have had eight mobilization plans. . . . There was duplication; there was conflict; there was confusion. Even the staff pattern was obscure because someone

70. Charles Schwarz to Steelman, 10 May 1949, Information Division, Entry 1, ibid.

71. Heller, *The Truman White House*, p. 111.

72. Steelman to Gilmor, 10 January 1949, NSRB Functions, Entry 1, RG 304, NA.

73. Reappraisal for Steelman, 21 December 1948, Entry 7, ibid.

had decided that this should be a stand-by operating nucleus organization. In an emergency, it was believed that the operators would
have to rush in and select their people to run the war. They had gone
out and gotten chaps who would be bang-up to run WPB functions in
wartime. They were already operators. They had come out of industry.
They knew how to turn the crank and make things go. But, they did not
like sitting down with paper and pencil, planning, and working things
out. They wanted to operate.[74]

Stowe's task force produced two reports. The
first, which provided a quick picture of the NSRB at
that stage of its development, was intended to provide
Steelman with a basis for making immediate budget decisions.[75] The more significant report, designated NSRB
Document 116, completely redefined the agency's mission, operational techniques, and relationships along
lines the Budget Bureau had been advocating for the
past year.[76]

The second report proposed two major jobs for
the NSRB. The first, which they called mobilization
planning, entailed the identification of the problems
the country would face in moving from a peacetime to a
wartime situation and the development of solutions to
those problems. The other task was to recommend policies and programs that would keep the country in a
"state of readiness" for war. This would include matters such as the stockpiling of strategic and critical
materials and the training of skilled manpower.[77]The
group devoted special attention to the relationships it
thought the NSRB ought to have with the other element
of the EOP. They stressed that:

The President's staff has a special responsibility to provide him with
complete and well-rounded staff advice. The submission of findings
and recommendations to the President without coordination with fellow staff agencies in the Executive Office would produce conflicting
and piece-meal advice, and impose upon the President the burden of

---

74. "The Role of the National Security Resources Board in National
Security," 13 January 1950, David H. Stowe Papers, HSTL.

75. Chairman's Staff Meeting, 17 January 1949, Entry 1, RG 304, NA.

76. NSRB Document #116, Office of the Assistant to the President
Files, Truman Papers.

77. Ibid.

coordinating those who were supposed to be helping him coordinate the Executive Branch. Joint staff work does not imply agreement, but it does imply joint consideration of matters of common concern, with a common presentation of issues and considerations and alternative answers.[78]

Steelman and Truman accepted this report as the basic charter for a redirected NSRB. Since they were trying to de-emphasize the decision-making role of the board in NSRB matters, they initially intended to present it to the board as a presidential decision. But then it became apparent that all of the members, with the possible exception of the defense secretary, were willing to officially adopt the document as board policy.[79] Realizing the advantage of having the board's official blessing and aware that they might resent a high-handed diktat, Steelman asked for and got their formal concurrence by mail ballot.[80]

The adoption of this mission and work program made the existing Eberstadt-designed NSRB internal organization inappropriate, so the Stowe group devised a new organizational scheme that was more compatible with the new direction. It was officially put in place in early September 1949.[81] The reorganization was accompanied by a realignment of personnel and, to a large extent, a restaffing of the agency.[82]

The administration's decision to revamp the NSRB was undoubtedly influenced by press reports that the agency did little or no work and the critical recommendations of the Hoover Commission task force headed by Eberstadt. That task force reported in November 1948. It noted that part of the agency's difficulties stemmed from its inability "to develop a sufficiently clear grasp of its own duties and potentialities," but the main problem was the president's failure to

78. Ibid.

79. H. Dewayne Kraeger to Steelman, 29 July 1949, NSRB Functions, Entry 1, RG 304, NA.

80. Steelman to NSRB Members, 8 August 1949, Steelman Chronological File, ibid.

81. NSRB General Order #26, NSRB Functions, ibid.

82. Stowe lecture to the Industrial War College, 13 January 1950, Stowe Papers, HSTL.

strongly support or adequately utilize the board. It recommended that the jurisdiction, program, and functions of the NSRB and its relationships with the other departments be promptly defined.[83] That is what NSRB Document 116 attempted to do, although not in a way Eberstadt favored.

CHAIRMAN SYMINGTON

After a year as acting chairman of the NSRB, Steelman had developed some strong views about the inappropriateness of the board's statutory charter. He believed that presidential staff assistance should be provided by people selected by the president and responsible to him. The NSRB violated that principle since it was headed by an interagency board instead of a presidential appointee. This, Steelman wrote, endorsed the idea of government by cabinet committee rather than by the president. He then described several problems that resulted from this arrangement:

1. The board members tended to represent the desires and interests of their departments instead of the overall views of a presidential staff. For example, "the minute wartime organization is mentioned, each department starts thinking in terms of what part of the wartime activities it should have."

2. The interagency board made it difficult to achieve coordination with the rest of the executive office because the problems encountered by the board cut across the interests of the Budget Bureau and the economic council.

3. The interagency board was a cumbersome device because each department had its own prejudices and predilections, yet if he failed to check all details with each member, it was "difficult to avoid assertions of prerogatives and jurisdictions by the departments."

---

83. Hoover Commission, *Task Force Report on National Security Organization*, Appendix G, pp. 16, 91.

4.   "Even though the Board is supposedly assisting the President, it is extremely difficult to keep the Board functioning on a confidential and informal basis. Any lineup of the Board for or against action in effect holds forth the possibility of the Cabinet lining up against the President."[84]

Steelman presented three possible remedies for the president to consider. His ideal solution was to abolish the board and replace it with a staff director who would operate in much the same manner as the director of the budget. But Steelman feared that such a drastic proposal would create too much political furor. Instead, he recommended that the board be retained—but in an advisory capacity to the chairman. This, he said, could be accomplished through a reorganization plan that would shift the board's power and responsibility to the chairman. Steelman told the president that if he could not accept either of these suggestions he ought to at least meet with the board and tell them that in the future he intended to deal with the chairman in the same manner as he dealt with his budget director. Truman approved Steelman's proposed reorganization plan in December 1949, but it was many months before the plan was sent to Congress for its review.[85]

The delay was for tactical and political purposes. A Budget Bureau analyst summarized the problem as follows:

Over the past year, NSRB and mobilization planning have been the subject of unfavorable comment and considerable public concern. Men like "elder statesman" Baruch and various columnists have charged various failings. The tense international situation stimulates a very strong public interest in the adequacy of our mobilization planning. Therefore, it is very likely that submission of a reorganization plan will be followed by hearings in which somebody will be called upon to testify regarding the success or failure of NSRB operations, the relationship of the Chairman to the members of the Board, and other

---

84. Steelman to Truman, December 1949, Steelman files, RG 304, NA.
85. Ibid.

difficult questions . . . might be exploited to particular disadvantage
in such a situation. . . . It would seem that a reorganization plan can
be submitted only under one of two alternatives: (a) if the present
Acting Chairman is willing to testify in support of the plan and discuss the internal operations and progress of NSRB, or (b) if a new and
highly acceptable Chairman is appointed and has had several months
experience under his belt and is then in a position to go up and testify in support of the plan.[86]

It was obvious that the bureau favored the second alternative and that Steelman would not welcome
the idea of testifying in defense of the NSRB before a
congressional committee. The result was Truman's nomination of the "highly acceptable" Stuart Symington to
be chairman of the NSRB.

Symington, who was secretary of the air force at
the time of his nomination, was from a socially prominent Baltimore family. He had gone into business in St.
Louis where he met John Snyder who in turn introduced
him to Truman. Symington began his government career
when, soon after he became president, Truman put him
in charge of surplus property. Then when the Air Force
Department was established by the National Security
Act, Symington became its first secretary. There he
came into conflict, first with Forrestal, and then with
Johnson because of his strident advocacy of a sev-
enty-group air force. Although he opposed Truman's
budget ceilings, he always managed to keep on good
terms with the president. The support he enjoyed in
Congress was probably a factor in his selection for
the NSRB job.[87] Symington was quickly confirmed by the
Senate on 3 April 1950. He began his tenure with the
support of Baruch who praised his "abilities and
courage."[88]

With the Symington appointment the Budget Bureau
urged quick action by the White House in sending the
NSRB reorganization plan to Congress because it had

86. Ralph Burton to Director, 6 January 1950 [sic], M1-21/50.1, Series 39.32, RG 51, NA.

87. *The Washington Post,* 15 October 1950.

88. OF 1295, Truman Papers, HSTL; Excerpts from Baruch speech, 18
May 1950, Fussell Memos, Entry 4, RG 304, NA.

to be submitted by the first part of May to take advantage of the existing presidential reorganization
authority. Another reason for haste was to permit
Symington to support the plan on it merits alone. If it
was delayed until after the new chairman had time to
administer the NSRB, he would inevitably be questioned
about his relations with the various department heads.
This would play into the hands of those who opposed
the reorganization because Symington was not likely to
testify that he could not get along with the board
members. Truman found this reasoning persuasive and
sent the plan to Capitol Hill in early May 1950.[89]

The proposal was designated Reorganization Plan
No. 25 of 1950. It transferred all of the functions of
the NSRB to the chairman and made the board purely
advisory to the chairman. The plan also established a
vice-chairman of the board who also required Senate
confirmation.[90] The plan went into effect in early July.
Robert J. Smith's nomination as vice-chairman of the
board was quickly approved on 20 July.[91]

By the time Symington assumed the chairmanship
in April, the NSRB had begun to function along the
lines that the White House and the bureau had long favored. What the board's 280 employees needed more than
anything else was strong leadership and Symington
seemed capable of supplying it. Two immediate objectives were to effectively activate departmental mobilization planning and a further strengthening of the
NSRB staff. Symington seemed to accept these goals,
sought to keep his staff small, and began to work
through the departments. But almost immediately the

89. Outline for discussion of NSRB, E2–58/47.1, Series 39.32, RG 51,
NA; Meeting with the President, 2 May 1950, Frederick J. Lawton Papers, HSTL.

90. F. J. Lawton to Truman, 6 May 1950, Reorganization PSF, Truman
Papers, HSTL.

91. House Document #590, 81st Cong., 2 sess. OF 1295, Truman Papers,
HSTL.

92. Key Points for NSRB Discussion, 12 April 1950, E2-50/49.1, Series 39.32, RG 51, NA.

93. Symington to Stephen Early, 19 June 1950, DOD, Entry 3, RG 304,
NA.

NSRB was wrenched in a new direction——this time by the Korean War.

11.
The
National Security Council,
1950-1952

By mid-January 1950, when James Lay replaced Admiral
Souers as the executive secretary of the National
Security Council, there were many indications that the
council's organization was beginning to disintegrate.
Since its creation it had met frequently and had
approved hundreds of recommendations, but its policy
papers failed to carry much weight because they
tended to skirt the major issues and to provide guidance that was too general for practical use. It had not
become Truman's primary adviser in national security
matters.[1]

As Lay looked at the situation he identified several causes for the decline in the council's effectiveness. These included:

1. Excessive attendance at council meetings which
    tended to inhibit discussion.
2. Truman's practice of not attending council meet-
    ings which had resulted in less sharply focused
    discussions and a practice of settling national
    security matters outside of the council mecha-
    nism.
3. Departments had begun to demonstrate a lack of
    confidence in the NSC staff and increasingly
    used *ad hoc* committees in its place.

1. Stanley Falk, "The NSC Under Truman, Eisenhower and Kennedy," p.
412.

4.   The absence of Joint Chiefs of Staff (JCS) membership on the NSC staff made it difficult for the council to anticipate the chiefs' position on issues.

5.   Chairmanship of the NSC staff by the State Department representative was causing resentment among the other members.[2]

As a first step to remedying some of these difficulties, Lay proposed to the council that it reconstitute and strengthen its staff. To replace the departmental consultants to the NSC, Lay suggested the creation of a senior staff composed of one representative designated by each council member, a military adviser from the JCS, and an intelligence adviser from the CIA. The most innovative aspect of this proposal was the requirement that these individuals be able to "fully and accurately reflect the views of their principals" and be able "to devote a large part of their time to council work." Lay expected that they would occupy the same level in the departmental hierarchy as the consultants but they would not be distracted from NSC work by the additional heavy operational responsibilities that burdened the consultants. Under Lay's plan, the existing NSC staff members detailed from the departments would become assistants to the senior staff group.[3]

When Lay first presented these proposals to the council in April 1950, the group failed to act on them. Lay then spent the next month quietly lobbying with the members and their representatives in an effort to sell his plan. In May, at a NSC meeting, Lay proposed that since he had found them all to be in general agreement with the basic thrust of his suggestions, the council should approve the ideas in principal. But Lay's ploy to get the NSC on record as favoring the changes failed when Louis Johnson moved instead for the creation of an *ad hoc* committee to work with Lay in developing a plan to strengthen the council. When the other members agreed with Johnson, a three-man

2. Lay, "Organizational History of the NSC," pp. 18-19.
3. Ibid., p. 20.

committee representing Defense, State, and the NSRB was set up. Named to this committee was Secretary of the Army Frank Pace, Deputy Undersecretary of State for Administration Carlisle Humelsine, and Special Assistant to the Chairman of the NSRB Thomas Lanphier.[4]

Lay's approach to solving the NSC's problems grew out of his long experience working within an interdepartmental framework. This led him to view staffs composed of departmental representatives as a natural and proper arrangement. He also remembered how effective consultants such as Kennan and Norstad had been in the early days of the NSC. So he was trying to create something similar to that system without its flaws. The Budget Bureau was not overly impressed with Lay's plan. They believed that, as a minimum, his proposal should require the Senior Staff people to remain in their own departments so that they would be available full-time to provide advice on NSC matters. But in the end the Budget Bureau reluctantly supported Lay's original proposal "if for no other reason than to forestall the further promotion of a far less satisfactory alternative."[5]

Sidney Souers believed that the quality of the discussions in the NSC declined whenever the number attending its meetings exceeded nine or ten. The admiral tried to limit attendance but failed because of the prestige associated with an invitation.[6] Another reason the group attending NSC meetings increased was because Secretary of Defense Louis Johnson was not adequately prepared for the discussions. To compensate he insisted upon being accompanied to the meetings by an inordinate number of advisers from the Defense Department.[7]

4. Sidney Souers to the President, 18 May 1950, NSC Meetings 1950, PSF, Truman Papers, HSTL. Lanphier was the pilot who shot down Admiral Yamamota's plane during World War II.

5. Miles to Stauffacher, 22 May 1950, M1-21/40.1, Series 39.32, RG 51, NA.

6. Henry M. Jackson, ed., *The National Security Council*, p. 108.

7. John Meck, "The Administration of Foreign and Overseas Operations of the United States Government, Memorandum on the National Security Council," p. 21.

Stuart Symington, as the first secretary of the air force, had been a member of the original NSC. When, as the new chairman of the NSRB he again became a statutory member of the council, he was disturbed by the large number of people who were attending NSC meetings and the effect this was having on the decision-making process. He described his concerns in a memo drafted to be sent to the president:

In the past, when the Council was run by Admiral Souers in the days of General Marshall and Mr. Forrestal, the number of people attending Council meetings was few enough to enable it to operate as a working committee. . . . At a recent meeting the President, the Vice President and the Secretary of the Treasury had a single assistant and the Chairman of the Resources Board had one. Nevertheless there were 33 people at the meeting, including eleven representatives from the Department of Defense alone. As Admiral Souers has pointed out, keeping the meetings down in size insures that people will do their homework. At the last two meetings the Secretary of Defense stated in front of the Council that he would like to see the President after the meeting with the Secretary of State in order to do business. But where does this leave the Vice President, the Secretary of the Treasury, and the Resources Board?[8]

Lay recognized these problems but he did not address them directly in his proposals to improve the council's operations. Another problem Lay did not raise grew out of the strained relations between Johnson and Secretary of State Dean Acheson. The bitterness of feeling between the two men was an important factor in the council's failure to perform its coordinating function since their attitude set the climate for relations between their departments. As relations became more and more strained, the departmental consultants assigned to NSC matters seemed to have given less and less of their attention to their council responsibilities and more to their regular jobs. The replacement of Souers by Lay was also a contributing factor in the consultants' declining diligence in NSC business.[9] Lay,

8. Symington draft, undated, NSC, Entry 3, RG 304, NA.
9. Meck, "The Administration of Foreign and Overseas Operations," pp. 22–23.

who regarded himself as the servant of the council rather than as the president's NSC man, was unable to deal with these deteriorating relationships as Souers might have done.[10]

As a career executive secretary, Lay was probably considered a mere functionary by Acheson, Johnson, and the other appointed officials. He could not take sides among them nor have much effect on their behavior. His only recourse was to propose changes in the council's procedures and organization and hope that they would be adopted by the members. It was his responsibility to see that somehow the mechanism functioned to facilitate and improve presidential decision-making. Yet he was aware that

meetings of the Council were not proving effective in meeting ever more difficult problems. . . . [T]he absence of the President meant that the Council members were expressing their views to each other rather than to their superior who was to make the final decision. Important points at issue were sometimes deferred or glossed over and decided in individual conversation after Council action, possibly by individual appeal to the President. Council members, with their staff officers in attendance, tended to rely on them for advice during the discussion instead of being fully prepared beforehand. All of these shortcomings at the Council table tended to encourage individual members to take their case directly to the President, who was thus put under pressure to make decisions without full knowledge of the views of other interested departments or agencies.[11]

It seems probable that this description of the NSC's difficulties was as much a reflection of Truman's unhappiness with the council's performance as it was of Lay's. How would Lay have known of the pressure Truman was under unless he had discussed it with him?

NSC 68 AND THE COUNCIL REORGANIZATION

Lay's attempts to reorganize the council were complicated by the concurrent development of a policy paper

10. Anna Kasten Nelson, "President Truman and the Evolution of the National Security Council," p. 372.

11. James Lay, "Suggestions to Further Strengthen the NSC," 19 January 1953, M1–1/1, Series 52.1, RG 51, NA.

later known as NSC 68. In January 1950 Truman had directed his secretaries of state and defense to make a
reassessment of "our objectives in peace and war and
of the effect of these objectives on our strategic
plans, in the light of the probable fission bomb capability and possible thermonuclear bomb capability of
the Soviet Union." It was indicative of Truman's attitude toward the NSC that he did not assign this task
to the council.

The preparation of the report further aggravated
the already tense relations between Acheson and
Johnson, but on 7 April the departments of State and
Defense, together with the JCS, submitted their analysis to the president. In summary they stated that the
Russian bomb capabilities "have greatly intensified the
Soviet threat to the security of the United States" and
this necessitated a "much more rapid and concentrated
build-up of the actual strength" of the country and its
allies.[12]

Truman of course realized that if he approved
this recommendation it would be a repudiation of the
intense efforts he had made for several years to impose tight ceilings on the defense budget. As he
sought a way out of this dilemma, he turned to Charles
Murphy for advice. Murphy, who had not been much involved in foreign policy issues before this time, was
overly impressed with the simplistic analysis the paper presented. He proposed that the president place
the report before the NSC. But since he was also aware
of the president's budgetary concerns, he suggested
that Truman ask Leon Keyserling, then chairman of the
economic advisers, to sit with the NSC to consider the
potential impact of the recommendations on the economy.[13]

Adopting Murphy's advice, the president on 12
April referred the report to the council where it received the designation "NSC 68." He asked the NSC to
develop more information and, most particularly, "a
clearer indication of the programs which are envisaged
in the Report including estimates of the probable

12. NSRB draft memo to the President, NSC, Entry 3, RG 304, NA.
13. Charles Murphy Oral History, HSTL, pp. 523–526.

costs of such programs."[14] Truman's request for a re-
examination of NSC 68 was considered by the council at
the same meeting at which Lay had proposed his restructuring of the council staff. As a result, the two
issues became intertwined.

On 20 April the NSC set up an *ad hoc* committee
to draft a position on NSC 68. The committee included
representatives from the Budget Bureau, the economic
council, the Treasury Department, and the Economic Cooperation Administration. The group was reluctant to
make an analysis without a war plan that described the
needs under various contingencies. But despite intense
presidential pressure and "Jimmy Lay's best efforts,"
the war plan did not exist and the Defense Department
refused to produce one.[15] As a result, the *ad hoc* committee made no report on NSC 68 until after the Korean
War had begun. Since the war created its own rearmament momentum, the immediate effect of NSC 68 on defense policy became blurred.

At its meeting on 18 May the NSC authorized the
ad hoc committee to "make recommendations with respect
to the organization of the government to implement the
conclusions of NSC 68." This linking of organization to
foreign policy was apparently the result of a suggestion from the Budget Bureau. The bureau was vigorously
opposed to the expenditures called for by NSC 68 and
complained that more money had been spent on the military establishment since V-J Day than the total national debt before World War II. Instead of rearmament
the bureau called for a better organized and more aggressive prosecution of the cold war using existing
resources.[16]

About a month before the onset of the Korean
War, Budget Director Frederick Lawton discussed the
bureau's NSC 68 concerns with the president. Truman
encouraged him to continue to raise questions and remarked that NSC 68 was definitely not "as large in

14. NSRB draft memo to the President, NSC, Entry 3, RG 304, NA.

15. Ibid.; NSC Action 302, 58th Meeting, 18 May 1950, PSF, Truman
Papers, HSTL; Thomas Lanphier to Stuart Symington, 17 May 1950, NSC,
Entry 3, RG 304, NA.

16. Thomas Lanphier to Stuart Symington, 17 May 1950, NSC, Entry 3,
RG 304, NA; NSC Action 302, 58th Meeting PSF, Truman Papers, HSTL.

scope as some of the people seem to think."[17] A few
days later Lawton told the president of the bureau's
interest in the organizational issues involved in
dealing with the cold war. Truman approved a study of
the problem by the bureau in coordination with the
NSC.[18] The bureau study eventually appeared as Annex
No. 9 to a later version of NSC 68. The creation of the
Pace-Humelsine-Lanphier committee was a part of the
same NSC action that authorized the *ad hoc* NSC 68
committee to undertake the bureau's broader cold war
organizational analysis. In this way Lay's NSC restructuring proposal was entwined with the bureau's
study.[19]

AVERELL HARRIMAN JOINS THE NSC

The restructuring of the NSC was further complicated
when it became necessary to incorporate Averell
Harriman into the council mechanism. Harriman had previously served Truman as ambassador in Moscow and
London and as secretary of commerce. In the spring of
1950 he was in Paris as the top field man for the
Marshall Plan and getting restless. However, it was not
easy to find a new job for a man like Harriman who was
an aristocrat, had great prestige, and was well aware
of both. Many were jealous of him and no one seemed
willing to step aside for him. But Dean Acheson, whom
Harriman had taught to row a shell at Groton, sought
to have a new position created for him. Although
Harriman had been his chief rival for appointment as
secretary of state, Acheson decided to persuade Truman
to take Harriman on as a special assistant for foreign
affairs. As an insider at the White House, Harriman
could be useful in persuading Truman to support the
NSC 68 arms buildup.[20]

On 8 June Souers told Truman that Harriman was
in town and that Acheson had had several meetings

---

17. Meeting with the President, 23 May 1950, Frederick J. Lawton
Papers, HSTL.

18. Ibid., 26 May 1950.

19. NSC Action 302, 58th Meeting PSF, Truman Papers, HSTL.

20. Dean G. Acheson, *Present at the Creation*, pp. 410-411; Walter
Isaacson and Evan Thomas, *The Wise Men* (New York, 1986), pp. 85, 510.

with him to interest him in becoming a special assistant to the president. His assignment would be "to serve as a coordinator in all matters relating to the North Atlantic Treaty . . . and interest himself in coordinating the implementation of various phases of NSC 68." Souers said that Harriman was interested in such an assignment but for prestige purposes was reluctant to accept it unless the president invited him to attend cabinet meetings. Truman solved the problem with the observation that any of his former cabinet officers were welcome to attend cabinet meetings if they returned to government service. The president thought the new position was "a fine solution" for Harriman's boredom with Paris.[21]

That afternoon Harriman met with Truman and they agreed he would assume his new duties in late July or early August. Acheson announced the appointment on 16 June lest rumors start that Harriman was coming back to become secretary of state. But when the Korean War broke out Harriman could not wait. He called Acheson from Paris and told him that he wanted to come back at once and asked him to "square it with the boss." He joined the White House staff as a special assistant on 27 June.[22]

Harriman's assignment was somewhat ill defined. He had assumed that Truman had in mind a position something like that later occupied by McGeorge Bundy and Walt Rostow under presidents Kennedy and Johnson. That is, he expected to be head of the NSC staff and the president's adviser on foreign and defense policy. But this would have left no room for Souers who was still serving as a "consultant." After Harriman came to work at the White House, Truman explained to him that Souers liked his job, did not want to quit, and he did not have the heart to fire him. Harriman was not happy with the decision but he stuck to his principle of never refusing a presidential order or request.[23]

21. Souers, Memorandum for the File, 8 June 1950, Sidney Souers Papers, HSTL.

22. Acheson, *Present at the Creation*, p. 411; Harriman statement in Francis Heller, ed., *The Truman White House*, p. 12; Isaacson and Thomas, *The Wise Men*, p. 511.

23. Lincoln Gordon Oral History, HSTL, pp. 136-137.

After the announcement of Harriman's appointment as a presidential assistant (but before he assumed the position), the Budget Bureau undertook a study to determine how he might attain maximum effectiveness. To get ideas bureau personnel interviewed various people then involved in the NSC process. William Sheppard of the State Department thought that Harriman should become a more aggressive and wide-ranging Souers because he had enough prestige to be able to go up to Louis Johnson and say, "Damn it, you don't know what you are talking about."[24] Don K. Price believed Harriman should not involve himself broadly in foreign affairs but should intervene only in those cases in which, because of urgency or lack of progress, top pressure was needed to get results.[25] Souers looked to Harriman to fill the gap that had developed in implementing NSC policy. He recommended that Harriman himself should sit on the council and have an observer assigned to the staff group. When asked, "who would do the kind of job vis-à-vis NSC policy articulation which he, Admiral Souers, now is doing on a temporary, emergency, special request from the President basis, Souers said that should be Harriman's job."[26] Although it appeared that Souers was willing to step aside for Harriman, he stayed on as a consultant through the remainder of Truman's term.

Most of those the bureau consulted about Harriman's role were curious about its scope. Would he be devoting his attention broadly to the coordination of foreign affairs on a worldwide basis or limit himself to advising Truman principally on the Marshall Plan and NATO countries? Although all agreed that the president himself had to be the ultimate authority and coordinator of foreign policy, some feared that Truman was too busy to spend the necessary time at this task. The bureau put this concern down to the familiar mis-

24. Conversation with Sheppard, 21 June 1950, NSC, Series 47.3c, RG 51, NA.

25. Interview with Price, 20 June 1950, ibid.

26. Conversation with Sidney Souers, 22 June 1950, ibid.

conception that the president was too occupied to be president.[27]

Others hoped that Harriman would fill the void that they believed the departure of Clark Clifford had left in the coordination of foreign affairs and in securing presidential resolution of interdepartmental conflicts. Although it was expected that Harriman would interject his own views into NSC discussion, there was some concern that if he became too strong an advocate of his own ideas he would merely become someone else for the president to coordinate. All the departments hoped that Harriman would limit the size of his own staff lest they develop as a rival instead of a help to State, Defense and the NSC groups.[28]

Harriman discovered his main chore was to coordinate the activities of the State and Defense Departments since Acheson and Johnson "were not getting along very well at that time." To do this he tried to bring the two secretaries closer to the president and defuse their battles rather than to superimpose himself as an individual between them and the president. He "tried to make it possible for meetings between the President and the secretary, whoever he might be, to be as fruitful as possible, and to put the President in a position to deal with the problems that came before them."[29] He saw his job as implementing policy—not making it—and in this way it was different from the positions later held by Henry Kissinger and McGeorge Bundy.[30]

Much of the success that the Harriman operation enjoyed was because of his close relations with Acheson. He became almost a member of the State Department, attending the secretary's staff meeting each morning and having access to all the department's information.[31] Harriman did not have the same rapport with Louis Johnson. But a few months after Harriman

27. "The Role of the Special Assistant for Foreign Affairs," Misc., Series 47.3c, RG 51, NA.

28. Ibid.

29. Harriman statement in Heller, *The Truman White House*, pp. 67, 155.

30. Nelson, "Truman and the Evolution of the NSC," p. 376.

31. Acheson, *Present at the Creation*, p. 411.

assumed his post Truman told Johnson "he'd have to quit." The president decided that Johnson had to be replaced when he realized that he had come "forth with a complex." Truman was puzzled by Johnson's behavior. "I don't understand what happened to him," he noted, "he talked out of turn to the press, the Senate and the House and he kept it up."[32] It was very painful for the president to fire his friend of thirty years.

Johnson was succeeded as defense secretary by General George Marshall. Harriman got along well with him. Even more important were Harriman's relations with the new deputy secretary of defense, Robert Lovett. Harriman and Lovett had known each other since childhood and had been partners on Wall Street.[33] Theodore Tannenwald, one of Harriman's aides, thought that it was this personal link that made the arrangement work. He recalled that "during this period, the three men—Lovett, Acheson, and Harriman—were very close to each other, knew how each other's mind worked, and had great respect for each other."[34]

With the departure of Johnson, much of the original impetus for Harriman's appointment was removed. For the next year he focused his attention on bringing urgent matters to the surface and seeing that they got the attention they deserved (the role that Don Price had suggested he play). John Meck, who studied the council's operations during this period, found that Harriman had "apparently fitted into the NSC picture without creating new problems," yet the hopes that many had had that the Harriman office would improve the implementation of NSC decisions remained unfulfilled.[35] With peace restored between the State and Defense Departments, Harriman again grew restless and sought a new assignment. He welcomed his appointment as the director of mutual security when that office was established in October 1951. Since the Mutual Security Act of 1951 made the director a statutory member

32. Longhand note, 11 September 1950, PSF, Truman Papers, HSTL.

33. Isaacson and Thomas, *The Wise Men*, 21.

34. Theodore Tannenwald statement in Heller, *The Truman White House*. p. 155.

35. Meck, "The Administration of Foreign and Overseas Operations," pp. 34.

of the NSC, Harriman maintained his place on the council.[36]

TRUMAN REORGANIZES THE NSC

While Harriman was trying to improve foreign policy
coordination through personal contacts, the efforts to
reorganize the NSC continued. During June 1950, the *ad
hoc* committee that had been appointed to work with Lay
on council problems met and considered various proposals. By mid–June Pace, Humelsine, and Lanphier had
agreed on a reorganization plan.[37] However, their proposal was never submitted to the NSC because of the
beginning of the Korean War and some disagreement
among the departments. Then it was preempted by the
president who decided to direct his own reorganization
of the NSC staff. The committee was discharged on 27
July.[38]

With the outbreak of the war in Korea, Truman
began to meet frequently with the NSC and use it as a
coordinating mechanism to direct the government's response to the crisis. Council meeting on 28 and 30
June were devoted primarily to Korea, and the president took an active part in revising the instructions
that were sent to General MacArthur.[39] Until the beginning of the war, the president had presided at only
twelve of the council's fifty-seven meetings. For the
rest of his term Truman chaired most of the meetings
of the NSC (he missed only nine of the next seventy-
one), but he still reserved his decisions on council
recommendations until after the executive secretary
had formally presented them to him.[40]

In May 1948 the NSC had established the practice
of meeting on alternative Thursdays but in early July
1950 Truman called for the council to meet weekly. The
president also directed "that all important recommen-

36. Lay, "Organizational History," p. 22.

37. Subcommittee conference, 13 June 1950, NSC, Series 47.3c, RG
51, NA; Thomas Lanphier to Jack Gorrie, NSC, Entry 4, RG 304, NA.

38. NSC Action 321, 62nd Meeting, PSF, Truman Papers, HSTL.

39. Souers to President, 30 June 1950, NSC Meetings 1950 PSF,
Truman Papers, HSTL.

40. Falk, "The National Security Council," pp. 405–416.

dations relating to national security be coordinated through the Council and its Staff for consideration at these regular meetings in order that all Council members may be completely informed."[41] In this way the Truman tried to deal with the complaints of Lay and Symington that the council was being bypassed by State and Defense in separate meetings with the president.

On 19 July Truman acted to implement the suggestions that Lay had made in April to restructure and strengthen the NSC. He sent identical letters to the statutory members, Acheson, Johnson, and Symington, as well as to Secretary of the Treasury John Snyder, who regularly met with the council, and to advisers Omar Bradley, chairman of the JCS, and the director of the CIA. In these letters he wrote:

I have been considering the steps which are now necessary to make the National Security Council of maximum value in advising me as to the major policies required in the interest of our national security as a result of the present international situation. It is my desire that all such policies should be recommended to me through the Council in order that I may readily have the benefit of the collective views of the officials of the Government primarily concerned with the national security. This result can be achieved only if there are frequent Council meetings at which the responsible officials may freely discuss specific recommendations on which there has previously been coordinated staff work.

To encourage free discussion he ordered that attendance at NSC meetings be limited to the statutory members and Snyder, Bradley, Bedell Smith, Harriman, Souers, and Lay. Others could attend only with the specific approval of the president.[42]

The other requisite for effective council meetings, according to Truman's letter, was "carefully coordinated staff work by the best qualified individuals

---

41. For the rest of 1950 the council averaged three meetings a month. The last two years of the Truman administration they meet less than twice a month. Ibid.; NSC Action 311, NSC Record 1950, NSC Meetings-Personnel, PSF, Truman Papers, HSTL.

42. Truman to Lay, 19 July 1950, NSC Meetings-Personnel, PSF, Truman Papers, HSTL.

who can be available for this task." To this end, the president said he was establishing a senior NSC staff group headed by the executive secretary. Truman asked each of the addressees to nominate one person for him to appoint to the group.[43]

The specification that these were to be presidential appointments was probably intended for the dual purpose of emphasizing that the NSC was the president's council and to give the positions additional prestige in the hope that the "best qualified" would accept the assignment. The appointment of the executive secretary as the head of the senior staff was designed to meet the objections of the Defense Department and the NSRB that the current arrangement of having the State Department representative act as coordinator of the NSC staff was unsatisfactory. There was a feeling that one individual could not be both an advocate of the State Department's position and an impartial chairman of the staff. Lay's direction of the senior staff was also "recognition that the work of the interdepartmental staff group which prepared reports for the NSC could be effective in serving the council only if the chairman of the group was personally cognizant, through regular contact with the President, of his desires and requirements regarding the work of the Council."[44]

Souers had been telling Truman for some time "that only he could press Johnson toward more effective corrective action" to make the council work.[45] The president's letter demonstrated he was now willing to make this effort and that he realized that Lay's proposed reforms would never be accepted unless he intervened. Truman knew that there had been objections to the idea that senior staff members should, by devoting a large amount of their time to NSC duties, act semi-independently of their departments. The JCS had also been cool to Lay's plan. The chiefs thought that if a senior staff was needed it should follow the mil-

43. Ibid.

44. Lay, "Organizational History," p. 19.

45. Conversation with Souers, 22 June 1950, NSC, Series 47.3c, RG 51, NA.

itary general staff model and make many decisions without referring the questions to the council level.[46]

THE SENIOR STAFF

On 3 August the president announced to the council his appointments to the senior staff. They were Ambassador Philip C. Jessup, state; Air Force Secretary Thomas Finletter, Defense; NSRB vice-chairman Robert J. Smith; William McChesney Martin, Treasury; Admiral E. T. Woodridge, JCS; and CIA director Admiral Hillenkoetter representing his own agency.[47] During the next two years, there was a complete turnover in this membership. Within a few weeks, Walter Bedell Smith became director of the CIA and he nominated deputy director William H. Jackson for senior staff membership. Jackson in turn was replaced by Allen Dulles in August 1951.[48] Finletter was succeeded by Washington lawyer Frank C. Nash that same year. Charles Bohlen replaced Jessup primarily because he was available and Acheson wanted to keep him busy. Bohlen, incidentally, did not think the paperwork generated by the senior staff contributed very much to NSC decisions because "every paper produced was so compromised and watered down to avoid disagreement that when it was finished it had about as much wallop as cambric tea."[49]

The membership of the senior staff expanded over the years in response to organizational changes prompted by the Korean War. When the Mutual Security Administration was formed, General Frank Roberts became its member on the senior staff. Roberts had served earlier as Harriman's personal representative. The establishment of the Office of Defense Mobilization (ODM) resulted in an expansion in the membership of both the council and the senior staff. J. Murray Mitchell was ODM's first representative on the staff

---

46. Meck, "The Administration of Foreign and Overseas Operations," pp. 23–24.

47. Minutes of the 63rd Meeting of the NSC, PSF, Truman Papers, HSTL.

48. W.B. Smith to President, 31 August 1950, NSC Senior Staff, ibid.

49. Charles E. Bohlen, *Witness to History, 1929–1969* (New York, 1973), p. 298.

but his lack of experience limited his effectiveness. His successors, Shaw Livermore and W. Y. Elliott, were more successful.[50] In April 1951 the Budget Bureau arranged to get advanced copies of the senior staff agendas so it could participate in matters in which it had a major interest. Then in August the bureau was invited to designate a representative to serve on a regular basis as an adviser to the senior staff. Robert Macy was named.[51]

Souers believed the consultant system he developed had "progressively deteriorated" because they were unable to predict the attitude of their superiors who sat on the NSC.[52] The creation of the senior staff significantly raised the organizational status of each department's representation, but this did not always improve the council's product. The ideal that Souers sought was for each council member to have a deputy in which he had confidence and who had enough time to engage in the thinking, exchange of views, and deliberation needed for planning. A group of such men, he argued, could, by sitting together and by debating among themselves, develop a broader point of view and better policies without surrendering the sovereignty of their departments. If this process was accompanied by council members who followed the development of the policies with their staff representatives, he felt they would get "pretty good results." However, if they downgraded their staff members, the process would suffer.[53]

The new senior staff initially met three or four afternoons each week but this soon declined to two meetings per week. The NSC staff, now rechristened the "staff assistants," met more frequently and did much of the basic research. Max Bishop, who had been the last coordinator of the NSC staff, usually accompanied Philip Jessup to the senior staff meetings. Similarly,

50. Herbert H. Rosenberg, "ODM: A Study of Civil Military Relations During the Korean Mobilization" (Ph. D. diss., University of Chicago, 1957), pp. 54–55.

51. Elmer Staats to Division Chiefs, 6 April 1951, NSC, Series 47.3c, RG 51, NA; Staats to Division Chiefs, 9 August 1951, M1–21, RG 51, NA.

52. Conversation with Souers, 22 June 1950, NSC, Series 47.3c, RG 51, NA.

53. Jackson, *National Security Council*, pp. 107–108.

Finletter was normally accompanied by General Spalding, who had been the Defense Department's NSC consultant before the reorganization, and James Hill, counsel of the air force. It is doubtful whether the senior staff ever devoted all their time to NSC work, although they were much more involved than the consultants had been.[54]

There is considerable evidence that the senior staff did not attain the objectives that Souers and Lay had hoped for. In 1952 William Yandell Elliott, then serving as the ODM senior staff member, described the staff and its work:

The Senior Staff . . . is made up of representatives who are in theory at the level of the Under Secretaries or non-Cabinet rank Secretaries in the Defense Department. In practice they are considerably junior even to the Assistant Secretary rank in many instances. The Senior Staff meets twice a week and performs the function of review of the papers presented by the Departments. They then prepare the issues for presentation to the NSC proper. In theory, at least, they brief the Secretaries of State, Defense, etc., for the weekly meetings of the NSC and for emergency sessions. The general evidence is that in practice the principal members of the Council spend a half-hour or less in many cases on this type of briefing and that the sessions of the Council are often somewhat perfunctory and the discussions are by no means searching or thorough, even on very important issues of policy.[55]

But it was not only the council members who did not spend enough time on council business; Lay thought the senior staff had similar problems. Although Truman was generally successful in obtaining the nomination of the senior people he asked for, Lay found that

in most cases these members have retained departmental responsibilities which made it impossible for them to devote sufficient time and attention to NSC work, or to display the initiative and drive required

54. Meck, "The Administration of Foreign and Overseas Operations," pp. 27-28; Lay, "Organizational History," p. 21.

55. Draft memo, W. Y. Elliott to Arthur Flemming, 23 December 1952, NSC Organization and Functions, White House Office "Project Clean Up," Eisenhower Papers, Dwight D. Eisenhower Library (DDEL).

to keep the NSC policies up to date, not to mention getting them ahead of the game. While the Senior Staff members must not become an ivory tower group, wholly divorced from the operations of the departments, they have tended to delegate the real development of policies to alternates or the heads of offices within their agencies responsible for the particular problems at hand. Long delays and incomplete policies or even, in a few cases, no policies at all, have sometimes been the outcome of this situation.

Lay began to use steering committees to partially compensate for the inability of senior staff members to devote sufficient time to council work or even to attend the meetings. He set up groups of three to five members of the senior staff whose departments were most directly concerned with the problems under consideration to meet separately to develop a paper. This permitted a "more thorough and comprehensive discussion, better team work, and faster action in the initial formulation of policy recommendations." The obvious difficulty with this practice was that it "placed the other Senior Staff members and their principals at an unfair disadvantage when they have subsequently been required to act on these recommendations, and has consequently occasioned some grumbling."[56]

After the senior staff had been in existence for six months, Lay sought Acheson's appraisal of the new organization. Apparently Jessup had been complaining about his assignment to the senior staff, for Acheson said that it was "hard to get the caliber of people needed for the work if the Senior Staff degenerated into a group which merely picked over papers which were drafted without any purpose in mind but just as 'papers.'" The secretary did not see much purpose in drafting papers that merely set down established policy. He believed one of the principal purposes of the NSC should be to get new and original thinking and analysis. He did not think the senior staff could be the source of all of these novel approaches, but the

56. Lay, "Suggestions to Further Strengthen NSC," 19 January 1953, M1–1/1, Series 52.1, RG 51, NA.

State and Defense departments could contribute if they worked together as they had on NSC 68.[57]

Being too heavily burdened with agency responsibilities was only one of the problems that developed within the senior staff. Too often its members tended to represent the particular interests of their agencies instead of serving the national interest. They also took too long to arrive at their recommendations. This was frequently due to an inability to agree and an unwillingness to send a paper forward unless it was generally agreeable to all concerned (as if acquiescence was the ultimate virtue). Too often they approached a problem on the basis of finding justification for decisions already made instead of attempting to make a searching objective analysis. By the fall of 1952 the membership of the senior staff had become so large that meetings became unwieldy and group discussion became difficult.[58]

In summary, it would seem that the Truman administration never overcame the inherent contradiction of expecting busy and important people to spend most of their time working outside of the organization with which they identified their career aspirations. The mild interest that Truman exhibited in the NSC was not enough to counter the tendency of senior staff members to view the assignment as a diversion from their basic interests and ambitions.

IMPLEMENTING POLICY

The council's role in the implementation of presidentially approved NSC policies was a controversial issue throughout the Truman years. The president, Souers, and Lay consistently maintained that the NSC was not an implementing agency; that this was the responsibility of the executive departments and agencies. To a degree this attitude probably reflected Truman's opposition to the Eberstadt Report which had advocated a

57. Memo of conversation, 26 January 1951, Acheson Papers, HSTL.

58. NSC Study, 2 February 1953, NSC Organization and Functions, "Project Clean Up," Eisenhower Papers, DDEL.

NSC that not only made policy but made sure it was carried out.

The president was determined to confine the council to giving advice on policies. This position was cogently expressed by Souers in a paper prepared for the Hoover Commission that outlined Truman's concept of the NSC. This paper, which had the president's approval, emphasized that the "Council does not determine policy or supervise operations . . . nor is it an implementing agency." If the council were to begin to coordinate the execution of policies, Lay argued, it

would radically alter the principle under which the Executive Branch operates, namely the various heads of departments and agencies are directly responsible to the President for the conduct of their operations. In effect, the Council as a committee would be interposed between the President and his Cabinet members and other agency heads. This is not the American way of Government.[59]

In keeping with this concept, Truman always designated a department or agency to assume primary responsibility for the implementation of a new policy paper at the time he approved it. In ninety percent of the cases responsibility was assigned to the State Department. Occasionally, after the beginning of the Korean War, he would assign responsibility jointly to two agencies.[60]

In 1948 the council adopted the position that the coordinating agency was responsible for assigning actions to other agencies to implement a particular policy and ensuring that the actions were taken. The coordinating agency was directed to periodically report to the council on the progress made in implementing the papers assigned to it.[61] Soon, however, the State Department complained that "whereas we were required to submit reports of progress of our implementation on NSC papers, no action was taken when we reported fail-

59. Lay, "Suggestions to Further Strengthen NSC," 19 January 1953, M1–1/1, Series 52.1, RG 51, NA.

60. Lay, "Organizational History," p. 26.

61. NSC Action 123, 6 October 1948, Modern Military Branch, NA.

ure of other agencies to carry out their assigned responsibilities."[62]

The Truman NSC never solved the problem of one
agency supervising the actions of another, but it did
provide that if two agencies differed about the interpretation of a paper or the methods of implementation,
the divergent views would be considered by the members of the council. If they could not resolve the
matter, the dispute was to be submitted in writing to
the president through the executive secretary.[63] Instances in which this remedy was used were rare. According to Lay, such cases ordinarily were "handled
directly by the Secretary taking the matter up with
the President, who, in turn, takes it up with the Secretary of the derelict department."[64]

The timing and content of the progress reports
were at the discretion of the reporting departments. In
theory Lay reported failures in the execution of policy to the president, but in practice he admitted that
it was "not particularly possible for the NSC to police
execution."[65] Initially, the progress reports were submitted every six months, but they became less and less
frequent as it became obvious that they served little
purpose. The reports usually contained two basic elements: (a) a summary of the actions taken to carry out
a policy and developments that affected the policy;
and (b) an assessment of the policy. The reports did
not recommend changes in policy but did indicate if
the policies were inadequate or in need of review. If
the council agreed that a review should be made, and
the president agreed, it was undertaken by the senior
staff.[66] In 1951 a small unit was established within the
NSC staff to receive and circulate these progress reports, but this procedure had little effect on their
use.[67]

62. Webb memo of conversation with Souers, 4 May 1949, *FRUS, 1949*,
vol. 1, p. 298.

63. NSC Action 242, 12 August 1949, Modern Military Branch, NA.

64. Interview with Lay, 14 June 1950, NSC, Series 47.3c, RG 51, NA.

65. Ibid.

66. Lay, "Organizational History," p. 26.

67. NSC Organizational Chart, 3 January 1952, NSC, Entry 304, NA.

Truman simply did not want the council involved in overseeing the implementation of policy. But others, particularly in the Defense Department, saw this as a major flaw in the NSC system. General James H. Burns complained

that we have a number of strands but no rope—no integration of the several programs or pieces of programs in the foreign field directed toward basic security objectives. . . . The President alone cannot in himself provide all orders needed for teamwork in our various security programs. He needs a general staff "arrangement."

Burns's solution was to make Harriman, together with a small staff, the driving force to make the implementation machinery work.[68] Many others hoped that Harriman's appointment would solve the problem of coordinating policy implementation, but this expectation was not fulfilled.

When, during the summer of 1950, the Budget Bureau's management analysts looked at the question of the NSC's role in implementation, they found Souers had given little attention to the problem. "His first thought on this score was that much of the implementing of NSC policy merely involved writing directives to the field within State." When asked whether some NSC machinery should be designed to follow through on policy decisions, the admiral conceded that in specific cases a committee could help coordinate the action, but he was opposed to the council accepting this role as a general responsibility.[69] In view of the president's concept of the NSC functions and the difficulty the council still faced in performing its basic policy advisory function, it is not surprising that Souers was reluctant to interject it into the quicksand of supervising departmental activities. He probably also realized that much of the underlying difficulty was because of weaknesses and limitations in departmental organization that could not be remedied by high-level coordination.

68. Conference with General Burns, 19 June 1950, NSC, Series 47.3c, RG 51, NA.

69. Conversation with Souers, 22 June 1950, ibid.

Shortly after the close of the Truman administration, Elmer Staats of the Budget Bureau summarized
the council's performance in implementation:

The assigning of responsibility for implmenting . . . is presently handled with a great deal of looseness. Most NSC papers requiring the
assignment of responsibility among the executive agencies for implementation and coordination of execution contain "boilerplate" language to the effect that, if the President approves the policies contained therein each department . . . concerned will assume its appropriate share of responsibility for putting these policies in effect,
with the Secretary of State taking general leadership in assuring
necessary interdepartmental coordination. The vagueness with which
this language is couched has often led to a considerable amount of
inaction. Related to this problem is the way that progress reports are
handled in the NSC. The reports are not fully used as instruments for
revising policy or reassigning implementation responsibilities. The
fact is that although these reports are regularly requested of the
agencies, little is done with them after they have been received by
the NSC, except that they are "noted" on the agenda and circulated
for information.[70]

To deal with some of these problems the Eisenhower
administration established the Operations Coordinating
Board to oversee the implementation of NSC policies.
Staats wrote his report prior to becoming the OCB's
first executive officer.

PROBLEMS

By 1951 the Truman NSC had reached it final configuration. The Korean War resulted in the creation of the
Office of Defense Mobilization (ODM). The president
named its director a regular member of the NSC.
Harriman was a NSC member by virtue of the statute
that established the Mutual Security Agency. Truman
regularly invited John Snyder or a representative of
the Treasury Department to attend NSC meetings. Since
each of these individuals and all the statutory members except the vice-president were entitled to have a
representative on the senior staff, that body also in-

---

70. "Implementation of Approved NSC Policy," 10 July 1953, M1-21,
Series 52.6, RG 51, NA.

creased in size. During his last two years, Truman began to relax his restriction on NSC attendance by nonmembers. Frederick Lawton of the Budget Bureau, Leon Keyserling of the economic council, the attorney general or his representative, and Millard Caldwell, the civil defense administrator, were frequently invited to council meetings. Caldwell even lobbied to have Congress make him a regular member but Truman and the Budget Bureau continued to resist any statutory expansion of council membership.[71]

Both the State and Defense Departments thought that this council was too large. These departments had their differences but each recognized that the other had large and legitimate interests in national security matters. However, they were less tolerant of the intrusion of the other council participants—NSRB, ODM, Mutual Security, and the Treasury—into what they considered to be their area of responsibility. Lay, who sympathized with their objections, thought the council members should be limited to the president, the vice president, the secretaries of state and defense, and someone representing the mobilization area. The others, Lay found, tended to become spectators or kibitzers with no real responsibility for or interest in the policies being considered.[72] Another observer found that the contribution of these members to the substantive matters before the council consisted of little more than their own personal views.[73]

Throughout the Truman administration, the size of the permanent NSC staff, made up of low-ranking civil servants, remained small. It functioned primarily as a secretariat that cleared the docket of necessary papers and insured that interagency disputes came up for discussion. With only a fourth of its two dozen members considered members of the "thinking staff," it never developed the capability of providing an independent reviewing function for the president or serv-

71. Lawton to Caldwell, 14 January 1952, M7–17/53, Series 53.2, RG 51, NA.

72. Lay, "Suggestions to Further Strengthen NSC," 19 January 1953, M1–1/1, Series 52.1, RG 51, NA.

73. Meck, "The Administration of Foreign and Overseas Operations," pp. 31–32.

ing as his devil's advocate.[74] Even the daily intelligence briefings that Lay gave Truman were prepared by the CIA instead of by the NSC staff that he headed. In this role Lay conceded that he merely acted as "the mouthpiece" for the CIA.[75] One reason Truman's NSC never made the jump from an interdepartmental coordinating mechanism to a group that developed presidentially oriented foreign policy was the inherent weakness of this NSC staff.

EVALUATION OF TRUMAN'S NSC

For the council to be more than a coordinating mechanism between the State and Defense Departments, the president had to believe that the NSC was important. He had to convey his interest in a device like the council and demand that it be used or department heads, who naturally wish to maintain their freedom of operation, would tend to merely give it lip service. But Admiral Dennison, Truman's naval aide, concluded from things the president had told him about the NSC "that he felt it was rather unnecessary."[76]

It must have been clear to his cabinet that Truman, until the time of the Korean War, viewed the NSC as a threat to his prerogatives. Even after the war began, he used it primarily as a coordinating medium instead of as an advisory group. According to Elmer Staats, Truman "preferred to operate much more informally; unlike President Eisenhower, he was not used to sitting down with a deliberative body and systematically going around the table for debate and statements of position."[77] It may also have been that he was simply not that interested in the proceedings. Clark Clifford recalled that since Truman was briefed

---

74. Cutler NSC Study, Notes of Study Group Conference, 13 February 1953, NSC Organization and Functions, "Project Clean Up," Eisenhower Papers, DDEL; W. Barton Leach, 3 February 1953, ibid.; W.Y. Elliott to Arthur Flemming, 23 December 1952, ibid.

75. Lay statement in Heller, *The Truman White House*, p. 233.

76. Dennison statement in ibid.

77. Staats statement in ibid.

each morning on international developments, he found council meetings repetitive and rather boring.[78]

Truman never relinquished his strict control over the NSC's agenda. When he chaired its meetings, according to Dennison, the president skillfully directed the trend and results of the discussions.[79] But his influence seems to have been a negative one. Although he decided which items could appear on the agenda, he rarely initiated questions for the council to consider. When he presided, he did not encourage the members to debate the issues. George Marshall remembered that "the President came in, sat down, went out. He was not a leader, a force at the table to bring out discussion."[80] The result was that these meetings did not sharpen the issues or provide options for presidential decision; instead, what emerged was the lowest-common-denominator advice from participating agencies. Paul Hammond found that even during the Korean War the NSC had little to do with either policy or overseeing the implementation of policy.[81]

Both of Truman's secretaries of state who served as members of his NSC were critical of the council's tendency to blur issues and produce generalized, sometimes meaningless, policy statements. George Marshall found the council "too much concerned merely with papers; too much a meeting of busy men who had no time to pay to the business before them, and, not being prepared, therefore took refuge either in non-participation or protecting their own departments." Marshall believed the papers the council considered were so compromised before they came to the table that they failed to state the pros and cons. Instead they merely presented *fait accompli* to be accepted or rejected or modified a little.[82]

Dean Acheson was similarly critical of "negotiated" papers. He believed that if there was a

78. Anderson, *The Presidents' Men.* p. 139.

79. Dennison in Heller, *The Truman White House*, p. 139.

80. Marshall interview by Robert Cutler, 19 February 1953, NSC Organization and Functions, "Project Clean Up", Eisenhower Papers, DDEL.

81. Paul Y. Hammond, *Organizing for Defense*, p. 233.

82. Marshall interview by Cutler, 19 February 1953.

real difference of opinion it was "important to sharpen it and not blunt it so that the President had before him all of the views." Acheson favored the adoption by the NSC of "doable" policies instead of generalized papers that purported to solve the difficulties of complex areas such as Vietnam or China. These, he felt, were useless and even dangerous. He gave, as an example of the latter, a policy that might state "we must support to the greatest possible extent the independence of Indo-China, give every aid short of American ground troops or whatever to these people, but on the other hand we must not commit the prestige of the United States to within any such degree, etc., etc."[83]

Evaluations of Truman's NSC range from Townsend Hoopes who called it "a revolutionary advance in responsible U.S. decision-making, an almost miraculous victory for organization principle, reason and coherence"[84] to George Marshall's "evanescent." One reason it has received such mixed reviews is because, although it obviously was a significant improvement over the chaotic procedures of the past, many thought it should have achieved more. At the close of the Truman administration, Budget Bureau analysts concluded that many of the criticisms of the NSC arose because of a

very high standard of expectancy [which] overlooks the fact that the coordinated and collective development of advice to the president on high national policy is inherently a cumbersome process. . . . An objective appraisal of the National Security Council must take into account the fact that measured against the situation of only a dozen years ago, the NSC represents a tremendous step forward.[85]

Souers came to a similar conclusion when he recalled that "it was not easy to fit the NSC into our governmental structure, and forward planning was difficult to accomplish."[86]

---

83. Princeton Seminar, 2 July 1953, Folder 2, Acheson Papers, HSTL.

84. Townsend Hoopes, *The Limits of Intervention* (New York, 1969), p. 4.

85. Appendix B, NSC, E2–50/52.1, Series 52.6, RG 51, NA.

86. Souers to Paul Y. Hammond, 14 December 1959, Council 1950–1953, Souers Papers, HSTL.

One wonders what the NSC might have achieved if Truman's personality and attitude had been different. Averell Harriman, many years later, admitted that "the National Security Council was not very important under Truman."[87] This view is substantiated by a contemporary analysis by the Budget Bureau that found that the NSC

plays a very limited role in questioning the adequacy of the departmental positions presented. Thus, policy issues are stated and resolved by default in terms of any effective challenge to the position of the major department concerned. Particularly when there is a latent feeling of opposition among the departments concerned, but no effective center of debate, this situation results in a "sterile" product from the NSC activity with each agency following its own course as a practical matter.[88]

Despite these negative judgments, the National Security Council, in the years 1947 to 1952, did achieve a substantial improvement in regularized coordination between the State and Defense Departments. A Budget Bureau analyst found this beneficial because it "permitted Defense to force State to deal with problems and has likewise permitted State to force Defense to give it a whack at problems which would otherwise be bound up in Defense alone."[89] But could it have been more? Many contemporaries thought so. The Budget Bureau, which was not given to extravagant statements, found that "on balance . . . it is possible to draw the conclusion that the NSC has not yet achieved working procedures which permit it to meet fully all of the criteria set for its performance."[90] In view of the high level of effectiveness that the council attained a few years later under Eisenhower, this understated evaluation by the bureau would seem generous.

---

87. Harriman statement in Heller, *The Truman White House* p. 154.

88. "Presidential Job in the Organization and Management of the Executive Branch," E2–50/52.2, Series 52.6, RG 51, NA.

89. Ed Strait to Files, 30 October 1952, E2–50.52.1, Series 52.6, RG 51, NA.

90. Appendix B, NSC, ibid.

12.
The
Mobilization Muddle

The Korean War had an overriding impact on the Truman administration. Declared or not, war meant an enlargement of presidential authority to control the economy. This in turn led to a struggle among the departments and agencies for a share in the additional power. The Executive Office of the President did not escape this bureaucratic competition.

The presidential staff most intimately involved in mobilization matters was the National Security Resources Board. Shortly before the invasion of South Korea, all the authority residing in the NSRB had been transferred from the board to its new chairman, Stuart Symington—ambitious, politically adept, and a vigorous Cold Warrior. If his agency was now authorized to direct the mobilization of the nation in support of a war effort, he would become one of the most powerful men in Washington. The main obstacle he faced was the conviction of the president and the Bureau of the Budget that the NSRB should be a staff planning unit with no operating responsibility or authority.

Since its establishment in 1947, Bernard Baruch had pushed the NSRB to draft standby legislation to grant additional authority to the president during an emergency. Baruch thought this legislation should be enacted during peacetime so that no time would be lost if a sudden crisis developed. But for several reasons Truman and his advisers initially opposed this strategy. They wanted to keep the NSRB in check and feared

Congress might reject the request. The president said he was reluctant to commit himself to a specific request for power without knowing what kind of an emergency they might face. To prevent any end runs Truman told Charles Murphy to edit any proposals for standby powers that the NSRB might try to send to Congress.[1]

As early as the fall of 1948 the NSRB staff had drafted an emergency powers act which they wanted submitted to Congress. They considered it their most significant project to date.[2] The draft bill specified that the powers would not be conferred short of war unless Congress, in a separate action, authorized them. The Budget Bureau warned Truman not to send the bill to Congress because if passed it might restrict his flexibility in the future.[3] The proposal was shelved by Truman who decided to send it to Congress only "if, as, and when the need for it arose."[4]

When war came in June 1950, the NSRB draft bill was resurrected to provide the basis for the mobilization statutes. The most important of these was the Defense Production Act which granted the president broad powers over production and economic stabilization. It gave the president authority to establish priorities and allocate materials, restrain credit expansion, and to accelerate and increase the production of essential materials, products, and services. All or part of five of the titles of the Defense Production Act were based on the original NSRB proposal.[5]

Anticipating passage of the bill, the departments and agencies began maneuvering to get their share of the additional power the president would have to delegate. Secretary of Commerce Charles Sawyer was advised to create an agency like the wartime War Production Board (WPB) under his jurisdiction. This idea

1. Truman to Murphy, 20 July 1948, Presidential Powers, Charles Murphy Papers, HSTL.

2. NSRB #44, M1-2, Series 39.32, OMB; Remarks of Arthur Hill, Legal Advisory Committee, Entry 1, RG 304, NA.

3. Roger Jones to Charles Murphy, 18 November 1948, Presidential Powers, Murphy Papers, HSTL.

4. Dean Acheson to James Webb, 5 May 1950, Memos of Conversations, Acheson Papers, HSTL.

5. Report of the Chairman, NSRB, PSF, Truman Papers, HSTL.

was strongly opposed by other departments who hoped
to have a major role in directing the mobilization effort.[6]

Because of the intense competition among the
various agencies for a share of the mobilization pie,
Truman tended to look to the disinterested organizational experts in the Budget Bureau for advice. Their
recommendations, made in late July 1950, assumed that
the Korean War would require only a limited buildup
that could be largely administered by existing agencies instead of a total mobilization of the economy.
The bureau suggested that the NSRB, on behalf of the
president, be made responsible for coordinating the
policies that the passage of the Defense Production
Act would require. But the bureau emphasized that all
authority for policy determination initially should be
retained by the president. Any formal delegation of
authority to the agencies should be done later on a
piecemeal basis.[7]

The bureau remained opposed to any assumption
of operating responsibilities by the NSRB. It admitted
that the NSRB was a good candidate for the mobilization role because it was an organization in being, had
an experienced staff, and, by virtue of its location in
the executive office, was in a good position to adjudi-
cate competing departmental interests, but found the
arguments against this option more compelling. It reasoned that the NSRB's mobilization planning work would
be needed now more than ever. But if the NSRB were to
be given operational control over mobilization, this
work would leave little time for or interest in planning. There was also the practical consideration that
if the NSRB became an operating agency, appeals from
its decisions could only be taken directly to the
president. "This would subject the President to a mul-
titude of day-to-day pressures, and at the same time,
he would be deprived of a major staff assistance." For
these reasons the bureau urged Truman to continue to

---

6. Herbert H. Rosenberg, "ODM: A Study of Civil Military Relations
During the Korean Mobilization," pp. 23-24.

7. Lawton to President, 28 July 1950, Defense Production Act, Series 47.3c, RG 51, NA.

use the NSRB as a staff that could help him to review the policies of those agencies who would be administering portions of the Defense Production Act.[8]

Although Truman accepted this recommendation, he wanted the NSRB to help him resolve mobilization disputes among his cabinet members. So the bureau developed these guidelines for the NSRB's coordinating activity: (1) It should review the actions of the departments involved to assure that they were consistent with mobilization plans; and (2) it should serve as the point of appeal from decisions of the secretaries of commerce, interior, or agriculture that might run counter to positions taken by other cabinet officers. "This second function may be looked upon, if it is not abused, as providing a means of bringing policy issues to the President, rather than providing a point of appeal on every action from one Cabinet officer's decision."[9]

The real question was how many of the disputes would be handled by the "coordinator" and how many would be referred on to the president for resolution. Symington strongly believed that the issues should be settled short of the president by an official clearly charged with that responsibility. The bureau defined for Truman three possible relationships he could have with the coordinator and recommended that he accept the following option:

No legal delegation of your authority for final decisions, but a public designation by you of an individual who is to be your top assistant for various purposes—to aid in your coordination of policies underlying industrial mobilization, to settle any issues which arise and which can be settled short of your decision, and to report to you issues which you should settle, together with alternatives and the pros and cons of them.[10]

The bureau did not specifically recommend that Symington be named to coordinate the mobilization ef-

8. Lawton to President, 28 July 1950, Defense Production Act, vol. 3, Stephen Spingarn Files, Truman Papers, HSTL.

9. Lawton to President, 10 August 1950, Defense Production Act, PSF, Truman Papers, HSTL.

10. Ibid.

fort, but Truman was reminded that if he did not designate the chairman of the NSRB for this role, he would need to assign it to someone else in the White House, the executive office, or someone entirely new.[11] In the end Truman followed the line of least resistance and named Symington.

Executive Order 10161 was issued on 9 September 1950, the day after the Defense Production Act became law. As the bureau had recommended, it created the Economic Stabilization Agency and delegated other mobilization authority to agencies. The chairman of the NSRB was told to coordinate these new functions and to resolve any interagency disputes that might otherwise require the attention of the president, but he was given no authority to direct or control their operations.[12] In practice Symington's coordinating powers were slight.

THE CEA AND MOBILIZATION

Under Leon Keyserling's leadership the Council of Economic Advisers took an active part in mobilization by preparing legislation, proposing administrative arrangements, and suggesting strategies for presidential leadership. During the summer, Keyserling and Gross contributed substantially to the drafting of the Defense Production Act.[13] In the past such matters had typically been the province of the Budget Bureau or the White House staff.

Since the Defense Production Act dealt almost exclusively with economic policy and control, the CEA's influence with the president was directly threatened as new or existing agencies were charged with directing various phases of the mobilization effort. The council, as a small agency, had no hope of obtaining a dominant position in such a massive undertaking. It attempted to maintain a significant voice in the nation's economic policy by offering its services directly

---

11. Ibid.

12. Report of the Chairman, NSRB, PSF, Truman Papers, HSTL.

13. Keyserling to Stephen Spingarn, 18 July 1950, Spingarn Files, Truman Papers, HSTL.

to the mobilization agencies, hoping to infiltrate their staffs and influence their policies.

When Executive Order 10161 assigned coordinating responsibility to the NSRB, Keyserling quickly moved to offer the council's services to Symington. He told the NSRB chairman that the council, "being divorced from daily operations, is in a unique position to help . . . distinguish the woods from the trees." Keyserling thought they "ought to be able to make some joint use of the resources of our agencies, because we are so completely in agreement about objectives."[14] They agreed on the need to speed up defense production and procurement but for different reasons. Symington was a hawk who sought full mobilization because he antici- pated a possible preventive war with the Soviets. Keyserling saw defense production as a politically ac- ceptable way to stimulate national economic growth. This alliance of convenience complimented the two men's organizational needs as well. Keyserling wanted the council to maintain its influence, and the NSRB was in a position to implement its advice. Symington, for his part, was short of skilled economists, so he wel- comed the staff support the council could provide.[15]

SYMINGTON'S STYLE

Each of the departments that were given a role in mo- bilization created new agencies (such as the National Production Authority in the Commerce Department and the Marketing Administration in the Agriculture De- partment) to exercise their new functions. Symington also set up new units in the NSRB to help him carry out his new responsibilities. For example, he organized an Interagency Controls Coordinating Committee (ICCC), with representation from all the agencies having con- trol responsibilities, to resolve any interagency is- sues and evaluate the effect of mobilization on the economy.[16]

---

14. Keyserling to Symington, 12 September 1950, Symington File, RG 304, NA.

15. Edward S. Flash, *Economic Advice and Presidential Leadership*, pp. 57-58.

16. Ibid.

Symington sought to build public cooperation and support for his efforts by setting up a National Advisory Committee on Mobilization Policy. It was made up of representatives from agriculture, industry, labor, and the public and included such luminaries as Murray Lincoln, Marion Folsom, Philip Murray, and Anna Rosenberg. The committee first met in mid-August while the defense production bill was being debated and twice monthly thereafter until Symington lost his coordinating function. Richard Neustadt cynically analyzed the advisory committee for the White House:

Symington kept his people happy—for a while—by the sheer personal pyrotechnics he displayed in chairing meetings, steering the discussion and dealing with the members individually and in groups. To this he added bread and circuses—a good show, with fancy briefings by high military and civil officers, *plus* lunch in the conference room, catered by the Statler and paid out of an NSRB slush fund. . . . Symington's Committee did not solve the problem of what does such an outfit do besides *receive* information.[17]

Labor was disappointed when Symington failed to select his vice-chairman from among its ranks. So to placate the unions he set up an *ad hoc* committee made up of various labor leaders to advise him. Soon labor representatives were placed throughout the NSRB staff, and three labor representatives participated in policy discussions by the board's directorate.[18]

During the early period of the Korean mobilization, Symington was solicitous of the views of the members of NSRB even though the board's function was now totally advisory.[19] He held eleven board meetings between 5 May and 20 October 1950. This equaled the total number of meetings during the entire previous history of the board. On major policy matters he consistently sought the views of board members before sending his recommendations to the president and tried to work out points of disagreement. From late October until mid-December he dispensed with formal board

17. Neustadt to Murphy, 5 April 1951, National Advisory Board, Murphy Files, Truman Papers, HSTL.
18. Report of the Chairman, NSRB, PSF, Truman Papers, HSTL.
19. Reorganization Plan No. 25 became effective on 9 July 1950.

meetings because he considered the Interagency Controls Coordinating Committee a more effective mechanism for resolving mobilization issues.[20] So long as Symington was charged with mediating interagency disputes relating to mobilization, he was able to do so effectively and no appeals were made over his head to the president.[21]

LIMITED MOBILIZATION

The period from September to December 1950 was an experimental time because no one really knew how best to administer a limited mobilization. The bureau had recommended a cautious approach and Truman had accepted it. To maintain flexibility, economic controls had been delegated to existing agencies so that they could be withdrawn easily and reassigned to temporary agencies if a greater emergency developed. The whole arrangement depended a great deal on voluntary cooperation. The NSRB had been assigned a carefully restricted role as a coordinator, but all legal authority had been retained by the president.

There were many tensions built into the situation. Neither Sawyer nor Symington was happy with the scheme, and the bureau seemed uneasy about the coordinating role it had reluctantly recommended for the NSRB. Symington continued to press for greater economic controls and a more rapid expansion of the economy even though Truman was clearly opposed to both. In meetings of the National Security Council the NSRB chairman had shown himself to be much more of a hawk than either his colleagues or the president.[22] It seems likely that the president must have had moments of inquietude about the behavior of his mobilization coordinator, but there was no indication that he intended to make a change.

---

20. Harry P. Yoshpe, "Planning for Defense: A History of the Role and Accomplishments of the National Security Resources Board," Draft, NSRB General Administration Folder, Series 39.28, RG 51, NA, pp. 28–29.

21. Edward H. Hobbs, *Behind the President*, p. 168.

22. NSC Action 315, 6 July 1950, 60th NSC Meeting, PSF, Truman Papers, HSTL.

In November the situation was altered dramatically when the Chinese intervened in force in Korea. As MacArthur's troops were thrown back, concern in Washington rapidly escalated to panic. In early December the dimensions of the problems raised by the military situation could only be dimly seen, but there was tremendous pressure to make some decisions. On 15 December the president proclaimed a national emergency. Part of the reason for the proclamation was to convince the American people that their leaders were doing something. It was also useful legally in the letting of contracts for mobilization.[23]

It was now clear that a higher level of mobilization would be required, but there were many views about what this level should be. Truman asked the Budget Bureau to review the existing mobilization organization and make recommendations directly to him if they believed changes should be made. Elmer Staats, Charles Stauffacher, and others in the bureau considered several alternatives they might propose to the president. Staats recalled that one of these was

to place the responsibility on the Chairman of the National Security Resources Board and that was the option favored by Symington. While the statute did not give the Chairman special legal authority, certainly the President by Executive Order could have designated him as his representative and, in fact, could have given him the power later given to the Office of Defense Mobilization. We, however, came to a different conclusion, namely that it would be better for the President to establish a new agency, leaving the National Security Resources Board in a somewhat dormant status but continuing to have an input to the mobilization planning.

The situation in Korea was then so fluid that it was impossible to make any assumptions about the probable duration of the war. The bureau planners argued about "whether it made any sense to pull out of the Commerce Department the resources which had been transferred there from the old War Production Board and thereby establish an agency which would have an uncertain

23. Robert J. Donovan, *Tumultuous Years: The Presidency of Harry S Truman, 1949-1953* (New York, 1982), p. 319.

life." Convinced that a significantly larger war effort would be required, they recommended that the president establish the National Production Authority, an independent mobilization organization.[24]

THE BUREAU PLAN

In retrospect there is little doubt that the Truman administration created a much more elaborate mechanism for economic mobilization than the Korean emergency required. This miscalculation was based on a breakdown in communications between Truman and his Budget Bureau and the demands of Charles E. Wilson. The episode began on 8 December 1950 when Budget Director Lawton spent half an hour with the president and his advisers presenting the bureau's plan to establish an independent National Production Authority. He explained that organizational adjustments were needed in the mobilization apparatus to assure an intensified administration of programs already in existence and to administer new programs that were now necessary. He stressed that any adjustments made should be consistent with any ultimate organizational structure planned for full mobilization. He gave the president a written summary of his recommendations and left.[25]

Specifically, Lawton proposed conservative adjustments in the existing mobilization arrangements, none of which even came close to the sweeping structure later adopted. Four alternative approaches were presented for the president's consideration. These were:

1.   Retain present structure; modify the existing industrial assignments to various agencies to provide greater integration.
2.   Create a separate NPA: make it a strong production programming center; retain NSRB in OWMR capacity.
3.   Make full priorities and allocations delegation to NSRB with

---

24. Staats to Alfred Sander, 27 October 1979.
25. Truman's Schedule, Notes of Truman, Richard E. Neustadt Papers, HSTL; Memo for the President, 8 December 1950, ODM, Series 47.3c, RG 51, NA.

understanding that NSRB would redelegate to operating agencies on a basis comparable with present setup; but that NSRB would establish stronger central programming and policy mechanism and exercise more direct operating control.

4. Make full priorities and allocations delegation to an independent NPA: provide for successive delegations to existing departments with understanding that NPA would establish stronger central programming and policy machinery; retain NSRB in a staff capacity on mobilization coordination.

After urging the president to select option #2 the bureau attempted to justify its recommendation.[26]

The NPA referred to in this recommendation was the National Production Authority which Charles Sawyer had set up earlier in his Commerce Department. The bureau now proposed that this be made an independent agency and given greatly increased powers. The effect would be to elevate the status of the agency in the eyes of both the public and industry and bring greater integration to the handling of industrial controls. Under this plan the NPA would assume the responsibility for production planning and business expansion controls that the NSRB was then exercising. Although the bureau recommended the NSRB assume additional functions such as foreign economic operations, Lawton proposed no increase in the power Symington had been given in Executive Order 10161.[27]

Lawton warned Truman that the selection of option #2 could cause some problems. One was the probable displeasure of Sawyer if the NPA was detached from the Commerce Department. Negative reactions could also be expected from secretaries Oscar Chapman and Charles Brannan (and of course from Symington) if some of their authority was transferred to an independent NPA. The budget director urged the president to choose whether the NPA or the NSRB would be the focus for coordinating industrial production. In making this decision Truman was cautioned to limit the NSRB to

---

26. "Alternative Approaches to Establishing a Strengthened Industrial Production Agency," 8 December 1950, Organization for Defense, PSF, Truman Papers, HSTL.

27. Ibid.

presidential problems so that it would not be rendered ineffective by wandering into areas that were not of the president's concern.[28]

The thrust of the recommendations was that a strong production programming center (like the World War II War Production Board) was needed at this stage in the Korean War. The bureau wanted the NSRB to be confined to its coordinating role but admitted this responsibility would increase as the tempo of industrial mobilization was stepped up.

Lawton left the meeting believing that Truman had approved alternative #2. He returned to his office and directed that work begin on an executive order to put the plan into effect. But (as the bureau later reconstructed the series of events) "the President apparently interpreted the Bureau's proposal as meaning something on the pattern of the old Office of War Mobilization and discussed the matter in these terms with the candidate for the directorship." As a result, the bureau and the president "got off on different tracks with respect to the organization formula to meet the contingency, without either discovering it until it was too late to repair the situation."[29]

THE ORIGIN OF THE ODM

Lawton had met with the president and his assistants on Friday. On Sunday Truman called Charles E. Wilson of the General Electric Company and invited him to come to Washington the next day for a talk. The two had gotten to know each other during World War II when Truman headed a Senate investigating committee and Wilson worked for the War Production Board. Wilson had not been much of a success during his wartime service, but Truman always felt that Charlie Wilson was just the kind of statuesque figure he wanted to be in charge if large-scale mobilization was ever necessary.

---

28. Ibid.
29. Background of Reorganization Plan #3 of 1953, "Establishment of New Office of Defense Mobilization," M7-51/52.1, Series 52.6, RG 51, NA.

He had made no secret of his intention to select Wilson if that time ever came.[30]

The next day, while the bureau was at work on the executive order establishing the strong production authority it thought the president had approved, Truman (unbeknownst to either the White House or bureau staffs) met with Wilson. He offered to appoint Wilson head of the NPA. But Wilson said he must have direction and control of the total mobilization effort or nothing. Truman, who deeply wanted the bipartisan symbol he believed Wilson represented, gave in.[31] He offered to appoint Wilson his "Deputy President" in charge of the mobilization program. Wilson, whose previous WPB experience had been frustrating, was suspicious and demanded that he be given the specific title, "Deputy President." Truman assured Wilson that he would have an opportunity to examine the terms of his appointment before committing himself to accept the position.[32]

Charles B. Stauffacher, the bureau's organizational expert and third-ranking officer, was the principal author of the existing mobilization structure as well as the most recent recommendation that Lawton had presented to Truman. While the president was meeting with Wilson, Stauffacher was busy preparing the draft executive order intended to transform the NPA from an appendage of the Commerce Department into the powerful and independent Defense Production Administration (DPA). The order would also authorize Symington to "coordinate generally" the entire mobilization program. On Tuesday, 12 December, Truman called Stauffacher and asked him to go to New York to discuss the new organization with Wilson. The president did not tell Stauffacher what he had talked to Wilson about, possibly because he was not aware that it contradicted the bureau plan.[33]

---

30. Charles Murphy Oral History, pp. 314–315, HSTL; Leon Keyserling Oral History, HSTL, pp. 142–143.

31. Richard Neustadt to Alfred Sander, 6 August 1987.

32. Rosenberg, "ODM," p. 34.

33. Ibid. pp. 33–35.

On Wednesday Stauffacher, believing that the president intended to make Wilson the head of the proposed DPA, called on the industrialist. He was startled to learn instead that Truman had offered Wilson the post of deputy president. Wilson demanded that the order establishing his position specify that he would have direct access to the president with a rank superior to cabinet officers. After Truman confirmed Wilson's account of their understanding, Stauffacher drafted an entirely new executive order (10193) that created the mighty Office of Defense Mobilization (ODM). Since the order did not use the term deputy president, Wilson was not entirely pleased with it, but on 14 December he accepted the appointment to be director of ODM.[34]

That same day Truman held a meeting attended by Steelman, Harriman, Murphy, Lawton, and Stauffacher in which he broke the news of the Wilson appointment and the establishment of ODM. While he said that he wanted Wilson to be regarded as a member of the White House staff, there was no more mention of a deputy president. (Presumably Stauffacher had been able to eliminate that faux pas.) The president seemed somewhat defensive about his decision.[35] Perhaps this was because he now realized the organizational implications of the ODM and knew it was too late to withdraw the offer to Wilson, or it may have been simply that he sensed that the others did not approve of his decision.

One of those who did not agree was Stuart Symington. When he learned of Truman's decision to invest coordinating authority in an ODM instead of the NSRB, he took the issue to the president several times. One one occasion when he raised the matter in a cabinet meeting it led to a "very warm discussion."[36]

But Truman was firm, so the executive order establishing the ODM was promulgated on 16 December. It specified that the director of ODM "shall on behalf of the President direct, control, and coordinate all mobilization activities of the Executive Branch of the Gov-

---

34. Ibid. pp. 36–37.
35. Ibid. p. 38.
36. Staats statement in Heller, *The Truman White House.* p. 170.

ernment, including but not limited to production, procurement, manpower, stabilization and transport activities." Wilson was given power as sweeping as Roosevelt had conferred on Byrnes in the midst of World War II. But the two situations were not really comparable. ODM was an overreaction to the Chinese intervention. Shortly after it was established, the battle lines in Korea stabilized and any thought of full mobilization was discarded. As Herbert Rosenberg, the historian of the ODM, observed, the agency "lived in an almost unreal world of `butter and guns' build up of partial mobilization."[37]

The ODM was an overall coordinating device like OWM had been. The bureau, in recommending the creation of the DPA, had seen the need for a production coordination authority similar to World War II's WPB. Since such an organization was still needed, in early January Truman signed Executive Order 10200 establishing the Defense Production Administration in pursuance of the original bureau plan. So to deal with the Korean "police action" Truman authorized a mobilization structure that approximated the World War II response. This in the view of the bureau was "a large jump from the original concept of proper restraint in setting up special machinery to something that could easily spell over organization at the top.[38]

THE ODM AND THE EXECUTIVE OFFICE

The ODM was handicapped by being designed to manage a situation that never materialized. The wave of patriotism sparked by the Chinese intervention soon ebbed as a military stalemate developed. The officials of the ODM never enjoyed the commitment of national purpose that could serve as the backbone of the mobilization effort.

Even if conditions had been more favorable, Wilson was not particularly well suited to head an organization like the ODM. As James Reston observed, Wilson had a history of getting what he wanted for a

37. Rosenberg, "ODM," pp. 12–13.
38. "Background of Reorganization Plan #3 of 1953, M7–51/52.1, Series 52.6, RG 51, NA.

while and then leaving in a huff. At one time during World War II he was head of production at the WPB while Eberstadt was in charge of raw materials. Wilson let everyone know he thought their two areas should be combined. After resisting this notion for a time Eberstadt resigned, but this caused such an uproar at the WPB that Wilson soon left as well. It was partly because of this experience with divided authority that Wilson had insisted that Truman give him extraordinary powers before agreeing to head the ODM.[39]

Charles Murphy, the president's aide, recalled Wilson as a sensitive person who "was at something of a loss" as the mobilization chief. His job, which initially overlapped Symington's to a large degree, involved "some of the most difficult problems in the Federal bureaucracy." Murphy concluded that "it just was not Charlie Wilson's bailiwick." Things seem to bother him and hurt his feelings. Soon it got to be a regular thing for Murphy to go over to Wilson's office "and sit for an hour or more so he could tell me his troubles and problems."[40]

Nor was the integration of the ODM into the EOP well planned. The White House staff (who were no longer sure whom they were working for) soon came into conflict with Wilson's staff. Difficulties arose between the two over manpower organization, shipping and transportation, and information policy. Since Truman had not bothered to think through the new organizational relationships, the White House staff did not know whether Wilson was to take over some of the functions they had been performing.[41]

The Budget Bureau tried to rescue the situation. It explained to Truman that from an organizational point of view he had "brought in a new Assistant President" but he had not arrived at an understanding with Wilson and the existing presidential staff about how they were to function and operate together. Everyone wanted to be cooperative and relieve the president

---

39. *New York Times*, 1 April 1952.
40. Murphy Oral History, HSTL, pp. 314-317.
41. Points for Discussion with the President, 22 January 1951, Defense Mobilization, Elsey Papers, HSTL.

of some of the burdens of mobilization, but they did not know what relationships Truman wanted to maintain with his staff.[42]

The bureau suggested that the answer was to regard the ODM as part of the "institutional" staff of the executive office instead of an addition to the White House staff. The president was reminded of the problems that had arisen in the past among the White House, the bureau, and the NSRB. These had been effectively solved by the development of proper staff understanding and working relationships. He was assured it could work again, but first there had to be some frank and free discussion of the matter and a clear indication of what the president wanted the relationship to be. The bureau thought Truman should hold a general conference on the subject after he had a private talk with Wilson.[43]

THE DEPARTURE OF SYMINGTON

Meanwhile, after his initial flare-up, Symington was a model of cooperation. He quickly arranged the mass transfer of over 500 trained NSRB personnel to the new emergency agencies.[44] These transfers were helpful in establishing continuity and permitting these agencies to more quickly attain operating effectiveness. However, the line was never effectively drawn between the NSRB's long-range planning function and the ODM's management of the mobilization effort. In early 1951 the overlap and duplication was particularly confusing. On the staff level, relations between ODM and NSRB were close because they were housed in the same building, had similar interests, and many former NSRB employees now worked for ODM. But this camaraderie did not extend to the leadership level. Symington simply became extremely circumspect about any NSRB activity that might possibly be interpreted as infringing on ODM responsibility. As a result, NSRB did very little.[45]

42. Ibid.

43. Ibid.

44. Truman to Symington, 3 January 1951, OF 1295, Truman Papers, HSTL; Symington Report, NSRB, PSF, ibid.

45. Yoshpe, *Case Study*, p. 41.

    While Symington was winding down NSRB opera-
tions (and probably looking for another job), members
of his staff were trying to define the distinction between NSRB and ODM and justify the continued existence of their agency. This search for a valid mission
occupied the attention of the NSRB for the rest of its
life. The most ambitious of these efforts was a paper
prepared by Francis Fussell in February 1951. Fussell
described the functions which the NSRB could perform
under existing presidential and legislative intents.
These included feasibility testing of existing mobilization plans to see if they would work and advising
the president in such areas as manpower utilization,
stockpiling, and the strategic relocation of industry.
His most imaginative suggestion was to have the NSRB
undertake a twenty-five-year economic strategic plan
covering such fields as minerals, petroleum, power,
water, communications, and transportation. Fussell admitted that to undertake such a far-reaching program
would require, at a minimum, presidential concurrence
and perhaps legislative action, but he clearly demonstrated that such a long-range plan was not only
needed but that it was not being done any place in the
government.[46] There were many similar papers written
that proposed various roles for the NSRB but none
were acted upon and the agency continued to drift.
    By early April it was generally known that
Symington would soon be named to head the Reconstruction Finance Corporation. This news prompted a
review of the NSRB's trials and tribulations by a member of John Steelman's White House staff. He wrote
that:

This outfit never had a chance. The first chairman was moved out because he misconceived the mission of the Board. Then there was the
fight on Mon Walgren's confirmation. After that, you [Steelman], as
acting chairman, could not devote enough time to it. The present
chairman is a high-power operator, not a planner. This history, plus
the present pressure of world events, with its emphasis on short-
range defense build-up, has reduced this agency to a laughingstock

------

46. "The Role of the NSRB in a Period of Actual Mobilization," 15
February 1951, Gorrie Files, Entry 4, RG 304, NA.

around town. Since the chairman is supposed to act as an adviser to the President, this reputation for ineffectuality does not redound to the President's credit, either.

With Mr. Symington leaving, I do not think the situation should be allowed to drift. The deliberate choice should be made either (1) to fill the chairmanship with an innocuous nobody, or let it remain vacant; reduce the staff to about five persons, and wait to see how the world situation develops, or (2) fill the chairmanship with the best man to be found, define a charter for the organization, and then proceed to beef-up the organization. . . . My chief point is that whatever is done about NSRB should be deliberate and considered. I think the President has an exposed flank there that his political opponents could exploit with devastating effect if they make use of their intelligence reports. I have reason to believe that the present situation in NSRB is of common enough knowledge not to escape the opposition's attention.[47]

The situation was "allowed to drift," but not because of a lack of suggestions. The bureau's organizational experts thought the next chairman should be a "short-haired guy who knows how to operate in a long-haired job."[48] Then word began to spread that Averell Harriman was being considered for the NSRB chairmanship. This caused consternation among the ODM staff. One warned Wilson that his organization would be threatened

if a statutory agency with functions largely overlapping those of ODM remains in operation and susceptible of being revised at any time. I would urge as strongly as I can that you make this a point of confidence with the President. It seems to me entirely appropriate that you take over the NSRB as Acting Chairman. . . . You could put anyone you chose in control and keep the operation in line with the functions of ODM.[49]

In early May Symington left the NSRB for the RFC. Since his vice chairman had resigned in February, the

47. Russell P. Andrews to John Steelman, 25 April 1951, NSRB Projects, Harold L. Enarson Papers, HSTL.

48. Arnold Miles to C. B. Stauffacher, 4 April 1951, NSRB, Series 47.3c, RG 51, NA.

49. W. Y. Elliott to Charles Wilson, 3 May 1951, ibid.

NSRB was left in the hands of Symington's executive assistant, Jack Gorrie. Truman named Gorrie acting chairman while he searched for a permanent head for the agency. Gorrie had been a reporter and writer in the early 1930s before becoming an internal revenue agent. Following the war, he served as an assistant to the governor of the state of Washington. In April 1949 he joined the NSRB as Steelman's executive assistant and continued in that job when Symington took over a year later.[50]

By mid-June Harriman was no longer under active consideration as the next chairman of the NSRB. With Gorrie in charge of a NSRB that had no viable mission, the ODM no longer felt threatened by its possible resurgence. Gorrie continued as acting chairman until October 1951 when he was given a recess appointment as chairman. But another eight months elapsed before his name was sent to the Senate and he was confirmed in the position. By default, Truman apparently had decided to fill the job with "an innocuous nobody" instead of a well-known political or industrial figure.

ODM TAKES OVER

While the NSRB was attempting to adjust to its fall from grace, Wilson was trying to get the ODM into operation. To help with organizational and production problems General Lucius Clay came to Washington as Wilson's principal assistant. When, after a few months, Clay returned to private industry, he was replaced by Charles Stauffacher of the Budget Bureau. Sidney Weinberg, who had a prominent role in World War II mobilization, served as a part-time special assistant to Wilson.[51] The ODM was never organized very concretely, but various individuals were assigned to general functional areas such as production programming, economic stabilization, manpower, health resources, and the scientific aspects of mobilization.[52] To help Wilson coordinate activities in the other agencies a Defense

50. Symington Files, Entry 3, RG 304, NA.

51. Murphy Oral History, HSTL, pp. 319–320.

52. W.Y. Elliott to Wilson, 30 March 1951, ODM, Series 47.3c, RG 51, NA.

Mobilization Board was set up. Consisting of the secretaries of defense, commerce, interior, agriculture,
treasury, and labor, together with the chairmen of the
NSRB, RFC, and the Federal Reserve Board, it served
many of the same purposes of the old NSRB when it was
coordinating mobilization.[53]

When it had become obvious that Truman intended
Wilson to be his sole agent for mobilization policy,
Leon Keyserling attempted to become Wilson's economic
adviser and to influence his policies as he had done
with Symington. This presented some delicate organizational difficulties because the CEA did not want to
concede that it was subordinate to the ODM. If it did,
it might have to relinquish its direct access to the
president. Truman told Keyserling that he did not intend for the council to be responsible to Wilson, but
he wanted Keyserling regularly to attend the weekly
ODM staff meetings. As a result, Keyserling became a de
facto member of the ODM organization. He felt that this
gave him "a good opportunity to know what was going
on in this field, to let Mr. Wilson have the benefit of
my advice (which he frequently took), and, not infrequently to differ with him." Although Keyserling maintained that he attended these meetings "as a representative of the President," Wilson was clearly in
charge and made the final decisions.[54] The council was
merely one voice that Wilson listened to, and since its
views were usually not in accord with his, its influence was not great.

The actual direction of mobilization was the responsibility of the new emergency agencies such as
Economic Stabilization, Defense Production, and Defense
Transportation. These agencies in turn reported to the
ODM. Wilson and his small staff devoted their attention
to: (1) the establishment of the major mobilization
policies and objectives; (2) meshing the policies of the
subordinate operating agencies and resolving issues
between them; (3) checking on the effectiveness of
agency operations; (4) phasing mobilization activities
into other national actions; (5) presenting the mobi-

---

53. ODM, 2 May 1951, ODM Misc., PSF, Truman Papers, HSTL.
54. Keyserling in Heller, *The Truman White House*, pp. 190–191, 216.

lization effort to the public, Congress, and other agencies; and (6) reporting to and advising the president on mobilization matters.[55]

ODM was, to a large extent, set up to deal with problems that never materialized. In many ways it was modeled after Roosevelt's OWM which was designed to be a conflict settlement point short of the president. FDR had called it into being because he was simply too busy with foreign policy and military strategy to serve as an arbiter among the nation's economic groups. But this was not the situation during the Korean War, nor did the need exist for the country to undertake a large scale mobilization. As a result, the ODM concerned itself largely with the production aspects of mobilization. But since production was the responsibility of the DPA, there was extensive duplication between the two.[56]

The ODM never did get on top of the military aspects of mobilization or the stabilization problem. But it was an effective coordinator and was able to push, expedite, and needle the operating agencies as no other part of the EOP was able to do. ODM was also useful as a symbol of unity for the mobilization program as a result of its public reports and relations with Congress.[57] Wilson became the spokesman and defender of the mobilization, took the lead on defense legislation, and undertook a comprehensive program of reporting to the public, both in speeches and through publications.[58]

By early 1952 the frustrations of Washington were taking their toll on the headstrong Wilson. In the spring Wilson thought he had convinced Truman to authorize a wage increase for steelworkers tied to an increase in steel prices. But when the head of the Office of Price Stabilization objected, Truman apparently changed his mind. When Wilson learned he had been overruled, he returned to his office and wrote out his

55. ODM Organizational Operations, ODM, Series 47.3c, RG 51, NA.

56. Appendix A, M7-51/52.1, Series 52.6, RG 51, NA.

57. Ibid.

58. Memo for Steelman and Lawton, 17 April 1952, ODM, M7-51/52.1, Series 52.6, RG 51, NA.

letter of resignation. Reston characterized Wilson as a "magnificent quitter" who always "leaves with a flourish. He always slams the door when he departs." The next day Truman named Steelman the acting director of ODM.[59] Steelman in turn was later replaced by Henry Fowler who served through the remainder of the Truman administration.

THE YOUNG STUDY

The NSRB was in a pitiful condition during its last two years. When Gorrie took over in the spring of 1951, his immediate objective was to eliminate the duplication with the ODM and rethink the NSRB's basic mission. Gradually much of the working relationship with ODM was clarified between Gorrie and Wilson, but the fundamental question of who was to plan mobilization remained. Because of the NSRB's preoccupation with reprogramming and restaffing, it did not attempt to press for a showdown on this issue. Similarly, ODM's concern with the current mobilization effort did not leave it much time to concern itself with full mobilization planning until after Wilson left. By that time the mobilization program had reached its projected base. This meant that the basic operating responsibilities of emergency agencies such as DPA had been fulfilled. Inevitably, they then began to encroach on the full mobilization area.[60]

As a result of DPA's aggressive and well-publicized efforts to move into the kind of long-range planning that NSRB had done before the Korean War, Congress took action to cut the NSRB appropriation because of the duplication they discerned in the functions of NSRB, ODM, and DPA. In early April 1952 the House by a voice vote reduced the NSRB from the requested $1,780,000 to $500,000.[61]

As the war wound down during the summer of 1952, the NSRB's professional staff had declined to twenty-nine people who were carrying on a minimal effort

---

59. *New York Times*, 1 March and 1 April 1952.
60. James L. Kuenen to Gorrie, 16 April 1952, Entry 4, RG 304, NA.
61. Ibid.

within the agency's statutory responsibilities.[62] Clearly, it was a caretaker operation designed to keep the NSRB in existence until an organizational decision was made among the competing mobilization agencies.

When the mobilization effort contracted, the competing agencies were confined to smaller and smaller areas of activities with an inevitable duplication of effort. Truman asked his staff to study the situation and provide him with a preliminary report. He stressed that as the emergency activities were reduced or eliminated he wanted "to preserve the original functions of the regular divisions of the Executive Office."[63]

During the fall, the report Truman asked for was prepared by John D. Young, a former employee of both the NSRB and ODM. Its most striking feature was a repudiation of the traditional view of the Budget Bureau that the NSRB should not be assigned an operational role because it was a presidential staff group. Young implied that there had been a continuing conspiracy to deny the NSRB its proper role. He wrote:

There is no compelling rationale to the old saw that planning and operating (or planning and direction) cannot be placed in the same institutional framework. In fact, the very opposite (in terms of the realities of administrative behavior) is and must be true. This rather strange dichotomy has been repeatedly used to achieve certain organizational ends or goals that people or groups did not want to admit directly. . . . The belief that the mobilization planning agency should only advise the President has little meaning. This approach has been used for devious and sundry reasons to deny the central planning agency effective authority.[64]

Young claimed that "attempts to split short-range from long-range planning has no real meaning in terms of a rationale for establishing separate structures."

---

62. "An Analysis of the Central Management Elements of the Defense Mobilization Program," 23 October 1952, Organizational Study, David H. Stowe Papers, HSTL.

63. Truman to David Stowe, 29 August 1952, Organization Study, Stowe Papers, HSTL.

64. Ibid.

He argued that planning becomes a fruitless and sterile undertaking if it is placed in an institutional setting that denies it a close working relationship with day-to-day actions and decisions in defense mobilization. He did not believe it reasonable to try to stockpile standby agencies to control prices, wages, rents, and materials since "organizations are still people with hopes, fears, ambitions, etc., they cannot be conceived of as inert matter." Young held that the only sound way to approach mobilization management was to devise a system of budgeting resources in terms of the major current and future demands. "Until some rather simple system to do this has been developed and made a part of the existing structure and processes of the government, the mobilization efforts, present and future, rest on shifting sands."[65]

To remedy the existing mobilization muddle, Young recommended that the ODM be gradually abolished in favor of a reconstituted NSRB that would be responsible for the direction, control, and coordination of the mobilization functions that remained. Since "NSRB" had "some bad symbolism connected with it," Young suggested its name be changed to furnish it with a "new store front."[66] Possibly because Young did not think these changes could be made before the spring of 1953, Truman took no action on the recommendation and left the problem for President Eisenhower.

THE END OF THE NSRB

When Eisenhower took office, the Budget Bureau prepared for him an extensive summary of the major organizational and management problems he would be facing. The NSRB-ODM matter was high on the list because Congress, in its appropriation for the NSRB, had provided monies only through 31 March 1953. This meant that an early decision had to be made to either consolidate the agencies or seek a supplemental appropriation.[67]

---

65. Ibid.

66. Ibid.

67. "The Presidential Job in Organizing and Managing the Executive Branch," E2–50/52.2, Series 52.6, RG 51, NA.

The bureau still believed that the NSRB chairman should not be given operational responsibilities, but this concern was now outweighed by the problem of securing the most able men to direct the mobilization work. It was, therefore,

the opinion of the Budget Bureau staff that the existence of three agencies for which the President must select and appoint a head . . . unduly complicates both the President's position in offering these jobs to various individuals and of explaining this organizational setup within the present program context to the Congress and the people. We would, therefore, recommend that the functions of these three organizations be consolidated and that the President effect the consolidation within the NSRB. It would be our further recommendation on the "concept" side that the President look upon the NSRB as an organization which could comprehend both operating and planning responsibilities by proper internal organization and allocation of responsibility.

In an enormous understatement the bureau said that this action would substantially simplify the problem of executive office organization.[68] Had they come to this conclusion in 1947 it would certainly have simplified the whole mobilization problem. John Young and the bureau ended up with about the same recommendation but they had arrived there by quite different lines of reasoning.

But Dwight Eisenhower was not inclined to trust recommendations made by a federal bureaucracy built up during twenty years of Democratic rule. Nor did he believe that career civil servants would help him fulfill his promise to reduce the size and increase the effectiveness of the federal government. Even before his inauguration he had formed a three-man Special Committee on Government Organization to advise him on restructuring the government. This committee, which was headed by Nelson Rockefeller, included the president's brother Milton and Dr. Arthur Flemming (lately of ODM). Its job was to develop recommendations for immediate improvements in the organization and management of the executive branch because the "entry of the new

---

68. Ibid.

Republican Administration provides a unique opportunity for substantial progress in this field."[69] One of President Eisenhower's first actions was to formally place Rockefeller's group in the Executive Office of the President as the President's Advisory Committee on Government Organization (PACGO).

By mid-February PACGO had recommended that the NSRB and ODM "be merged into a single central defense mobilization staff agency to the President" bearing the name Office of Defense Mobilization.[70] This recommendation was supported by the new budget director, Joseph M. Dodge. Perhaps one reason ODM was chosen as the name for the combined agency was that John Taber, chairman of the powerful Ways and Means Committee of the House, thought the NSRB was "just no good" and the "direct opposite of a security board."[71] Another probable reason was that Arthur Flemming, who had been in charge of manpower for Truman's ODM, was Eisenhower's choice to be the acting head of the new ODM. And, of course, the new name would provide the "new store front" that Young had suggested.

Dodge explained to Taber that the acting director of ODM (Flemming) would supervise the work of the NSRB until formal merger took place and that all employees of the NSRB were being given terminal notices. (Actually a limited number of selected employees of the NSRB were later transferred to ODM to carry on certain high-priority work of the board.) Dodge denied any intention

to eliminate the statutory functions now vested in the NSRB. The general idea is in the direction of a possible change of name rather than statutory responsibilities, have its operations reorganized, and have the same individual who is appointed to head ODM also head the NSRB. The NSRB would be the forward-planning arm of the project and the

69. Special Committee on Government Organization, 12 January 1953, Administration No. 3, PACGO, Eisenhower Papers, DDEL.

70. Memo No. 2, 14 February 1953, No. 62, PACGO, Eisenhower Papers, DDEL.

71. William Carey to Director, 6 February 1953, E3-1/1, Series 52.1, RG 51, NA.

present ODM-type organization would continue the operating side of the project.[72]

When Eisenhower accepted the PACGO recommendation, the bureau prepared Reorganization Plan No. 3 of 1953 which consolidated within one agency in the EOP "mobilization planning activities aimed at the eventuality of future war, similar activities with a current emphasis, and controls regarding stockpiles." It created a new ODM, transferred to its director the functions of the NSRB chairman, and abolished the NSRB. Further, it transferred to ODM the stockpiling policy and program authority then exercised by the service secretaries and the Munitions Board.[73] While Eisenhower sought a suitable businessman to serve as the director of this ODM, Flemming continued to serve as acting director. When that search failed to find an appropriate candidate, Flemming accepted a regular appointment to the post.[74]

CONCLUSION

Thus ended the Truman administration's experiment in mobilization planning. It had been an unsuccessful effort for many reasons. One was the undefined nature of its assignment. The NSRB had little to help it in establishing its role and work programs except the World War II mobilization experience. This model proved inappropriate in many ways. Another burden it carried was a flawed organizational concept that held that a board made up of cabinet members could direct a presidential staff group.

The NSRB had been unlucky in the men Truman had selected to lead the agency. Hill had worked for Forrestal and Eberstadt instead of the president, Walgren was rejected by the Senate, and Symington

72. Dodge to Taber, 12 February 1953, M7-2/2, Series 52.1, RG 51, NA.

73. Dodge to Eisenhower, 1 April 1953, M7-51/53.1, Series 52.1, RG 51, NA.

74. Lauren L. Henry, *Presidential Transitions* (Washington, D.C., 1960), pp 560-561.

tried to use the NSRB to further his own political ambitions. During the long Steelman hiatus, the agency
simply drifted.

Until almost the very end the Budget Bureau organizational theorists sought to confine the NSRB exclusively to a planning role. It is still to be demonstrated that that alone is a viable function for a
staff group in the EOP. For many years much of the energy of the NSRB was spent in resisting this definition
of its responsibilities. By the time the bureau re-
treated from this position too little time remained for
the Truman administration to make the adjustment.

But fundamentally a presidential staff group is
only effective if a president is willing to accept its
advice. This in turn depends upon his belief that the
staff can be useful to him in dealing with the problems
of his office. The NSRB (and the NSC) were hampered
from the beginning because they were created, not to
meet the felt needs of the president, but by historical
and political forces beyond his control. Harry Truman
was determined to control and limit these staff groups
because he believed that one of their purposes was to
limit his presidential prerogatives.

By the end of the Truman administration it was
clear that many wrong turns had been taken in the administration of the mobilization program. Although
there was still general support for the idea that there
should be a presidentially directed mobilization planning staff, the existing organizational arrangements
were in a shambles.

13.
Conclusion

A future historian comparing the structure of the Executive Office of the President as it existed in 1939 and 1952 might logically conclude that it had evolved in response to the growing complexity of the federal government, the dramatic preeminence of American military and economic power, and the increasing expectations placed upon the president. No doubt these were factors. However, a close examination of the circumstances within which the executive office developed reveals that the egos of the actors involved and the twists and turns of the decision making process in the bureaucracy, the White House, and the Congress were the primary forces that molded the president's staff.

The three elements of the EOP that were created because a president felt he needed help in meeting his managerial responsibilities were the Bureau of the Budget, the White House Office, and the various mobilization agencies. The bureau was created by Congress for its own purposes, but the initial impetus had come from Taft's desire to control the federal budget and through it, the agencies. The bureau's functions expanded significantly after 1939 as first Roosevelt and then Truman (under Harold Smith's tutelage) realized it could be useful in dealing with many of the problems they faced. This staff prospered as budget directors skillfully used the rising demand for presidential leadership to demonstrate that their organization had the skills and experience to advise the president effectively.

Then, of course, it was Franklin Roosevelt who sought the formal establishment of the White House Office as part of the EOP and it was Truman who eventually organized and expanded the office. It was also presidential initiative that resulted in the establishment of emergency mobilization organizations during World War II and the Korean conflict. When war required the mobilization of the nation's resources, Roosevelt and Truman responded by creating a myriad of temporary agencies to coordinate the effort. Eventually, both presidents decided to install a mechanism within the executive office to coordinate the coordinators.

But presidential involvement in the creation of the other major elements of the executive office was much more tenuous. On the surface the National Resources Planning Board would seem to owe its existence to Roosevelt's need for an antidepression staff arm. In fact, the NRPB became a part of the executive office primarily because of the president's uncle's long association with the organization and the personal interest of the members of the Brownlow committee in the planning function in general and that board in particular. It disappeared, not because the country had outgrown its need for economic planning, but because a combination of its bureaucratic and congressional enemies were determined to bring it down.

The Council of Economic Advisers was a congressional creation imposed on a reluctant Truman. The impact that the council had on national economic policy was limited because Truman, probably resenting the council and uncomfortable with professional economic advice, excluded it from his pattern of decision making. The council contributed to its own plight by failing to deliver a product the president found useful. Divisions within the council further impaired its effectiveness. Nourse sought to make the council a professional advisory group solely responsible for presenting objective economic advice to the president. In contrast, Keyserling believed that the council should be an active agent for executive policy formulation and a spokesman before Congress and the public for the administration's economic policies.

There were many forces at work leading to the creation of the National Security Council, but Truman's desire for staff assistance in the formulation of foreign and defense policies was not one of them. Forrestal shared the concern of many wartime governmental leaders who believed that the coordination of politico-military policy had been haphazard and needed to be systematized to counter Soviet threats. He sought to exploit this sentiment to sidetrack military unification. But he lost control of the definition of the NSC as the legislation moved through the White House on its way to Congress. As a result, the council that emerged was merely a pale imitation of the powerful policy-making instrument that Forrestal had envisioned. Truman, ever wary of efforts to invade presidential prerogatives and coached by the Budget Bureau, effectively asserted his control over the fledgling NSC.

For several reasons the Truman NSC was ineffective. Each agency continued to follow its own course with little reference to NSC pronouncements since they found many of the security council's policy statements too vague and general to be applied to the realities of departmental operations. The NSC played a limited role in questioning the adequacy of departmental proposals and in following up on policy execution. Since the Truman council did not develop into an effective center for debate, its products were sterile.

The National Security Resources Board was the culmination of Bernard Baruch's long crusade to institutionalize mobilization planning on the presidential level. Truman considered the board, like the NSC, an unwanted invasion of his authority but he was forced to accept them in order to realize the larger benefits of the unification of the armed forces. The NSRB was a flawed organization from the beginning. The experiment of heading a presidential staff agency with a board composed of a majority of the president's cabinet was doomed to failure because of its obvious internal inconsistencies. Disputes over the agency's proper role, inadequate leadership, and the enigma of planning wartime mobilization in peacetime plagued the NSRB's efforts to become an effective staff for the president. The advent of the Korean War and the resulting mobilization muddle eliminated any chance that the NSRB might assume a productive place in the executive office.

Over time, some EOP units prospered if their missions reflected the president's priorities and declined if they did not. For example, the Budget Bureau fitted in well with Truman's desire to control federal expenditures but the NSRB was not in accord with his concept of a mobilization agency. But some units are able to persist "without regard to any reasoned design of the Executive Office or even a rough order of the president's priorities."[1] Truman's economic council survived by competing with other parts of the presidential staff and courting favor with congressional committees and the Bureau of the Budget.

WHOSE EXECUTIVE OFFICE?

One of the enduring questions about the EOP is whether the president alone should determine the nature of his staff support or whether Congress should establish the president's staff structure by statute and require Senate confirmation of his nominees to head the various staff agencies. Many of the executive office difficulties during the Truman years can be traced directly to the fact that all of the new staff groups (CEA, NSC, and NSRB) were created by Congress rather than the president. In the process the executive office was transformed from virtually a unitary organization built up within the Budget Bureau to a loose arrangement consisting of several separate agencies largely headed by boards. For several reasons the tendency of the legislature to impose advisers on the executive proved to be an unworkable strategy for designing a presidential staff organization.

---

1. John Helmer, "The Presidential Office: Velvet Fist in an Iron Glove," p. 64.

One of the flaws in this approach is rooted in the constitutional separation of powers. Harry Truman was determined "to see that the functions of the Presidency [were] not infringed upon by either the legislative branch of the Government or the judicial branch." He later recalled that he had had a continual fight when he was president to maintain the integrity of his office.[2] Even a president less sensitive to this issue than Truman would be reluctant to have Congress mandate the source of his advice and assistance.

It is a truism that presidential staff units flourish only if the president accepts their advice. To be receptive to the work of a particular staff group the president should feel the need for its help before it is created. In the case of Truman, a decision (particularly by a Republican-controlled Congress) that he needed advice on economic policy, national security affairs, and mobilization planning was certain to be resented. Truman accepted his new staff assistance with good grace and tried to work with them, but he did not do so with much conviction or enthusiasm. If they had been created as a result of executive action, the results would undoubtedly have been better.

Each of these staff units was set up by Congress to perform functions that were only dimly perceived by their sponsors. Since Truman did not want them, and had little notion why they were created, he offered no guidance. As a result, each of these agencies had to devise its own raison d'être by a laborious procedure of trial and error. They all had a strong will to survive but this process did not produce a complete, balanced, or integrated presidential staff office.

One reason Congress seized the initiative and acted to augment the executive office was because between 1944 and 1947 the presidents failed to sponsor a reorganization of the presidential staff. Their default was not intentional. As FDR's third term drew to a close, Harold Smith told him "that history will show that your greatest contribution to Federal administration was the conception and establishment of the Exec-

---

2. Truman to John F. Kennedy (January 1953?), PACGO, No. 8, Eisenhower Papers, DDEL.

utive Office of the President." Smith hoped that during his fourth term Roosevelt would be able to organize the executive office so that it could become "an effective instrument of government."[3] FDR promised to talk to Smith about the executive office when "he had a little more time" but soon he was dead.

Smith then tried to interest Truman in staff matters but the budget director resigned before he had made any significant progress. When Smith left the bureau, he warned Truman "that failure to do something to tighten the organization of the Executive Office may prove to be as much of a stumbling block" to him as it had been to Roosevelt.[4] Webb also talked of reorganizing the executive office and Truman seemed interested, but again more pressing matters intervened and nothing was done.[5] In the end neither president considered the development of an institutionalized staff important enough to take priority over other concerns. So the economic council, the NSC, and the NSRB were created because Congress wanted them and insisted on them. Two of them remain today in the executive office "whipsawed between presidential initiative and congressional resistance (or vice versa)."[6]

THE EOP AND THE CABINET

Another recurring question about the executive office is whether presidents would resist the temptation to use their institutional staffs to subvert the line authority of their cabinet officers. There is no doubt that during the Kennedy, Johnson, and Nixon administrations the EOP became a "bloated command post" that arrogated to itself many of the decisions formerly made in the departments and agencies.[7] But the executive offices of FDR and Truman did not exercise this kind of operational authority. Why not?

3. Smith to Roosevelt, 9 November 1944, BOB Misc. 1945-53(1), PSF, Truman Papers, HSTL.

4. Smith to Truman, 3 May 1946, ibid.

5. Truman to James Webb, 3 October 1946, ibid.

6. Helmer, "The Presidential Office," p. 60.

7. Don K. Price interview in "News for Teachers of Political Science," APSA, no. 28 (Winter 1981), p. 30.

Had the EOP been available to him when he entered the White House Roosevelt might well have used it to extend his personal control over the executive branch. As Cordell Hull could attest, FDR was perfectly capable of ignoring a department head and using his own agents to carry out departmental functions. But FDR's EOP did not come into existence until his management style of working through unofficial agents rather than institutionalized staffs was firmly established. Soon he was presiding over a rapidly expanding federal government in the midst of a world war. By 1943 he had realized that he could no longer hope to coordinate economic mobilization alone. He responded by delegating this task to Jimmy Brynes. It was Congress, not the president, who tried to institutionalize mobilization coordination by creating the Office of War Mobilization and Reconversion.

Even the expanded executive office of the Truman period was quite primitive by today's standards.[8] But it was substantial enough that the president could have used it to centralize operational decisions in the EOP. Still, it did not happen. Indeed, Truman has been taken to task for not making a more spirited use of the staff he assembled. He did not permit it to become a shadow cabinet with great influence throughout the government nor did it intrude in foreign policy. As Patrick Anderson has pointed out, "Even Clifford's primary importance lay in his intellectual and political influence on Truman, rather than in the authority he exercised over the executive departments."[9]

There are probably several reasons why Truman's White House staff did not wield the power of some of its successors. Truman, after all, was the first president to have a large White House staff and a significant executive office staff. It took time to adjust to the problems of administering the massive postwar federal bureaucracy. And, Truman only gradually gave up on his desire to manage the government through his cabinet. As long as he held to this concept, he would

8. George Elsey speech to the Society for Historians of American Foreign Policy, Annapolis, Md., 25 June 1987.

9. Patrick Anderson, *The Presidents' Men*, p. 108.

be loath to permit his personal staff to exert influence within the departments. Finally, Truman saw his
staff as an instrument to render personal service to
him. He laid out their assignments and these rarely included spurring some action in the bowels of the bureaucracy. Since many of the staff had experience and
contacts in other parts of the government, they were
well equipped to perform this function, and they sometimes did so, but they had to proceed with caution.[10]

EOP COORDINATION

Although the EOP has a common mission to serve the
president, it has always been essentially a paper organization. It was even more fragmented during the
Truman years than it is today. Technically, of course,
the president himself is the official head of the executive office. But Truman made little effort to assume
such a role, and since he had no chief of staff, the
EOP was leaderless during his administration. Whatever
efforts that were made to get the various units to
function as a coordinated presidential staff came periodically from the Budget Bureau. As early as October
1946 the necessity of bringing more order to the various presidential messages prompted the bureau to seek
some understanding with the economic council and the
OWMR concerning responsibilities in the preparation of
these documents.[11] This inaugurated an effort that was
to continue, with varying degrees of success, for the
remainder of the Truman administration.

Nevertheless, the EOP remained an unstructured
organization. There was no consensus among the career
staff members that the executive office should be
centrally controlled. One bureau analyst thought the
problem of coordination endemic because "the various
parts of the Executive Office are largely self-contained with no processes or structure to provide the
necessary cohesion of the whole."[12] Bert Gross pre-

10. Alan D. Harper, *The Politics of Loyalty: The White House and the
Communist Issue, 1946-1952* , p. 242.
11. D.C. Stone to Director, 17 October 1946, Series 39.3, RG 51, NA.
12. Ralph Burton, "Presidential Leadership," 26 May 1948, Presidential Staff Assistance, 1946-1949, E2-5, Series 39.32, OMB.

dicted that the method of "coordinating the Executive coordinators will continue to be a problem more of esprit de corps and intangibles than of mechanical reforms."[13] As the Truman administration drew to a close, Herman Somers could wonder, "Is the Executive Office something real or only a convenient tag?"[14]

The Hoover Commission urged the president to establish a permanent coordinating mechanism in the EOP, but Truman would not institute such a change unless pushed to do so by his staff. But the bureau, as an institution, was not enthusiastic about being "coordinated" and the rest of the executive office felt no responsibility in the matter. Apparently the bureau did not think it really vital to establish a coordinating authority and feared that it would be perceived as grabbing for more power if it advocated it too strongly. During those years, the bureau leaders thought informal organization and relationships more important to the executive office than formal structure.[15] In this way the tradition was established that has resulted in the EOP remaining a synthetic organization.

THE EOP TODAY

Since the end of the Truman administration, the EOP has become a well entrenched part of the federal establishment. There is now both an Old and a New Executive Office Building, fifty percent more staff, and, in budgetary terms, the EOP has grown eightfold. The original five units established in 1939 had increased to eighteen by 1977. It is no longer possible to separate the White House from the rest of the executive office when describing the president's essential staff support.[16]

13. Bertram M. Gross and John P. Lewis, "The President's Economic Staff During the Truman Administration," *American Political Science Review* 48, no. 1 (March 1954): 119–120.

14. Herman Somers, "Executive Office of the President," The Brookings Institution, May 1951, E2–50/51.2, Series 39.32, RG 51, NA.

15. R.E. Neustadt to Herman Somers, 4 August 1949, Chronological File, June–Sept. 1949, Richard E. Neustadt Papers, HSTL.

16. Helmer, "The Presidential Office," p. 57.

The old Budget Bureau, now called the Office of Management and Budget, is still the premier element of the EOP. Eisenhower integrated the NSRB into the Office of Defense Mobilization which, after the end of the Korean War, was recast as the Office of Civil and Defense Mobilization. From Kennedy through Nixon it was known as the Office of Emergency Planning Preparedness. It was Eisenhower who made the chairman the real head of the Council of Economic Advisers when he reorganized the council along the lines initially recommended by the Hoover Commission. The National Security Council, through the antics of Oliver North, is probably the best known and least understood of the presidential staff units. The parts of the EOP that were established and refined during the Truman years have proven to be the most durable as well as the most significant.

Bibliography

MANUSCRIPT COLLECTIONS

Acheson, Dean G., Papers. Harry S. Truman Library, Independence
    Missouri.
Ayers, Eban, Papers. Harry S. Truman Library.
Blough, Roy, Papers. Harry S. Truman Library.
Clark, John D., Papers. Harry S. Truman Library.
Clifford, Clark, Papers. Harry S. Truman Library.
Colm, Gerhard, Papers. Library of Congress, Washington, D.C.
——————. Harry S. Truman Library.
Elsey, George M., Papers. Harry S. Truman Library.
Lawton, Frederick J., Papers. Harry S. Truman Library.
Neustadt, Richard E., Papers. Harry S. Truman Library.
Nourse, Edwin G., Papers. Harry S. Truman Library.
Pace, Frank Jr., Papers. Harry S. Truman Library.
Price, Don K., Papers. Herbert C. Hoover Library, West Branch, Iowa.
Rosenman, Samuel I., Papers. Harry S. Truman Library.
Smith, Harold D., Papers. Harry S. Truman Library.
Souers, Sidney, Papers. Harry S. Truman Library.
Spingarn, Stephen J., Papers. Harry S. Truman Library.
Stowe, David H., Papers. Harry S. Truman Library.
Turner, Robert C., Papers. Harry S. Truman Library.
Webb, James E., Papers. Harry S. Truman Library.

ORAL HISTORIES

David E. Bell. Harry S. Truman Library.
Ewan Clague. Harry S. Truman Library.
Joseph G. Feeney. Harry S. Truman Library.
Neil H. Jacoby. Dwight D. Eisenhower Library, Abilene, Kansas.

Roger W. Jones. Harry S. Truman Library.
Keyserling, Leon H. Harry S. Truman Library.
Frederick J. Lawton. Harry S. Truman Library.
Charles S. Murphy. Harry S. Truman Library.
Edwin G. Nourse. Harry S. Truman Library.
Frank Pace, Jr. Harry S. Truman Library.
Don K. Price. Herbert C. Hoover Library.
James H. Rowe. Herbert C. Hoover Library.
Walter S. Salant. Harry S. Truman Library.
James L. Sundquist. Harry S. Truman Library.

UNITED STATES GOVERNMENT PAPERS

Dwight D. Eisenhower Papers. President's Advisory Committee on Government Organization (PACGO). Dwight D. Eisenhower Library.
Dwight D. Eisenhower Papers. White House Office "Project Clean Up." Dwight D. Eisenhower Library.
Files of the National Security Council. "Organizational History of the NSC," James S. Lay to J. Kenneth Mansfield, 30 June 1960. In possession of author.
Harry S. Truman Papers. Official Files. Harry S. Truman Library.
Harry S. Truman Papers. President's Secretary's Files. Harry S. Truman Library.
Harry S. Truman Papers. White House Office Files of Clark M. Clifford, George M. Elsey, Harold L. Enarson, Charles S. Murphy, Stephen J. Spingarn, John R. Steelman, David H. Stowe, and Raymond Zimmerman. Harry S. Truman Library.
"Machinery to Assist the President." AM Project 174, June 1944–November 1945, E2-5, Series 39.32, Office of Management and Budget, New Executive Office Building, Washington, D.C.
Records of the Bureau of the Budget. Office of Management and Budget, New Executive Office Building, Washington, D.C.
Records of the Bureau of the Budget. Record Group 51. National Archives.
Records of the National Security Resources Board. Record Group 304. National Archives.
U.S. Senate, Committee on Naval Affairs. Ferdinand Eberstadt. *Report to the Secretary of the Navy. Unification of the War and Navy Departments and Postwar Organization for National Security.* 79th Cong., 1st Sess.

CORRESPONDENCE WITH CONTEMPORARIES

George M. Elsey   Richard E. Neustadt
Don K. Price   Elmer B. Staats
James L. Sundquist   James E. Webb

BOOKS AND DISSERTATIONS

Acheson, Dean G. *Present at the Creation: My Years in the State Department.* New York: W.W. Norton, 1969.

Altschuler, Alan A. *The Politics of the Federal Bureaucracy.* New York: Dodd, Mead, 1968.

Anderson, Patrick. *The Presidents' Men.* Garden City, N.Y.: Doubleday, 1969.

Bailey, Stephen K. *Congress Makes a Law: The Story Behind the Employment Act of 1946.* New York: Columbia University Press, 1950.

Baruch, Bernard, M. *The Public Years.* New York: Rinehart and Winston, 1960.

Berman, Larry. *The Office of Management and Budget and the Presidency, 1921-1979.* Princeton, N.J.: Princeton University Press, 1979.

Bohlen, Charles E. *Witness to History, 1929-1969.* New York: W.W. Norton, 1973.

Brownlow, Lewis. *A Passion for Anonymity.* Chicago: University of Chicago Press, 1958.

Burns, James MacGregor. *Presidential Government: The Crucible of Leadership.* Boston: Houghton Mifflin, 1965.

——————. *Roosevelt: The Lion and the Fox.* New York: Harcourt, Brace, 1956.

——————. *Roosevelt: The Soldier of Freedom.* New York: Harcourt, Brace, Jovanovich, 1970.

Caro, Robert A. *The Years of Lyndon Johnson: The Path to Power.* New York: Vintage Books, 1981.

Clark, Keith and Legere, Laurence J.. *The President and the Management of National Security: A Report by the Institute for Defense Analysis.* New York: Praeger, 1969.

Clawson, Marion. *New Deal Planning: The National Resources Planning Board.* Baltimore: Johns Hopkins University Press, 1981.

Dawes, Charles G. *The First Year of the Budget.* New York: Harper and Brothers, 1923.

Donovan, Robert J. *Tumultuous Years: The Presidency of Harry S Truman, 1949-1953.* New York: W.W. Norton, 1982.

Egger, Rowland. *The President of the United States.* New York: McGraw-Hill, 1969.

Ferrell, Robert H., ed. *Dear Bess: The Letters from Harry to Bess Truman.* New York: W. W. Norton, 1983.

——————, ed. *Off the Record: The Private Papers of Harry S. Truman.* New York: Harper & Row, 1980.

Flash, Edward S. *Economic Advice and Presidential Leadership.* New York: Columbia University Press, 1965.

Gould, Louis. *The Presidency of William McKinley.* Lawrence, Kansas: University of Kansas Press, 1980.

Graham, Otis L. *Toward a Planned Society: From Roosevelt to Nixon.* New York: Oxford University Press, 1976.

Hammond, Paul Y. *Organizing for Defense: The American Military Establishment in the Twentieth Century.* Princeton, N.J.: Princeton University Press, 1961.

Hand, Samuel B. *Counsel and Advise: A Political Biography of Samuel I. Rosenman.* New York: Garland Publishing, 1979.

Harper, Alan D. *The Politics of Loyalty: The White House and the Communist Issue, 1946–1952.* Westport, Conn.: Greenwood Press, 1969.

Heclo, Hugh, and Salamon, Lester M., eds. *The Illusion of Presidential Government.* Boulder, Colo.: Westview Press, 1981.

Hillman, William. *Mr. President: The First Publication from the Personal Diaries, Private Letters, Papers and Revealing Interviews of Harry S. Truman.* New York: Farrar, Straus and Young, 1952.

Heller, Francis, ed. *The Truman White House: The Administration of the Presidency, 1945–1953.* Lawrence, Kans.: The Regents Press of Kansas, 1980.

Henry, Lauren L. *Presidential Transitions.* Washington, D.C.: The Brookings Institution, 1960.

Hobbs, Edward H. *Behind the President.* Washington, D.C.: Public Affairs Press, 1954.

Hoover, Herbert. *General Management of the Executive Branch.* Washington, D.C.: U.S. Government Printing Office, 1949.

Hoopes, Townsend. *The Limits of Intervention.* New York: David McKay, 1969.

Huthmacher, J. Joseph. *Senator Robert F. Wagner and the Rise of American Liberalism.* New York: Antheneum, 1968.

Ickes, Harold L. *The Secret Diary of Harold L. Ickes.* vol. 3, *The Lowering Cloud.* New York: Simon and Schuster, 1955.

Isaacson, Walter, and Thomas, Evan, *The Wise Men.* New York: Simon and Shuster, 1986.

Jackson, Henry M., ed. *The National Security Council.* New York: Praeger, 1965.

Jones, Joseph. *The Fifteen Weeks.* New York: Viking Press, 1955.

Karl, Barry D. *Executive Reorganization and Reform in the New Deal.* Chicago: University of Chicago Press, 1963.

——————. *The Uneasy State: The United States from 1915 to 1945.* Chicago: University of Chicago Press, 1983.

Kennan, George F. *Memoirs, 1925–1950.* Boston: Little, Brown, 1967.

King, Anthony, ed. *The New American Political System.* Washington, D.C.: American Enterprise Institute for Public Policy Research, 1978.

Marx, Fritz Morstein. *The President and His Staff Services.* Chicago: Public Administration Service, 1947.

May, Ernest R., and Neustadt, Richard E. *Thinking in Time: The Uses of History for Decision Makers.* New York: Free Press, 1986.

Meck, John F. "The Administration of Foreign and Overseas Operations of the United States Government, A Staff Memorandum on the National Security Council." Study for the Brookings Institution, March 1951.

Millis, Walter, and Duffield, E. S., eds. *The Forrestal Diaries.* New York: Viking Press, 1951.

Morrow, William L. *Congressional Committees.* New York: Charles Scribner's Sons, 1969.

Neustadt, Richard E. *Presidential Power: The Politics of Leadership.* New York: John Wiley & Sons, 1960.

——————. "Notes on the White House Staff Under President Truman." June 1953, Manuscript, Harry S. Truman Library.

Nourse, Edwin G. *Economics in the Public Service.* New York: Harcourt Brace, 1953.

Parrett, Geoffrey. *America in the Twenties: A History.* New York: Simon and Schuster, 1982.

Polenberg, Richard. *Reorganizing Roosevelt's Government: The Controversy Over Executive Reorganization, 1936-1939.* Cambridge: Harvard University Press, 1966.

Pringle, Henry F. *The Life and Times of William Howard Taft.* 2 vols. New York: Farrar & Rinehart, 1939.

Ramsey, John W. "The Director of the Bureau of the Budget as a Presidential Aide, 1921-1952: With Emphasis on the Truman Years." Ph.D. diss., University of Missouri, 1967.

Rosenberg, Herbert H. "ODM: A Study of Civil Military Relations During Korean Mobilization." Ph.D. diss., University of Chicago, 1957.

Roth, Harold H. "The Executive Office of the President: A Study of Its Development with Emphasis on the Period 1939-53." Ph. D. diss., The American University, 1958.

Schlesinger, Arthur M., Jr. *The Coming of the New Deal.* Boston: Houghton Mifflin, 1959.

Schilling, Warner R., Hammond, Paul Y., and Snyder, Glenn H. *Strategy, Politics, and Defense Budgets.* New York: Columbia University Press, 1962.

Silverman, Corrine. *The President's Economic Advisers.* Inter-University Case Program Series No. 48. Birmingham: University of Alabama Press, 1959.

Somers, Herman M. *Presidential Agency: OWMR* Cambridge: Harvard University Press, 1950.

Stein, Herbert, ed. *American Civil-Military Decisions.* Birmingham: University of Alabama Press, 1963.

Sundquist, James L. *The Decline and Resurgence of Congress.* Washington, D.C.: The Brookings Institution, 1981.

Thompson, Kenneth W., ed. *Portraits of American Presidents.* Vol. 1, *The Roosevelt Presidency.* Washington, D.C.: University Press of America, 1982.

———————, ed. *Portraits of American Presidents*. Vol 2, *The Truman Presidency: Intimate Perspectives*. Lanham, Md., University Press of America, 1984.

Truman, Harry S. *Memiors*. Vol 1, *Year of Decisions* Garden City, N.Y.: Doubleday and Company, 1955.

———————. *Memiors*. Vol 2, *Years of Trial and Hope*. Garden City, N.Y.: Doubleday and Company, 1956.

———————. *Public Papers of the Presidents of the United States, 1946*. Washington, D.C.: Government Printing Office, 1962.

U.S. Department of State. *Foreign Relations of the United States, 1948*. Vol. 1, part 2. Washington, D.C: Government Printing Office, 1976.

U.S. Department of State. *Foreign Relations of the United States, 1949*. Vol. 1. Washington, D.C: Government Printing Office, 1976.

U.S. Senate, Committee on Government Operations, Subcommittee on National Policy Machinery. *Organizing for National Security*. vol. 2, *Studies and Background Material*. Washington, D.C.: Government Printing Office, 1961.

Weaver, Warren, Jr. *Both Your Houses: The Truth About Congress*. New York: Praeger, 1972.

Wildavsky, Aaron. *The Politics of the Budgetary Process*. Boston: Little, Brown and Company, 1964.

Yoshpe, Harry B. *A Case Study in Peacetime Mobilization Planning: The National Security Resources Board, 1947–1953*. Washington: GPO, 1953.

———————. "Planning for Defense: A History of the Role and the Accomplishments of the National Security Resources Board." Draft, NSRB General Administration Folder, Series 39.28, Record Group 51, National Archives.

ARTICLES AND PAPERS

Blum, Albert A. "Birth and Death of the M–Day Plan." In *American Civil–Military Decisons*, edited by Harold Stein. Birmingham: University of Alabama Press, 1963.

Brownlow, Lewis. "A General View." *Public Administration Review* 1, no. 2 (1941).

Colm, Gerhard. "The Executive Office and Fiscal and Economic Policy." *Law and Contemporary Problems* 21 (Autumn 1956).

Cuff, Robert. "Ferdinand Eberstadt, the National Security Resources Board and the Search for Integrated Mobilization Planning, 1947–1948." *Public Historian* 7 (Fall 1985)

Falk, Stanley. "The National Security Council Under Truman, Eisenhower and Kennedy." *Political Science Quarterly* 79 no. 3 (September 1964).

Fisher, John. "Mr. Truman's Politburo." *Harpers Magazine* 202, no. 1213 (June 1951).

Gordon, Kermit. "The Budget Director." In *The Presidential Advisory System*, edited by Thomas E. Cronin and Sanford D. Greenberg. New York: Harper and Row, 1969.

Greenstein, Fred I. "The Modern Presidency." In *The New American Political System*, edited by Anthony King. Washington: American Enterprise Institute for Public Policy Research, 1978.

Gross, Bertram M., and Lewis, John P. "The President's Economic Staff During the Truman Administration." *The American Political Science Review* 48, no. 1 (March 1954).

Gulick, Luther. "Conclusion to Symposium on Executive Office." *Public Administration Review* 1, no. 2 (1941).

Hamby, Alonzo L. "The Vital Center, the Fair Deal, and the Quest for a Liberal Political Economy." *American Historical Review* 77, no. 3 (June 1972).

Hammond, Paul Y. "The National Security Council As a Device for Interdepartmental Coordination: An Interpretation and Appraisal." *The American Political Science Review* 54, no. 4 (December 1960).

——————. "NSC–68: Prologue to Rearmament." In *Strategy, Politics and Defense Budgets*, edited by Warner R. Schilling, Paul Y. Hammond and Glenn H. Snyder. New York: Columbia University Press, 1962.

Heller, Walter. "Economic Advisers." In *The Presidential Advisory System* by Thomas E. Cronin and Sanford D. Greenberg. New York: Harper & Row, 1969.

Helmer, John. "The Presidential Office: Velvet Fist in an Iron Glove." In *The Illusion of Presidential Government* edited by Hugh Heclo and Lester M. Salamon. Boulder, Colo.: Westview Press, 1981.

Hobbs, Edward H. "An Historical Review of Plans for Presidential Staffing." *Law and Contemporary Problems* 21, no. 4 (Autumn 1956).

Koistinen, Paul A. C. "The 'Industrial–Military Complex' in Historical Perspective: The InterWar Years." *The Journal of American History*, 56, no. 4 (March 1970).

May, Ernest R. "The Development of Political-Military Coordination in the United States." *Political Science Quarterly* 70, no. 2 (June 1955).

Mackenzie, G. Calvin. "The Paradox of Presidential Personnel Management." In *The Illusion of Presidential Government* edited by Heclo, Hugh, and Lester M. Salamon. Boulder, Colo.: Westview Press, 1981.

Nelson, Anna Kasten. "National Security I: Inventing a Process (1945–1960)." In *The Illusion of Presidential Government* edited by Heclo, Hugh, and Lester M. Salamon. Boulder, Colo.: Westview Press, 1981.

Nelson, Anna Kasten. "President Truman and the Evolution of the National Security Council." *The Journal of American History* 72, no. 2 (Sept 1985).

Neustadt, Richard E. "Approaches to Staffing the Presidency: Notes on F.D.R. and J.F.K." *The American Political Science Review* 57 (December 1963).

——————. "Presidency and Legislation: The Growth of Central Clearance." *The American Political Science Review* 48, no. 3 (September 1954).

Nourse, Edwin G. and Gross, Bertram M. "The Role of the Council of Economic Advisers." *The American Political Science Review* 42 (April 1948).

Pemberton, William E. "Struggle for the New Deal: Truman and the Hoover Commission." *Presidential Studies Quarterly* 16, no. 3 (Summer 1986).

Porter, Roger B. "The President and Economic Policy." In *The Illusion of Presidential Government* edited by Heclo, Hugh, and Lester M. Salamon. Boulder, Colo.: Westview Press, 1981.

Price, Don K. "Staffing the Presidency." *The American Political Science Review* 40, no. 6 (December 1946).

Rossiter, Clinton L. "The Constitutional Significance of the Executive Office of the President." *The American Political Science Review* 43 (December 1949).

Sander, Alfred D. "Truman and the National Security Council, 1945–1947." *The Journal of American History* 59, no. 2 (September 1972).

Sautter, Udo. "Government and Unemployment: The Use of Public Works before the New Deal." *The Journal of American History* 73, no. 1 (June 1986).

Schick, Allen. "The Problems of Presidential Budgeting." In *The Illusion of Presidential Government* edited by Heclo, Hugh, and Lester M. Salamon. Boulder, Colo.: Westview Press, 1981.

Schilling, Warner R. "The Politics of National Defense: Fiscal 1950." In *Strategy, Politics and Defense Budgets* edited by Warner R. Schilling, Paul Y. Hammond and Glenn H. Snyder. New York: Columbia University Press, 1962.

Seligman, Lester G. "Presidential Leadership: The Inner Circle and Institutionalization." *The Journal of Politics* 18, no. 3, (August 1956).

Seligman, Lester G., and Covington, Cary R. "The Comparative Institutionalization of Presidential Roles." Paper presented at the annual meeting of The American Political Science Association, Washington, D.C., August 1979.

Souers, Sidney. "Policy Formulation for National Security." *The American Political Science Review* 43, no. 3 (June 1949).

Steele, Richard W. "The Great Debate: Roosevelt, the Media, and the Coming of the War, 1940–1941." *The Journal of American History* 71, no. 1 (June 1984).

——————. "Preparing the Public for War: Efforts to Establish a National Propaganda Agency, 1940-41." *American Historical Review* 75, no. 6 (October 1970).

Steelman, John R., and Kraeger, H. Dewayne. "The Executive Office as Administrative Coordinator." *Law and Contemporary Problems* 21, no. 4 (Autumn 1956).

Index

About the Author

ALFRED DICK SANDER is Professor of History at Purdue University, Calumet. He is a graduate of Miami University and The American University (Ph.D. 1955). A former analyst at the National Security Agency, he has served as department head, dean and chief academic officer at Purdue. He was awarded an individual grant by the Ford Foundation to support much of the research for this book.